Perspectives on the Family
in Spain

Perspectives on the Family in Spain, Past and Present

DAVID S. REHER

CLARENDON PRESS · OXFORD
1997

Oxford University Press, Great Clarendon Street, Oxford OX2 6DP

Oxford New York
Athens Auckland Bangkok Bogota Bombay
Buenos Aires Calcutta Cape Town Dar es Salaam
Delhi Florence Hong Kong Istanbul Karachi
Kuala Lumpur Madras Madrid Melbourne
Mexico City Nairobi Paris Singapore
Taipei Tokyo Toronto
and associated companies in
Berlin Ibadan

Oxford is a trade mark of Oxford University Press

Published in the United States by
Oxford University Press Inc., New York

British Library Cataloguing in Publication Data
Data available

Library of Congress Cataloging in Publication Data
Reher, David Sven.
Perspectives on the family in Spain, past and present / David S. Reher.
Includes bibliographical references and index.
1. Family—Spain—History.   I. Title.
HQ649.R44 1997 96-34857
306.85'0946—dc20

ISBN 0–19–823314–0

1 3 5 7 9 10 8 6 4 2

Typeset by Best-set Typesetter Ltd., Hong Kong
Printed in Great Britain by
Biddles Ltd., Guildford & King's Lynn

Acknowledgements

This book has been many years in the making. I first became interested in Spanish family history at the outset of my doctoral dissertation over two decades ago. Since then, even when involved in research on other topics, questions and issues concerning the family in Spain have always been present, and I have found myself coming back to this fascinating subject over and over again. By bringing together many of these concerns in this book, I hope to be able to shed light on some of the central issues which have affected family formation and development in historic and contemporary Spanish society.

An intellectual undertaking of this sort would never have been possible without institutional, intellectual, and personal support. This I have found in generous abundance over the years. A grant from the Ministerio de Educación y Ciencia of Spain and leave given me by the Universidad Complutense de Madrid enabled me to take a year off from my teaching responsibilities in order to put together the final manuscript. Most of the book was written at the University of California at Berkeley, where the Demography Department gave me much-needed technical and material support. The assistance given to me by the Cambridge Group for the History of Population was essential for the microsimulation analysis used in this book.

I greatly benefited from the intellectual input, technical assistance, or archival help of many colleagues and friends. Josep Bernabeu Mestre, Pamela Camille, Enriqueta Camps Cura, Maimen Díez Hoyo, Patrick Galloway, Eilidh Garret, Jesús Leal Maldonado, Ronald Lee, Massimo Livi Bacci, Elisa Martín, José Antonio Ortega Osona, Vicente Pérez Moreda, Roger Schofield, Richard Smith, Richard Wall, and Zhongwei Zhao were all willing to give my ideas and intuitions their critical scrutiny. Arturo Ortega Berruguete designed and printed all of the maps used in this book and Guillermo Reher helped define the content and layout of a number of them. Zhongwei Zhao and Jim Oeppen helped run the microsimulations I used. Antonio Reher, Vince Reher, Charis Baz, Josh White, and Carl Mason gave me help with computing. Begoña Gómez Garay provided diligent archival assistance. My family and my friends were patient and kind enough to put up with me and my ideas regarding a project which for them must have often seemed larger than life. All of these people have contributed in different ways to much of what is good and useful in this book. I have incurred a great debt to all of them.

Contents

Figures

Maps

Tables

Appendix: Detailed CAMSIM Microsimulation Results

1 The Big Picture and Smaller Perspectives

> The people of Perojales used to say that the Peñarrubias were like swifts:
> one of them came, fixed up the nest, formed a family and disappeared with
> it, without anyone knowing where they went or why. After a while, another
> Peñarrubia showed up and restored the old family homestead, etc. etc.
>
> (José María Pereda, *De tal palo, tal astilla*, 1880)

When brigadier Rey died in 1841, his two children, Juan and Perfecta, had just
married. Juan's wife, María, died very young and left him with a toddler
named Pepe who would one day become an engineer and a man of science.
Juan's sister, Perfecta, married Manuel María José de Polentinos, a man of
wealth and debauch who took her to live in Madrid. He led a life of ruin until
death also took him at a young age. By then Perfecta had a very young
daughter, Rosarito, and was mired in the debts left by her husband. She called
on her widowed brother Juan to help her out. He was able to patch things up
and she eventually returned to her village of origin, Obrajosa, where she raised
her daughter. Years later, when young Pepe Rey had become a man of means
and Rosarito a beautiful young woman, their parents Juan and Perfecta suggested that they marry each other in order to keep the family wealth intact and
to care for each other and for their parents. In *Doña Perfecta* (1876), Benito
Pérez Galdós described a family which pulled together when faced with adversity. This was not always the case. When little Lazarillo lost his father to
the law and to war, his mother was forced to turn to prostitution and other
desperate means in order to survive (anonymous, *Lazarillo de Tormes*, 16th
c.). Eventually she turned Lazarillo out to fend for himself in the difficult and
often cruel world of sixteenth-century Castile. Things were not much different
for young Manuel, whose infancy had been spent in Soria and who came to
Madrid to live with his widowed mother, who had become a maid in order to
survive (Pío Baroja, *La Busca*, 1904). Just like Lazarillo, he ended up having
no choice but to struggle for survival, this time in rough and tumble *fin de siècle*
Madrid (Moral, 1974).

The same themes appear in the admirable Catalan genealogies compiled
recently by Andrés Barrera (1990: 385–420). All of them are stories of successful families: successful in maintaining intact for generations their family lineage, their family property, their family homestead. In all of these genealogies,
carefully planned marriage and inheritance strategies and judicious use of
property and other economic assets were successful despite untimely deaths to
the chosen heirs, their wives, and children, despite profound economic trans-

formations in Catalonia, despite wars and upheaval. In these cases the family and the family lineage prevailed; they are success stories. Matters did not necessarily turn out that way; risks were numerous and survival strategies were not always adequate. Whether it was a Catalan family lineage or a Castilian nuclear family, the obsession with survival, with stability, and, if possible, with well-being was common to all families.

Risk, uncertainty, and death; dysfunctional and resilient families; family loyalties, brokered marriages, social and moral strictures; survival and stability; property, wealth, and poverty. The themes are always the same: the family, always the family. Its presence is ubiquitous in Spanish literature, in Spanish society; in its history and in its life. The family fulfilled a dual function, one for its own members and one for society as a whole. When times were good, a person's family was a source of comfort and well-being; when they turned sour it might well be his only source of support. It was commonly held that the only truly indigent people in Spanish society were those who for one reason or another had no family. Until very recently, and even today, the family ended up being the last social and economic safety net for its own members. For society as a whole, the family was the key to social and economic reproduction; it educated and socialized the young; it provided social stability. It is difficult to overestimate the importance of the family for Spanish society.

The key role played by the family was not lost on thinkers, reformers, the Church, or political authorities. Its well-being was considered essential for the well-being of society and if problems were perceived, measures were taken to guarantee its health. While these were not always successful, they were always taken. The legal underpinnings for succession, inheritance, and intra-familial relations were already well-developed by the early Middle Ages, and had acquired many of their modern trappings by the reign of the Catholic Kings towards the end of the fifteenth and beginning of the sixteenth centuries. As Castile slid into a period of profound crisis during the early years of the seventeenth century, reformers (*arbitristas*) considered that impediments to marriage and family formation were at the root of many of the severe social and economic problems affecting the kingdom. As a result, at the behest of the Count-Duke of Olivares in 1622 the *Junta de Reformación* proposed a series of measures designed to facilitate marriage, fertility, and family formation. This veritable family policy included a cap on dowries, a recommendation that charitable foundations help create dowries for orphans or poor young women, tax exemptions and other special privileges for newly-weds and for all those who had six or more male children, and certain penalties for those who had not married by 25 years of age (Elliott, 1986: ch. 3; Martín Rodríguez, 1984: 259–66). Over three centuries later, the Franco regime showed the same concern over marriage, family formation, and fertility when it adopted a number of measures between 1941 and 1971 designed to encourage large families by means of different basically fiscal benefits (Campo, 1991: 78–88). Even today, with Spain run by left-of-centre democratic governments, incentives for family formation, fertility, child care, and access to housing are central to the social policy of the government.

Everyone had a stake in the well-being of the family: the young and the old, the rich and the poor, the powerful and the weak. It was and probably still is commonly perceived as central to social stability and cohesion, personal welfare and public authority. The importance of the family was recognized by all, then and now. This importance is not specific to Spain; but certain defining characteristics of family forms and their historical development are. This book is an attempt to sketch the main contours of that specificity and to deepen and widen our understanding of the family in Spain.

Family Studies, Family History

Despite its importance, the empirical study of the family as a social institution is a comparatively recent phenomenon and dates from the pioneering research of some of the first relevant figures in the field of the social sciences. The work of Frédéric Le Play, which was centred on the micro-analysis of a selection of families, family budgets, the distribution of household labour, and other related subjects, was and still is essential for any viable understanding of the family.[1] Rowntree (1901, 1910) and Chayanov (1925 [1966]), whose works centring on family economies have been particularly useful for my own study, are also pioneers in the field. All of these thinkers ended up emphasizing the role of the family as an institution which mediated between individuals and society, was subject to economic, social, cultural, and demographic constraints, and was itself capable of influencing society. With differing emphases they portrayed the family as conditioned by and able to condition the world around it, as dependent and independent variable. This duality has marked most of the work done in the field of family history during this century, and in many ways will form the *leitmotiv* of this book.

In recent decades, the field of family history has acquired a maturity and a dynamism all its own, making it an essential point of departure for any study of the family. With the avowed goal of relating the lives of individual families to those of their members and to the larger social, economic, and political realities within different historical contexts, the growth of this field has been phenomenal both in terms of the number of publications generated and the depth and sophistication of the issues addressed.[2] Recently Tamara Hareven, one of the field's most relevant figures, summed up some of the immense changes which have taken place:

Over the two decades and a half of its existence, family history has moved from a limited view of the family as a static unit at one point in time to an examination of the family as a process over the entire lives of its members; from a study of discrete domestic structures to the investigation of the nuclear family's relations with the wider kinship group; and from a study of the family as a separate domestic unit to an examination of the family's interaction with the worlds of religion, work, education, correctional and welfare institutions, and with processes such as migration, industrialization, and urbanization. (Hareven, 1991: 96)

As so often happens, the growth of this field can be traced to certain seminal ideas and to the methodological innovations which enabled researchers to ascertain their validity. In many ways the starting point for family history as an autonomous discipline can be traced to *L'Enfant et la vie familiale sous l'ancien régime*, first published by Philippe Ariès in 1960. In his study of childhood, Ariès argued that during the Middle Ages, and until much more recently for the lower classes in society, the family was characterized by its public nature, by its sociability, by its ties of loyalty. During that period, childhood as a distinct age of life did not exist, as young children went straight from infancy into a world in which they mixed freely with adults both at an economic and a social level. 'The family fulfilled a function; it ensured the transmission of life, property and names; but it did not penetrate very far into human sensibility' (Ariès, 1962 edn.: 411). It was a family in which realities such as apprenticeship loosened the emotional bond between parents and children. At some point during the Early Modern period, the 'sociable' family was replaced by the 'private' or 'modern' family, based on a desire for privacy and a craving for identity: the members of the family were united by feeling, habit, and their way of life. In the modern family, childhood became an age of life, mainly because it was recognized that a child was not ready for life until he had been subjected to special treatment and been given an education for life. The new family 'shrank from the promiscuity imposed by the old sociability', and was originally a middle-class phenomenon.

Not only had Ariès attempted to identify the origins of the 'modern' family; he also had laid the foundations for a debate as to which type of family best prepares children to function in a complex, modern society: the sociable family of the past or the intimate family of the present. His work was particularly timely because it first appeared in a period in which demography, economics, and education were teaming up to prolong the duration of childhood to a startling degree, one which could not even have been imagined in historical times. This linking of past family patterns with present family concerns was among the most significant of Ariès's contributions. Equally important was the fact that he did not hesitate to use a wide variety of sources, ranging from iconography and memoirs to demographic data, to approach the topic of childhood. Even though not all family historians ended up being directly concerned with the origins of the modern family, Ariès gave the field a direction (a working hypothesis) and a methodological orientation.[3] In a sense he had given it the intellectual acceptability it needed to grow.

The other seminal contributions were more strictly methodological, but no less important. During the latter part of the 1960s, Peter Laslett and other collaborators became interested in verifying the validity of the commonly held notion that the conjugal family arose as a by-product of the Industrial Revolution, and that earlier family forms had been by and large complex and multi-generational. He claimed that most of what was known about earlier family forms was based on subjective or literary evidence, and that a more scientific or verifiable basis of evidence was required. He pointed to the ubiquitous ecclesiastical and secular household listings existing all over Europe as a potential source of useful data, and he devised a basic classification scheme which was applicable almost everywhere in Europe and in many other areas of the world as well.[4] The volume in which the method was first described, along with the main results coming from a conference organized in 1969 by the Cambridge Group for the History of Population and Social Structure on the subject of the comparative history of the household and the family, appeared in 1972.[5]

The results were extremely exciting because Laslett seemed to have made a case for the existence of the nuclear, conjugal household in certain areas of Europe dating as far back as the sixteenth century or perhaps even earlier, long before any modernization of society had taken place. More important than the substantive results, however, was the fact that Laslett had unearthed a source of data and proposed a classification scheme which was universally available and applicable. It was the tool that family historians had been waiting for. Even though his findings, his source material, and his method immediately became the centre of a lively debate, with many often-justified doubts and criticisms being raised, the importance of his efforts should not be under-estimated.[6] Today, more than 25 years after the Laslett bombshell, family historians invariably continue to use the household as a key source of data on the family and to apply some sort of household classification scheme. In this book, I am guilty on both counts.

The importance of Ariès and of Laslett for the field of family history was not the result of specific ideas or methods. Their influence was far greater because they gave family historians a basis upon which they could build new hypotheses, new methods, new lines of enquiry. They helped lay the basis for an entire field of research. No family historian can escape their influence; yet the field long ago went far beyond the original questions, sources, and methods which they proposed.

The development of family history in Europe was always strongly influenced by a wide range of social sciences. The works of its pioneers are those of persons who approached the field from other areas of interest: Le Play was an anthropologist, Chayanov an economist, Ariès a cultural and social historian, and Laslett in many ways a historical sociologist. This cross-fertilization has proved to be enormously fruitful. Demography is a case in point. During the 1950s, Louis Henry, a demographer by profession, devised the method of family reconstitution, which enabled researchers to reconstruct the reproductive histories of married couples directly from parish archives (Fleury and Henry, 1956). Even though family reconstitution is often considered a method more specific to historical demography than to family history, it proved to be the key to the scientific understanding of the demographic role families fulfilled. Since their beginnings, historical demography and family history have been complementary fields and their influence on each other has been considerable.

Many of the more recent advances in family history can be traced to the influence of other social sciences. During the decade of the 1970s, household studies dominated much of the output in family history, though results were often criticized because of the strictures imposed by simple household analysis at one point in time. The inability of the household, for example, to reflect wider familial relations eventually led to a sharp increase in studies based on the kin group, and on the relationship between the nuclear family and its members with the wider kin group. Kin studies have meant that new data sources had to be used, and a balance between quantitative studies and 'thick description' based on a variety of qualitative sources was attempted (Wheaton, 1987; Hareven, 1991: 109–11). This type of focus, clearly inspired by the work of anthropologists, has enabled researchers to tackle such issues as the kin structures underlying networks of familial solidarity or the importance of the kin group in determining the intensity and direction of migratory flows.[7] Work on the family life cycle and the individual life course, as well as studies of the way in which family micro-economies worked within the context of macro-economic structures and fluctuations, are other examples of how the influence of other social sciences, sociology and economics in this case, have helped the field of family history to enlarge and reformulate the analytical framework for many of the central issues affecting family life in historic contexts.[8]

It is not my purpose here to give an overview of the recent developments in the field of family history, which has already been done far more competently by Tamara Hareven (1987, 1991), but rather to point to the dynamic nature of the field and to the close relations linking it to other areas of the social sciences. On both these points, the results offer little doubt: family history continues to be in a state of rapid renovation and much of this is due to the influence of anthropology, sociology, economics, and demography. Beyond these different areas of enquiry, however, in my opinion there are two major challenges facing the field of family history today. One of them is to explore in greater depth the extent to which families were able to establish viable survival strategies in diverse and often changing social, economic, and ecological circumstances. It is unquestionable that families were decision-making units and that they devised strategies destined to protect their members and to ensure the maximum benefit for themselves. Families were constrained by the prevailing economic structures and trends, by social structures, by cultural factors, and by their own demographic and economic realities. All of this can be imagined without ever looking at the historical record. The challenge is to actually document these strategies, evaluate how efficient they were and how they affected the societies in which families lived. A good deal is already known about marriage and inheritance practices in Europe, but much less is known, for example, of just how families used the human capital at their disposal and what implications these had on local economies and societies. The potential issues which can be raised are many, but all of them point to the interaction of families with their social, economic, and cultural environment, and to the family as an intermediate institution between people and society.

By extension, a second major challenge is to take up once again the issue of long-term change in family patterns and its relation to the entire process of historical change. The rise of the modern family was central to the work of Ariès and many others, and the work carried out on proto-industrialization was an attempt to place family strategies at the centre of the process of the transition to an industrial economy. There are other issues, however, which are every bit as challenging, though perhaps somewhat less ideologically charged. The effects of the demographic transition on patterns of family formation and on networks of family solidarity; the interaction between the family and the growth of the State, especially in areas of education and welfare; the role of the family in the process of urbanization of historic societies; property management, inheritance practices, and marriage strategies in times of demographic growth and demographic decline, in a full world or in a relatively empty one. These are but some of the issues which warrant further research; many more could be mentioned. They are the 'big' issues which demand imaginative research and generous answers. All of them, however, have the common denominator of the family in its dual role as an institution buffeted by the tides of history, but an active agent of those same processes of historical change.

Initially, major growth areas of family history were concentrated in central and northern Europe and in the United States, with the Mediterranean region lagging behind. In recent years all of this has begun to change. In Italy the works of Barbagli, Delille, and Kertzer, all of which appeared between 1984 and 1985, did much to stimulate an intense interest in the field which has yielded excellent results.[9] In Spain and Portugal growth in interest in family history has paralleled Italy's, though it started later and as yet is somewhat less developed. Much of the initial interest was generated by research groups in Barcelona, Murcia, Palma de Mallorca, Bilbao, Santiago de Compostela, and Lisbon, most of which eagerly emulated much of what was good, and some of what was bad, in French, English, and, to a lesser extent, Italian family history. In 1987 David Kertzer and Caroline Brettell surveyed recent developments in Italy and in the Iberian Peninsula. Their paper is fitting testimony to just how young the field was and how indebted it was both methodologically and conceptually to advances coming from northern Europe. Fortunately, Kertzer and Brettell's paper is now dated. The contours of the Iberian family history landscape are quite different from those they described, even though a certain amount of imitation of approaches coming from France and England can still be perceived. Nevertheless, the number of publications and, more important, their quality has increased substantially in the past few years. Today a number of authors, most of whom are quite young, are in the process of leading family history in Spain into its maturity. Much of their work will be used in the course of this book.

If a simple survey of those persons working in family history in Spain were carried out, it would not be difficult to see that the cross-fertilization which characterized the development of the field elsewhere in Europe also exists in Spain. Historians have learned certain methods and concerns of the social sciences; anthropologists, economists, sociologists, and demographers have renewed their interest in the past. The result has been quite positive. More than any single discipline, anthropology has provided us with much of what we know of traditional and historic family patterns in Spain. Here the pioneering work of Julio Caro Baroja and Carmelo Lisón Tolosana has been very influential, as has a tradition of local ethnographic studies.[10] Demographers, and especially historical demographers, have also become extremely active in this field, and much of the current production in family history is written by them.[11] Sociology and economics have also been influential, especially in conceptual and methodological terms.[12] This interdisciplinary nature of family history is likely to continue and deepen in the coming years.

Family history in Spain shares many of the same challenges confronting family history in other areas of Europe. Despite its recent growth, however, it is still a very young field and lacks much of the conceptual and methodological depth present elsewhere. In Spain, therefore, family history has before it two additional challenges. Developing a greater methodological sophistication which, whenever possible, is specific to the nature of the Spanish archival material is one of them. The other is to deepen and widen our empirical knowledge of family patterns in this culturally diverse country enough so as to be able to generate some working interpretative hypotheses which, in turn, will provide the basis for meaningful debates of their own regarding the development of the family in Spain. This is the only way in which the field will achieve the maturity it deserves. This book will hopefully be a useful contribution to this task.

The Family in Spain: This Book and its Perspectives

In this book I propose to sketch the basic contours of family development in Spain from the seventeenth century to the present. This is no small assignment, especially since the cultural, economic, and social complexity of this country tends to make generalizations exceedingly risky. In many ways, it is impossible to speak of the Spanish family, except perhaps in strictly contemporary society, simply because it did not exist. Even so, it is time that an attempt was made to evaluate these complexities in family forms and well as their variations over time. This would be an impossible task without attempting to bring together the different lines of the research which has been so vibrant in recent years; and a substantial part of the book will be based on that research. Editorial constraints and lack of requisite local studies will make it impossible at times to focus on key local factors and processes, or even to give an account of the substantial amount of sub-regional and societal heterogeneity which has always characterized Spain, and continues to do so today. This book is more a point of departure than one of arrival. Analytical perspectives must be deepened, widened, and made more sophisticated before our understanding of the family becomes a truly viable one. This book will not propose any definitive vision of the family in Spain. It should rather be understood as a signpost midway on the road to an acceptable understanding of the family.

Throughout this study, the family will be considered in its dual role as the guarantor of social, economic, and demographic reproduction of society, and as an institution designed to defend, protect, and assure the survival and well-being of its own members as best as possible in often difficult and adverse circumstances. The work of anthropologists, ethnographers, and family historians in Spain has been strongly influenced by the family in its role in the process of social, economic, and cultural reproduction. This can be seen in the emphasis so often placed on questions of succession, family systems, and basic modes of familial organization, as well as on the family as the key repository of certain cultural characteristics. This approach is quite necessary and addresses important issues, yet it is only a part of the entire picture. The family must also be seen as a group whose major purpose is simply to assure the survival and well-being of its members. In this sense, 'the family' becomes 'families', and their importance for society becomes their importance for their own members. Families were the context within which the young were educated and socialized; they were the primary source of welfare for those members who were vulnerable for one reason or another; they were the source of authority, of loyalty, and of social behaviour. This perspective of the family as an intermediate institution, linking the individual to society as a whole, the survival of family members to that of society, is useful because it reminds us that while the State and society had a great stake in the family, individuals did as well. From one perspective the family was a key part of a larger reality, and from the other it was that larger reality.

The ability of families to carry out either of these functions was constrained by cultural, demographic, economic, and ecological realities. Families also acted on their own environments, helping to shape key economic, social, and cultural characteristics of society. In this sense, families were both subjects and objects of their historical time, their societies, their destinies. It is extremely important to see the family as a decision-making group where short- and long-term strategies were implemented to achieve their dual goal of perpetuating society and of surviving as best as possible. Sometimes their capacity for decision-making was substantial and successful, and other times it was not. Yet the rationality was always there, and it was always constrained by outside forces. Pinpointing the ability of families to act on their surrounding world and estimating the effects of structural constraints on family development is of the utmost importance. This is the only way we will eventually be able to describe, albeit imprecisely, the role the family and families played in the process of social change.

Large-scale explanations linking the family to social and economic change are attractive, but they are only as good as their empirical base. In Spain, one of the most famous of these was the role which family systems are thought to have played for peasant living standards and for the industrial revolution in Catalonia. In this explanation, the practice of impartible succession led, by and large, to higher peasant living standards and eventually created the human capital made up of those siblings with no access to family property, which was to prove invaluable for the take-off of Catalan commercial and industrial development during the eighteenth and nineteenth centuries.[13] In seeming contradiction, in the other great region of Spain in which succession is impartible, the Basque Country, the major prevailing historical interpretation of the stem family has been to link it to questions of cultural identity which by nature were opposed to the social and economic changes, as represented by industrial, liberal, and decidedly non-nationalistic Bilbao.[14] Other general explanations like these exist, but too often they offer contradictory, ideological, and idealized visions of reality. It is not my purpose to enter into the relative merits of this or that attempt to link the family to historical change. My point is that these hypotheses are often based on wholly inadequate empirical knowledge of family forms and the way they interacted with processes of historical change. The family must be related to change, and change to the family, both at a local and at a general level. Explanatory hypotheses, however, are only as good as the building blocks they are based on. In order to do this, work must begin from the bottom up.

Undertaking a comprehensive, systematic study of the family at all of these levels of enquiry is beyond the purpose of the present book. The current state of research on the family in a society as complex as Spain's makes any project of this kind impossible. If this study is to be at all useful, decisions must be made and priorities established. This is a book of perspectives rather than a definitive treatise on the family in Spain. It could not have been written without the now-burgeoning field of family studies, but it is not going to be a mere summation of the results of those studies. In so far as it is the product of current research, however, it is constrained by the depth and quality of that research. Yet it is also strongly influenced by my own attitudes towards certain methodological, analytical, and substantive issues. These interests have contributed to the way I have conceptualized many of the questions raised and discussed in the book. By sharpening certain analytical perspectives, by advancing some useful working hypotheses, by making use of certain types of innovative data and methods, by attempting to look at society as a whole rather than this or that region or locality, I hope that these pages will prove to be useful and influential for future research in what is still a very young field. Some of the criteria underlying these perspectives are outlined in the following paragraphs.

While examining some of the interactions between the family and social, economic, and political change can be done within closely defined historical periods, a long-term perspective on family development tends to yield more rewarding results.[15] It enables us, for example, to view the family before, during, and after major historical developments such as the demographic transition or the process of modernization of Spanish society. Our earliest date of enquiry, normally the seventeenth century, has been determined by the existence of adequate source material and does not imply that major historical change has been restricted to recent centuries. This study will end in contemporary Spain; any other ending date would be arbitrary and basically unjustifiable from a conceptual standpoint. The family today has its roots in the family of the past, and these are everywhere visible. Moreover, the intensity of change taking place in Spain during the second half of the twentieth century has been so great that it enables us to see the family in the throes of change perhaps more clearly than at any other point of Spanish history. I believe that historians should not be afraid to bring their studies up to the present, just as social scientists must make greater use of historical perspectives. They have much to learn from each other. Linking the past to the present is a major challenge.

By implication, this means that in the course of this book long-term transformations in family life will receive more attention than sudden and intense, but perhaps less-lasting developments. Here continuity and continuities will tend to prevail, and the type of change we see will be gradual and lasting rather than intense and immediate. This is not to say that sudden breaks with the past did not occur. But when they did, more often than not their effects were not lasting. When change was lasting, it tended to be gradual and tended to be perceived only gradually by families.

The interactions of the family with the rest of society and with its own members will be viewed as multiple and multi-directional. The traditional way in which the family has been viewed by historians, anthropologists, and sociologists has been as an institution subject to the constraints of historic time, economic and social realities, and cultural factors. Less attention has been paid to the family as an agent of historical change or as a key element influencing the make-up of society as a whole. The role of the family as a cushion designed to defend and protect its own members from the potentially negative processes in the rest of society has been largely ignored. All of these perspectives will be present in this book; all of them are essential to our understanding of the family.

The family as institution is not the only focal point of this book. Families were also the context within which numerous events influencing people's lives took place. Family demography, practices of infant care and feeding, the way in which people confronted their options on the marriage market, or the way in which decisions to migrate were made may not have had more than indirect implications for the size and age structure of the co-resident domestic group, but they were carried out within the context of the family and as such were themselves forms of family life. The individuals who make up families and the events which take place within families are also legitimate subjects of this enquiry.

Generally speaking my analysis of the family will be restricted to those relationships which can be empirically verified. By implication, then, it will not always be possible to tackle some of the 'big' questions linking the family to the processes of change as we might wish. The transformation of a large kin-based group held together by wide-ranging allegiances into one based on private ties to the immediate kin group, the privatization of public family life, and the replacement of the authority based on lineage by the sentiment emanating from the conjugal group are all processes of great interest which have been tied in one way or another to the Industrial Revolution and to the modernization of society. They are all subjects of keen importance; but they cannot be adequately explored until more is known about their timing, their importance, or their pace of change. With these and other issues, I shall opt for a more humble but probably a more useful approach, one based on concrete issues and verifiable hypotheses. The role of the family in the process of industrial change is a case in point. Apart from lofty theoretical and ideological rhetoric, specifying those interactions is a very risky affair. Yet evaluating migratory decisions, for example, in terms of individual family strategies and decision-making processes is readily possible; and these ended up being an integral part of the process of economic continuity and change. Family issues will only be tackled where they can be verified in some way; for the most part, speculation is not a fundamental part of this book.

Certain issues affecting or characterizing families and family life have not been raised at all, either because there is not enough adequate documentation available to study them correctly, or because my own research interests have never been oriented in that direction. Family conflict, dysfunctional families, the perception of parental authority, and the role of sentiment in family relations are among them. Future studies will have to address issues like these if a thorough understanding of the family is to be reached.

Defining the family is not always an easy matter and has been an ongoing source of controversy for family historians. The conjugal unit, the co-residential domestic group, the larger kin network, and the development of kin groups over time are all manifestations of the family. All of them form different and complementary aspects of an institution which was and is able to demand ties of allegiance and authority. Each is a perspective which has advantages and disadvantages; none is complete by itself. For historical demographers the conjugal family has been the object of numerous family reconstitutions and the basis for our understanding the demographic reproduction of families and of societies. Household studies, so ubiquitous among family historians and among sociologists, are central to our understanding the basic shape of families who lived, ate, and often worked together. The kin group, which was essential for transmitting family property, for certain survival strategies, for the socialization of the young, and for the care of the elderly, has been the point of departure for numerous anthropological studies. Genealogical studies follow the development of kin groups over time and enable us to evaluate, for example, the success or failure of the survival strategies they used.

Each of these perspectives can lead to a useful understanding of certain aspects of the family, yet none of them has a lock on just what the family is or was. The conjugal family is only the biological family; the household is essentially a spatially constrained kin-based entity; and the larger kin group may have had little or no meaning for its members, especially beyond those links stemming from the original nuclear family (siblings, aunts and uncles, cousins, etc.). This multiplicity of perspectives can create a certain analytical confusion and has generated often needless controversies among students of the family. Each is valid; each is closely dependent on available documentation, ubiquitous for the household and for demographic patterns and relatively scant for the larger kin group. In the course of this book, no attempt whatsoever will be made to define the family in only one way, in terms of only one data source or analytical perspective. Demographic reproduction, co-residence, and kinship networks are interrelated aspects of the family. No viable perspective of this institution can be achieved without making use of all of them.

Whenever possible, I will attempt to render a coherent view of the family in Spain as a whole, as well as its diversity in the different cultural, economic and social, and historical contexts holding in the country. This is not always feasible, especially when our understanding of family forms must be based on local studies where coverage is uneven at the very best. It will often be impossible to portray the variety of Spanish experience adequately. In many parts of the book, analytical perspectives of the family will be proposed which are entirely new in Spain. When these are based on local data, as they often are, the results will be no more than working hypotheses whose validity in other historical and regional contexts will have to be evaluated in the light of future research. This book, in fact, contains a mixture of approaches. Some of them are global and are based either on disparate local studies or on census material, while others make use of innovative methodological or conceptual approaches, often based on very local data, to suggest potentially fruitful lines of future research.

Many different types of source material have been used. Local data include parish registers and secular (*padrones*) or ecclesiastical (*liber status animarum*) listings of inhabitants. Much of what we know about the demographic function of the family is based on parish registration, and practically all of what is known

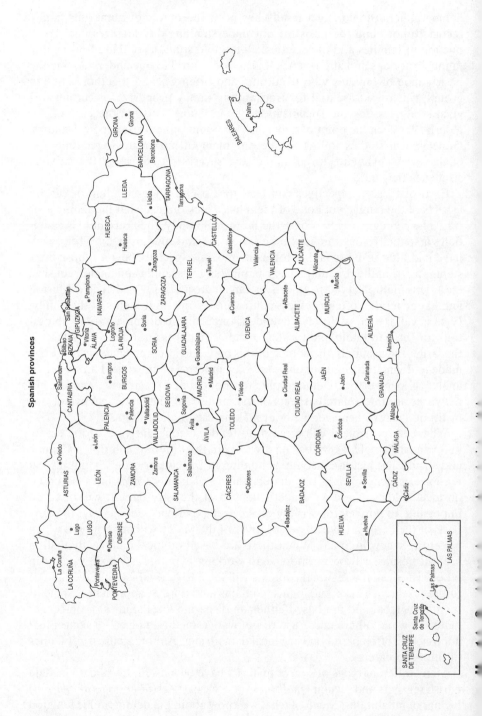

Spanish provinces

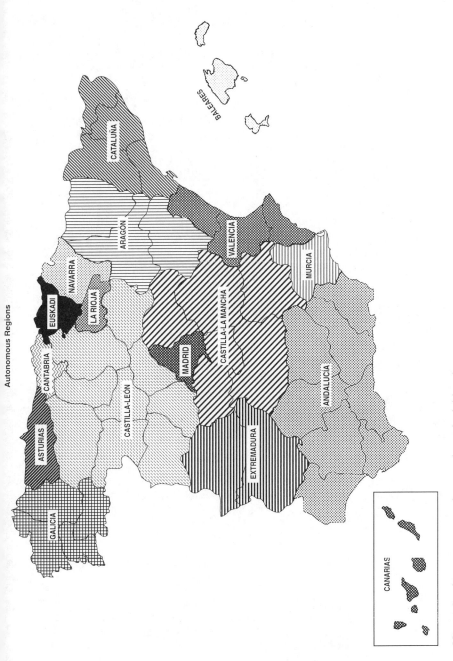

Map 1.2 Autonomous regions and provincial borders

Autonomous Regions

BALEARES

CATALUÑA

ARAGÓN

VALENCIA

MURCIA

NAVARRA

LA RIOJA

EUSKADI

CASTILLA-LA MANCHA

MADRID

CANTABRIA

ANDALUCÍA

ASTURIAS

CASTILLA-LEÓN

EXTREMADURA

GALICIA

CANARIAS

Other places and districts mentioned in the text

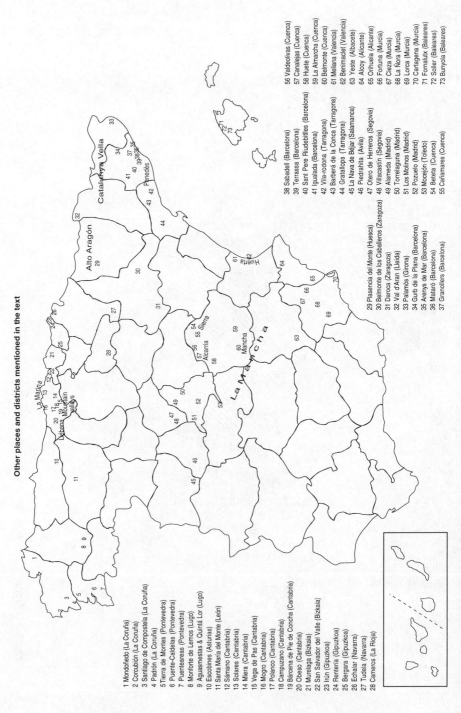

1 Mondoñedo (La Coruña)
2 Corcubión (La Coruña)
3 Santiago de Compostela (La Coruña)
4 Padrón (La Coruña)
5 Tierra de Montes (Pontevedra)
6 Puente-Caldelas (Pontevedra)
7 Puenteareas (Pontevedra)
8 Monforte de Lemos (Lugo)
9 Aguasmestas & Quintá Lor (Lugo)
10 Escobines (Asturias)
11 Santa María del Monte (León)
12 Sámano (Cantabria)
13 Solares (Cantabria)
14 Miera (Cantabria)
15 Vega de Pas (Cantabria)
16 Mogro (Cantabria)
17 Polanco (Cantabria)
18 Campuzano (Cantabria)
19 Bárcena de Pie de Concha (Cantabria)
20 Obeso (Cantabria)
21 Murelaga (Bizkaia)
22 San Salvador del Valle (Bizkaia)
23 Irún (Gipuzkoa)
24 Rentería (Gipuzkoa)
25 Bergara (Gipuzkoa)
26 Echalar (Navarra)
27 Tudela (Navarra)
28 Cameros (La Rioja)

29 Plasencia del Monte (Huesca)
30 Belmonte de los Caballeros (Zaragoza)
31 Daroca (Zaragoza)
32 Val d'Aran (Lleida)
33 Palamós (Girona)
34 Gurb de la Plana (Barcelona)
35 Arenys de Mar (Barcelona)
36 Mataró (Barcelona)
37 Granollers (Barcelona)

38 Sabadell (Barcelona)
39 Terrassa (Barcelona)
40 Sant Pere Riudebitlles (Barcelona)
41 Igualada (Barcelona)
42 Vila-rodona (Tarragona)
43 Barberá de la Conca (Tarragona)
44 Gratallops (Tarragona)
45 La Nava de Béjar (Salamanca)
46 Piedrahíta (Ávila)
47 Otero de Herreros (Segovia)
48 Villacastín (Segovia)
49 Alameda (Madrid)
50 Torrelaguna (Madrid)
51 Los Molinos (Madrid)
52 Pozuelo (Madrid)
53 Mocejón (Toledo)
54 Beteta (Cuenca)
55 Cañamares (Cuenca)

56 Valdeolivas (Cuenca)
57 Canalejas (Cuenca)
58 Huete (Cuenca)
59 La Almarcha (Cuenca)
60 Belmonte (Cuenca)
61 Meliana (Valencia)
62 Benimaclet (Valencia)
63 Yeste (Albacete)
64 Alcoy (Alicante)
65 Orihuela (Alicante)
66 Fortuna (Murcia)
67 Cieza (Murcia)
68 La Nora (Murcia)
69 Lorca (Murcia)
70 Cartagena (Murcia)
71 Formalux (Baleares)
72 Soller (Baleares)
73 Bunyola (Baleares)

Map 1.3 Other places and districts mentioned in the text (with provincial and regional borders)

about family co-residential patterns is taken from local listings of inhabitants. Census data have also proved to be invaluable in estimating the regional variability of certain demographic, economic, and co-residential aspects of family forms. All censuses since 1860 have been used in this book, as have vital statistics, published annually in Spain since 1900. Notarial archives are the source of much of what we know about inheritance and succession. Finally, a small number of ethnographic interviews of elderly peasants have proved to be very useful in deepening our understanding of certain aspects of family forms and family life. Much of my personal research has been carried out in the province of Cuenca and elsewhere in central Spain. In other areas, my knowledge is completely dependent on the number, quality, and coverage of other local studies. All national perspectives are my own. Specific characteristics of the data, the methodology used, and the origin of the source material will be discussed in the course of this book. The administrative districts of Spain as well as those places cited in the text are shown in Maps 1.1–1.3.[16]

Above all I hope this book will prove useful to all those who are interested in the family in Spain, whether or not their interest is professional, whether or not it is primarily historical, whether or not they are family historians, anthropologists, demographers, economists, or sociologists. It is a book for researchers, for students, and for all people with any curiosity about the development of the family. The book has a quantitative base, as will become apparent in the numerous tables and figures it contains, but I have attempted to make the text as accessible as possible. Sophisticated statistical techniques have been deliberately avoided; there is no econometric analysis and most tabular data contain only simple percentages and frequencies. This numeric base, however, is essential because it is the only way we can ascertain the real dimensions of families and of kinship networks, of demographic behavior and of co-residence patterns, of family economies and of migration patterns. It is also the only way the real parameters of change can be evaluated. Crafting a readily readable text in which issues and implications are clearly stated and discussed has been central to my entire effort. Whether or not this has been successful will have to be judged by my readers.

Notes

1. See Le Play (1858, 1864, 1867, 1877–9). Since Le Play and his collaborators made use of a wide selection of families taken from several European contexts, his work has had special influence in many countries. For a recent publication of a sample of the families he took from Spain, see Le Play (1990).
2. For an excellent overview of recent developments in the field, see Hareven (1991). An earlier useful paper on the same general topic can be found in Hareven (1987). See also Stone (1981), the collection of papers in Laslett (1987), and Hareven and Plakans (1987).

3. The works of Edward Shorter (1976) and Lawrence Stone (1977) have been among the most important ones to be dedicated to the subject of the formation of the modern family.
4. The original classification scheme can be found in Laslett (1972). It was subsequently refined by Hammel and Laslett (1974).
5. See Laslett and Wall (1972).
6. Two recent and critical articles, one regarding the relative stability of co-residential pattern over very long periods of time and the other on the questionable prevalence of the notion that the complex family characterized pre-modern Europe, are examples of the fact that many aspects of Laslett's original postulates continue to provoke lively debate. See Ruggles (1994*a*) and D. S. Smith (1993).
7. The work of Plakans (1984), Netting (1981), and Segalen (1985) are but three examples of this type of kinship study. Viazzo's study of Alagna in the Italian Alps is an excellent example of the type of analysis which an interdisciplinary approach based on anthropology, family history, and historical demography can yield (Viazzo, 1989). On this last point, see also Segalen (1981) and Sabean (1990).
8. For an overview of developments in life-course studies together with a useful bibliography, see Elder (1987). The field of family economies, which was long dominated by the entire debate over proto-industrialization, is now beginning to tackle some new issues. For a recent overview of the present state of this debate, see Rudolph (1992). Whether or not he is cited, the influence of the work of Gary Becker (1981) and other economists on the economics of the family is pervasive.
9. For a good example of the work being done in the field of family history in Italy, see the monographic issue of the *Journal of Family History* (vol. 15, no. 4, 1990). In that issue, the papers by Barbagli and Kertzer, Viazzo and Albera, and Da Molin are of special interest for an overview of the field. See also Viazzo (1989) and Da Molin (1990*b*).
10. In Portugal, anthropologists account for much of the best work done on historical family patterns. For useful examples of this type of work, see O'Neill (1984) and especially Brettell (1986). For an early overview of the field in Portugal, see Rowland (1984). For a brief overview of the importance of both history and anthropology for our understanding of the family, see Bestard-Camps (1991).
11. A substantial amount of the work being done on family history can be found in the publications of the Asociación de Demografía Histórica (ADEH). Within the next year, for example, the ADEH is directly or indirectly organizing two seminars which will be dedicated wholly or partially to the subject of Spanish and Portuguese family history.
12. For a useful overview of family sociology in Spain, see Iglesias de Ussel and Flaquer (1993). See also Flaquer (1990).
13. On this, see Vicens Vives (1954). See also Barrera (1990: 21–31).
14. This type of interpretation was essential to Basque nationalism, especially in its initial stages. On this, see the works of Arana-Goiri (1980) and Aranzadi (1932). See also Urrutikoetxea Lizarraga (1993: 255–7) and Elorza (1978).
15. Long-term perspectives on the relationship between the family and historical change have largely been ignored by most family historians in Spain. This has ended up having extremely negative implications for the development of family history in this country.

16. Map 1.2 represents the autonomous regions of Spain, which is the official administrative division of the country used in recent years. This map is actually quite similar to that of the historical regions of the country, with certain notable exceptions. Castilla-León historically was called Castilla la Vieja (Old Castile) and León and included Cantabria and La Rioja, which today have administrative autonomy of their own. Historically, Castilla-La Mancha was actually called Castilla la Nueva (New Castile) and included the province of Madrid.

2 Patterns of Co-residence in Spain

Establishing the basic patterns of co-residence is essential for any analysis of the family. While it is clear that the family transcends the co-residential domestic group, it is also true that many aspects of family life take place within the household. It is the most readily accessible of all family units, mainly because in many historical sources the co-residential domestic group is the basic unit of aggregation. Here I am mainly referring to national census returns (data are collected by family unit), local listings of inhabitants (*padrones* in Spanish), and *liber status animarum* (*libros de matrículas*). All of these sources are constrained by the prevailing definition of household (*hogar*), and by the fact that at times, especially before the latter part of the eighteenth century, parts of the population may not have been enumerated and the age distribution of the resident population is often missing. Another problem affecting these data is that they tend to portray residential patterns in a static way, rather than dynamically as we might well imagine family development processes to have been. Yet local listings are ubiquitous, at least from the eighteenth century on, and their analysis enables us to draw a fairly accurate picture of how residential patterns were distributed throughout the country and how they developed over time.

In Spain the recent growth in interest in family history has revolutionized our understanding of patterns of co-residence.[1] One of the first achievements of this admittedly young field has been the identification of a significant diversity of family forms on the peninsula. The existence of regional characteristics of household structure, formation, and dissolution has been related to the relative homogeneity of inheritance practices and socio-economic structures within different regions (Rowland, 1988). It has also been suggested that the regional patterns which seem to have characterized the co-residential group in Spain were quite consistent within any given region. In most of central and southern Spain, household structures seem to have always been dominated by the nuclear family, and where complexity existed, it was normally for reasons unrelated to inheritance. The only areas of the Iberian Peninsula where levels of complexity were high seem to have been located above a line stretching from northern Portugal in the west, running just south of the northern coastal mountain ranges into the Basque Country, and then along the Pyrenees, swinging down into Catalonia. In these areas inheritance practices and social and demographic structures differed markedly from the rest of the country (Douglass, 1988*a*).

Establishing these regional, ecological, social, and economic dimensions of co-residence is central to this book. In order to assess its parameters adequately, I will make abundant use both of published census data and of the now significant number of local studies evaluating household structures. Each of these sources has advantages and drawbacks. Published census data afford the only truly representative sample of co-residence patterns for the entire country, though these data do not exist before the second half of the nineteenth century and normally census categories preclude anything but the crudest measures of co-residence. Local studies offer a much greater wealth of information, but the degree to which they represent the experience of society as a whole is always suspect. Before the eighteenth century, few listings contain the requisite data for assessing household structures; after that date, while adequate data exist in most places, regional coverage has often been uneven. Even though for the eighteenth century there are a large number of local studies, some of which make use of sizeable regional samples, there are entire regions in which no studies at all have been carried out. The number of monographs on nineteenth-century society is surprisingly smaller, and for the early part of the twentieth century few large-scale studies exist. This uneven coverage is particularly unfortunate because it is precisely during this last period that Spanish society underwent a process of demographic, social, and economic modernization which was to have profound affects on family life.

Where requisite data exist, the Laslett–Hammel system of classification will be used. This system seems particularly well suited to most European contexts, mainly because the key defining element within the household is the kin group. Moreover, it has been used within the context of most of the research projects on the family in Spain. Contemporary household classification schemes are not very distant from those proposed by Laslett, and thus ready comparisons are available. Basically, in this classification the key concept is that of a conjugal unit which may be formed by a married couple, a married couple with children, or either the father or mother with their offspring. Households with more than one conjugal unit are considered 'multiple family households', and those with additional kin which do not make up a family nucleus are considered 'extended family households'. Households without any family nucleus are classified differently.[2] When the available data make this type of classification impossible, alternate proxy measures will be proposed.

Together, these measures will enable us to outline the basic regional and sub-regional patterns of co-residence in Spain and their development from the beginning of the eighteenth century until nearly the present. The picture that emerges will be one of regional stability, as those areas of relatively complex household structures in the eighteenth century and probably earlier continued to be so over two centuries later. While important changes in the family occurred over the period, they seem to have had relatively little effect on basic regional distributions. The key to this stability was unquestionably the stability in regional patterns of succession to headship and inheritance. Land availability, population growth rates, economic activity, and patterns of settlement were also important, though they cannot account for the basic regional distribution of co-residence.

Spain in 1970

Our assessment of co-residence patterns in Spain will begin at the earliest date for which adequate indicators can be generated for the entire country. The 1970 census in Spain is the first one to have an entire section dedicated to household composition. The census divides co-residential units into the following categories: (1) those without any conjugal unit or 'family nucleus' , including households with only one person, and those with groups of related and unrelated persons; (2) households with only one conjugal unit, independent of whether or not co-resident kin are present; (3) households with two kin-related conjugal units; and (4) those with three or more conjugal units. Combining categories 3 and 4 gives a unit of analysis which is directly comparable to the multiple households used in the Hammel–Laslett household classification scheme. Despite difficulties inherent in ascertaining the precise weight of extended households, some authors have generated useful though approximate measures.[3] In the published census results, all household classifications appear for provinces, provincial capitals, towns over 50,000 inhabitants, and 'urban' (>10,000), 'intermediate' (2,000–9,999), and 'rural' (<2,000) areas. These data represent the experience of the entire country and enable us to anchor our discussion of co-residence on a sound empirical footing.

If the weight of complex (census categories 2.3 + 3 + 4) and of multiple (categories 3 + 4) households are used as indicators of the basic living arrangements holding in Spanish provinces, an extremely clear regional pattern appears (Maps 2.1 and 2.2). Greatest complexity can be found in Galicia, followed at a considerable distance by Catalonia and other areas of northern Spain. In Galicia 13.6 per cent of all households had two or more conjugal units, as opposed to 9.1 per cent in Catalonia and 6.5 per cent in the Basque Country. The Spanish average was 5.8 per cent. Generally speaking, all of the provinces with relatively high percentages of multiple family households were located in the northern part of the country or in the Canary Islands.[4] Levels near or above the national average can also be found in the south-western part of the country (especially in the provinces of Seville, Huelva, and Badajoz). Much of the central and south-eastern areas of the country had extremely low levels of complex living arrangements. This general north–south division in Spain suggests a basic pattern which is not unexpected and corresponds very generally with those sections of the country where partible or impartible succession prevailed. In the following pages I will attempt to assess the extent to which this pattern was also evident during earlier periods of Spanish history.

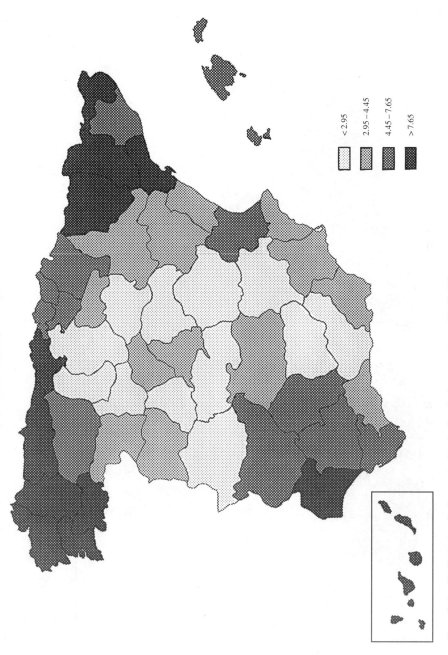

Map 2.1   Multiple family households in Spain by province, 1970 (%)

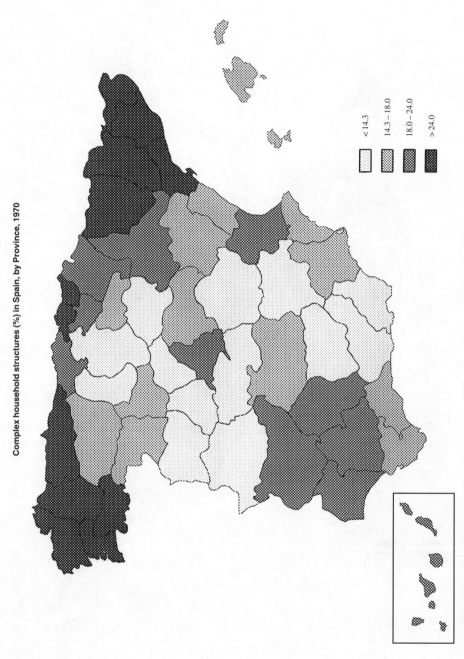

Map 2.2 Complex household structures in Spain by province, 1970 (%)

Household Structures before 1900

Tracing the stability of these patterns through the Spanish past is impossible without making use of local studies of family and household structures. Fortunately, these sorts of studies are now relatively abundant. Taken separately, questions may arise as to how representative the samples used in a number of them are, but together they constitute a fairly sizeable sample of household

Table 2.1   Household structures in spain before 1920

Region and place	Date	n	Nuclear (%)	Extended (%)	Multiple (%)	Complex (ext + mult)	Source
Galicia							
Galicia (interior)	1752	22,600	62.5	14.4	10.0	24.4	Dubert García (1992a: 89, 400)
Tierra de Montes	1752	354	56.2	15.8	9.6	25.4	Fernández Cortizo (1982)
Orense (town)	1752	773	66.4	9.6	1.8	11.4	Dubert García (1992a: 424)
Santiago de Compostela	1752	4,177	65.5	9.6	4.2	13.8	Dubert García (1987: 1992a: 424)
Monforte de Lemos (town)[a]	1708–61	1,342	67.5	10.0	5.8	15.8	Dubert García (1992b: 37)
Lugo (town)	1752	677	68.3	11.6	7.0	18.6	same
Cantabria							
Solares, Mogro[b]	1578–82	216	67.4	7.7	10.1	17.8	Lanza (1991: 355)
6 villages[c]	17th c.	672	73.2	3.2	12.1	15.3	same
Santander (town)	1752	681	74.7	3.2	1.9	5.1	Lanza (1991: 354)
Provincial sample	same	30,435	70.7	4.4	6.1	10.5	same
Basque Country							
Vizcaya (provincial sample)	1885–82	17,927	63.5	17.8	7.6	25.4	Ortega Berruguete et al. (1988: 136; 1989: 68)
Vizcaya (rural)	1885–92		59.5	18.9	15.6	34.5	Ortega Berruguete et al. (1988: 136)
Vizcaya (semi-urban)	1885–92		62.6	18.4	9.2	27.6	Ortega Berruguete (1989: 68)
Vizcaya (industrial)	1885–92		77.8	14.9	2.1	17.0	same
Bilbao (town)	1885–92		53.9	19.1	3.5	22.6	same
Bergara (Guipúzcoa)	1658		51.3	25.0	17.1	42.1	Ibañez et al. (1994)
Irún (Guipúzcoa)	1766	235	63.4	5.5	27.7	33.2	Urrutikoetxea (1992: 145)
Irún (Guipúzcoa)	1845	797	64.6	12.4	16.4	28.8	Urrutikoetxea (1992: 152)
Rentería (Guipúzcoa)	1857	178	54.5	10.1	32.6	42.7	Cruz Mundet (1991: 485)
San Salvador de Valle (Vizcaya)[d]	1877–1913	3,635	76.5	15.7	1.9	17.6	Pérez Fuentes (1993: 156)
Navarre							
Provincial sample (rural and urban)	1786	11,585	62.9	7.2	22.1	29.3	Mikelarena Peña (1992a: 131–2; 1995)
Echalar	1842, 1861	653	63.1			29.6	Douglass (1988b: 82–3)
La Rioja							
Logroño (town)	1752, 1797		75.9	7.3	1.4	8.7	Lázaro and Gurría (1992: 106)
Cameros	1752	1,797	71.7	10.0	2.5	12.5	Gurría (1984: 66)

Table 2.1   (cont.)

Region and place	Date	n	Nuclear (%)	Extended (%)	Multiple (%)	Complex (ext + mult)	Source
Catalonia							
Gerona (town)[e]	1720–1800		55.2	6.3	13.3	19.9	Simón Tarrés
Barberá	1776	116	43.1	25.9	24.1	50.0	Isaevich (1984: 246)
Gratallops	1800	218	58.7	21.5	17.4	39.0	Roigé Ventura (1989: 12)
Sant Pere de Riudebitlles	1849	316	67.1	15.2	14.2	29.4	Torrents i Rosès (1993: 263)
Navarcles	1857	295	58.3	19.7	18.3	38.0	Ferrer i Alòs (1987: 572)
Vila-rodona	1889, 1901	936	68.5			25.2	Comas d'Argemir (1988: 147)
Val d'Aran	1900, 1920	604	57.2	22.1	7.7	29.8	Roigé Ventura (1993: 171)
Balearic Islands							
Bunyola	1824	399	77.7	8.0	4.8	12.8	Moll Blanes (1988: 246)
Fornalutx	1824	232	67.2	12.9	6.5	19.4	same
Soller	1824	1,332	69.6	11.6	7.3	18.9	same
Valencia							
Meliana	1753, 1791	358	67.4	12.5	14.9	27.4	Garrido Arce (1992a: 67; 1992b: 86)
Murcia							
Cieza, Fortuna	1756	1,579	86.2	3.5	0.4	3.9	Chacón et al. (1986: 175)
Cartagena (town)	1756	7,064	85.9	4.1	0.0	4.1	Chacón (1987: 143)
Lorca	1771		78.3	5.5	0.4	5.9	Hurtado Martínez (1987)
La Ñora[f]	1850–1901	2,091	87.9	3.7	0.6	4.3	Martínez Carrión (1988: 96)
León							
Santa María del Monte	1752	328	79.6	5.8	0.6	6.4	Behar and Frye (1988: 20)
New Castile							
Cuenca (rural sample)	18th c.	778	80.8	4.1	0.4	4.5	Reher (1988: 6)
same	1800–50	2,762	82.1	4.9	0.8	5.7	same
same	1851–1900	3,947	85.8	4.2	1.8	6.0	same
Cuenca (town)[g]	1724–1844	3,273	73.2	7.3	1.5	8.8	Reher (1990: 194)
Los Molinos (Madrid)	1751	92	81.4	4.4	0.0	4.4	Soler Serratosa (1985: 148)
Andalucia							
Granada (town)	1752	5,724	65.1	14.4	1.6	16.0	Casey and Vincent (1987: 177)

Notes: Whenever data taken from more than one date or from more than one place have been combined, unweighted averages have been used.

Normally the sample size refers to the number of households, though in some cases it is not clear whether the author refers to the number of households or to the number of persons.

When data from one of the categories is missing, it either means that the author did not include it in the cited publication or that the classification used was not completely compatible with the Hammel–Laslett system used here.

[a] Data from Monforte de Lemos are taken from 1708, 1752, and 1761.
[b] Solares 1578, Mogro 1582.
[c] Obeso 1605, Pie de Concha 1605, Miera 1607, Sámano 1627, Polanco 1673, and Campuzano 1683, 1684, and 1686.
[d] Dates: 1877, 1887, 1900, 1913.
[e] Dates: 1720, 1755, 1800.
[f] Data taken from listings in 1850, 1879, 1885, 1895, and 1901.
[g] Data taken from 1724, 1800, and 1844.

structures in Spain over much of the eighteenth and nineteenth centuries.[5] It is unfortunate that most of these studies have been disproportionately centred on villages in the northern areas of the country. This is partially the result of the keen interest generated by the stem family and its different manifestations in Spain, and partially a product of the research priorities of historians and anthropologists in these regions. Nevertheless, recognizable and consistent patterns emerge from the data presented in Table 2.1.

Household structures have been classified basically according to the Laslett–Hammel typologies, and are presented here as percentage nuclear, extended, and multiple. It is important to note that none of these categories constitute proof by themselves of the existence or absence of the stem family. More precisely, they are simply indicators of living arrangements. Stem family succession may or may not be present in any of them; and complex living arrangements could be entirely independent of succession. They do, nevertheless, give us an excellent idea of how households were arranged in different parts of the country.

An initial conclusion which can be drawn from Table 2.1 is that the basic regional pattern of co-residence described for 1970 appears to have held since at least the eighteenth century, and possibly quite a bit earlier. Despite some widely varying results, generally levels of household complexity seem to have been notable in Galicia, the Basque Country, Navarre, and Catalonia, and moderate or very low in studies centred on other parts of the country.[6] The only areas of the northern part of the country with data in the table which show relatively low levels of complex households are Santander and especially La Rioja. There is also some indication that in Valencia and to a lesser extent in the Balearic Islands extended or multiple households were not as uncommon as in other parts of the country.

These data provide a rich testimony to the amount of quality research which has been done in recent years on the structures of the co-resident domestic group. While each of them deserves abundant detailed comment, taken together they basically suggest that the regional distribution of living arrangements did not seem to have changed very much over the past three centuries. Further proof of this can be found if census-based indicators are used. While before 1970 these sorts of indicator are much poorer than the ones derived from local studies, they do have the great advantage of covering the entire country evenly. In this way they supplement the all-too-evident gaps in the local studies. The most readily accessible of these indicators is the mean household size (MHS), which can be calculated beginning with the census of 1860 by dividing total population by the number of census returns (*cédulas*). While it is unquestionable that the mean household size is strongly influenced by living arrangements, it is also subject to prevailing levels of fertility, mortality, nuptiality, migration, and the presence of co-resident servants or other individuals unrelated to the kin group.[7] Despite its imperfections, it provides a valuable approximation to regional patterns of complexity and how they evolved over time.

In 1860 the regional distribution of mean household size is quite familiar. The 13 provinces with the highest MHS were all located in the northern part of Spain, and these were followed by Madrid (due probably to the importance of domestic servants in Madrid households) and by the Canary Islands. Intermediate levels can be found in the Balearic Islands and in Valencia, with other provinces in the central and southern parts of the country showing far lower values of MHS. Sixty years later in 1920, even though changes had occurred, the basic patterns continued. Fourteen of the 15 provinces with highest MHS were located in the northern areas of the country and in the Canary Islands, and lowest values were once again in central and southern Spain. This basic pattern had hardly changed by 1960. The demographic transition and the massive overseas migration flows had introduced important transformations over time, but not so much as to obscure the basic similarity in patterns.[8] This can also be seen in Table 2.2, which contains a matrix of bivariate correlation coefficients of MHS over time, together with the percentage of multiple households taken from the census of 1970 and used earlier in this chapter. The abundance of significant coefficients points to the stability of basic regional patterns. While they tend to weaken with the passage of time, due probably to factors largely unrelated to family structures themselves, the similarities are undeniable. It is also interesting to note the significant correlation coefficients with the indicator of the percentage of multiple households, which are especially strong with regional distributions taken from the nineteenth century. Despite changes in fertility, mortality, and migration, census-based mean household size suggests that regional distributions of basic co-residential patterns underwent few substantial changes between the nineteenth and twentieth centuries. After 1940 families ended up becoming generally smaller because the number of children at home diminished. Yet the presence of co-

Table 2.2   Mean household size and percentage of multiple households: matrix of bivariate correlation coefficients

Date and indicator	1860	1877	1897	1920	1930	1940	1960	% mult. 1970
1860	1.000	0.787**	0.566**	0.589**	0.486**	0.292	0.432**	0.602**
1877		1.000	0.845**	0.792**	0.687**	0.513**	0.511**	0.496**
1897			1.000	0.852**	0.802**	0.629**	0.537**	0.392*
1920				1.000	0.947**	0.820**	0.663**	0.469**
1930					1.000	0.891**	0.704**	0.405*
1940						1.000	0.788**	0.250
1960							1.000	0.418*
% multiple (1970)								1.000

Significance: * < 0.01 ** < 0.001.

resident kin outside the conjugal family unit continued to be high in the northern part of the country, just as it had been during the eighteenth century.

Sub-regional Diversity

The rather straightforward regional patterns of co-residence which have been proposed in the preceding pages may well not do justice to more complex realities. Intra-regional variability was likely greater than has been suggested. Specifically local factors often played an important role in conditioning inheritance practices, and demographic, economic, and historical realities also tended to differ by district, social group, or urban/rural residence. Society was basically heterogeneous and ascertaining the extent to which this influenced household structures is essential if complexity of family forms in Spain is to be adequately understood.

A very useful point of departure for this discussion lies in the district-level data contained in the censuses of 1860 and 1887 in Spain, which have been studied by Fernando Mikelarena Peña (1992*b*) and by Reher *et al.* (1993). Even though we are restricted to very simple measures of household complexity such as mean household size, the 476 judicial districts existing in the entire country enable us to get at some important issues affecting family residence patterns. Despite certain discrepancies in the way in which the census data were gathered in 1860 and 1887, the results from both studies are quite comparable.[9]

Both studies make use of MHS as the basic indicator of household structures, but end up proposing other measures less sensitive to demographic and economic realities. Noteworthy, but not surprising, is that the regional and sub-regional distribution of MHS in both censuses is very similar (Map 2.3). Once again the highest values are to be found along the Pyrenees from Catalonia to the Basque Country, and from the western part of Cantabria through most of Galicia. Areas of the south-west and along the eastern and south-eastern parts of the country also had relatively high MHS, as opposed to the central plateau (*meseta*) and parts of Andalucia, which had low MHS. Perhaps more interesting, however, is the variety visible within different historical regions. The only region with a certain degree of homogeneity seems to have been Catalonia, where relatively high MHS prevailed in most areas. The other classic stem family regions were quite different. In the Basque Country and Navarre, the northern mountainous areas showed high levels of complex living arrangements, but along their southern flank mean household size diminished noticeably. The situation in Aragon was even clearer: only the northern parts of the region close to the Pyrenees (basically the province of Huesca) were characterized by high levels of complex living arrangements, as opposed to the central and southern areas, where household size was very small. In Galicia household sizes were far higher in the central and eastern parts of the

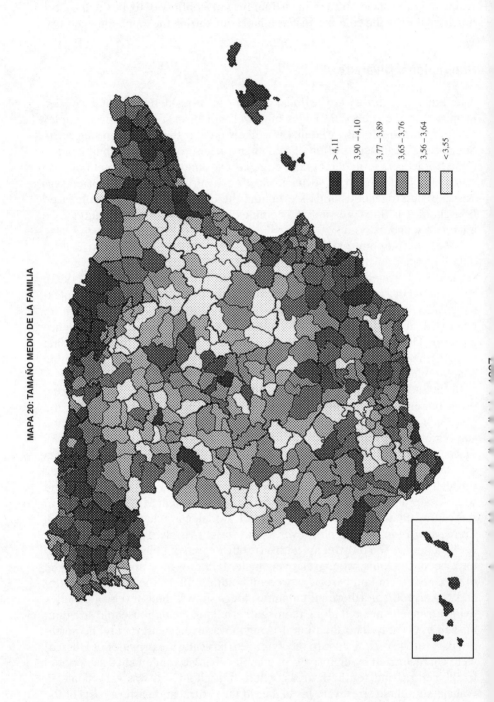

MAPA 20: TAMAÑO MEDIO DE LA FAMILIA

> 4,11
3,90 – 4,10
3,77 – 3,89
3,65 – 3,76
3,56 – 3,64
< 3,55

region than in the western coastal areas, possibly the product of male migration to America, which was strongest precisely in those districts. The region of
Valencia was also one of great diversity. While the rich 'Huerta' stretching
west and south from the city of Valencia had fairly high values of MHS, the
entire western part of the region was characterized by very low values. Much
the same occurred in the south-east, where household size was far higher along
the coast than it is in those districts lying further inland.

In order to minimize the effects of fertility, mortality at young ages, and sex-
specific migration, and to approximate better the complexity of household
structures, both studies have proposed alternative indicators. One of those
used is based on the number of adults (above 21 years of age) in 1860 or female
adults (above 25) in 1887 per household.[10] This indicator was designed to take
into account household complexity derived either from the presence of more
than one conjugal unit within the household or the presence of other adult kin.
This last aspect may or may not have been related to patterns of family
succession, and was likely quite sensitive to adult (female) celibacy levels. The
results for 1887 are summarized in Map 2.4. The major difference can be seen
in Galicia, where practically everywhere the levels of the indicator were
among the highest in Spain. Even though mean household size was only
moderate due to male emigration to America, other indicators suggest that
complex household types were quite frequent.

Finally, Fernando Mikelarena also presents indicators of the number of
married and widowed persons per household, and the number of married and
widowed women per household. Both of these tend to reflect mainly the
weight of actual conjugal units integrating Spanish households in 1860. His
results (1992b: 24–5) suggest that the only areas in which values are high were
located in Catalonia, the northern parts of Aragon, Navarre, and the Basque
Country. These are the regions in which the stem family was typical and where
appreciable percentages of households tended to have more than one conjugal
unit. Yet it is surprising to note that in Asturias and Galicia these indicators
give no indication at all that levels of household complexity were high. This
tends to contradict not only the results derived from local studies based mainly
on the eighteenth century, but also those in 1970 which were based precisely
on the number of households with more than one conjugal unit. When, on the
other hand, Mikelarena uses all adult persons per household irrespective of
their marital status as an approximate measure of household structures, his
results show that complexity was indeed high in both regions. While it is well
known that high levels of female celibacy were essential to relatively large
family sizes in Galicia and Asturias (unmarried women did not live alone),
local studies have also shown that levels of multiple households there were
considerably higher than in most of the rest of the country.[11]

Even this census-based approach does little justice to the great intra-
regional and even local variations which can arise in patterns of co-residence.
Yet not all areas experienced the same degree of variability. Fortunately,

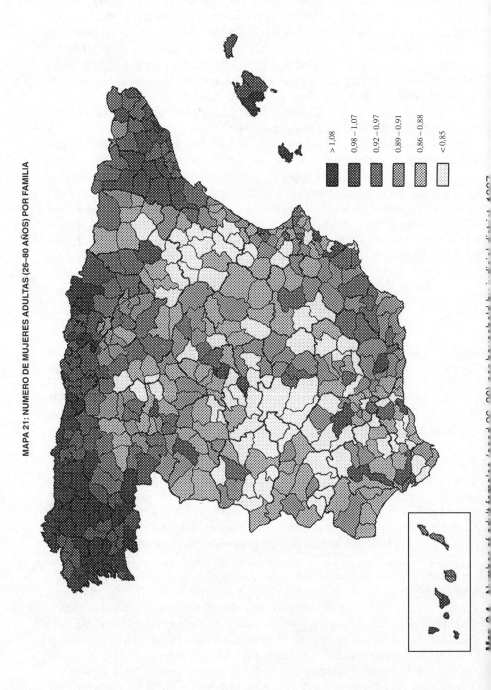

MAPA 21: NUMERO DE MUJERES ADULTAS (26–80 AÑOS) POR FAMILIA

ambitious regional studies exist for Galicia, Cantabria, the Basque Country, Navarre, and Cuenca which enable us to assess this sort of diversity.[12] A brief overview of existing results will be instructive on this count. From the data presented in Table 2.3 it is evident that in the three regions noted for high proportions of complex household structures there was considerable variability, as opposed to the other two regions, where structures were somewhat more uniform.

During the central part of the eighteenth century Galicia seems to have been fairly clearly divided into a central-eastern region encompassing the southern half of the province of Lugo and the northern half of Orense, where complexity was considerably higher than in other areas to the north, south, and west of the region.[13] In the Basque Country, the southern parts of the region had appreciably lower levels of complexity than the more northern districts. The situation was much more pronounced in the adjacent province of Navarre, where household complexity was very high in the central and northern part of the region, and moderate to low in the south. In Navarre, at least, this difference appears to have been a long-standing one, likely present during

Table 2.3 Household structures in spain before 1920: intra-regional variation

Region and place	Date	n	Nuclear (%)	Extended (%)	Multiple (%)	Complex (ext + mult)	Source
Galicia							
West Galicia	1752	18,335	64.2	13.2	8.9	22.1	Dubert García (1992a: 400)
East Galicia	1752	4,265	57.3	18.5	13.6	32.1	Dubert García (1992a: 400; 1992b: 37)
Cantabria							
La Marina	1752	17,722	73.0	4.1	5.6	9.7	Lanza (1991: 354); see also Lanza (1888: 138)
Mountain valleys	1752	9,702	71.9	4.5	4.5	9.0	same
Liébana	1752	2,330	63.5	5.7	12.5	18.2	same
Navarre[a]							
Areas from Pamplona north to Pyrenees	1786	3,592	50.8	9.5	32.5	42.0	Mikelarena Peña (1992a: 131–2; 1995)
Central Navarre	1786	4,134	60.1	6.8	27.7	34.5	same
Southern districts, near Ebro river	1786	3,859	76.9	5.2	8.1	13.3	same
Cuenca (New Castile)[b]							
Sierra	1800–1901	1,817	82.0	6.0	0.7	6.7	Reher (1988)
Alcarria	1800–1901	1,756	83.8	3.8	0.9	4.7	same
Mancha	1800–1901	3,923	83.0	3.8	0.4	4.2	same

[a] Mikelarena Peña divides Navarre into eight districts' which for the purposes of this table have been reduced to only three. Unweighted averages have been used.

[b] These are previously unpublished data coming from a research project on the family in Cuenca. Each district represents an area of the province with different geographic and economic structures.

the late Middle Ages, and is not dissimilar to the geographical limits of the Basque language in 1857 (Berthe, 1984).[14] In other regions, sub-regional differences do not appear to have been so pronounced. This is especially true in the districts (*comarcas*) of Cuenca, where at no time do appreciable differences in household structures appear.

In explaining the differences, or the lack thereof, most of the authors cited here have pointed to inheritance practices as the key variable in determining the weight of complex households in society. In those regions where a given type of inheritance, be it partible or impartible, was practised uniformly, appreciable sub-regional differences in household composition never appeared.[15] In other regions, such as Navarre or Aragon, where this was not the case, regional uniformity in patterns of co-residence practically disappeared. Where inheritance practices were more uniform, sub-regional differences tended to be more reduced, and demographic and other economic factors are sufficient to explain the observed variations. In other words, the great general regions characterized by complex and large households, or by nuclear and small ones, ended up being defined essentially by the existence or not of partible or impartible inheritance practices. When the prevailing norms dictated that one member of the family was to inherit the family home and farm and end up co-residing with his or her parents, co-residential groups were large and household structures complex. When all heirs participated equally in inheritance, as was the case in the great majority of the country, households tended to be small. Within each of these general regions, variations in the size and make-up of households ended up being determined by demographic realities, marriage markets, patterns of family solidarity, and the constraints of the household economies.

This being the case, when controlling for economic position or place of residence within a given region we can expect observed differences in household structure to be the product of a combination of these factors. Levels of complexity should vary by wealth and by the existence of property, especially rural property. Wealthier families were in a better position to house kin, and may well have needed them as a supplementary form of household labour. For them, inheritance tended to loom larger than for other sectors of society. Property, itself often closely tied to wealth and social position, was another factor influencing certain patterns of co-residence. The structures of inheritance were only socially and economically significant when there was property to be bequeathed. These ideas receive strong support from the different local monographs in which household structures have been classified by the occupation of the household head. Households headed by the well-to-do in society tended to have higher levels of complexity than other social groups. This can be seen clearly from the data contained in Table 2.4, which have been taken from several different studies of family structures in widely varying contexts. The results are clear: the wealthier the social group and whenever there was property to be transmitted in one way or another, levels of co-residential

Table 2.4   Percentage of complex household structures by occupation and wealth

Region	Date	Occupational category	Complex (ext + mult)	Source
Galicia (sample of rural areas)	1752	Salaried artisans	20.6	Dubert García (1992*a*: 120)
		Day labourers and farmers	25.1	
		Nobles	30.5	
		Administration and commerce	25.5	
Navarre (sample from central area)	1786	Peasant farmers	47.2	Mikelarena Peña (1995: table 4.9)
		Artisans	33.0	
		Day labourers ·	18.3	
Balearic Islands (Bunyola, Fornalutx)	1824	Peasant farmers (*labradores*)	20.7	Moll Blanes (1988: 248)
		Day labourers	12.0	
Logroño[a] (town)	1752–94	Day labourers	4.8	Lázaro and Gurría García (1992: 108)
		Farmers	12.7	
		Artisans	11.3	
		Services	12.7	
		Privileged	17.4	
Cuenca (rural sample)	1800–1970	Day labourers	3.6	Reher (1988: 151)
		Farmers	6.1	
		Artisans	5.1	
		Services	5.3	
		Professional/ privileged	6.4	
Cuenca (town)	1800, 1844	Day labourers	9.5	Reher (1990: 194)
		Industry/artisans	10.0	
		Services	13.5	
		Prof./Adm./ Privileged	15.0	
Santander (Cantabria) (town)	1752	Privileged/ merchants	17.0	Lanza (1991: 356)
		Farmers	4.8	
		Sailors	2.3	
		Artisans	3.7	
Granada (Andalusia)	1752	Privileged	240	Casey and Vincent (1987: 177)
		Artisans	18.2	
		Day labourers	11.3	
Vila-Rodona (Catalonia)	1889, 1901	Peasant landowners (>6 hectares)	46.5	Comas d'Argemir (1988: 150)
		Peasants and sharecroppers (0.5–6 hectares)	29.6	
		Landless peasants	14.6	
Sant Pere de Riudebitlles (Barcelona/Catalonia)	1849	Pagesos (peasant farmers)	32.9	Torrents i Rosès (1993)
		Paper makers	28.8	
		Other artisans	31.9	

Table 2.4   (cont.)

Region	Date	Occupational category	Complex (ext + mult)	Source
La Ñora (Murcia)[b]	1850–1925	Services	7.5	Martínez Carrión (1988: 102)
		Peasants	5.3	
		Day labourers	8.3	
		Annual income	Complex (ext + mult)	
Cuenca (rural sample)[c]	1817	<200	2.3 (254)	Reher (1988: 178)
		200–499	5.2 (488)	
		500–999	2.8 (408)	
		1,000–2,499	5.4 (537)	
		2,500–4,999	12.2 (151)	
		>5,000	15.0 (80)	
	1910–30	200–499	0.0 (33)	same
		500–999	2.4 (132)	
		1,000–2,499	4.0 (189)	
		2,500–4,999	10.7 (145)	
		>5,000	11.0 (122)	

[a] Weighted average from 1752, 1770, 1784, and 1797.
[b] Unweighted average from 1850, 1879, 1901, and 1925.
[c] Data refer to annual income expressed in *reales* in 1817 and in *pesetas* in 1910–1930. Sample size in parentheses.

complexity were higher. Within every different context, artisans, people in the services sector, day labourers, or landless peasants showed lower levels of household complexity than did peasant farmers, the professional and privileged groups of the society, or large landowners.[16] The rural areas of the province of Cuenca provide perhaps the most eloquent example of this positive relationship between kin co-residence and wealth. Both at the beginning of the nineteenth century, and then again one century later, in a region characterized by the absolute predominance of simple family households, families with higher incomes invariably had higher numbers of co-resident kin.

If place of residence is controlled within given regional contexts, interesting and not unexpected results emerge. Urban patterns of co-residence roughly reflected the general geography of rural co-residence in Spain. Relatively high levels of household complexity in urban areas persisted precisely in those regions characterized by complex family forms. This is apparent from the examples shown in Table 2.1 taken from historical studies, as well as those in Table 2.5, which contains a selection of provinces taken from the census of 1970. In both cases, towns located in the northern parts of the country had higher levels of household complexity than towns in other parts of the country. Despite this, however, it is also interesting to note how levels of complexity diminished in the towns situated in regions of complex family forms, but hardly varied or even increased in those characterized by nuclear households.

Table 2.5 Percentage of households with two or more conjugal units by place of residence, Spain, 1970

Province	Place of residence				
	Total	Capital	Urban	Intermediate	Rural
La Coruña	13.8	6.2	5.6	7.9	18.8
Barcelona	7.6	6.3	7.1	9.7	13.5
Vizcaya	6.6	5.7	5.9	7.2	10.5
Sevilla	5.9	5.4	5.5	7.1	5.5
Badajoz	6.0	5.4	5.8	6.3	5.7
Madrid	3.6	3.8	3.7	2.2	2.0
Granada	2.8	3.0	3.2	3.0	2.3
Spain	5.8		4.9	5.5	8.0

Note: Urban, >10,000; intermediate, 2,000–10,000; rural, <2,000.

These results can be seen both in the historical monographs and in the 1970 census.

The reason for these patterns is quite clear. Generally speaking, levels of complexity were always higher in those regions where more or less impartible patterns of inheritance were practiced, and lower where they were not. Since the boundaries of these regions in 1970 were much the same as two centuries earlier, the basic pattern remained unchanged. However, in those regions where complex household structures tended to be important, kin co-residence was always less significant in urban areas, mainly because for most urban residents inheritance was much less important than in rural areas. Even though some families did maintain links to land and homes located in rural areas, and thus tended to perpetuate these practices in towns, the role of inheritance in determining patterns of co-residence was invariably lower. People for whom family formation was more dependent on their economic activity than on inheritance were always more numerous in towns. In fact, in many ways towns were filled precisely with those people who had been ex-cluded in one way or another from the inheritance of the family farm. Impart-ible inheritance, and complex living arrangements, were basically a rural reality.

In the areas of Spain in which partible inheritance practices prevailed, this urban/rural dichotomy did not necessarily occur. There, the relative com-plexity of family forms did not depend on the patterns of succession, but rather on links of solidarity within the family. The nephew studying at school, the unmarried sister, the widowed mother-in-law, or the newly married couple were the sources of complex structures, not the heir apparent and his spouse. Wealth was also a key factor here because normally the wealthier families were more prone to having co-resident kin. None of these realities, however, were anchored in rural life. Data taken from both historical monographs and from the 1970 census suggest that in the nuclear family regions, levels of complexity in urban areas were similar to or even higher than those holding in the surrounding rural areas.

The Effects of Time, 1700–1970

Over the past century, a profound process of demographic and economic modernization has taken place in Spanish society. A demographic transition has occurred, society has become urbanized, periods of massive out-migration have come and gone, farming has given way to industry as the chief mode of economic activity, and a traditional society and its values have been replaced by a fairly mature consumer society. The extent to which these momentous changes have affected the basic living arrangements of Spaniards is an open question. Earlier in this chapter rather convincing proof was given of the stability of the regional patterns of co-residence in Spain over at least the past three centuries. The extent to which changes took place within different regions is more difficult to know because few studies attempt to track systematically patterns of change over prolonged periods of time.

An initial approach to this question can be derived from an admittedly inadequate comparison of some of the historic regional samples presented earlier and data taken from the 1970 census classifications. The samples used are not strictly comparable mainly because the historical studies have made use of much smaller samples, often based on the experience of only a few villages. Yet there are two categories present both in the Laslett–Hammel classification system used in the historic data and in the 1970 census: the proportion of households occupied by only one person, and the proportion of households with two or more conjugal units. Results suggest that despite other transformations, in most areas the weight of multiple households did not change appreciably between the pre-industrial era and 1970. With the exception of Navarre and to a lesser extent of Catalonia, the importance of households with more than one conjugal unit remained basically the same (Table 2.6). In many cases, levels of complexity actually increased by 1970. While a

Table 2.6 Percentage of households with two or more conjugal units by region, pre-1900 and 1970 compared

Region/Province	pre-1900	1970
Vizcaya	7.6	6.6
Galicia	10.0	13.6
Navarre	22.1	5.9
Cantabria	6.1	7.7
Catalonia	16.2	9.1
Baleares	6.2	4.5
Cuenca	1.2	2.3
La Rioja	2.0	3.5
Murcia	0.4	4.1
Granada	1.6	3.0

Note: For pre-1900 data, only unweighted averages have been used.
When a provincial sample has not been available, the unweighted
average of available studies has been used.

large part of the observed variation may well have been the result of demographic and economic factors totally unrelated to inheritance and succession within given family systems, the data suggest that the component of family forms dictated by inheritance continued to exert a considerable influence on patterns of co-residence as recently as 1970.

More useful data can be derived from local studies which follow the development of family structures at regular intervals before and during the process of modernization of Spanish society. Very few of those published cover such an extended period of time, but the ones that do provide valuable insights into the development of household structures over time. For purposes of comparison, my own study of family forms in rural areas of the province of Cuenca between the eighteenth century and 1970 will be used together with Xavier Roigé i Ventura's 1993 study of the Aran Valley (Val d'Aran). Neither of these studies cover strictly comparable periods of time, and while one is a fairly sizeable provincial sample, the other centres on a very small rural district. But each one evaluates family forms in sharply contrasting contexts. In rural Cuenca, simple household structures were predominant, whereas in the Aran Valley, nestled in the Catalan Pyrenees, the stem family was prevalent and complex living arrangements abounded.[17] In many ways, these contexts are typical of the two different family systems predominant in Spain. The results from these two studies are summarized in Figures 2.1–2.4.

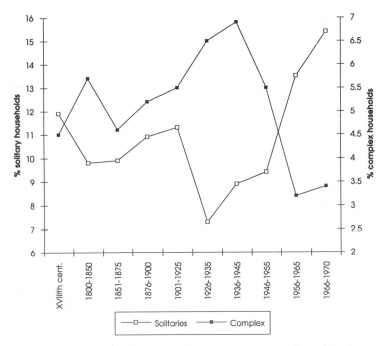

Fig. 2.1 Solitary and complex household structures in Cuenca, 1700–1970

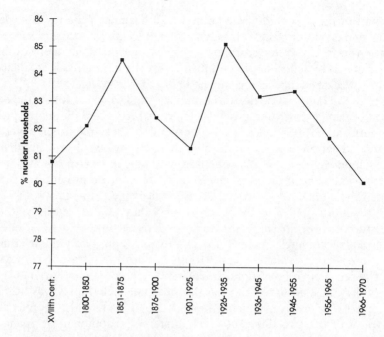

Fig. 2.2 Nuclear household structures in Cuenca, 1700–1970

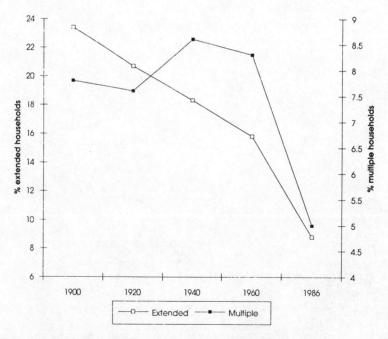

Fig. 2.3 Complex household structures in Val d'Aran, 1900–1986

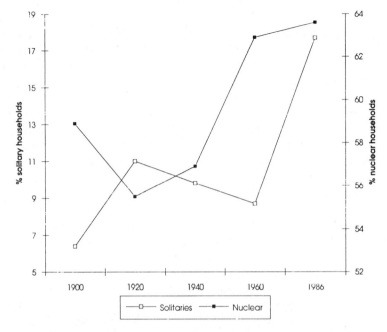

Fig. 2.4 Solitary and nuclear household structures in Val d'Aran, 1900–1986

Interesting contrasts emerge when comparing both studies. In Cuenca, the incidence of complex households rose from the middle of the nineteenth century until approximately 1940, and declined sharply thereafter to nearly half the levels reached earlier. In the Val d'Aran, on the other hand, the importance of complex households appears to have declined consistently from the beginning of this century. If we look closer, however, multiple family households seem to have held their own until 1960, as opposed to extended households, which declined sharply throughout the twentieth century. In both the Val d'Aran and Cuenca, there was a significant rise in solitary households, dating from 1940 in Cuenca and from 1960 in the Val d'Aran. Nuclear households, on the other hand, followed quite different trajectories, increasing in importance in Aran after 1920, mainly at the expense of extended family households, as opposed to the consistent but small declines occurring in Cuenca after 1930.

Despite important changes occurring with complex family forms, certain regularities also appear. Much as occurred when comparing recent census data with earlier historical studies, at least until 1970 levels of multiple households both in Cuenca and in the Val d'Aran were roughly comparable with those holding decades earlier.[18] The same cannot be said of the presence of other kin within the household, which declined consistently from the beginning of the century in Aran and after 1940 in Cuenca. In Cuenca co-resident kin were almost never involved in household succession; and in Aran the presence of collateral kin declined drastically as opposed to the number of ascendant or descendent kin potentially in line for succession, which remained relatively stable (Roigé, 1993: 165).[19] In other words, in both contexts the decline in co-resident kin appears to have affected those persons unrelated to succession. In more recent years, however, there is strong evidence that the importance of the stem family has been diminishing appreciably in the Val d'Aran, and any vestige of household complexity has practically disappeared in Cuenca.

Cultural and demographic factors help explain these patterns. In both contexts, the rise of solitary households was unquestionably the result of an increasing life expectancy which was much more pronounced among women than among men. Moreover, both areas were affected by currents of out-migration which became especially intense after 1950–60. People who might have remained at home with their parents, for example, had now moved to Barcelona, Valencia, or Madrid to establish households of their own. The increase in the importance of solitary households is one of the most salient changes affecting the family in Spain during the second half of the twentieth century, and has continued unabated until the present. Declining fertility also reduced the numbers of children at home, as well as the potential youths who might have co-resided with other kin as nephews or grandchildren. Finally, after mid-century diminishing levels of female celibacy and earlier age at marriage also tended to reduce the pool of celibates who under other circumstances might well have co-resided in other kin households. These demographic changes were part and parcel of more far-reaching economic and social changes which rendered family support systems decreasingly important for important sectors of society. As a result of these processes, between 1940 and 1970 mean household size diminished in Spain by over 10 per cent, and simple household structures tended to become more prevalent everywhere. This trend towards smaller households with simpler structures has continued until the present.

When inheritance was involved, however, considerably greater stability was evident than in nuclear family areas. In those regions characterized by stem family systems, inheritance was used to tie the heir to the family homestead, while his or her siblings became decreasingly involved in different co-residential arrangements. Ultimately, however, the resiliency of these family systems was also going to fall prey to many of the same social, economic, and demographic forces which had been affecting other types of co-residential domestic groups for decades.

Some Preliminary Conclusions

In the course of this chapter we have attempted to give a general overview of patterns of co-residence holding in Spain during the past three centuries. Data have been used both from the rapidly growing number of local studies and from available published census material. While the regional coverage of the data is as yet inadequate, and the census indicators leave much to be desired, we have been able to give a reasonably complete portrait of the basic structure of the co-residential domestic group in Spain and its development over more than two centuries. Certain general characteristics have become quite clear.

In Spain there was a very strong and persistent regional pattern of household structures. Stretching along the northern coastal areas, from Galicia to the Basque Country, and then again along the Pyrenees to Catalonia, the domestic group tended to be fairly large and relatively high percentages of households had complex structures. In these areas it was not uncommon to find complex structures in between 20 and 40 per cent of all households, and mean household size was often in excess of 5. Even though this region was not entirely uniform, and areas like Cantabria and the southern reaches of the Basque Country, Navarre, and Aragon had far lower levels of complexity, it was clearly set apart from much of the rest of the country. Elsewhere simple household structures and low mean household sizes prevailed. There it was not uncommon to find complex structures in well below 10 per cent of all households, and MHS normally below 4. While this region is probably not uniform either, lack of local studies makes it difficult to identify many of the existing variations. In the case of Valencia and the Balearic Islands, some historic household studies have suggested that levels of complexity were somewhat higher than in the central and southern parts of Spain and lower than in the north. Within these general regions, the complexity of co-residential units varied appreciably by wealth, economic occupation, and place of residence. This variance was never strong enough to obscure the general regional distribution of household structures on the peninsula, but within given contexts was often quite important.

The regional pattern of family forms in Spain is similar to that of inheritance patterns in the country. In those areas in which impartible patterns of inheritance prevailed, marriage led more or less directly to household formation, households tended to be small and were made up primarily of the conjugal family. Where inheritance was more or less impartible, whenever one heir was clearly favoured over his or her siblings, relatively high proportions of households had co-resident kin present for reasons of succession. These might have constituted a second conjugal unit, or been ascendant kin; but their presence was invariably related to matters of succession to headship. This was the single most important defining element in the size and complexity of family forms in Spain.

Everywhere kin might have also been present for demographic, economic, and social reasons. Celibate sisters, nieces and nephews, and widowed mothers were typical co-residents in Spanish households. The number of children and servants at home influenced household size, but not its structure, and also varied appreciably for reasons of demography and migration and according to the needs of family economies. The weight of these groups, however, was never large enough to alter the basic regional configuration of family forms in Spain.

It should be noted, however, that even in the areas of greatest household complexity such as the mountainous areas of Navarre or Catalonia, household size and complexity was never more than moderately high when compared to other areas of Europe. Household sizes between 4.5 and 5 may have been high in Spain, but were a far cry from the 5–9 holding in Tuscany, the Balkan Peninsula, or other parts of the continent. The 20–30 per cent of households with two or more conjugal units was far below the 30–50 per cent common in areas characterized by complex family forms.[20] In other words, even though these were areas of considerable complexity and specialized inheritance patterns, they were so relative to the rest of Spain, but not to areas in other parts of Europe. Even in the areas of impartible inheritance, significant parts of the population did not participate in these forms. Because of this, household complexity and size was never more than modestly high in these areas of Spain.

Notes

1. The number of publications in the field is now quite significant and is growing fast. The work of Francisco Chacón Jiménez (1983, 1987a, 1987b) and Robert Rowland (1987a, 1987b, 1988) have both been instrumental in stimulating research in the field. Their approaches to the family, and those of most of the recent work being done in Spain, have emphasized household analysis.
2. For a detailed description of this classification scheme, see Laslett (1972) and Hammel and Laslett (1974).
3. In earlier papers Fausto Dopico (1987a) and Lluis Flaquer and Juan Soler (1990) made use of 1970 census data in their analysis of complex household structures in Spain. In order to do this, they subdivided the census categories into the standard Laslett classifications, and generated an index of household complexity (called Ic by Dopico). In so doing, they made census category 2.3 ('a nuclear family with other persons, none of whom is in the domestic service') the equivalent of Laslett's 'extended' household. Since the census does not specify whether or not the non-servant co-residents were kin-related to the conjugal unit, their index tends to overstate household complexity and the results must be interpreted with care. For comparative purposes, I have also used this indicator.
4. 17 of the 19 provinces with the highest levels of complex living arrangements were located in these regions.
5. Data prior to 1700 tend to be scarce because local *padrones* seldom list members of the household or the kin relations holding therein.
6. Some authors have used household classification schemes in their studies which are not fully compatible with the one used here. In those cases, I have regrettably been unable to make use of their data. Examples of these are the papers by J. M. Pérez

García (1988*a*: 6) on Benimaclet in the 'Huerta' district of Valencia and P. Saavedra (1985: 125–7) on areas of the province of Mondoñedo in Galicia.

7. Most local studies use the mean household size as a standard indicator of family forms and until now it has been used with census data on two occasions. See Mikelarena Peña (1992*b*: 22–34) and Reher (1993: 48–52).

8. Three examples of these effects are readily apparent from the data used. During the 19th century, there were times when some of the provinces in Galicia and Asturias had relatively low household sizes, due mainly to the fact that a considerable part of their male populations had migrated to South America. Again, during the early years of the 20th century, the delay in fertility decline of most of the areas along the northern coast tended to boost household size in those regions. Finally, in 1960 persistently high fertility in areas of southern Spain led to household sizes there often comparable with those holding in the northern parts of the country.

9. In 1860, the definition of the basic census unit was very close that of the household itself, whereas in 1877 and in 1887 as well this is not quite so clear. In the census of 1860, a census return (*cédula*) was filled out for every household, no matter how many conjugal units lived in it, but in 1877 and 1887 instructions were given to census takers to use different census *cédulas* whenever a conjugal unit was 'economically independent', even though it lived in the same household with other units (Mikelarena, 1992*b*: 18–19). Even though this leads to a higher number of census returns in 1887 than in 1860, with a corresponding decrease in mean household size (from 4.35 to 3.82), the regional distribution of MHS from both censuses is quite similar (bivariate correlation coefficient of 0.787**). The greatest disparities between them emerge for the province of Huesca, where MHS was uniformly high in 1860, but only modestly so in 1887.

10. For other studies in which similar indicators have either been proposed or used, see Rowland (1987*a*: 133–6), Parish and Schwartz (1972), and Mendels (1978).

11. On this point, Mikelarena's results appear to be slightly contradictory.

12. Unlike the other regional samples, in the Basque Country data have been aggregated not by district, but rather by urban/rural residence.

13. The division of the data in Table 2.3 into 'eastern' and 'western' Galicia does not do justice to the complex geographical patterns which emerge from the data (Dubert García, 1992*a*: 103).

14. Fernando Mikelarena Peña has suggested that this linguistic coincidence is evidence of the ethno-cultural heritage which helped foment stem-family forms in the centre and north of Navarre, as opposed to nuclear family forms in the south (Mikelarena Peña, 1992*b*: 26–31; 1995).

15. Even in Catalonia, however, where a certain uniformity seems to have existed, some authors have noted widespread diversity in family forms, with a greater persistence of stem families in what has been called 'Catalunya Vella', in the northern part of the region (Barrera González, 1990: 80–5).

16. The only exception to this was in La Ñora (Murcia), where day labourers had higher levels of complex household structures than other social groups.

17. In 1900, 31.2 per cent of all households in the Val d'Aran had complex structures, as opposed to 5.5 per cent in Cuenca.

18. In Cuenca levels of multiple family households varied by only 0.8 per cent over a period of 100 years, whereas in Aran they increased by 0.5 per cent.

19. This same process has been observed in parts of the Aragonese Pyrenees as well (Comas d'Argemir, 1984).
20. These levels of household size and complexity can be found, for example, in Mishino, Russia (82.3 per cent complex, 9.0 MHS), in Bologna (34.8 per cent complex), in Fagagna near Trieste (43.1 per cent), in seven Hungarian villages (31.8 per cent complex, MHS of 5.4), in Estonia in the eighteenth century (30.3 per cent, 6.9 MHS), in Serbian villages (MHS of 6.5), and in Belgrade during the eighteenth century (31.8 per cent, 5.7 MHS). See Czap (1983:123–9), Angeli and Belletini (1979: 160), Morassi (1979: 205), Andorka and Faragó (1983: 289–93), Palli (1983: 211–15), Halpern (1972: 409–17), and Laslett and Clarke (1972: 391–4). It would not be difficult to find many more examples of this sort of household complextiy.

3 Family Systems and their Implications

Introduction

The domestic group provides us with a readily accessible but ultimately unsatisfactory look at family systems. The household is a meaningful manifestation of the family, but it is constrained by time and especially by space. It is evident that the family itself transcends the household, though in practice it is exceedingly difficult to define its precise dimensions, which may vary from one culture to another and from one family to another. Nevertheless, it is traditional among anthropologists, and among many family historians as well, to see the family as a more or less diffuse kin group capable of organizing itself and of making the decisions necessary to assure its continuity. It is often seen as a key element of social stability, mostly because the logic of family preservation has ended up being identified with the logic of social reproduction. Whether or not this family-based approach to the understanding of social structure is valid is not at issue here. What is clear is that living arrangements, property transmission, household formation and dissolution, social position, and even many aspects of economic activity were all, to a greater or lesser extent, the product either of decisions made within the family or of legal and customary practices based on the logic of family reproduction. Contributing to the understanding of the origins, dynamics, and implications of the different family systems existing in Spain is the central purpose of this chapter.

Over a century ago, Frédéric Le Play (1877–9) identified two fundamental types of family system: the patriarchal family with its stem-family variant, and the 'unstable' or nuclear family.[1] For him, the key defining element of these systems was the way in which family property was transmitted. Whereas in stem-family systems, more or less impartible inheritance practices implied that the selected heir married and co-resided with his parents, in 'unstable' family systems, partible inheritance led to the continual subdivision of family patrimony, and ultimately made family continuity impossible. Most authors have agreed with the emphasis Le Play placed on inter-generational property transmission as the key to succession and to family systems.[2] Much as the geography of co-residence suggests, both of these family systems existed on the Iberian Peninsula.[3] While considerable work has been done on the nature of family systems within specific contexts on the Iberian Peninsula, there are few comparative surveys spanning the entire country.[4]

The legal context of inheritance and succession, forged to a large extent during the Middle Ages, will be an essential starting point for this story.

Customary inheritance practices also played an important role in moulding the often very general legal norms to suit the needs of the different family systems in Spain. An adequate understanding of these systems cannot be reached without understanding both the legal and the consuetudinary aspects of succession.[5] Once again an examination of the available data will lead to a discussion of the geography of 'two Spains', one of relatively partible and the other of relatively impartible succession practices. Yet it will become apparent that the Spanish mosaic was far richer than this simple geographic distinction might suggest, as impartibility did not have the same origins or implications in Galicia as in Navarre, and partibility had a very different meaning for, say, the landed peasant in Andalusia and the artisan in Cuenca.

Theories as to the origins of the different family systems in Spain will be discussed, as will their implications. Family systems were not neutral, and carried with them economic, demographic, and cultural consequences. Ultimately, our approach will emphasize the cultural component of different modes of familial organization and perpetuation. These systems came into place for a mixture of juridical, historical, economic, political, and ecological reasons. Once established, however, they helped constitute normative cultural patterns for a large part of the population. In many ways, this cultural 'inertia' helps explain the stability of different systems practically to the present, a stability which is often surprising in the light of the economic, social, and political modernization which has taken place in Spain over the course of the past century.

Theory and Practice of Succession in Spain

As with so many other aspects of Spanish historical development, the characteristic differences in family law originated during the Middle Ages, when the Christian principalities adapted different versions of Roman, Visigothic, and Muslim law. The main difference between these three legal traditions in so far as succession was concerned lay in the amount of freedom given a testator. Under Roman law a person had complete freedom of bequest, under Visigothic law he was free to dispose of one-fifth of his property as he chose, and under Muslim law it was normally one-third. It was during the Reconquest that these legal traditions were adapted to the needs of the different regions of Christian Spain, which were faced with the challenge of colonizing the territories gradually being taken from al-Andalus. By the dawn of the Early Modern period, these legal constructs were fairly well defined, and only suffered modest revisions until the elaboration of the Civil Code in 1889. Even then, however, the basic regional pattern of family law hardly changed.[6]

The Castilian legal code held sway in the vast majority of the peninsula with the exception of territories located immediately to the south of the Pyrenees. The Laws of Toro (1505) brought together different medieval traditions, and established a system of succession which hardly varied for almost four centuries. It was a system based on limited freedom of bequest, a portion of the estate called the *legítima* which went to the mandatory heirs (*herederos forzosos*), and a part of the *legítima* called the *mejora* which could be used to benefit (*mejorar*) one of the heirs. When there were no legally mandated ascendants or descendants, the testator's freedom of bequest was complete. If he had descendants he could freely bequest only one-fifth of his entire estate. The other 80 per cent, called the *legítima*, was divided into three parts. Two of them had to be left to his legitimate descendants in equal shares, regardless of their gender or position in the family. The last third of the *legítima* could be given to any mandatory successor the testator chose and, if so, was called the *mejora*. The only important innovation introduced by the Civil Code of 1889 was the increase in the part of the inheritance which a person drawing up the will could use freely (from 20 to 33 per cent of the estate), and the division of the *legítima* into two equal parts, one for equal distribution among mandatory heirs and one for the *mejora*.[7] The estate of any person dying without drawing up a will (*ab intestato*) was divided equally among his legitimate descendants, even though they might have been the issue of different marriages.[8]

Within the Castilian system, most inheritance was transmitted *mortis causa*, though informal arrangements were often made with both the testator and his offspring present. Any legal transmission of inheritance taking place *inter vivos* was centred on the dowry or marriage portion. Parents were legally obliged to provide their daughters with a dowry which amounted to half of their part of the *legítima*. Save in very wealthy families, the dowry seldom amounted to more than some immediate effects used to set up a new household. During a woman's married life, her husband had the right to administer her dowry, though it had to be turned over either to the surviving spouse or to her legal heirs upon death. In Castile the authority of husbands over their wives' property was considerably greater than in other parts of Spain, though it was never complete. Apart from the dowry, they also administered any other estate their wives had brought with them to marriage through inheritance, as well as any wealth accrued during their marriage (*bienes gananciales*). Upon death, however, all of this property had to be returned to their spouses or to any direct heirs.

Even though it is common to consider that the Castilian system of succession leads to partible inheritance practices, in fact it gave a person a considerably wide range of possibilities to give preferential treatment to one of his heirs should he so choose. The mechanisms by which this might take place were centred on the part of the estate which a person could freely dispose of (one-fifth before the proclamation of the Civil Code in 1889, and one-third thereafter), and on the discretionary use of the *mejora*. Any testator who wanted to accrue a sizeable part of his estate in only one heir could bequeath both of these parts of his estate to him, as well as the portion of the *legítima* due the chosen heir by law.[9] Within a pre-1889 context, for example, with three surviving offspring, a person could have bequeathed as much as 64.1 per cent of his estate to his designated heir; and under the Civil Code this would have increased to 77.8 per cent of his estate.[10] Whenever families used the *mejora de tercio y quinto*, the relevance of the estate received by the designated heir would have only been marginally less than that received by the 'universal heir' in those areas of Spain characterized by impartible inheritance practices. The use made of these options provided by the prevailing legal system was the key to whether or not inheritance was truly partible in areas where the Castilian legal system prevailed.

Under the umbrella of Castilian inheritance law, consuetudinary practices led to a number of different types of succession. The key to all of these was the use made of the *mejora* as a means to favour differentially one heir over his siblings. In **Castile** itself, as well as in Extremadura, León, Andalusia, and Murcia, the practice of partibility seems to have been almost complete, whereas in Galicia, Asturias, Guipúzcoa, and, to a lesser extent, Santander and Valencia, different restrictions tended to be imposed on the system so that partibility was never really complete. These practices will centre our attention over the next few pages.

The province of Cuenca provides an excellent example of nearly perfect Castilian partibility.[11] There the key to understanding succession can be found in the fact that very few people ever even bothered to draw up a last will and testament. For those who did not, inheritance was by definition completely partible. Had this only been the case for day labourers, for example, it would not have been significant because, for the most part, they had very little to bequeath. Yet it is a behaviour pattern which seems to have been ubiquitous in the province and among all social groups. Despite the difficulty in estimating the percentage of people drawing up legal wills in rural areas, where notaries normally covered several different villages, only between 10 and 20 per cent of those adults with property seem to have actually made out a will.[12] Those that were drawn up were either to give parts of the estate to some institution outside the family (like the Church), to forestall potential problems, to compensate a son or daughter who had been especially helpful to his or her parents during a period of illness, or to assure the education of younger children.[13] Wills were also used to make sure that each child received an equal share of the inheritance, after certain parts of the estate had been received earlier as wedding gifts.[14] Finally, many wills also stipulated some type of economic or moral support of the widowed spouse, though conditions might also have been imposed.[15] It is extremely rare to find a legalized will in which there is some indication of the intent to benefit one child at the expense of his or her siblings.

The transmission of people's estates in Cuenca, then, was basically done without making use of legal wills; the partible norms of succession *ab intestato* applied in the vast majority of cases. Even though this type of transferral of estate property was technically post-mortem, in fact it was agreed upon *inter vivos* by means of *hijuelas*. These documents, especially frequent in the Mancha, contained an account of all goods and property a young couple had received from the day of their engagement until their wedding, and were used to even out the share each of them had in the inheritance of their parents.[16] In other words, in *hijuelas* the patrimonial estate corresponding to each child and given in usufruct at marriage was set out. They referred to an inheritance which was known well before the death of the parents, and was generally negotiated among all the heirs.[17] In other contexts the *hijuelas* were in fact a full-scale partition of all the family possessions which were going to be bequeathed at the death of the parents. Perfect equality was never completely possible, and family tensions were bound to occur. Since the *hijuelas* were private documents, should litigation occur their legal validity could be called into question. It seems however that there was remarkably little actual litigation involving family succession. Even though occasionally some heir may well have felt unfairly treated, every person interviewed insisted on the fact that without exception all inheritance was divided into equal shares, thus confirming much of what appeared in wills drawn up during the eighteenth and nineteenth centuries.[18]

Considering that the great majority of people died without ever having drawn up a will, strictly partible inheritance had to prevail. It is interesting to note, however, that in Cuenca and probably in almost all of Castile, equality of inheritance was much more than a legal imposition; it was an integral part of the customary practice of succession and was essential to people's expectations. Without question, strictly partible inheritance was normative behaviour, and the fact that few people made use of legalized wills is a testimony to just how deep-seated the practice was.

From a strictly legal standpoint, with the exception of the dowry and other wedding gifts, succession *ab intestato* could only take place upon the death of a person's parents. Had this been completely true, marriage would have depended to a large degree on the mortality of the parental generation. In reality, however, access to inheritance normally took place long before death, though what was transferred was the usufruct of the estate rather than the actual property itself. The economic effects, however, were similar. Transferral of usufruct might have taken place at the moment of marriage of a descendant, upon the death of one of his parents, or when his parents were too aged to continue working in the fields by themselves.[19] In none of these cases was the entire inheritance necessarily transferred, though that might also happen. Generally the dowry tended to be composed of goods which helped a daughter set up her own household. More frequent was the practice whereby upon marriage a young couple was able to have the usufruct of part of their future inheritance. This was normally an informal exchange, and often took the form of a wedding gift or the access to a part of the estate listed in the *hijuela*.[20] Any wedding gift or advance on inheritance ended up being evened out in the end when the parents actually died.

It is unclear just how much this system varied in other parts of Spain where partible inheritance practices prevailed.[21] Generally speaking, in the entire region women played a relevant role in property transmission because they always conserved their patrimony and bequeathed it separately to their offspring, even though during marriage it was administered by their husbands. Dowries were generally insignificant, and their exact content might vary by region.[22] In Cuenca, however, other informal property transferrals took place at marriage which were not officially a part of the dowry. The extent to which this type of process took place in other regions under the Castilian legal traditions is not known. The fact that dowries were only of relative importance in much of the region should not make us lose sight of the fact that family estates were essentially a two-sex affair, and that this patrimony in most cases, especially in rural areas, was far more important than possessions accumulated during marriage. From an economic standpoint, in areas of strictly partible inheritance like Castile, Murcia, Andalusia, or Extremadura succession was a far more complicated affair than in those areas where impartibility prevailed because everyone participated fully in the process, not just the chosen heir and his parents.

Galicia, Asturias, Guipúzcoa, and partially Santander and Valencia were other areas of Spain subject to the Castilian legal tradition in which strictly partible inheritance practices were not universally followed. In all of them, the discriminatory use of the *mejora* was the key to their own particular practices of succession. In **Galicia**, prevailing levels of household complexity give forceful evidence of the existence of certain restrictions on partible inheritance, though there is no agreement on the exact nature of the predominant form of succession. Some years ago, Carmelo Lisón Tolosona (1976: 305–6; 1987: 84–8) identified three different patterns: one typical of the mountainous areas of the interior, in which the eldest male son married and co-resided with his parents, eventually inheriting most of the family patrimony; another in the coastal villages, where a daughter was chosen, married, and co-resided at home with her parents; and finally in Orense one of equal division of property and neo-local residential patterns.[23] Lisón's work is attractive and has been quite influential, though the geography of succession he describes is not entirely compatible with that of co-residence which has appeared in recent research on eighteenth-century Galicia, in the district-level data in the 1860 and 1887 censuses, and in the 1970 census returns.[24] While this evidence is by no means conclusive, it does suggest the need for more research on the subject.

Recent innovative work has been done on household structures and inheritance patterns in parts of eighteenth-century Galicia.[25] Even though much of this work on succession practices does not cover Galicia as a whole, the thoroughgoing use of notarial archives enables us to get a better view of inheritance patterns in parts of Galicia during the Enlightenment. In the rural areas around Santiago, almost half the wills benefited one heir preferentially and, of these, males were the preferred heirs in nearly two out of every three cases. Normally the designated heir (*millorado*, in the language of Galicia) was the first born, and was constrained to live *a una mesa y manteles* with the testator (sharing the same table). In this way the traditional Galician figure of the '*casado en casa*' (married son or daughter at home) was created.[26] In the town of Santiago de Compostela itself, the situation was similar except that the proportion of wills containing a *mejora* was lower (about one-third) and sharp differences by occupational category were apparent (Dubert García, 1992*a*: 184–95). Dowries and other forms of donation were complementary forms of assuring co-residence and preferential succession.

The situation portrayed for the area around Santiago suggests that it was not uncommon to give preferential treatment to an heir in a person's testament, and this brought with it the obligation to reside with and to care for the parental family. While the eldest male child tended to be preferred, enough female offspring received the *mejora* to suggest that it was a practice which affected both sexes fairly widely. It is unclear just what happened to the siblings who did not receive preferential treatment, save the fact that they never lost their part of the *legítima*. For Dubert García (1992*a*: 265) these mechanisms were used basically for two reasons: to assure the welfare of the parents as they grew older by means of co-residence with the younger generation, and to maintain the viability and integrity of the family farm. The situation he has portrayed is interesting but ends up raising a number of questions. The most important of these refers to just how extended the practice of the *mejora* was, because the fact that between one-third and one-half of all wills contained a *mejora* does not tell us just how many families used this procedure. Judging from the relatively modest levels of household complexity in eighteenth-century Galicia, we might suspect that a not-insignificant proportion of the population did not use the *mejora*, and may not have even bothered to draw up wills.[27] Moreover, we might suspect that the protection of the integrity of the family homestead afforded by these practices was less than complete because the process of fragmentation of land became a hallmark of Galician history during the eighteenth and nineteenth centuries.

There also appears to have been more than one type of household succession in **Asturias**, with strictly partible inheritance prevailing in the mountainous southern part of the region, and modified impartibility in the more northerly areas. Most authors seem to conclude that the preservation of the family household was assured because a single heir tended to be chosen over his siblings. The process, though, was not one of simply choosing the heir and giving him a *mejora*. Before that moment, there was a period in which the family property was administered by only one child, normally the eldest son, even though it still belonged to both parents and would eventually devolve upon all of the legitimate heirs.[28] The way in which this was done was through a pre-marital donation, called *heredamiento familiar* in Spanish, which was normally given by elderly parents to one of their children, giving him the right to manage and conserve the family homestead and *casería* (the family home).

This donation did not include property rights, but rather opened a period in which the family farm was worked jointly by the entire family, and was run by the person who would eventually become the preferred heir. During the period, the chosen offspring had the obligation 'to dress, feed, and educate' his unmarried siblings, as well as to pay their trip as emigrants to America. The reception of the donation normally carried with it the obligation of co-residence with the older generation. When he married, in his marriage contract he was promised a *mejora* which consolidated his role as favoured heir. This process seems to have been more a strategy of ensuring old-age support and of maximizing the efficiency of the family farm, and only secondarily one of maintaining the family property intact from one generation to the next.

A recent anthropological study has identified a totally different inheritance practice, based on equal distribution of all family property to the legitimate heirs, in the small village of Escobines, located in the mountains of the southern part of Asturias near León (Fernandez and Fernandez, 1988: 127–30). Within this context, families seem to have attempted to prevent the fragmentation of their holdings by promoting marriage unions between close relatives or even sibling marital exchange. It is unclear just how common these practices were and, based on the available information, it seems premature to generalize for the entire region. Nevertheless, it is unlikely whether any of these property-consolidating measures have been very successful over the past two centuries, a period in which property fragmentation and emigration became common themes of Asturian life.

In **Cantabria (Santander)** partible succession seems to have been widely practised, with the exception of some districts in the western part of the region, such as the Liébana Valley, where the chosen heirs often received a *mejora*. This was given on the condition that the chosen heir remain at home with his retired parents and with any other unmarried siblings.[29] During the eighteenth century in this district, however, wills were drawn up in approximately one-third of all possible cases, and of those, only about 35 per cent expressly gave a strict *mejora de tercio y quinto* to a chosen heir. Even though this estimate is only approximate, it suggests that in only around a quarter of all cases was a special heir signalled out (Lanza, 1988: 153–5). Assuring the care of elderly parents seems to have been of paramount concern when families decided whether or not to choose only one heir and to constrain him to co-residence with his parents.[30] In most cases this was only done by relatively wealthy peasant farmers (*labradores*) whose estates were large enough to make selective succession worth while and where heirs had few chances of complementary employment outside the home (Lanza, 1991: 361–3). In the rest of Santander partible succession seems to have been adhered to in the vast majority of cases well into the present century.[31]

Succession and family systems in the rest of Spain, where for the most part Castilian legal traditions were not in effect, were not uniform either. In **Catalonia**, where Roman law prevailed, a key difference was that the part of one's possessions that one could freely bequest was far higher than anyplace else in Spain, amounting to 75 per cent of the total estate. There was no *mejora* in Catalonia, and a person made universal heir with, say, two other siblings stood to acquire as much as 83 per cent of the family estate.[32] It has been suggested that the Catalan system of succession probably originated in the early Middle Ages, as the Carolingian feudalism existing in the Hispanic March became a Christian beachhead on the Iberian Peninsula against the Muslim-dominated lands to the south (Terradas, 1984: 15–42). It was probably during the Early Modern period when the stem-family system in Catalonia consolidated and spread to most sectors of society (Barrera González, 1990: 27–31).

The key to succession was a donation called *heretament* in Catalan, made in the marriage contract[33] whereby the parents promised their estate to their chosen heir. This donation was absolutely irrevocable and included the estate not at the moment at which the marriage agreement was made, but at the death of the parents. Until that time, the parents remained fully in possession of their own property, which they could administer as they pleased. The only restrictions on his inheritance was that the designated heir respect the *legítima* of the other direct descendants, though this in reality normally amounted to very little. In the marriage contracts there was normally an additional clause naming the first-born male child of the newly-wed couple heir in case his parents should die suddenly without settling their estate (*ab intestato*). In this way, marriage contracts and the entire issue of succession in Catalonia always ended up including three generations.[34]

In theory, the chosen heir was supposed to be the person with greatest 'moral and intellectual conditions' to carry on the family tradition. In practice, however, it was the eldest son (*hereu*) or, if there were no male heirs, the eldest daughter (*pubilla*). The rest of his siblings were compensated with a dowry or with the part of the estate stipulated by law, which normally consisted of either money or, if not, of land or goods which were basically marginal to the family estate. It was the *hereu* (or the *pubilla*) who decided just how these compensations were to be made. Should a person die without having chosen an heir in his own marriage contract or that of his son, or without having left a last will and testament, his estate was divided among all of his descendants. This, however, seems to have been very rare, even among families with little property. Donations, marriage contracts, dowries, and wills seem to have been essential parts of the life of most Catalan families.[35] In the donation, the parents reserved the usufruct of the family estate until their death, and the *hereu* promised to follow the indications of his father with respect to the administration of the household. In turn, the father promised to keep the *hereu*, his wife, and his children 'in his house and in his company' and provide them with all that was necessary for their sustenance. Thus the marriage of an *hereu* meant the initiation of a prolonged period of apprenticeship in the management of his father's holdings; full control was only gained at his father's death. The duration of the period of co-residence of both generations of a

Catalan stem family, then, was closely tied to the age at marriage of the *hereu* and the life expectancy of his parents.

Within this general context, a number of variants can be identified. The pre-eminence of patrilineal primogeniture and of patrilocal co-residence was most strictly followed in what is called *Catalunya Vella* (literally 'Old Catalonia'),[36] among peasant farmers (*pagesos*), and in areas characterized by relatively dispersed patterns of settlement and by rural economies based on cereal production (Barrera González, 1990: 4, 73–85). Other studies, however, have shown that primogeniture was also widely practised in areas outside of the *Catalunya Vella*, though perhaps less completely than in the more northerly zones.[37] In certain parts of the western Catalan Pyrenees, the chosen heir was the first-born but not necessarily the male, and in Tortosa it might have been the youngest son who co-resided and cared for his parents (Barrera González, 1993: 143). All of these variants, however, led to impartible succession in one form or another.

Until the middle part of this century, the most generalized practice was that the young heir and his wife would co-reside and eat with their parents, and with unmarried aunts and uncles and any other unmarried siblings who still remained in the parental household, called the *casa pairal*. In more recent years, there is some evidence that many chosen heirs tend to maintain a separate residence so as to assure themselves greater independence and privacy. This 'nuclearity' of some Catalan stem families, however, should not be confused with formulas of partible succession, because the *hereu* is still considered the heir of the family lineage and his is the family estate. As recently as 1979, in the village of Gurb de la Plana, located in the northern part of the province of Barcelona near the town of Vic, 84.6 per cent of the chosen heirs co-resided in the parental household, either directly with the family itself, or in a part of the same house which had been set up for them (Barrera González, 1990: 170–2, 372–7).[38] In Catalonia, the *casa pairal* became the centre of rural life, and was not only the place of co-residence of the heir, his parents, and his spouse and offspring, but also where the other siblings lived before they married, and even for more or less prolonged periods after they had departed. In many ways the *casa pairal* symbolizes the tight links between the *cap de casa* (the eldest male in the stem family), the *hereu*, his wife (the *jove*) and their children, and the other siblings (*cabalers*) who often resided far away, but who used the family stem for both economic and personal support.[39]

Roman law had originally governed succession in **Valencia**, with a reduced *legítima*, one-third or one-half of the inheritance, depending on the number of surviving heirs; but as a consequence of the War of Spanish Succession at the beginning of the eighteenth century the Castilian legal tradition was imposed throughout the kingdom. It was not infrequent for families with land in the rich irrigated Huerta to the west and south of the town of Valencia to benefit a selected heir, normally a son, with a *mejora de tercio y quinto*.[40] This, however, was normally not effective until the death or the retirement of the elder generation, and most donations made at marriage consisted of enough property to help a young couple get started in their married life (Garrido Arce, 1992*b*: 95–6). Sometimes these donations carried with them the obligation of co-residence and of caring for the elder generation, though it is unclear just how frequent this practice was. While it is unquestionable that this strategy was at least partly designed to maintain the family farm relatively intact, much as the modestly high levels of complex co-residential patterns have suggested, it would be hazardous to guess at just how widespread it was.[41] Moreover it is not uncommon to find parents actively concerned about promoting equality among their heirs (ibid. 100–3). It is quite possible that during the eighteenth century in Valencia, the system of inheritance was in a process of transition toward more or less complete partibility. By the middle of the nineteenth century, there are indications of the presence of complex household structures only in some areas of the region, and by 1970 levels of complexity in Valencia itself were slightly below the average holding for the country as a whole (Flaquer and Soler, 1990: 118).

Originally in **Aragon** the legal norms of succession dictated that all descendants had a right to participate equally in succession, though in 1307 this was modified for the nobility so that they could choose a universal heir, as long as other heirs were compensated as much as was felt to be necessary (*quantum eis placuerit*).[42] In 1311 the Cortes of Daroca extended this right to all citizens. Within this legal tradition, donation *inter vivos* of all property in favor of one heir was admitted, as long as other direct descendants received enough for food and dowries.[43] In this sense the donation was very similar to the *heretament* in Catalonia and was made as a part of the marriage agreement, with the exception that in Aragon there was no *legítima* to speak of, and the family was not constrained to choose the eldest son and could opt for any offspring they preferred regardless of their sex.[44] In the marriage contract, the heir and his spouse took on the obligation to co-reside in the parental household, under his father's authority, together with any siblings remaining at home.[45] In some cases, succession was not stipulated in the marriage contract, but rather in the last will and testament of the head of the family. When this formula was chosen, the father retained complete control over his estate until the end of his life.[46] The decision as to which child would succeed to headship was made by both parents together or, in their absence, by a family council.[47] The practice of designating a universal heir seems to have been widespread only in the very northern part of Aragon, near the Pyrenees. Over much of the rest of the region, with few exceptions, inheritance seems to have been partible. This is why there is little or no indication of the presence of the stem family south of the province of Huesca.[48]

As in Aragon, there were two different types of property devolution in **Navarre**, though the legal underpinnings were somewhat different. In the northern two-thirds of the region, one child normally received the vast majority of the family property, whereas in the south, inheritance was divided equally among all of the heirs.[49] During the Middle Ages a noble heir had almost complete freedom to distribute his estate as he saw fit, as long as a small amount of property was given to each child,[50] while for peasant farmers all property had to be distributed equally among the direct heirs. In practice, however, all sectors of society made use of this privilege. From a strictly legal standpoint, then, succession in much of Navarre was unlike any other region in Spain because only there did a testator have complete freedom of bequest. In the rest of Spain, all inheritance law stipulated a greater or lesser proportion of the estate which necessarily had to be left to the legitimate heirs.

In practice, in northern and central Navarre inheritance devolved upon one heir, though male primogeniture did not necessarily apply (Douglass, 1971: 1106–7). As in the rest of the Pyrenees, the sole heir was normally designated in his marriage contract, and this carried with it the obligation of co-residence with the parental generation. Other siblings could remain in the household as long as they were celibate and submitted to the authority of the heir and his parents. When they married, these siblings were provided with a dowry, but the amount was purely discretionary.[51] Many years ago Yaben noted that this type of impartibility was used mostly by well-to-do farmers and sharecroppers, but much less among the families of merchants and civil servants, 'which are unstable in Navarre like everywhere else' (Yaben, 1916: 72–4).

In much of the **Basque Country**, especially in Vizcaya and areas of neighbouring Alava, the entire question of succession was geared to maintaining the estate within the family. Any kin to the fourth degree of kinship became 'stems' of the family property, and in the absence of any direct descendants or ascendants were bound to receive the family estate. In this way, the permanence of the landed property within the family was assured. Under normal circumstances the father or the mother could designate one child as heir, irrespective of his sex and position in the family, as long as they left some land to the other direct heirs.[52] The donation was made *inter vivos*, often at marriage, and was in many ways similar to the practice used in Aragon.[53] Much as occurred in northern Navarre, the chosen heir was not necessarily the eldest male.[54] Unlike the situation of the *hereu* in Catalonia, in some parts of the Basque Country once the heir married and the co-residence of both families began, even while owing his father respect and filial obedience, the heir became the primary authority at home and ran the family homestead as he felt was best (Douglass, 1973: 111–12; 1975: 33–49, 163–4). In other areas, however, headship was not attained until the death of the parental generation (Urrutikoetxea, 1992; Arbaiza, 1994).

A stem-family system was also apparent in the province of Guipúzcoa, where the Castilian legal system prevailed. Unlike Vizcaya, the designated male or female heir received a *mejora* which was promised in the marriage contract, and which carried with it the obligation of co-residence with the parental generation, the reception of a dowry from the spouse who was marrying into the family, and the obligation of respecting the *legítima* of the other heirs.[55] Even though there is ample evidence of the use of the *mejora* in the final will and testament, the marriage contract was where the basic agreement was set out. Normally the designated heir received only the usufruct of the property, and had the obligation of co-residing 'at the same table and in the same company' (*en una misma mesa y compañia*) with his parents and spouse in the family *caserío*.[56]

Judging from available empirical studies, the stem family was fairly widespread in the rural areas of the central and northern parts of the Basque Country, though probably less so in the southern part of the region. The basic north–south geography of family systems so characteristic of Aragon, Navarre, and to a lesser extent of Catalonia appears to have existed in the Basque Country as well. Central to succession was the importance attributed to the family *caserío* (*baserria* in Basque), which not only was the essential unit of rural production but in many ways the symbol of the Basque Country itself. Thanks to the norms of succession in most of the region, these *caseríos* often remained within the same family for generations on end.

From Inheritance Patterns to Family Systems

Understanding the geography of succession in Spain is essential to understanding the nature of family systems present on the peninsula. It is, however, only part of the picture. Families developed within contexts which were defined by the prevailing legal system, by tradition, and by a whole host of other social, economic, geographic, demographic, and cultural realities. Families were not just passive fixtures stuck on a relatively unchanging historical landscape; they were active players, attempting to make the most efficient use possible of their inherited structural constraints. At times these structures worked directly in favour of certain families or social groups, and other times families had to sort through negative contexts as best they could so as to secure the greatest possible well-being for the family group as a whole. Active decision-making might affect single households, or it might be a matter for the larger kin group; but it was always present. While it is unquestionable that individual families 'worked the system' as best they could, it is also true that certain behaviour patterns can be observed that were common to given social groups, geographical and ecological contexts, or historical periods. At times decisions affected the entire issue of social reproduction, while in other contexts these decisions were designed to facilitate certain key transitions for the family and its members, especially those relating to marriage and death.

Understanding the ability of families to deal with the challenges of life informs a number of chapters in this book. Here I would like to address the issue from the standpoint of the general social reproduction of families and family systems. It is an attempt to look at the way customary practices ended up shaping legal and traditional structures, making them more flexible than they might have otherwise been. Doing this correctly, however, is not an easy task. When faced with this challenge, many historians limit themselves to making a series of generalizations about family organization, such as those based on, say, differing household structures by social group. This type of approach is ultimately insufficient and unsatisfactory because it does not allow us to get at the real mechanisms of decision-making, the way in which families actually functioned. The only way to flesh this out adequately is to look at the system from the inside out, in terms of the way individual families sorted out their destinies within the contexts they had 'inherited'. In Spain this type of work has only been done by some anthropologists and by very few historians.

The following paragraphs are an attempt to piece together certain aspects of family behaviour in different contexts on the peninsula. It is by no means a complete portrayal of how family systems and social reproduction really worked. This will only be possible when more innovative research has been done along lines still fairly uncommon among most family historians. My attempt will be impressionistic, rather than thorough. It will be based on extremely interesting work done by historians like Fernando Mikelarena and Llorenç Ferrer. Some of the examples will be taken from stem-family areas of Spain, and others from areas where partible succession prevailed. The way in which both areas are approached will not be strictly comparable, mostly because the basic research has not addressed exactly the same issues. The results will, however, be illustrative of the way families coped with the traditions they inherited. All of the examples used will point to the importance of flexible and informed decision-making for how family systems really functioned.

In areas of impartible succession, an ongoing concern for families was what to do with children who were not the designated heirs. The very nature of the system of succession tended to force these children into a pattern of downward social mobility, an outcome that families attempted to avoid as much as they could. Non-heirs were members of the family group, and social rank was to be defended wherever possible. At the same time, however, this defence of the family members had to be done without endangering the stability of the family estate. In a series of recent articles, based primarily on a number of family genealogies referring to central Catalonia during the eighteenth and nineteenth centuries, Llorenç Ferrer has been able to identify how different groups in society made differential use of a common inheritance system based on the nature of their access to economic resources and the strategies they saw fit to follow.[57] For the most part, Ferrer has centred his analysis on the behaviour patterns of three social groups: well-to-do peasants, the lower nobility, and the commercial bourgeois. He has shown how each of them sought in different ways the coveted balance between the security of the family line and the well-being of members of the family group.

Well-to-do peasants were quick to take advantage of an inheritance system which helped keep their property intact and, more than any other social group in Catalonia, were the ones who glorified the family homestead, the *masía*, and the style of life surrounding it. Downward mobility for non-heirs was an unwanted by-product of this system. Whenever possible, daughters were married to other heirs (*hereus*) though their dowries were generally smaller than those entering the household via the marriage of the family *hereu*. In other words, young women were obliged to marry heirs of less well-off peasant families, and thus tended to move down the social ladder. Other options, such as remaining celibate at home, entering a convent, or marrying non-heirs of other families were not preferred strategies for this group. For sons the situation was somewhat more difficult. With little property to inherit, if indeed any at all, celibacy for them was the norm. It was difficult for them to marry female heiresses (*pubillas*) because these preferred male heirs. Sometimes they learned a trade to supplement their own inheritance, but mostly they abandoned the family homestead to migrate to larger towns or to enter the Church in positions which had fixed rents attached to them. This last option was doubly advantageous for the family because not only did it save money on the *legítima* due these sons, but also upon their deaths the capital accruing through the ecclesiastical rents reverted back to the family. By the mid-nineteenth century, economic transformations under way in Catalonia had changed much of this. Instead of entering the priesthood, non-inheriting males, often subsidized by their families, began to study to be lawyers, architects, or other liberal professionals. At the same time, heirs gradually began preferring wealthy women from industrial urban families as their spouses. Eventually, the heirs themselves began leaving their farmsteads in the hands of *masovers* (sharecroppers or small landholders) and moving to the major towns. This entire process ended up being central to the history of Catalan modernization and economic growth.

For the lower nobility things were somewhat different. Basically these families lived from fixed rents. By implication, this meant that over time they had declining income. Unlike the well-off peasants who chose to keep their family estates intact, it was legally impossible for the lower nobility to put any of its property on the market in order to generate income. In this way, it was imperative for them to maintain their rents they had. Consequently, non-heirs suffered. Among males there was extremely high celibacy, with as many as two to three males per generation entering the clergy. Since dowries were at a premium, many daughters also went into convents, certainly far more than among peasant families. In fact, often dowries were not paid in cash, but in return for yearly pensions, a practice which brought short-term gain and long-term hardship to these families. One possible solution for these families was to encourage weddings between daughters and sons of wealthy industrial and merchant families who were looking for ways to promote their own upward social mobility. Marriages like this, however, also demanded significant dowries, and could create hardship for these families. Other strategies existed, but none of them was fully satisfactory. Ultimately this cash-strapped lower nobility was destined to decline in importance within Catalan rural society.

The commercial bourgeoisie was in an entirely different position, mainly because its income was not fixed nor was it tied to the land. This gave bourgeois families much more flexibility in defining the best possible strategies to implement. Daughters would often be married to young men who entered the family business, and their dowries often included a share of the future earnings of the family firm. Unlike other social groups, the outlook of non-inheriting males of bourgeois families was not entirely negative. Whereas in the rural world non-heirs either had to leave or be strictly subordinate to the heir, in the merchant households they often became key players in the family businesses. In this way, the distinction between the heir and the non-heir, so central to rural Catalan society, gradually diminished. Their share of the *legítima* was often hard to pin down, mainly because non-heirs also helped generate a more or less significant part of the family wealth through their participation in the family business while still at home. Within this context, it was fairly simple to guarantee the well-being of the entire family, downward social mobility of non-heirs was infrequent, and out-migration was much less important than in rural areas.

In the central and northern parts of rural Navarre, similarities and differences in the system of social reproduction with respect to Catalonia can be identified. Here too there was a universal heir, though the eldest male was not necessarily the first in line for succession. Unlike central Catalonia, however, the structure of landholding in Navarre led to numerous small farms, and thus the income families could generate and the flexibility they had were more reduced than among the groups of Catalan society analysed by Ferrer. In Navarre, concern for the fate of non-heirs was central to family strategies. Basing his study on two villages in Navarre (Larraun and Obanos), Fernando Mikelarena (1995) has been able to identify a system of dowry circulation designed to protect the interests both of the family and of the non-heir. He has found that normally non-inheriting sons received more than their legally mandated share of the *legítima*, especially if they were able to abandon the family homestead and marry the heiress of some other estate. The amount a non-heir might receive was decided by his parents, and depended on the social and economic position of the family, the amount of money available to them, or the importance of the wealth the son himself had been able to generate on his own initiative. With non-heir females, the contribution of the family to boosting their dowries was probably even greater than with men, because women were less able to generate additional income on their own. Mikelarena has found that there was no true circulation of dowries, by which families spent about as much as they received on dowries, and that benefiting non-inheriting children so that they could maintain their social status was often done at a net economic loss to the family itself. In this sense, families became risk-takers in order to assure the reproduction of social status among their offspring. And they were not always successful at it.[58]

When families were faced with situations characterized by economic duress, other less desirable options were available to them. The social degradation of those not destined to inherit the family estate or celibacy within the parental household were not always avoidable options. This was especially true when the parental household had fallen into debt due to its efforts to marry off the siblings or for some other reason. In either case, the son occupied a singularly disadvantageous position on the marriage market, one which invariably led either to marrying downward from a social standpoint or to remaining unwed in the parental household. Those who did remain at home were doubly advantageous for the family because not only did they not make use of their dowry, but they also contributed to the family labour force, at least during their economically active years. Independently of people's preferences, however, the advisability of this second strategy was strictly dependent on how many economic options the family could muster for those children and adults remaining in the household.

The examples presented here, based on case studies in Catalonia and Navarre, are necessarily schematic. They are but a pale outline of what was certainly a very complex reality, one which varied not only by social group, as Ferrer has shown, but also by economic status, by where people lived and the way in which their incomes were derived, and by a number of other human and structural factors characterizing their households. For one, it would have been very useful to have had further information about other social groups in these regions, such as Catalan sharecroppers and tenant farmers (*pagesos*) or even day labourers, or families from Navarre for whom migration to Pamplona or San Sebastián, together with the upward mobility which that may have brought with it, was a realistic option. Nevertheless, the quandary posed by children not destined to inherit, but for whom families struggled to avoid the downward social mobility so embedded in the entire system of succession, is evident throughout.

In all of the cases cited, however, the options available to families were severely conditioned by their own economic and demographic realities. For example, manipulating the opportunities for marriage for heirs and non-heirs alike was a definite possibility for all families. As Ferrer has pointed out, age at marriage, for example, was very high for heirs in well-to-do peasant families in Catalonia, thus reducing the frequency of headship turnover in the family line, and allowing for heads to generate enough income to compensate those who were not heirs. Among non-heirs, on the other hand, celibacy was frequently very high. In fact, stem-family regions on the peninsula were frequently those characterized by fairly restricted marriage opportunities. More important, however, is that these family systems were invariably based on low rates of population growth, population densities which enabled families to generate the income necessary to fulfil their social expectations, and a growing economy. If any of these underpinnings failed, the entire system might come toppling down. In many ways, both the legal and traditional structures as well as the strategies devised by families were subject to forces which often escaped the control of those families struggling to survive and even to prosper. Moreover, it would also be most interesting to be able to observe succession strategies of families according to their concrete demographic constraints, such as the number, age, and gender distribution of their offspring surviving past early childhood. These are variables which often escaped the control of families, but which must have been essential in conditioning the options available to them. Much, much more research remains to be done on this issue throughout Spain, especially in stem-family regions.

In areas of partible succession, as was the case on most of the peninsula, the concern for those who did not inherit did not exist, mainly because everyone had access to his or her share of the inheritance, if indeed there was any. In these contexts, at least from the standpoint of the family as a whole, there were no first-and second-class households, and behaviour was substantially different from what we have just described. Yet even in these areas families designed strategies to assure the well-being of their members. While the way in which strategies were implemented were strikingly different within different family systems, the desire to protect and promote family members was typical everywhere.

In Castile inheritance was fundamentally divisible, wills were seldom used, and when one child received a *mejora* it was normally in return for some special act of service towards his or her parents, such as caring for them in illness or during their old age. In areas of León, for example, the divisibility of inheritance was taken so seriously that all children received a part of every type of property owned by their parents (Behar, 1986). Underlying this type of behaviour was the belief that all children had an equal right to the products of their parent's property and to the property itself. Everyone participated equally in the fortunes or the misfortunes of the family. By implication, children were expected to take up residence near their parent's home whenever possible, help them with their land, care for them during their old age, and basically function as an enlarged family unit. In these areas, the meaning of family transcended that of the household far more clearly than in areas where one heir and one homestead embodied the family and its goals better than any other member of the kin group.

Beyond the question of inheritance and succession, in Castile family systems are probably best viewed in terms of the mechanisms of solidarity, economic activity, and even parental authority they generated; and they are mechanisms which invariably spanned individual households, linking them together in an effective way. These links were most clearly evident upon marriage and then again during old age. Parents did whatever they could to guarantee a home for each of their children upon marriage, and subdividing the parental home or setting up some other type of temporary residence, no matter how poor it might be, was not uncommon.[59] Newly-weds often shared table with their parents, much as parents did with their children when they grew older. This reality is brought out by behaviour patterns holding in the town of Cuenca during the central years of the nineteenth century.[60] As in all areas of partible inheritance, marriage led to household formation for everyone and the availability of housing might become a major constraint on the ability of a couple to get married. Nevertheless, a closer look at the Cuenca data suggests that marriage led directly to household formation only about half the time, with other couples spending between one month and three years residing in one of two parental households (Reher, 1990a: 213–15). This co-residence had nothing to do with property devolution, and seems to have been a part of family strategies whereby the effective links between parents and their offspring did not end with marriage.

Once the newly-weds were able to set up their own households, there continued to be a marked tendency for them to reside in the immediate vicinity of at least one of the parental households (74 per cent of all couples) (ibid. 217–19). Whether or not this was by choice or because of the way in which housing was found within the neighbourhoods of residence is unclear, but spatial proximity invariably facilitated ongoing contact among family households. Furthermore, residential proximity did not just affect couples immediately following marriage, but seems to have characterized many family groups over extended periods of time. A case in point is three branches of the same family which migrated to Cuenca during the latter years of the eighteenth century from nearby villages (ibid. 222–6). All three branches took up residence in the upper part of the town in the parish of San Pedro and either entered into agriculturally related activities (tenant farmers) or became unskilled day labourers.[61] Once in the town, and over a period of three generations, this family ended up reproducing itself within a well-defined neighbourhood in the upper part of town.[62] Property transmission and jobs, as well as marriage patterns of children who wed persons from the same neighbourhood, contributed to this situation. Underlying these social and economic considerations, however, there seem to have been other family-related reasons which might have been still more important in influencing behaviour.

The spatial development one can observe from this genealogy probably owes its specific form to the existence of a family in which the distinct branches created systems of mutual assistance. This led to a pronounced tendency for family members to circulate among family households. Examples of this circulation might be women whose husbands were absent and who spent a year in a sibling's household, grandchildren staying temporarily with one of their grandparents, widowed parents circulating among the households of their offspring, or the nieces and nephews residing in a family household while their parents were absent. In the long run this function of family solidarity was probably every bit as important in conditioning human behaviour as were other social and economic factors. It is fitting testimony to the way families established networks with specific spatial dimensions.

A by-product of this was that the staunchly nuclear households so prevalent in town were rife with movement and were anything but stable. In Cuenca an index of familial change was developed to evaluate the 'permeability' of the household (ibid. 229). The result showed that while the household had a stable core (the head and his wife), it was surrounded by increasingly mobile family members. Within this context, between 11 and 12 per cent of all offspring present in the household either entered or left home in any given year, and between 50 and 60 per cent of co-resident kin did likewise.[63] By implication, this means that household structures were also prone to change frequently: a typical Cuenca household changed its basic structure 4.1 times over its hypothetical 40-year existence and could be reasonably expected to have had 'complex' household structures for between six and seven years.[64] This transient nature of household structure adequately reflects the life experience of children who were born into Cuenca families, or of the young married couples starting them.

It could be argued that the evidence I have presented for the existence of functional family networks in a nineteenth-century Castilian town is purely circumstantial, and that the levels of spatial proximity and kin circulation observed do not constitute sufficient proof of family ties. While strictly speaking this objection is well founded, what has been presented here is about as close as we can come to actually observing family systems in action in historical contexts where interviews are not possible. It is convincing, albeit circumstantial, evidence that the reality of family systems in Cuenca, and probably everywhere else that partible inheritance was the norm, are only understandable if we go beyond individual households and get at the kin group as a whole.

While these behaviour patterns may have also been present to a certain extent in stem-family areas, I am convinced that their importance was far less noteworthy than in areas where inheritance was divided up equally among all the children. In stem-family systems, the meaning of the family had a great deal to do with property and inheritance, with the heir, and with the family homestead. Non-heirs, in most cases, were bound to leave the family home, often taking up residence at a great distance. Where partible succession prevailed, on the other hand, family systems were not based on property and they had little to do with any given family household. In these systems, the basis of family was for the most part devoid of any need to perpetuate the family economy, had nothing to do with the family farmstead, spanned a large number of households, and was measured more in terms of solidarity than anything else.

Demographic and economic constraints impinged on family development in areas of partible succession just as they did where the stem-family prevailed, yet the way in which these constraints were played out were quite different. In areas of family systems based on the equal division of inheritance, marriage age and intensity might vary, but seldom as a direct result of family strategies; the young might migrate, but never because of dictates embedded in the structure of the system itself; and young men and women might join the clergy, but much less clearly as a result of family strategies than in the stem-family areas of the peninsula.[65] The ability of these two systems to meet the real needs of people is very much a matter of debate, a debate which must be informed by further empirical work in both areas. What is clear, in any case, is that the way in which these needs were met was very different in each context.

Origins and Implications of Family Systems

This wealth and complexity of family behaviour notwithstanding, legal and traditional confines of succession continued to be the most important factor in defining the basic geography of family systems on the peninsula. That is why the regional nature of family forms is invariably so sharp. Two fundamentally different family systems have existed in Spain for centuries. One of them was predicated on the fact that one heir was chosen over his siblings to inherit most of the family estate and to live and care for his parents. The other was based on a reality in which inheritance was divisible, and co-residence with related kin was seldom if ever based on succession to the headship of the family property. The general north–south division of the peninsula probably dates at least from the Middle Ages, though the Early Modern period was one of consolidation, especially of the stem family (Terradas, 1980; Berthe, 1984; Barrera González, 1990: 85).

There is little agreement as to why the stem family ended up prevailing in certain areas and not in others.[66] Some authors have related it to the existence of the power of feudal lords as opposed to the central monarchy; others have considered it ecologically constrained to mountainous areas with dispersed settlement patterns, pastoral or mixed rural economies, small farms, and widespread access to land; and still others have noted that it was typical of communities in which collective organization was essential.[67] None of these explanations prove to be very useful in Spain, because historical and ecological realities often do not conform to expectations.[68] That is not to say that the stem-family regions did not have important aspects in common. They did; but none of these seems able to explain the geography of family forms by themselves.[69]

There is also ample evidence to suggest that the stem-family systems themselves were far from uniform in Spain. In many ways it seems ill-advised to consider the stem family of the Pyrenees and the Basque Country together with the family systems existing in the western part of Santander, Asturias, Galicia, or even Valencia. In one area use was made of a legal system which encouraged the selection of a universal heir, while in the other legal norms basically encouraged partibility. Where the Visigothic legal tradition held, impartibility was always incomplete and had to be achieved via the *mejora*; but in areas of Roman tradition this was not the case. Even though appreciable levels of co-residence can be observed in both contexts, neither the legal roots nor the strength and durability of the stem family in the Pyrenees from the

Basque Country to Catalonia were comparable to those of the stem family in Galicia or Asturias.

In those areas where the stem family did exist, and may even have been the predominant form of family organization, there are ample indications that often appreciable sectors of the population continued to use partible inheritance and lived in nuclear families. Earlier it was shown that family residential arrangements often varied sharply by district or by social group. This heterogeneity was present everywhere in Spain, but it was most visible in the northern part of the country, noted for the stem family. The empirical data referring to different family systems are as yet limited, but the fairly reduced levels of household complexity and low mean household sizes holding in most of northern Spain suggest that even in areas in which the existence of the stem family was unquestionable, it is quite possible that sizeable parts of the population never participated in this type of family organization.

Even if impartible inheritance had been practised by every single family, a sizeable proportion of families would have ended up living in nuclear family households at any one moment in time. The designated heir and his family resided in a nuclear household during the years after both his parents had died, and before his own chosen heir had married.[70] Any other sibling who married a non-heir and lived locally was also constrained to live most of his life in a nuclear family household, unless he too was able to amass an estate and start a stem family of his own. Under these conditions, it is highly unlikely that all or even most of the households would have shown stem-family living arrangements. This would only have happened in a family system characterized by extremely large, joint families like those existing in Russia or in the Balkan Peninsula. These, however, never existed in Spain.

Some years ago, a group of researchers undertook to simulate the household structures which should have emerged had stem-family rules of succession been applied uniformly within a given community.[71] In so doing, they estimated a series of expected household structures under three stem-family rules of household formation, under differing demographic regimes.[72] This sort of exercise yields purely theoretical results, but if the postulates of the authors about household formation and the incidence of migration are correct, they give us a reliable estimate of the percentage of households which should have stem-family co-residential patterns whenever that rule of succession is universally applied.[73] The actual results indicate that under primonuptial rules of household formation, between 38 and 49 per cent of all households should have had stem-family types of organization, 29–44 per cent for primoreal rules, and only around 15 per cent for ultimonuptial rules. If complex households are used, instead of specifically stem-family households, the proportions should be 46–54 per cent for primonuptial, 36–48 per cent for primoreal, and 18 per cent for ultimonuptial. Since this last rule was seldom applicable anywhere in Spain, we can expect between 29 and 49 per cent of all households to have stem family structures, and between 36 and 54 per cent to have complex structures, with between 37 and 55 per cent of all households having nuclear structures.[74] In other words, there should be about the same percentage of complex and of nuclear household structures in those areas where stem-family rules of succession were universally applied.

Reviewing the empirical data presented in the past chapter, it is clear that nowhere in Spain were proportions of stem families anywhere near as high or those of nuclear families anywhere near as low as was suggested by the simulation results. Percentages of complex co-residential arrangements varied between 15 and 25 per cent in Galicia, between 25 and 35 per cent in rural areas of the Basque Country, near 30 per cent in Navarre, and between 25 and 40 per cent in village case studies taken from rural Catalonia. Levels comparable to those of the simulation results were only found among well-to-do peasants in Vila-Rodona in Catalonia, among peasant farmers in central Navarre, and in the northern areas of the province of Navarre. Otherwise, the results suggest that over half the families in Galicia, one-third of those in the Basque Country and Navarre, and about one-fourth of those in Catalonia were not involved in stem-family types of succession. This does not mean that stem-family systems were not present there, or that impartible succession was not widely practised. Rather it suggests that even in rural areas of the north, society was heterogeneous and different family systems co-existed within given regions, social classes, and even villages.

Everywhere the need to assure support for the elderly was a cornerstone of stem-family systems. In this sense they were a type of retirement contract in which the elder generation gave a preferential part of the inheritance to one heir in return for his remaining in the family household and caring for his ageing parents. The existence of this intent is unquestionable and, at least in theory, the elderly should have been better protected in areas of stem-family forms and complex household structures than elsewhere. In practice, however, it raises a number of questions. For one, we have no proof whatsoever that the elderly enjoyed more favourable living conditions in stem-family areas than elsewhere, or among the families who did not make use of impartible inheritance even where it was widely practised. In stem-family areas it is not uncommon to find family conflicts in which the elder generation complained that now that their heir had taken over the estate, they were treated miserably.[75] Care of the aged was not merely a function of retirement contracts and co-residence; it transcended the household and was a matter of importance for the entire kin group.

Stem-family systems were also predicated on the need to guarantee the continuity of the family estate, and to prevent excessive fragmentation of the land. On this point the success of these systems appears to have varied widely. In Catalonia, for example, the defence of the *casa pairal*, the family estate, and the family name was central to the entire system of succession, perhaps even more so than the protection of the elderly. In Galicia, on the other hand, the stem family appears to have been centred on the overriding need to protect the elderly. This difference may have been the consequence of the fact that in Galicia Castilian law prevailed, marriage contracts were less important than in Catalonia, and the amount of one's estate which could be left to a designated heir was considerably less than in Catalonia, Aragon, or in much of the Basque Country. By and large stem-family systems existing in areas of the Castilian legal tradition appear to have always been weaker than those in areas where Roman law prevailed, and less effective in preserving the unity of the family homestead. The exceptional nature of family systems in Guipúzcoa may have been due to the fact that the Castilian legal tradition existed within an extremely pervasive Basque cultural context, both in Guipúzcoa and in neighbouring Navarre, Vizcaya, and France, which placed extremely high values on the unity and stability of the family *caserío*.[76] As opposed to Catalonia, and to a lesser extent in the Basque Country and the northern part of Navarre, where a certain amount of stability seems to have always been present, in Asturias and Galicia fragmentation of holdings became a major and ongoing characteristic of nineteenth- and twentieth-century history. When the regime of Francisco Franco undertook the major task of attempting to regroup scattered holdings all over Spain into economically viable farms, nowhere was its task more difficult than in Asturias and Galicia. In fact, in those regions fragmentation was far more severe than in any part of Castile, where partible inheritance had always prevailed for the entire population.

It is a basic misconception to consider the progressive fragmentation of land to be an exclusive characteristic of one type of family system and not of another. Fragmentation occurred when rural population growth was not compensated by out-migration, the creation of jobs in the non-agricultural sector of the rural economy, and the number of people remaining celibate. This sort of population pressure was only moderate in much of Spain, at least before the twentieth century, but not in Galicia and Asturias. The demographic pressure on rural resources in Catalonia, for example, was neutralized by the growth of rural industries and by the ready opportunity to migrate to the town of Barcelona and other industrial centres. In Asturias and Galicia, on the other hand, population growth ended up being extremely rapid, the growth of rural industry could not keep pace, and local urban areas did not prove attractive enough to absorb excess rural population. In Castile, high mortality kept population growth rates generally lower than in the north-western part of the country, and thus the problem was never as acute.

Within this context, family inheritance systems were never more than a partial defence against land fragmentation. In Catalonia, where the stem family was much more deeply implanted than in Galicia, the result was a controlled process of growth within a fairly dynamic rural and urban economy. In Galicia and Asturias, however, the family system proved practically useless, and the result was an extreme process of fragmentation, high out-migration, and restricted nuptiality. Had Catalonia been subject to equally high demographic pressure within a stagnant economy, even though the stem family might have slowed the process of fragmentation, it is extremely unlikely that it could have prevented it.

Different family systems had very concrete implications for the actual form which landholdings took between one generation and the next. Where the stem-family prevailed, a certain continuity could be observed over time, since the bulk of a person's real estate was given to only one heir. In this way, it was not uncommon to find that a field or farm had belonged to one family for generations. Where partible inheritance prevailed, however, the situation was far more complex. Since a young married couple inherited property from four different people (the husband's and the wife's parents), every generation ended up creating a family farm, which only lasted the life of that couple. By the next generation it was divided up again among each of their heirs who, in turn, joined it with the property of their own spouses to form new farms. Even though this process of estate dismemberment and reconstruction took place every generation and made property inherently unstable, at a societal level it did not necessarily lead to instability and excessive fragmentation. As long as population pressure was not too great, people normally found ways of supporting their families adequately from one generation to the next. In much of Spain, the instability of the family farm ended up being an essential part of the stability of the social and economic system.

It is commonly held that one of the by-products of most stem-family systems was the selective discrimination of non-heirs who were either condemned to celibacy or out-migration. The marriage of the heir was of primary concern to the family, because he was the one who would secure the family lineage.[77] For other siblings, marriage was not nearly so simple. Each had to be supplied with a dowry, and even then their value on the marriage market was limited. The exception might be a daughter who married an heir from a neighbouring family. If there were more than two surviving children, however, the others faced what has been called structural discrimination (Bourdieu, 1962). This led to higher celibacy and ultimately to an important undercurrent of out-migration. As the popular Catalan expression put it, *el primer fill hereu, el segón capellà i el tercer advocat.*[78] Thus, we would expect stem-family areas to show relatively higher levels of celibacy. Though not uniform on this point, Spanish census data give some confirmation to this hypothesis.[79] Nuptiality, however, had many determinants, and family systems were only one of them.[80] Out-migration also tended to be generally high in the rural areas of much of the northern part of the country. Migration and nuptiality were characteristic compensatory mechanisms for all populations faced with situations in which rates of demographic growth outstripped the carrying capacity of rural economies. The difference was that in stem-family systems they were at least in part a structural by-product of succession, whereas in nuclear family areas they were more a result of individual choice and chance.

Conflict is an integral part of all families, and the family in Spain was no exception. Both stem-family and nuclear family systems were rife with family conflict, though the form it might take was not necessarily the same in each of them. In nuclear family areas, where partible inheritance was the norm, family quarrels often arose when dividing up the family estate into lots.[81] It is not uncommon to find that some siblings might feel that another had received, say, a more productive field, one situated closer to the village, or one in some way more valuable than his own lot.[82] It is interesting to note, however, that these quarrels seldom spilled over into litigation. This was probably because the lots were normally drawn up by or in the presence of the parents, and therefore a culturally mandated moral authority of the parents kept complaints within bounds. Moreover, for the vast majority of families the amount of property in question was quite small and the *hijuelas* used in allotting the estate made any eventual litigation a problematic matter.

In stem-family areas conflict also existed, but it was structurally different.[83] Once again cultural norms kept most conflict from spilling over into litigation, as the right of the testator to bequeath and of the universal heir to receive the majority of the estate was basically accepted by the entire society. Disagreements over the distribution of inheritance normally applied to the *legítima* due each of the heirs, often a relatively small part of the total estate, but could be a sensitive issue when it was the designated heir, as in Catalonia for example, who determined which lot each of the siblings received after the death of their father.[84] In stem-family systems, however, conflict between the designated heir and his parents with respect to running the estate or to the way either party should be treated was not uncommon, because during the years of co-residence each family was dependent on the other in numerous ways.[85] This sort of inheritance-related inter-generational conflict would have been much less frequent in nuclear family systems.

Patterns of family solidarity, especially in so far as care for the elderly was concerned, were also structurally different for different forms of family organization. Underlying all else was the basically unquestioned respect children owed parents, the awareness that 'blood runs thicker than water' and that the larger family group had certain ties which entailed obligations and privileges no other member of society could demand. Inter-generational support was also linked to property, though in different ways. In areas of stem-family organization, support was directly related to the co-residential arrangements stipulated in the marriage contracts and thus fell preferentially on the shoulders of the universal heir and his family. This is not to say that other siblings were not affected, but the main responsibility clearly belonged to the heir. For nuclear families, however, any prolonged co-residence of a married son was exceptional. Thus inter-generational support had to rest on the shoulders of all of the siblings or, if there was an unmarried daughter (or son) who might have been promised the *mejora* of the family house itself, the elderly parents might reside with her. As the extremely low levels of permanent celibacy suggest, however, the solution of the unmarried daughter was only used in a minority of cases. Property and inheritance were also important in this context, because the actual transferral of inheritance did not take place until the death of the father or the mother, but its influence was less immediate and pervasive than it was in stem-families.

The economic and social changes taking place in Spain during this century, which have acquired great intensity during the past three or four decades, have had a profound effect on the family. These changes have affected the rural family everywhere in Spain, but only in the stem-family areas have they threatened the prevailing mode of familial organization. Everywhere there is evidence that the stem family, which has characterized family systems in the northern part of the peninsula for centuries, is in a state of extreme decadence, and some say may be about to disappear.[86] The privileged position of the chosen heir in these systems has been progressively undermined by the modernization of Spanish society. A century ago, being the designated heir was the key to marriage and to economic and social stability; today it is just the opposite. The demographic transition has had markedly deleterious effects on the stem family, basically because it has turned what used to be a temporary co-residence with the parental family of, say, 10 or perhaps 15 years, into one which now lasts throughout the heir's productive life (Moreno Almárcegui and Torres Sánchez, 1993: 199). Advances in life expectancy may be perceived as a positive change by the aged, but certainly not by their children. The economic modernization of society has meant that most opportunities have been generated in urban areas and in the industrial and especially the services sector, making rural production decreasingly profitable.[87] Moreover, the advent of consumer society in the past few decades has led to a situation in which the traditional position of the peasant has come to be seen as a handicap more than an advantage.

Today few would want to be a chosen heir, especially if that meant living with one's parents for 30 or 40 years after marriage and working a traditional homestead while one's siblings were making a career for themselves in Barcelona, Bilbao, or La Coruña. Ultimately it is not surprising at all that economic and social modernization has brought about this severe crisis for the stem family in Spain. More noteworthy, perhaps, has been the ability of the system to resist the forces of change which have been operating in Spanish society for much of this century for such a long time. This in itself is fitting proof of the depth of the roots of family systems in the country. While it is too early to predict the disappearance of the stem family in Spain, the critical transition it is undergoing is evident. The implications of this crisis for these societies and for their ideological underpinnings remain to be seen.

Notes

1. For a useful overview of the implications of some of Le Play's ideas for patterns of family solidarity, see Wall (1983).

2. In a moderately dissenting opinion, Comas d'Argemir (1992) argues that inheritance alone is not sufficient, and must be understood within the context of social reproduction.

3. Curiously, the three Spanish families studied by Le Play all came from the north (Galicia, Cantabria, and the Basque Country), yet none showed any sign of stem-family organization. See Le Play (1990).

4. Among these, contributions from anthropologists such as Carmelo Lisón Tolosana (1976*a*, 1977), William Douglass (1988*a*), and J. Contreras (1991), have been most useful. Of special interest is a recent paper by Fernando Mikelarena Peña (1992*b*), a family historian and a historical demographer by profession. For useful comparative perspectives covering only those areas of Spain characterized by complex family forms, see Barrera González (1993). See also Kertzer and Brettell (1987).

5. A number of authors feel that the specifically legal aspects of succession are much less important than customary practices, demographic and economic realities, and ecological contexts. See, for example, Alonso (1947: 149), Mikelarena Peña (1992*a*: 135–7; 1992*b*: 40–3).

6. This overview of the legal basis for inheritance in Spain will only cover those aspects directly related to my discussion of family systems, and even then will steer clear of the many complexities inherent in this type of jurisprudence.

7. When a parent chose to specially favour an offspring, he could impose restrictions or conditions on the bequest, as long as these did not affect the part of the *legítima* due each of the other heirs (Gacto, 1987: 53–4).

8. Should no descendants exist, there were complex norms governing succession at different levels of kinship (ascendants, collaterals, illegitimate children, spouses, etc.). In Castile, the spouse was fifth in line for succession. In other areas of Spain, succession *ab intestato* was basically similar to that holding in Castilian law in so far as legitimate descendants were concerned, though other levels of succession could be quite different.

9. This was often called the '*mejora de tercio y quinto*'. This terminology was imprecise since from a legal standpoint only the *tercio* (third) was part of the *mejora*, which had to be bestowed on a legitimate heir, whereas the *quinto* (fifth) belonged to the part of the estate the testator had freedom to do with as he chose (Gacto, 1987: 51–3).

10. Before 1889, this would be the sum of the 20 per cent he was free to dispose of, plus the third of the *legítima* called the *mejora* (one-third of 80 per cent = 26.4 per cent), plus a third of the remaining two-thirds of the *legítima* corresponding to his heir by law (one-third of 53.6 per cent = 17.7 per cent). Had there been four surviving children, the proportion would have been 59.8 per cent, and with only two, 73.2 per cent. After 1889, with two or four surviving children, the proportion given the designated heir would have been 83.3 and 75.0 per cent respectively.

11. For further reading on the practically complete partibility of inheritance in areas under Castilian law see, for example, Pérez Díaz (1966: 81–8), Freeman (1970: 67–70; 1979: 114–17), Brandes (1971: 120–3), Gilmore (1980: 158–61), Behar (1986: 66–88). Much of the material on Cuenca in the following paragraphs is taken from Reher (1988: 202–16).

12. Ethnographic evidence, taken from interviews of elderly peasants, suggests that basically people did not want to go to the trouble or expense necessary to file a last will and testament. 'The ones who went before the notary were those who smelled

problems' (interview no. 1). 'A will? People didn't do that. They were not willing to spend the 25 pesetas it cost to make out a will' (interview no. 7).

13. On her deathbed, Manuela Monreal of Belmonte (1824) gave her house to her daughter who had taken care of her for 19 years, which 'is not even half of what I owe her'. María Muñoz de Zerdosa, from Canalejas, willed to her son Sebastián de Zerdosa, 'as a *mejora*, and due to all of the good he has done me and my husband', half of a house 'which he does not have to share with his siblings'. Examples such as these are abundant. Interviews have suggested that the use of the *mejora* was extremely exceptional.

14. In Beteta, for example, after enumerating all of the goods (furniture, a calf, etc.) he had given to his children and their spouses, Carlos González ordered that his three children make sure each received his fair share (*'que se igualen entre sí'*).

15. In Belmonte in 1822, Manuel Manzano gave his house to his wife in usufruct until her death, and then to his six children. In Canalejas in 1765, Antonia de Alcázar willed her husband 200 ducats, 'because of the great love and affection we have had'. Juan José Marquina y Brionés of Priego in 1792 willed the house to his wife so that she and his daughter might live there together. Should her daughter marry and leave, 'my wife can still remain there'. Finally, in the will of Micaela Bonillo (Belmonte, 1824), it states that the usufruct family house and a mill are to be left to her husband 'if his children approve, and as long as he does not remarry'.

16. They were private documents made between the parents and their children, although normally drawn up by local experts in this practice called 'poor lawyers' (*abogados de pobres*). In some areas of La Mancha at the beginning of this century, the value of the 'wedding gifts' amounted to between 3,500 and 6,000 pesetas. This amounted to approximately one to two years of an average family's income at the time. The people actually drawing up the document charged three to four pesetas (Costa, 1902*b*: 177–8).

17. Even so, normally the deviation from the actual value of the inheritance was rather small (ibid. 88).

18. 'They usually made up lots. Sensible people from the village were called in and would assess the value of the different fields. They were usually the uncles. They made up the *hijuelas*, which were a type of private contract. . . . They had legal validity as long as the families respected them; an *hijuela* given by your father was sacred. But their validity with respect to the notary and to the registry of property was more doubtful because you see the property was never really registered. It was a document that never made it to the desks of the tax collectors' (interview no. 1). 'They used to set up as many lots as there were children' (interview no. 10). For a perspective on the *hijuelas* in another context, see Behar (1986: 68–88).

19. In areas of León, for example, as parents grew older they often distributed their land among their children in exchange for income (López Moran, 1902: 253). These agreements existed in many places and normally were not formalized in any sort of legal manner.

20. This practice was brought out in a number of ethnographic interviews. 'They might allow their children to work some land when they married, but the owners were always their parents. His or her father might say, for example, "this is going to be your land and so you should work it, but it doesn't belong to you yet"' (interview no. 4). 'When children got married, their parents used to give them a little bit of land and, if they could, a mule and some wheat . . ., but when it came time to divide

things up, everything was made equal' (interview no. 8). 'If they had two houses, his or her parents gave them one and also allowed them to sow something. They continued to be tied to their families in the use of land, even though they lived independently. They continued to work the fields of their parents. They might receive some sheep as well. It was a wedding gift. Then it was put in the *hijuela*' (interview no. 1).

21. Higher levels of household complexity which have appeared in certain parts of Andalusia may suggest that in those areas at least certain minority sectors of the population may not have participated fully in partible succession. On this subject, see, for example, Pitt-Rivers (1961) or Moreno Navarro (1972: 144).

22. On the subject of dowries and the entire question of gender and property transmission, see Brettell (1991: 348–53). On the same subject in Murcia, see Chacón (1987*b*: 160–6). In this last case, the author gives considerably greater importance to women's dowries, though this may be due to the fact that most of the families selected in his samples belonged to the elite of Murcia's society.

23. For inheritance patterns in Orense, see also Tenorio (1982).

24. In 1970, for example, the percentage of multiple family households in Orense was almost the same as for Galicia as a whole (12.4 per cent as opposed to 13.6), and is high enough to indicate the presence of certain types of impartible succession.

25. Of especial interest on this point is the work of Camilo Fernández Cortizo (1982, 1988), Pegerto Saavedra (1985), and Isidro Dubert García (1987, 1992*a*).

26. For more complete details, see Dubert García (1992*a*: 184–265, 428–32).

27. The number of wills used by the author in, say, 1790 for both Santiago and its surrounding area was 87, far fewer than the total number of property-owning adults who probably died that year (Dubert García, 1992*a*: 186). With a population of over 15,000 in 1787, the city of Santiago de Compostela alone had around 250–300 adult deaths per year.

28. On this subject, see, for example, Pedregal y Cañedo (1902), Fernández Martínez (1953), and Prieto Bances (1976: 957–8).

29. For information on inheritance practices during this period, two recent publications of Ramón Lanza (1988: 141–82; 1991: 359–63) are of great use.

30. A type of retirement contract also existed called the *alargo de bienes*, in which parents gave a chosen child the usufruct of the land as long as they were cared for. This, however, did not necessarily mean that the child was going to be the preferred heir (Lanza, 1988: 151–2). Retirement arrangements also existed in other parts of Castile, though they were seldom formalized.

31. On the prevalence of partible inheritance among the *Pasiegos* in Santander, see Freeman (1979: 114–17). For a contrary view emphasizing the existence of at least some form of impartibility, see Christian (1972).

32. 75 per cent came from the part of the estate freely given by the family head, plus another 8.3 per cent corresponding to his part of the *legítima*.

33. Called *capítols matrimonials* in Catalan.

34. For a valuable description of Catalan succession practices, see Barrera González (1990: 92–104). See also Hansen (1977: 84–8), Terradas (1980), and Ferrer i Alòs (1987).

35. For an overview of the empirical and cultural importance of marriage contracts for Catalan succession practices, see Barrera González (1990: 131–61).

36. This was the part which was north of the Hispanic March originally set out by Charlemagne.
37. An example of this might be the village of Sant Pere de Riudebitlles, located in the Penedès district to the south of Catalunya Vella, with concentrated settlement patterns, viticulture, and paper mills. Within this context primogeniture was practised widely by all social groups. See Torrents i Rosès (1992, 1993).
38. 10.9 per cent lived in a completely different house. This practice of separate residence is considered quite natural by young couples, is tolerated by parents, but is a source of alarm and worry for grandparents (Barrera González, 1990: 339).
39. On this point see, for example, Hansen (1977: 84–7).
40. For information on inheritance in the Huerta of Valencia during the 18th century, see Pérez García (1988*a*, 1988*b*, 1989), Benítez Sánchez-Blanco (1992), Garrido Arce (1992*b*). See also Garrido Arce (1992*a*, 1995).
41. In the village of Meliana in the Huerta, for example, the *mejora* was used in about one-half of all wills, but it is impossible to know how many families died without leaving any will at all (Garrido Arce, 1992*b*: 94). Similar proportions seem to have held elsewhere in the Huerta (Pérez García, 1989).
42. On the subject of succession and inheritance in Aragon, see Martín-Ballestero y Costa (1902*a*), Costea (1949), Lisón Tolosana (1966), Comas d'Argemir and Pujadas (1980), Comas d'Argemir (1991), Moreno Almárcegui (1992), Moreno Almárcegui and Torres Sánchez (1993).
43. The medieval custom had it that all other heirs would receive 10 *sueldos jaqueses* (10 coins from Jaca) as payment for their part of the inheritance. In fact, they normally received a proportion of the hereditary estate determined by the family.
44. In this way, the Aragonese system ended up being somewhat more flexible than the one in Catalonia, where the eldest son was invariably made heir. Nevertheless, at least in the village of Plasencia del Monte among the lower nobility during the 17th and 18th centuries, the son was the chosen heir in almost 80 per cent of all cases (Moreno Almárcegui, 1992: 78–80).
45. The formula used might read as follows: 'Both future spouses, once they have been married, will be obliged to reside, inhabit, and live in the place, house, and company of their parents and future in-laws (house of the husband's family), under the obedience, respect, administration, government, and headship of said parents, or of the surviving parent, forming together one great family and helping each other mutually and reciprocally' (Moreno Almárcegui and Torres Sánchez, 1993: 196).
46. In Plascencia del Monte (Huesca), by the second half of the 18th century marriage contracts were used in about half of all marriages, and were preferred to wills when designating a universal heir in about 70–80 per cent of all cases (ibid. 197–8).
47. Two variants of this system existed, though they were not widely practised outside of the very northern part of the region near the Pyrenees (Alto Aragón), and even there they were not frequent. In one case the *heredamiento* could be made *in solidum*, which meant that two siblings could be named as universal heirs as long as they and their spouses lived with the elder generation, thus forming a joint family household. This donation implied that both couples would make the first male child born to either of them the universal heir of the entire estate. The second variant was when both spouses were the universal heirs of their respective family property. At first they were obliged by custom to live in the household of the parents of the

husband, and later with the parents of the wife. In these cases a type of family consortium might be created which was administered by the four ascendants.

48. Even though Carmelo Lisón Tolosana found some indication of the joint household in the village of Belmonte de los Caballeros in the province of Zaragoza, he only found it among the very wealthy ('because economic affluence is the *conditio sine qua non* of this type of family') (1966: 166–9). Mostly inheritance here was equally divided among all children (1966: 162). See also Moreno Almárcegui (1992: 72–5).

49. The classic work on Navarrese inheritance and marriage contracts is by Yaben (1916). On this subject, see also Caro Baroja (1958, 1972), Douglass (1971, 1975, 1988*b*), and Mikelarena Peña (1992*a*, 1992*b*, 1992*c*, 1993, 1995).

50. In Navarre tradition had it that this compensation would be five coins and a *robada* of land (a small parcel).

51. See Douglass (1971: 1100–14; 1975: 33–5), Mikelarena Peña (1995).

52. The exact expression in Spanish is: '*con algun tanto de tierra, poco o mucho*'.

53. For more on Basque inheritance practices, see Caro Baroja (1958, 1976), Douglass (1975: 43–6; 1988*b*), Urrutikoetxea (1992).

54. In his study of the Vizcaya village of Murelaga, William Douglass (1975: 44–6) found that preferential male primogeniture succession only took place in 31.4 per cent of the families he studied, and a male heir was chosen in two-thirds of all cases. In the Navarrese village of Echalar, male primogeniture was even lower (18 per cent of all cases), and the male was chosen in 58 per cent of all cases. In both contexts, when the eldest male or female was not chosen, it was most often an intermediate sibling.

55. During the latter part of the 18th century in Irun, approximately one-third of those heirs receiving a *mejora* were female (Urrutikoetxea, 1992: 242).

56. See Urrutikoetxea (1992: 235–52; 456–7; 1993: 252–3). In only about 11 per cent of the marriage contracts studied was the transmission of property made with no conditions.

57. See Ferrer i Alòs (1991, 1992, 1993, 1994, 1995, and forthcoming).

58. Yaben (1916: 119) stated that he had observed some peasant families who had been ruined by the fact that they had 'too many children and had given dowries which were too generous'.

59. Household listings are filled with households clearly belonging to groups of siblings, or to a father and his sons, which are located at the same address on the same street.

60. The data, taken from linked household registers and family genealogies, provide an interesting glimpse at the way families actually functioned and some insight into the way family strategies were implemented. Much of this material comes from Reher (1990*a*: 207–43). At this time, Cuenca had between 6,000 and 7,000 inhabitants.

61. During the first half of the 19th century, Cuenca had 14 parishes.

62. All of the second-generation descendants living in town were born in the original parish of San Pedro. 10 per cent of the members of the following generation were born in neighbouring parishes and nearly 85 per cent in San Pedro, with none born anywhere else in town. Even in the fourth generation, a little over half of the offspring were born in the parish of San Pedro.

63. This estimate does not include movement caused by births and deaths.

64. Basic structural changes refer to changes between solitary, nuclear, extended, or multiple households, and not to changes within any of those categories. See Reher (1990*a*: 234–9).

65. In 1887, the weight of the clergy in stem-family regions of the peninsula, especially in the Basque Country and Navarre, and to a lesser extent along the Pyrenees and in Catalonia, was far greater than in those regions of partible inheritance. Even so, it is important here to bear in mind that the extent to which these nuns and priests originally came from the regions where they lived is unclear. See Reher *et al.* (1993).

66. Here we will follow the ideas of Mikelarena Peña (1992*b*: 34–3) and Douglass (1988*a*: 1–4) closely.

67. See, for example, Goldschmidt and Kunkel (1971), Berkner and Mendels (1978), Burguière (1986), Douglass (1988*a*), Comas d'Argemir (1991), Barrera González (1993).

68. For example, while the importance of feudal control may have been important in Catalonia or Aragon, it certainly was not in most of the rest of the northern region; and settlement patterns were not dispersed in many stem-family areas of Catalonia and Navarre. There is considerable ecological unity in the north, with mountain valleys, small farms, and high levels of access to property, but other areas of the Iberian Peninsula with similar ecological characteristics give no indication that the stem family was ever present.

69. One of the most evident of these is the fact that the areas where the stem family flourished were precisely those in which Muslim domination was felt least.

70. This means that in stem families, as adult mortality declined over the course of the demographic transition, the years spent co-residing with the elder generation were bound to increase, as was the overall weight of these complex living arrangements in society.

71. See Wachter *et al.* (1978). The computer software used for the simulation is called SOCSIM and was devised at the University of California at Berkeley.

72. Simplifying considerably, the researchers solved for primogeniture and ulti-mogeniture (where either the first-born or the last-born surviving son married and brought a spouse into the family household). These two provide, so to speak, an upper and a lower bound on stem-family proportions. Since the simulation is based on marriages, the authors called these rules 'primonuptial' and 'ultimonuptial'. Considering that historical reality may have fallen somewhere in between these sets of two rules, they also devised the 'primoreal' rules of co-residence, in which a series of preference rules were introduced based on the age and sex of the members of the household and of the rest of the community. See Wachter *et al.* (1978: 29–42).

73. Generally speaking, households with more than two conjugal units with an ascendant–descendant relation, or ones with one nucleus with a lineal relative not a member of any nucleus and in an ascending or descending relation, are considered to be indicative of the presence of the stem family. In the original Laslett classification system, these households would be types 4a, 4b, 4d, 5a, 5b, and perhaps 5d and 5e (Laslett, 1972: 31). This indicator tends to exaggerate the importance of the stem family because in a number of cases the presence of co-resident kin may well have had nothing at all to do with succession and property.

74. For a complete summary of these results, see Wachter *et al.* (1978: 43–64).

75. In other European countries, there is abundant documentation pointing to the existence of frequent conflicts between parents and their children because of economic agreements regulating retirement and old age. See, for example, Gaunt (1983: 262–8).
76. For the importance of Basque cultural contexts for family systems, see Mikelarena Peña (1992*a*).
77. In Catalonia, the most typical union was that of an heir with a non-heir with a dowry; marriages of heirs of two different families (an *hereu* with a *pubilla*) were infrequent (Barrera González, 1990: 199–202; 1993: 153–4). Closed marriages between two families, a type of sibling exchange, were also frequent in Catalonia (Ferrer i Alòs, 1987: 605–16, Barrera González, 1990: 172–88).
78. The first son is the heir, the second a chaplain, and the third a lawyer.
79. While in Galicia, Asturias, and parts of the Basque Country, for example, celibacy for both sexes was relatively high, and sometimes extremely high, in Catalonia it was only moderate. Much the same held for age at marriage. Nevertheless, nuptiality generally was more restricted in these areas than in most of the rest of the country.
80. For more details on this subject, see ch. 6.
81. For examples of the often contentious nature of succession in areas of partible inheritance, see, for example, Freeman (1970: 69–70; 1979: 114–19), Aceves (1971: 66–7), Gilmore (1980: 158–61).
82. There is a Castilian aphorism to the effect that 'Brothers and sisters have not quarrelled because they have not divided up the inheritance yet' (*Los hermanos no han reñido porque no han partido*).
83. On this subject, see Hansen (1977: 100–4), Barrera González (1990: 294–302, 343–450), Urrutikoetxea (1993: 254–255).
84. The potential for conflict among siblings was still greater during the 20th century, when for inheritance tax purposes people tended to declare their estates to have far less value than they actually did. In these cases, there was normally a tacit agreement between the father and the *hereu* as to how the inheritance should be distributed. A typical conflict might ensue if the *hereu* decided not to honour such an agreement and to insist on the declared value of the estate (Hansen, 1977: 101–2). There is no reason to think that this type of conflict was specific to the 20th century or to Catalonia.
85. In the Basque Country, where in many cases the designated heir was completely in charge of the family estate, this type of conflict may well have been less significant (Douglass, 1973: 111–12).
86. See, for example, Douglass (1975: 136–49, 178–9, 182–91), Hansen (1977: 104–6, 153–4), Barrera González (1990: 365–77; 1993: 243), Celaya Ibarra (1993: 28–9), Comas d'Argemir (1993: 232–3, 240–1), Roigé i Ventura (1993: 164–6).
87. Certain transformations in rural industries, especially relating to viticulture in Galicia, the Basque Country and Navarre, and Catalonia, are exceptions to this trend.

4 The Stages of Life

The household, the larger kin group, and the individual; all are vantage points which must be used if we are to reach a viable understanding of family forms and family life in historic Spain. Each is different; each yields different types of results. Earlier, I used the co-residential unit and the kin group as the core of my analysis of living arrangements and family systems. In this chapter aspects of the family developmental cycle will be discussed not only in terms of the household and the larger family, but of the individual as well.

The effects of time on families is a central feature of people's life experience. Here I am not referring so much to historical as to human time. Life can be simply and meaningfully classified into stages, extending from infancy and early childhood to retirement, old age, and decrepitude. Each of these stages was dictated by an individual's biological and physiological development, and entailed very different roles for a person within his family group. Everyone was essential for the social, demographic, and economic reproduction of the family, yet the position a person occupied within the household, whether or not he was a net provider or a net receiver of aid, whether the authority over the family unit lay with him or not, and whether the role he played meant that his main activity took place inside the family home or elsewhere were all dependent on a person's stage in life.

The household itself also had a developmental cycle, which was dependent on the age and sex of its members, and especially of its head. The needs and the make-up of the co-residential group changed as the age structure of headship changed. In this sense, the stages of life of individuals were linked to the development of households, not only in a metaphorical way but also in real life. A type of dynamic synergy was created and played out over people's life spans, a synergy linking the individual, the household, and the larger family group in a type of three-dimensional triangle in which the stages of life of each ended up affecting the life course of the others.

Ultimately my analysis will point to the importance of questioning the meaning of the deceptively stable household patterns discussed in earlier chapters which characterized most areas of Spain over the past three centuries. The results will underscore the existence of a great variety of living experiences both within society and over the life course of individuals. The household will be shown to be a profoundly permeable and dynamic unit, continually mediated by inflows and outflows of people, wealth, and support. The family will be shown to be the primary source of social and economic welfare for persons in need of support, especially the very young, the widowed, and the aged. This essentially familial nature of social welfare will only be modified with the advent of an effective and universal national social security and retirement system, and that only dates from the middle decades of the twentieth century. The dynamics of family support take place both within households and across them, as the extended family makes its importance felt everywhere in Spain, largely independent of the basic family systems and co-residential patterns holding in any given region.

Since many of these matters normally only receive marginal attention in much of the literature published on Spanish family history, our information tends to be sparse and geographically unrepresentative, and affords only a rudimentary view of the major issues. Much use will be made of the Cuenca data base, even though it can only be considered representative of a Spain in which inheritance was divisible and population primarily rural. The extent to which many of the issues raised here are applicable to other Spanish contexts can only be ascertained in the light of future research. Even then, the available historical sources are hardly adequate for the task, and only afford a glimpse of issues we might expect were very complex.

Marriage and Household Formation

Everywhere in Spain, the formation, development, and demise of households were strictly linked to the demographic facts of life. Births, deaths, marriages, and migration were all essential catalysts of change in the life of a household. Chief among these was marriage because it marked the onset of household formation for a very large majority of young couples, just as it also initiated the 'empty nest' period of the parental household when children were no longer present. Births and migration were very important in determining the actual size and age and sex composition of the domestic unit. Death did the same, and was also the key to the ultimate disappearance of the family household. All of these contributed to what can be called the life cycle of the household, which started small and young, grew larger as the parents aged, and ultimately became small once again.

Marriage was unquestionably the most important of all of these life-cycle events. It led to demographic reproduction and set in motion a series of mechanisms which were essential for the survival of society. Marriage-related mobility was a source of redistribution of active population and, as long as it was accompanied by some sort of property devolution, as it normally was, it heralded the foundation of separate family economies and the diversification of previously existing ones. This seems to have been the case in much of western Europe, where marriage implied certain property transfers in dowries and other types of marriage portions and in most cases led to neo-local household formation. In so doing, marriage became an important catalyst for individual and household development, stimulating change not only for newly-weds, but for their households of origin as well. Spain was not exceptional here; everywhere marriage was an essential element of social reproduction.

Where partible inheritance and nuclear families prevailed, as was the case in most of the country, marriage and household formation went hand in hand. An example of this is given in Figure 4.1, where the similarity in the proportion of married men and the proportion of male household heads in each age group indicates that a marriage invariably led to the formation of a separate household.[1] This example has been taken from the town of Cuenca in 1844, but could have come from almost anywhere in central and southern Spain, and from many of the regions of the north as well. Marriage and family formation were interdependent acts, and were sensitive to many of the same social and economic factors. Marriage was a necessary prerequisite for household formation, but a marriage could not take place unless a young couple had achieved a certain amount of economic independence with which to set up its independent household (R. Smith, 1981: 618).

In areas where stem-family systems were prevalent, the relationship between marriage, headship, and household formation was necessarily somewhat different. Marriage led more or less directly to household formation only for those young adults who had not been designated heir. For heirs, however,

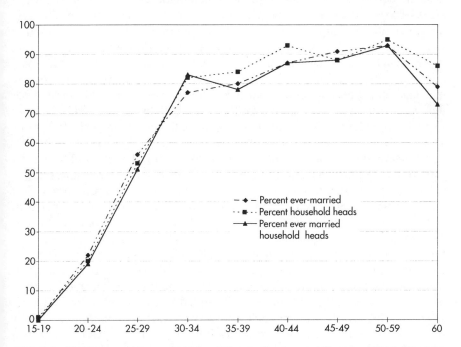

Fig. 4.1 Marriage and household formation in the town of Cuenca, 1844 (% males in each age group)

even though marriage initiated a period of profound transformation for the family, it did not lead to the formation of a new, autonomous household. Since headship was and is a culturally constrained concept, in stem-family contexts empirical data might yield ambiguous and contradictory results. For example, data on headship and marital status by age such as those used in Figure 4.1 would have shown markedly different patterns in those regions in which the elder generation retained headship, as opposed to areas where it did not. In the first case, headship rates would have lagged far behind marriage rates, at least for the designated heirs, only reaching similar levels as the elder genera- tion died off. Where headship devolved upon the younger generation, much as occurred in some parts of the Basque Country and Navarre, marriage and headship would also have gone hand in hand, even though neo-local house- hold formation was only practised by a part of the population. The marriage of the heir automatically meant a change in household headship, even though the only real change would have been the entry into the household of a new son- or daughter-in-law.

With nuptiality and household formation so closely linked for such a large part of Spain, the determinants of nuptiality ended up having a very direct effect on family formation. Migration patterns, mortality, marriage markets, and economic conditions were all central to rates of household formation. In fact, the closest proxy indicator of age-specific household formation rates in areas where neo-local patterns prevailed would have been age-specific first marriage rates. By implication, this suggests that rates of household formation were probably far lower and peaked at later ages in those regions and among those social groups characterized by relatively late and restricted male nuptiality. It is extremely difficult to generate data regarding age-specific marriage and especially household formation rates, but it is not implausible that rates of household formation differed sharply by region and over time, quite independent of whether or not neo-local household formation rules prevailed.

In most Spanish regions, then, the custom of neo-local household formation subsequent to marriage was common enough to be considered a normative cultural behaviour pattern, and can be summed up in the aphorism *casado casa quiere*, which implied that any married woman wanted a home of her own (Pitt-Rivers, 1961: ch. 1).[2] Originally the result of inheritance practices, econ- omic needs and opportunities, the availability of housing and land, and cul- tural attitudes, these patterns had probably been in existence for centuries. Even though economic and social factors were still central to the timing of marriage and household formation, to a large extent it had become a norma- tive behaviour pattern and therefore it tended to transcend individual deci- sions. In other words, young people expected to start up a household of their own when they married, and were unwilling to marry when this was not a realistic possibility.

Yet the link between marriage and household formation was not necessarily an immediate one. In many different contexts more or less prolonged periods of co-residence in the household of one set of parents was accepted, encouraged, and often even mandated. In the Vega de Pas of Santander, for example, until fairly recently newly-wed couples tended to co-reside either with the bride's or the groom's family, often for as long as a year. Susan Tax Freeman (1979: 131–3) has related this practice to the finalizing of the marriage portions and insists that this co-residence was essentially designed to facilitate the independence of the new household once it was formed. A similar pattern appeared in the nineteenth century in the town of Cuenca, where linking yearly population enumerations to registered marriages has yielded results suggesting that some type of temporary co-residence took place in nearly half the marriages considered in a random sample (Reher, 1990a: 213–16).[3] This type of co-residence lasted one year for 41 per cent of the sample couples, and for at least three years for almost a third of the marriages. In fact, in Cuenca co-residence immediately subsequent to marriage was the cause of over 40 per cent of all multiple households in town.

Just how widespread these customs of temporary co-residence were is unknown, but they were probably fairly common in much of Spain, quite independent of the prevailing family system. Since by and large the practice was unrelated to property devolution, it is best understood within the context of the help given to young couples designed to facilitate their transition to the married life. This transition was not always an easy one, because setting up a household required an initial outlay of capital which young persons normally did not have. Except in those cases in which a sole heir was designated, the dowries, marriage portions, and advances on the usufruct of inheritance which devolved upon young couples at marriage were normally only enough to give them an often rather precarious beginning to married life. They needed assistance and sought it within their own families. Temporary co-residence with the parental family was one way to help them on their way. Other means of helping also existed: newly-weds might be invited to eat either with their parents or with other members of their extended family during the months following the wedding; parents might also give the couple some grain or other food products; the rent on a home might be paid by one of their families for a period of time; or both families might collaborate in fixing up a shed, stable, or barn which the newly-weds could use as a temporary residence.[4]

All of this was designed to help out during the first months of marriage so that the young couple could get its own family economy going. The widespread practice of leaving land in usufruct to children upon marriage meant that during the initial years of marriage, the young family's economy and those of its parental households might well be mixed economies, and it was not infrequent for members of the younger generation to help out on the land of their parents, which would one day be theirs. As the years went by, parents died and the estate of the young couple grew as property was received from each of the four parents through inheritance. The basic direction of family support, which went from the older to the younger generation, was not completely reversed until the parental generation, had reached old age.[5]

The Family Life Cycle

The concept of the household developmental cycle is intuitively attractive because it illustrates that the needs, composition, age structure, and sex ratio of the co-residential unit changed over the life course of its components. A household was young when a family was formed by a young couple, matured as children were born and grew up, and aged as the children left home and the household became an empty nest. This conceptualization of the formation, growth, and decay of the family household is primarily based on the reproductive cycle of conjugal family units, though the forces at work influencing changes were only partly related to the process of reproduction.

Defining the 'age' of a household presents certain important difficulties. For one, the concept of life course or life cycle generally refers to individuals, and not to groups, and households were made up of a number of different individuals each of whom was at a certain point of his or her own life. The way this is normally done is by pegging the 'age' of the household to the age of its head. In other words, households headed by persons 25–29 years of age would be considered 'young', while those headed by persons, say, 55–59 would be 'old'. In the best of cases this is only an approximation, and in some contexts it might actually obscure more than clarify the reality at hand.[6] Another difficulty concerns the fact that the developmental cycle is a cohort-specific concept, but the data generally available are based on the experience at one point in time of a number of different cohorts. It is, however, the only readily accessible way to classify households by the stage they are at in their developmental cycle, and it will be used here.

All over Spain household structures varied substantially by age of the household head, though the importance of certain co-residential patterns and the way they developed over the life cycle were markedly different within different family systems. In order to illustrate this, in Figures 4.2 and 4.3 I have used examples taken from the area around Pamplona (Navarre), located in one of the classic stem-family regions of Spain, together with data from the Asón valley in the eighteenth century in the eastern part of Cantabria in the north, La Ñora (Murcia) in the south-east, and Cuenca in the central or central-eastern part of the country.[7] Each of these last three places is located in regions where differing intensities of partible inheritance prevailed.

The incidence of complex household structures around Pamplona was extremely high at young ages, and diminished steadily thereafter. In Cantabria and in Cuenca, the patterns were more U-shaped, being slightly higher at younger and especially at older ages. In Murcia no discernible life-cycle development can be seen. In all of these contexts, however, the cycle of nuclear

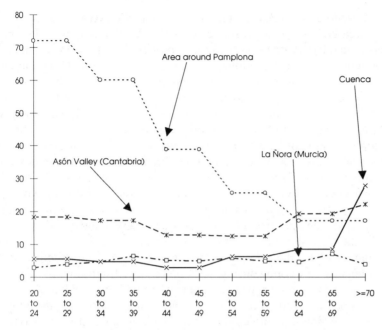

Fig. 4.2 Complex households by age of head in four Spanish contexts (%)

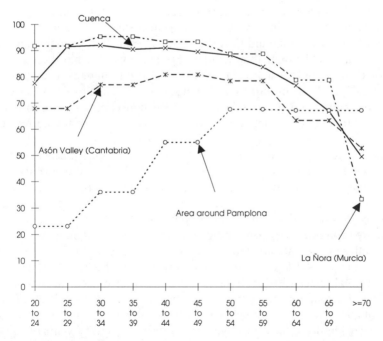

Fig. 4.3 Nuclear households by age of head in four Spanish contexts (%)

family households was basically the same, though intensity varied: their importance increased during the early years of the developmental cycle, and decreased precipitously once the head approached the age of retirement. The exception once again is Pamplona, where the incidence of nuclear households grew over the life course until it stabilized at about 50 years of age.

In areas of partible inheritance and widespread prevalence of nuclear households, the reproductive cycle and patterns of family solidarity were central to the shape the household took over the life course, whereas in the stem-family context of Pamplona, inheritance-related co-residence dominated the observable patterns. In Pamplona, the high incidence of complex households among 'young' families in reality reflects the co-residence of young heirs in their parental households. Tradition, however, dictated that the young heir become household head upon marriage. Had the parental generation retained headship, as it did in parts of the Basque Country and in most of Catalonia, for example, the highest levels of complexity would have been reached among the 'older' families. This does not necessarily mean that the age structure of these households was very young during these years. In fact, subsequent to marriage it was probably at its oldest, because the young couple co-resided with more or less elderly parents, and there were as yet no young children in the family. The progressive decline in complex households and increase in nuclear ones was the product of death in the older generation and marriage in the younger one. By the time a household head was 40 or 50 years of age, both co-resident parents had probably died, thus turning complex structures into nuclear ones. Upon the marriage of his own chosen heir, headship automatically passed to the younger generation, and thus the parents became co-resident family in a 'young' household rather than heading up their own. Within the universe of complex households around Pamplona, important changes also took place over the life cycle, as multiple family households practically disappeared (67.3 to 1.4 per cent), and the weight of extended households increased between three and four times, mainly due to the effects of death on the co-residential group.[8]

Inheritance-related co-residence of the designated heir was the key element defining the development of the household over the life course of its head in stem-family regions, but had little or no importance elsewhere. In nuclear family regions co-residential patterns over the family life cycle were fundamentally determined by the demographic constraints of reproduction and death, by economic concerns, and by patterns of family solidarity. The excellent quality of the Cuenca data set helps bring a number of these factors to light. In Figures 4.4 and 4.5 household structure is shown by the age of the head.[9] In male-headed households, the incidence of nuclear households predominated throughout the entire life course, though relative levels of importance of all types of structure changed significantly by age. People living alone were fairly important at young ages, but between 25 and 50 years of age there were few solitary households. After 50 the importance of people alone increased ever more rapidly, and by the time male household heads reached the

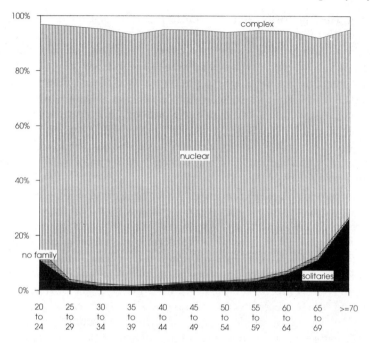

Fig. 4.4 Household structure by age of head, male-headed households, Cuenca

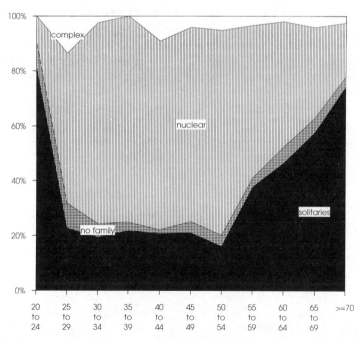

Fig. 4.5 Household structure by age of head, female-headed households, Cuenca

'third' age (the age of retirement), more than 20 per cent of all households were made up of men living alone. Households with people living together but not forming a family nucleus were never very important, except perhaps at 20–24 years of age, when a certain percentage of unrelated men lived together, normally in work groups. Complex households grew in importance before heads reached 35–39 years of age, when it was not uncommon for widowed parents to live with them, and then again after 55, this time due mainly to the temporary co-residence of newly-wed children.

Households headed by women were far less numerous than those headed by men, especially at younger ages, and their developmental cycle was substantially different (Table 4.1).[10] The importance of nuclear households was far lower, solitary households represented between 20 and 70 per cent of all households, and complex family forms were only modestly important, except when the female head was very young and her husband absent (Figure 4.5). Elderly widows living alone were a characteristic trademark of rural Spanish society. These differences in the life-cycle pattern of male- and female-headed households were the result of cultural norms which stipulated that a male was head whenever he was present, and because the incidence of remarriage was greater and life expectancy considerably lower among men than among women. This led to the predominance of nuclear household structures at far higher ages among men than among women. Despite the traditional 2–3 year age difference at marriage, wives ended up outliving their husbands; and when a spouse did die, it was far easier for a widower to remarry than it was for a widow. Past 50 years of age, men could still count on living with their wives and with offspring who remained at home, whereas for women, except in the few instances in which they lived with other kin, only the presence of children at home kept them from living alone. The permanence of children in households headed by a widowed parent, however, declined with age but hardly differed at all by sex.[11]

Within the context of partible inheritance and the overwhelming prevalence

Table 4.1 Proportion of female-headed households in Cuenca by age of head, 1750–1970

Age of head	Total households	Proportion female-headed
20–24	176	0.063
25–29	939	0.023
30–34	1,271	0.034
35–39	1,342	0.048
40–44	1,318	0.058
45–49	1,200	0.104
50–54	1,252	0.139
55–59	973	0.186
60–64	959	0.253
65–69	724	0.265
70 and more	965	0.382

of nuclear co-residential patterns, the presence or absence of children in the household and the effects of adult mortality were the primary determinants of household size over the life course. During the early years of a couple's life this was basically a consequence of their own process of demographic reproduction, minus the effects of mortality. Once women ceased having children, normally at about 40 years of age, the amount of time children remained at home and the effects of adult mortality gave household size its particular shape. This process can be see quite clearly in Figure 4.6. The number of persons at home steadily increased until male heads were between 45 and 49 years of age, and declined rapidly thereafter. Households were only very small before male heads had reached 30 years of age, and after 65, though at no stage did the mean household size dip beneath two. Female-headed households were always much smaller. Once again the absence of the male helps explain differences which were often in excess of one person per household, especially during the central years of life (35–60), because not only was the spouse missing but women whose spouses were absent tended to give birth to fewer children.

The entire question of children in the household can be more adequately seen in Figure 4.7, which juxtaposes the number of children at home and their mean age. Young couples had few children and all of them were very young. Before 30, the average number of children per family was less than one, and their average age well below five. As the age of the household head rose, so did

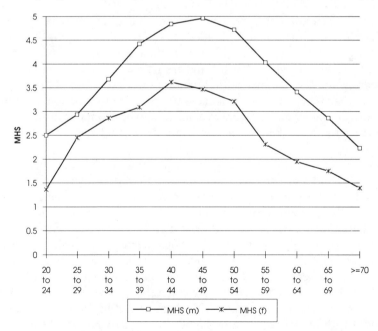

Fig. 4.6　Mean household size by age and sex of household head, Cuenca

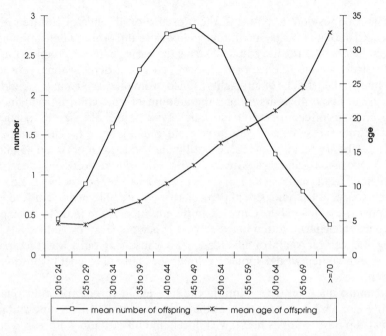

Fig. 4.7   Mean number and age of offspring by age of household head, Cuenca

the number of children at home and their mean age. 45–49 marks the age at which families had the greatest number of children. At that point there were nearly three children per household, and their average age was about 13. This was the age at which for the most part women had completed their childbearing and the majority of their children were still living at home. Only after heads had reached 50 years of age were they able to count on the fact that the majority of their children were in a position to be economically productive. Before that moment their economic usefulness could never be more than marginal.

After this period the number of children at home steadily decreased as they left their parental households via marriage or migration. By the time a household head was 55–59 years of age, fewer than two children remained at home, and this number dipped below one a decade later. Demographic and economic factors determined these patterns. Age at marriage in Cuenca was between 24 and 26 over much of this period, and the mean age of childbearing was between 30 and 31. Thus, in the absence of mortality, a woman married at 25 would have had her last child when she was about 40 years of age, and this child would have reached marriage age when the mother was near 65 and the father closer to 70. This explains why there was still almost one child per household with an average age of slightly below 25 when the head was between 65 and 69 years of age.

Children abandoned their parental home at marriage and, save in exceptional circumstances, normally did not return during the course of their lives. Therefore, the presence or absence of older children in the household was determined to a large degree by the incidence and age of marriage. In those societies in which marriage age was high, or was increasing, households would tend to have more adult children than where marriage age was low. It can also be shown that the levels of celibacy, especially permanent celibacy, were positively related to household size and complexity. Galicia offers a good example of this because very high levels of male and especially female celibacy ended up being a prime factor determining the relatively complex co-residential patterns existing there, at least during the nineteenth and the early part of the twentieth century. Extremely low percentages of never-married household heads, especially past 30 years of age, suggests that in the absence of out-migration, never-married sons and daughters normally remained at home to care for their parents or co-resided with their married siblings.

Marriage was not the only reason that sons and daughters abandoned their parents' households. At young ages significant proportions of children left their homes either to live with some member of their extended family as nephews or grandchildren or to seek temporary employment. Adolescents often held jobs outside the household at a relatively young age in order to supplement their family income and to save up for their own marriage. The timing and intensity of this type of departure from the household were conditioned by the requirements of the family economy, by the relative population pressure on local resources, and by the economic opportunities existing elsewhere (Hajnal, 1982; R. Smith, 1984). In Spain, the life-cycle farm servant so

Table 4.2 Percentage of children residing in parental household by age and date

Urban Cuenca

age group	1800		1844	
	males	females	males	females
0–4	92.1	96.7	91.6	98.4
5–9	96.1	93.8	90.8	91.7
10–14	81.1	79.7	88.0	88.1
15–19	65.8	50.9	76.3	51.7

Rural Cuenca (both sexes)

age group	18th century	19th century	20th century
0–4	95.8	95.5	97.7
5–9	94.7	94.2	96.6
10–14	84.7	91.3	94.9
15–19	72.3	85.1	90.8

Source: Reher (1988: 167; 1990: 201).

characteristic of the English countryside had little if any importance, at least after the eighteenth century. If farms were large enough to require significant non-family labour (principally in the southern half of the country), there was generally an abundant supply of landless day labourers to fill those needs. Even so, the incidence of child and adolescent migration still had a substantial effect on families. Despite the difficulties involved in measuring the incidence of this type of movement, available urban and rural studies suggest that from 10 to 20 years of age, between 7 and 40 per cent of all youths lived in households other than those of their families (Table 4.2). This mobility affected girls more than boys, was higher in urban areas, and tended to diminish over the course of the present century.[12] This was likely a characteristic of families everywhere, though probably the age structure and intensity varied markedly by social, economic, and regional context. Its effects on the family household should not be underestimated, either for the co-residential domestic group or for its economy.

The presence of kin in these households was never very high, and it varied distinctly by the age of the household head (Figure 4.8). When the head was young, kin were relatively abundant and their mean age was quite low. They were the cousins and perhaps the unmarried siblings of young heads, some of whom were not yet even married. As the age of household heads increased, the numbers of kin stabilized at a much lower level (approximately one for

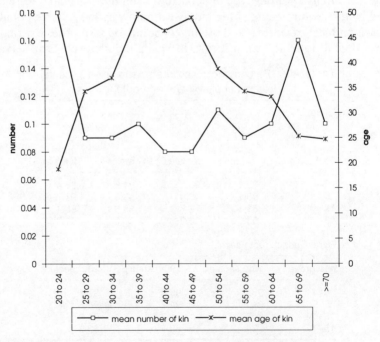

Fig. 4.8 Mean number and age of kin by age of household head

every 10 households), but their mean age rose sharply. Kin age was highest in households of people between 35 and 50, as parents, especially widowed parents, came to live with couples who were just entering the summer of their maturity. It was a period in which their children were still quite young, and their co-resident parents likely collaborated in the process of caring for and educating their grandchildren. After 45–50 the number of kin present in the household rose, as their age declined. It was then that kin presence in the household involved temporary post-marital co-residence of young couples, or perhaps those whose marriage had been cut short by the death of a spouse and who were taking refuge in households of their parents. Elderly household heads were not normally accompanied by kin from the same generation. Only when couples were very young were co-resident kin from the same generation. Subsequently, they were first from an older and then a younger generation than that of the household head.[13]

The Life Course and the Individual

Up until this point our perspective on the family has been one taken from the vantage point of the household itself, and specifically from that of the age of the head or the age and sex make-up of the household. Since people normally saw their lives not so much in terms of their family, but in terms of themselves living in different family contexts, an individual perspective over the life course is complementary and useful for our general discussion.[14] The likelihood of residing in differently structured households is portrayed in Figures 4.9 and 4.10. For both men and women, the incidence of complex living arrangements was fairly constant over the life course, oscillating between 6 and 9 per cent of each age group, though at all ages it was somewhat higher for women. This situation changed after about 60 years of age, when the propensity towards complexity increased appreciably for men, and nearly tripled for women. The age profile of solitary residence was quite similar. Before 20 years of age people seldom lived alone. Between 20 and 24 for women and 20 and 29 for men there was a slight increase in its incidence, though it continued to remain low until about 45 years of age for both sexes. After that it increased slowly for men, and more rapidly for women, reaching very high proportions for people of the 'third age'. Above 70 years of age, about 20 per cent of all men and just under 40 per cent of all women lived by themselves. In the case of elderly women, nuclear household structures represented only a minority of their living arrangements. In general terms, women were more likely than men to live in complex households at all ages, and in solitary ones at higher ages, mainly because superior male mortality and a lower incidence of remarriage among women led to a society with more widows than widowers.[15] They were the ones most likely to end up either living alone or moving in with their married children.

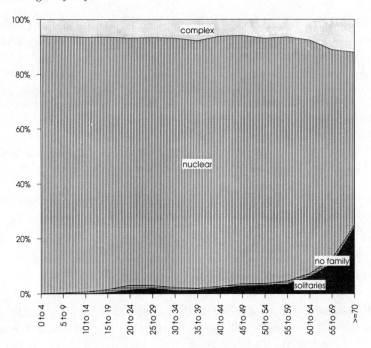

Fig. 4.9 Household structure by age of males, Cuenca, 1700–1970

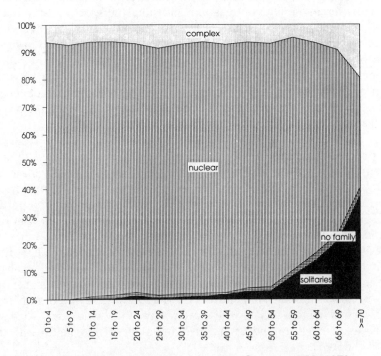

Fig. 4.10 Household structure by age of females, Cuenca, 1700–1970

The reproductive cycle of both the family and of the household is forcefully brought out if the mean size of the households people lived in at different stages of their lives is charted (Figure 4.11). Two clear cycles are visible, one which starts at birth and finishes at marriage, and the other starting at marriage and continuing into old age. The first cycle reached its peak when children were about 10 years of age, because at that stage they probably had both younger and elder brothers and sisters and both of their parents were still living. At this juncture, there were on average nearly six people per household, despite the fact that kin or servants were never numerous. Between 10 and 25 years of age, size diminished as older siblings married and started households of their own, as new children were no longer born into the family, and as parents gradually began to die. The duration of this cycle was, in fact, very nearly the same as the time parents and especially women invested in bearing and rearing their offspring.

The same cycle was repeated a second time in a person's life, only this time he or she was the parent forming his or her family. The duration of both cycles was just about the same, because they were determined by the same set of circumstances. The slight lag in the household cycle of men as opposed to women was the result of the fact that men tended to marry women about 2–3 years younger than they were. With the end of the second cycle and the departure of the children from the home, household size continued to diminish as death progressively reduced the number of surviving people at home. At

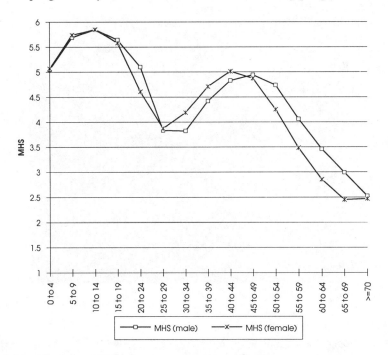

Fig. 4.11 Mean household size by age and sex, Cuenca

these ages women invariably ended up living in smaller households than men, as death made its age-old preference for men known, and in so doing ended up making life for their surviving widows that much more solitary. Even so, mean household size always remained well above two, even at older ages, thus suggesting that living alone was always a minority experience in rural Cuenca and probably most everywhere else in Spain during the period under study.

A person's position in his household was very much determined by his sex and age (Figures 4.12, 4.13, and 4.14). Before 20, the vast majority of persons were children in their parental households. After that, the importance of children diminished very quickly, as they married and set up their own households. This change came earlier and more quickly for women, but affected both sexes. Whereas at 15–19 nearly 95 per cent of all people resided with their parents, by 25–29 it was 34.4 per cent for men and 22.1 per cent for women. By 30 years of age, few children remained with their parents and by the time they had reached 50 years of age they had practically disappeared as household members, save for the occasional female spinster who lived with her parents. As in so many other cases, this pattern was the result of the nearly universal link between marriage and household formation, together with the gradual death of the parental generation. Had the context of the data been an area of Spain with restricted nuptiality, the percentages of co-resident offspring at higher ages would have been much greater.

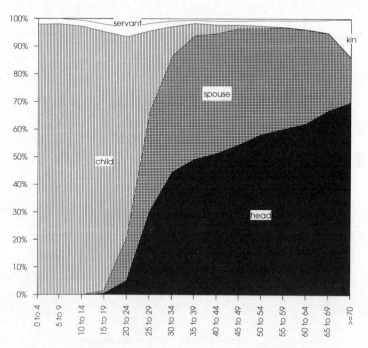

Fig. 4.12 Position in household by age, both sexes, Cuenca, 1700–1970

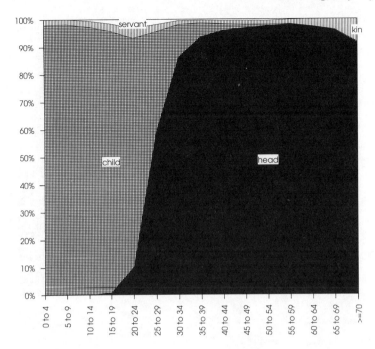

Fig. 4.13 Position in household by age, males, Cuenca, 1700–1970

The great majority of men went directly from being children in parental households to heading their own. After 35–39 years of age, levels of male headship continued to increase very gradually until they peaked at 55–59 years of age. It was then that men were still young enough to head their own households and the last of their children were just leaving home via marriage. From that moment on, headship among males declined sharply as increasing numbers began to co-reside with other family households, often those of their married children. For women the pattern was much different. Taking the combined position of head and spouse, women ascended to this position at a younger age, but retreated from it at a far more precipitous rate than did men. For the truly aged women, almost 20 per cent lived as kin in family households, as opposed to about 8 per cent of men. Female headship was practically non-existent before 30 years of age, but increased steadily thereafter. By the time women were over 60 between 35 and 45 per cent of them headed their own households, and the majority of them lived alone.

Demographic Modernization and the Length of Shared Life

Up to this point, the central role marriage and death played for where and with whom people lived has received considerable empirical support. During the

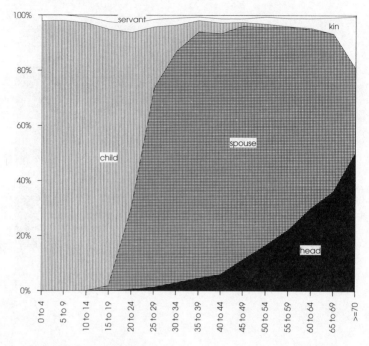

Fig. 4.14   Position in household by age, females, Cuenca, 1700–1970

period under study, however, all demographic variables underwent profound transformations. This was especially true with mortality, which went from a life expectancy at birth (e_0) of 25–30 years during the eighteenth and a good part of the nineteenth centuries to one of near or above 60 during the central decades of this century. Marital fertility was never very high (pre-transitional I_g just above 0.600), though the fertility transition did not start in the province of Cuenca until after 1920. Over this period marriage age increased substantially, though celibacy remained fairly low throughout.[16] Despite the rather tardy onset of the fertility transition in Cuenca, these demographic changes had a profound effect on the living arrangements of people. Some of these effects can be seen in Figures 4.15 to 4.23, in which household data have been grouped into three periods: from 1750 to 1880, well before the onset of the demographic transition; between 1881 and 1930, when the transition was in full force with its concomitant reductions of fertility and mortality; and from 1931 to 1970, when the historic demographic transition was being completed. Our data on household living arrangements are eloquent testimony to the effects of these transitions.

Demographic change led to a larger and generally older family group.[17] An acceptable general indicator of these changes is the mean household size over the life course, which both grew and changed its basic age structure (Figure 4.15). Lowest household sizes were invariably reached during the first period,

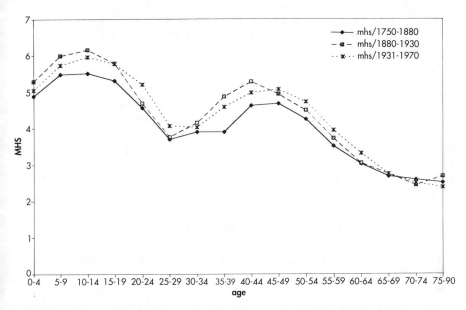

Fig. 4.15 Mean household size over the life course and over time

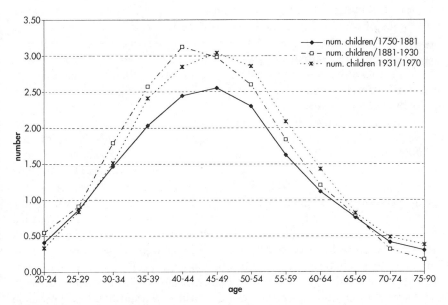

Fig. 4.16 Presence of children at home over time, by age of head

and the highest ones can be found between 1880 and 1930, when mortality was falling rapidly and fertility remained unchanged. In the final period, maximum size was somewhat lower but it peaked later and, in higher age groups, MHS was almost always highest. Here, during the early years of life the effects of lower fertility can be seen, though still lower mortality and higher age at marriage make themselves felt in higher age groups. Children at home are the key to many of these differences (Figure 4.16). During the central decades of this century, there were fewer children during the early years of the household life cycle. By the time the household head had reached 50, however, his co-resident offspring were more numerous than ever before as later marriage and increased life expectancy kept them at home longer. Demographic change had no effect on the number of co-resident kin in the household, but mean age grew by more than 10 years in certain age groups, as increasingly elder kin, often widowed parents, were taken in by their children (Figure 4.17).[18]

Many of the practical consequences of improving mortality conditions were more pronounced among men than among women, though for both, demographic modernization led to important changes in the household. Unquestionably the most important of these was that the threshold of vulnerability which people invariably crossed as they grew old became relatively less significant in each age group and, just as important, tended to occur later in people's lives. The initial decline in mortality had an enormous impact on people's welfare. This can be seen, for example, in Figure 4.18, where a continued decline over time in the per centages of single-person households, especially after the 40–44 year age group, can be observed. For the very old, the relative importance of those living alone had diminished by almost 20 per cent by the middle decades of this century. An interesting aspect of these data is the rise in the percentage of solitary households in the 20–24 year age group, which may in part have been due to small sample size, but which also suggests that over time progressively delayed age at marriage led to higher levels of young adults living by themselves.[19]

Important differences by sex emerge as men seem to have benefited far more from the prolonged periods of co-residence with their spouses or children than did women (Figures 4.19 and 4.20). For men past 55–60 years of age, the incidence of living alone declined on the order of one-third to one-half the levels holding between 1750 and 1880, as opposed to women, where the decline was about 15–20 per cent. Since the propensity to live alone for a given sex was basically dependent on the length of life of the other sex, men ended up benefiting from these changes relatively more than women basically because the gains in life expectancy of women far outstripped those of men. Parallel to these changes was the substantial increase in the number of persons of the third age living in nuclear households (Figure 4.21) and an increase in incidence and lengthening of the period in which women lived as spouses in their own households (Figure 4.22). This lengthening of cohabitation was

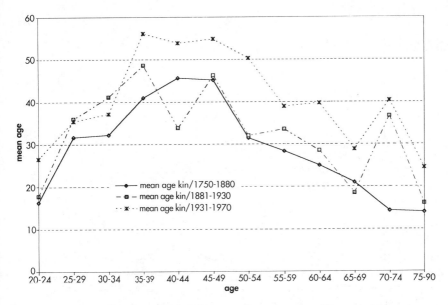

Fig. 4.17 Mean age of co-resident kin over time, by age of household head

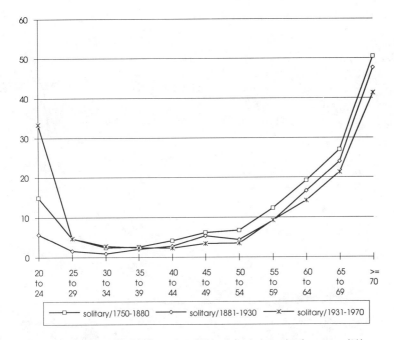

Fig. 4.18 Solitary households by age of head and date, both sexes (%)

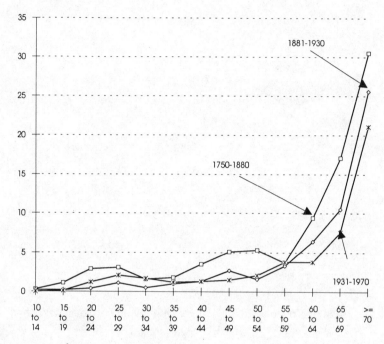

Fig. 4.19   Men living alone by age and date (%)

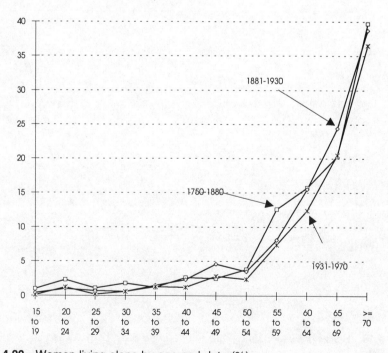

Fig. 4.20   Women living alone by age and date (%)

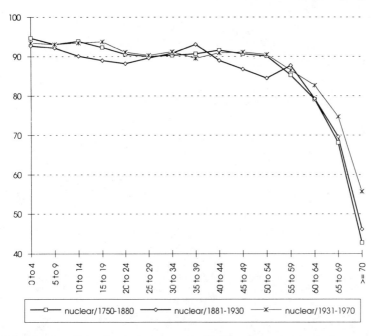

Fig. 4.21 Persons living in nuclear households by age and date, both sexes (%)

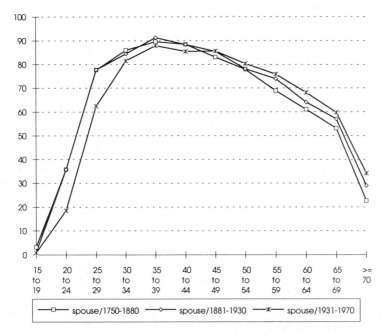

Fig. 4.22 Women currently married to household head by age and date (%)

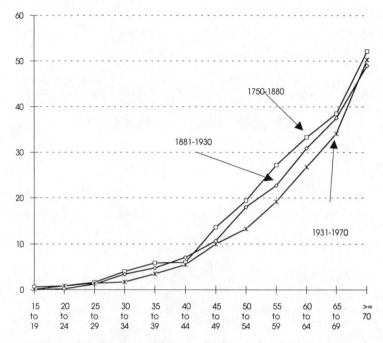

Fig. 4.23   Women heading households by age and date (%)

visible despite the much-reduced incidence of spouses at younger ages, itself the result of later ages at marriage.[20] One of the most eloquent examples of the implications of these changes can be found in the percentage of women heading households, which underwent drastic reductions visible as early as the 30–34 year age group (Figure 4.23).

Mortality reduction had a substantial and beneficial effect on the welfare of everyone in society. Nowhere, however, were the benefits more visible than for the elderly, as ever-increasing percentages of people prolonged the part of their life in which they were able to live with someone else, mainly their spouses. In so doing, they were pushing back the limits of the vulnerability that invariably affected people who lived alone and more generally those whose spouses had died. Had we been able to chart the same relationships with data from the 1980s and 1990s, it would be apparent that the incidence of living alone was far lower still than it was in the 1930–70 period. In many ways, increased life expectancy was alleviating young married couples of a measure of the responsibility that they would have had to share for the welfare of their parents during old age. On the other hand, however, it also meant that old age lasted longer and that an increasing percentage of the population was going to survive the 'third' and enter the 'fourth' age (Laslett, 1989). This has ended up bringing about an entirely different set of problems which will be taken up in other parts of this book.

The Stages of Life, the Limits of Vulnerability, and Family Support Mechanisms

People were keenly aware that life had different stages, each of which brought with it a certain role for them within the family and the household. These stages were understood by everyone, and they provided the framework for the inter-generational transfers of wealth and property, of education and company, of support and love. It is impossible to realistically understand the family without understanding the different stages of life and the fact that inter-generational transfers were at the very essence of its unity, flexibility, and durability. Some stages such as early childhood were completely dependent, at least in so far as material contributions to the family and household were concerned, while others were not. Yet material contributions to the welfare of the family were not the only ones considered important, as families more than any other social or political institution understood that wealth and utility included all those elements, be they material or immaterial, which contributed to their survival and happiness. Everyone had a vital role to play, one which was profoundly related to his or her stage of life. Explaining some of the ways in which these inter-generational transfers were materialized is the purpose of the following pages.[21]

Early childhood was a time when persons were completely dependent on their parents for material, emotional, and educational support. In turn, children were the key to the future survival of the family and were a present source of satisfaction for their parents as recipients of their love and as the living example that the parents were fulfilling their social, cultural, and familial obligation to assure the reproduction of the family and therefore of society. At a very young age, however, these children entered another stage in which they made an active contribution to the material welfare of the family group as they prepared for marriage and departure from their parental household. After marriage and until at least 50 or 60 years of age, parents first cared for their own young children, then provided food, shelter, and education for the entire family group, and ended up helping their newly-wed children or their own parents. In turn they received their share of the inheritance of their own parents, together with the satisfaction derived from their role as the prime source of family welfare and survival. After the family nest had been abandoned upon the marriage of their children, elderly people contributed to the welfare of their family by advancing the usufruct of their possessions to their children, or by assisting in the socialization of their grandchildren. In turn they received the material and emotional support of all of the younger generations of the family. The material and immaterial inter-generational links often transcended the limits of the household, as the extended family made its importance felt. Even though family conflict did exist, and some people may have made every effort not to participate in the entire system of family and social reproduction, it is unquestionable that this was normative behaviour for society as a whole.

In all societies, but especially in those characterized by high mortality, risk was a basic fact of life and risk management was central to the strategies of all families.[22] People knew that under normal circumstances an important percentage of children would die, and that after a certain age parents also would begin to die and that the family group would have to become increasingly active in their welfare. But risk also entailed uncertainty, as death could well be unexpected either in its intensity or its timing. The only protection from the effects of death at young ages was to have many children, a fact that characterized Spanish society until the levels and the variability of infant and child mortality began to undergo substantial decline towards the end of the nineteenth and the beginning of the twentieth centuries. In the case of adults, however, an untimely death might leave a family group or an individual in a particularly disadvantageous situation. An example of this might be a woman with young children whose husband had died at an unexpectedly young age. She and her children ended up being particularly vulnerable as the earning power of the family declined drastically. As will become clear shortly, the incidence of vulnerability was considerably higher than might be imagined.

Where nuclear households represented the majority of people's living experience, the implications of vulnerability might well be abject poverty, especially if the conjugal unit had to depend exclusively on its own resources for survival. This situation has been called the 'nuclear hardship hypothesis' by some researchers, and implies that even though nuclear families might be considered an 'ideal' type of co-residential arrangement, they were more exposed than other types of household to the potentially deleterious effects of risk (Laslett, 1988). Where nuclear household structures represented the dominant type of co-residence, the applicability of this hypothesis is unquestionable. The extent to which it is pertinent in the part of Spain where the stem family predominated is unknown. With both the parental generation and that of the heir and his family living in complex co-residential units, exposure to the negative implications of risk was reduced though not eliminated. For members of the family outside the stem itself, it is not at all clear whether those who experienced hardship were any more or less likely to receive support from other family households than elsewhere in Spain.

Minimizing the potentially negative implications of risk was of primary importance for families and for society. Poor laws such as those existing in England, whereby the community as a whole took responsibility for the social welfare of those who could not fend for themselves, by and large did not exist in Spain. Before the twentieth century, the Church or certain municipal or royal institutions did provide a type of social safety net whereby desperately poor or ill individuals could find shelter and food. Hospitals and the dispensing of alms are good examples of the type of activity they undertook. Beneath that level, however, risk management and social welfare were first and foremost the responsibility of the family. People looked to it for help, and normally found it there. Mechanisms of familial support transcended the household and implicated the entire extended family, though most directly those who came from the original conjugal family unit. In doing this, the family played an essential role in the welfare and stability of Spanish society, much as it does to this day.

Charting vulnerability over the life course can never be more than an approximate exercise, mainly because the categories used are arbitrary and often do not reflect the true situation of families. It can best be considered a function of a person's age and the type of household he lived in. Early childhood and old age were ages normally characterized by a person's depend-ence on others for support and often for survival. People living alone, especially at older ages, were probably the most precarious of all groups in rural society in Spain. In many cases they were completely dependent on outside support for their primary economic necessities, and were often com-pletely alone. Household listings are filled with elderly paupers, and suicides were not an uncommon cause of death among them. In most cases important, even elaborate mechanisms of familial support were a key element in their social welfare.

Demographic realities made vulnerable women more numerous than vul-nerable men, and economic realities made them poorer. This was especially true with widows since normally they were unable to be as productive econ-omically as their husbands. This is not to suggest that they did not make a significant contribution to their family economy. They did, and it is commonly held that they worked longer hours than the men of the household. Ultimately, however, from a strictly economic standpoint their role was complementary. The death of a husband in a rural context, especially if there were no surviving working-age male children in the household, could only be partially compen-sated by his widow. The same of course was true when it was the wife who died. Nevertheless, since remarriage for men was far more frequent than for women, and since a man's role in agricultural production and in wage labour was normally more relevant than a woman's, the overall situation of the family suffered less. On the other hand, the important part of the woman's work-load dedicated to the house itself was more easily carried out by other women of a wider age range than was male labour.[23] The result was that not only were there more vulnerable women than men, but they were also generally worse off economically. This is brought out forcefully in the data on household income available for certain household listings during the first decades of this century in rural Cuenca. In all cases, male-headed households had annual incomes nearly 2.5 times higher than female-headed households (Table 4.3). Controlling for marital status and using only widowed household heads, general levels of income decline, but the male advantage continues to be enormous.[24]

Single-parent households were at a distinct disadvantage mainly because all members of a household had specific roles to play, roles which could not be fully carried out by anyone else in the family. This was particularly true with

Table 4.3 Mean annual household income by sex and marital status of head, Cuenca, 1910–1930

	All households		Widow- or widower-headed	
	income	n	income	n
male-headed households	6193.2	526	4226	29
female-headed households	2826.4	44	2790	41
total	5925.5	570	3385	70

Note: Mean annual income measured in Spanish *pesetas*.

the parents, since they were the chief providers for the family. If a spouse died, the situation might be entirely reversed or its effects mitigated if the head remarried fairly quickly. This was an option far more open to men than it was to women. This is brought out very clearly in Figure 4.24, which shows the incidence of single-parent households with children present over the life course.[25] During early childhood, there was little difference by sex, as the percentages rose from 2 to nearly 15 per cent of the entire population of each age group. Between 20 and 29, men showed a greater likelihood of living in single-parent households, mainly because they married and started families of their own at a higher age than did women, and thus resided in their parental households longer and allowed more time for the death of one of their parents. After 30 years of age, however, women showed a tendency nearly twice that of men to live in and to head single-parent households. In old age these percentages declined because by then marriage had removed most of the children from their parental households.

The implications of living in this type of household varied substantially with age. In the years immediately preceding marriage, when people were fully productive in economic terms, living in a single-parent household probably only meant that a greater part of one's economic activity had to be dedicated to helping out his family household and his remaining parent. It is possible that this sort of situation may have led to a postponement of marriage or in just a few cases the forgoing of marriage in order to care for the parent. On the other hand, the death of a parent also meant that the younger generation had earlier access to its part of the inheritance. If there were young children in the household, they would initially be the hardest hit by a marriage terminated by death, because they were deprived of the economic and personal welfare afforded by one of their parents. In the long run, however, it was the parent who suffered most, and more often than not these parents were women. At first the economic and social implications of raising a family alone were the most visible effects of hardship, and they affected both the parent and the children. Later, however, economic and personal deprivation were confined to the individual himself.

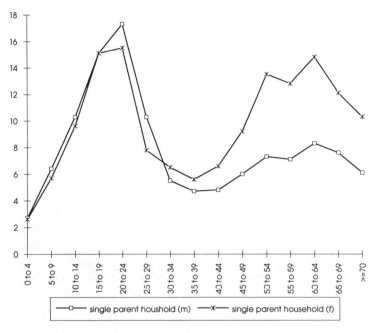

Fig. 4.24 Population living in single-parent households by sex, Cuenca (%)

A number of these considerations underlie the summary information contained in Figures 4.25 and 4.26. Not all of the groups shown were necessarily equally 'vulnerable', but all were so potentially. People living alone or in the company of persons other than their families were not necessarily in a precarious situation, especially when they were young, but as they grew older the likelihood of poverty among them was extremely high. Persons in single-parent households might only experience indirect hardship, especially just before marriage, but helping to maintain a single-parent household was not a desirable situation for anyone.[26] The sum of all the categories represents the total importance of potentially vulnerable persons in society.

Differences by age and sex of this 'index' of vulnerability varied enormously. A significant proportion of the population was always potentially vulnerable. Only for the very young (0–4) did this threshold affect fewer than 5 per cent of the population. Otherwise, nearly or above 10 per cent of the population was always experiencing situations of potential hardship, though the concrete meaning varied considerably with a person's age. After about 50 years of age for men and 40 for women, levels of hardship increased dramatically, nearly doubling every 10 years for women. By the age of 70 half of all women were in potentially vulnerable situations. For men the rate of increase was far lower, though nearly one-third of them were living in situations of hardship at 70 years of age. After 40 years of age, demographic, social, and

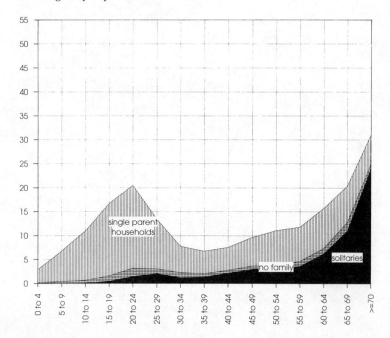

Fig. 4.25 Cumulative percentage of potentially vulnerable male population by age, Cuenca

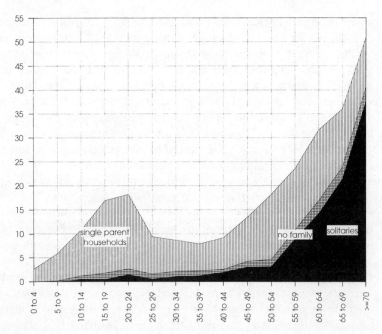

Fig. 4.26 Cumulative percentage of potentially vulnerable Female population by age, Cuenca

economic factors made women both more numerous and much poorer than
men.

With demographic modernization, relative levels of vulnerability diminished considerably, even while the total number of years people lived in those
situations may well have increased. This can be seen in Figure 4.27, where I
have charted vulnerability over the life course and over time for men and
women together. The results are an eloquent testimony to the pervasive effects on the family of the demographic transition. During the early stages of
life, the likelihood that a child was to live in a potentially vulnerable household
diminished by up to one-third between the initial and the final periods. It was
past 45–49, however, when improvement was most visible and most significant
from a social and economic standpoint. In those age groups, people living in
potentially difficult situations diminished by between 10 and 25 per cent over
the course of the past century. Only among the very old did vulnerability
increase, basically because gains in life expectancy were far greater for women
than for men. Since by mid-century age at death was already quite high, the
effects of this gap are not really visible until very high age groups.

Risk and hardship, then, affected people at all ages, though it was greatest
for adult women and especially for the elderly. The way in which hardship, real
and potential, was managed was central to the welfare of all and the key to a
great part of the social stability which had characterized rural society in Spain
for so long. Without the state-run welfare systems, which only came into
existence during the central decades of this century, most risk management
took place within the family and was based on inter-generational wealth flows

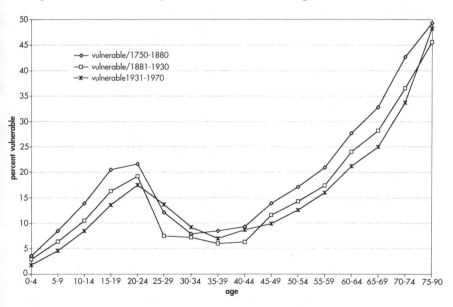

Fig. 4.27 Potential vulnerability over the life course and over time, both sexes
combined, Cuenca

which involved each member of the family in the welfare of all. Oftentimes these flows took place within the household, but not always. Parents were the key to family welfare throughout much of their adult lives. They provided for their children when they were very young, were essential in helping them get started in married life, and often assisted them in raising their own children.

As they aged they were increasingly in need of support from their children and other members of their extended family. This support normally transcended the household because by that time for the most part the children had departed to start up households of their own. Neo-local household formation, however, did not necessarily imply a clear break with the parental household, and oftentimes meals and economic activities were shared. Family support mechanisms transcending the household were facilitated by residential proximity as young couples showed a marked tendency to set up their own households in the immediate vicinity of at least one of their parental households. When dealing with household listings, it is a ready occurrence to find members of the same family living on the same street and often next to each other. A good example of this can be found in the town of Cuenca during the middle years of the nineteenth century, where almost three-quarters of a sample of newly-weds set up their own households in the same neighbourhood as at least one of their parental households (Reher, 1990*a*: 218).

The tendency for families to maintain residential proximity went beyond the first years following marriage and the strictures of the original conjugal family, as families tended to develop within certain neighbourhoods or villages. Whereas in a rural context, a certain degree of residential proximity within the same village was inevitable, living next door or across the street from one's parents was a matter of decision. The same can be said of urban environments, where families often developed within certain neighbourhoods. Shared economic interests and especially the awareness that the extended family was necessary for the welfare of each of its members were central to behaviour patterns in which residential proximity facilitated the links between households and between members of that family.[27] The circulation of kin among family households is further proof of the viability of family support systems. Co-residents often were elderly, widowed parents, who spent periods in the households of each of their children. In some contexts this custom was called *ir por meses* and meant that an elderly person would spend a month or so in the household of each of his children, at a time when he might well continue to maintain a separate household of his own. Even when he was alone, however, many of the same sources of support were readily available to him.

The family welfare system appears to have worked well when hardship was moderate. In cases of extreme necessity, however, especially when they were related to health, its ability to provide adequate support would have been severely compromised. During most of the period under study, these situations were exceptional. Long-term degenerative illnesses were relatively un-important until recently, and the desperately poor could always receive alms from the Church or the public authorities. Within this context, children were essential to hardship management in Spanish society, because without them none of these support mechanisms could exist. They bore the brunt of caring for their aged parents. The way in which this inter-generational support of the aged was materialized differed appreciably in stem-family areas, where it was mainly the responsibility of the designated heirs, as opposed to other regions, where it was shared more equally by all of the siblings. But the basic process was the same, as it was the younger generation which took charge of the welfare of the older one. Even though family conflict existed, it is ex-tremely infrequent to find people challenging the basic age-dependent flows of support which characterized the system. As one peasant said: 'First the chil-dren lived off of their parents, and then the parents lived off of their children. That is just the way it was.'[28] The truly desperate people were those who had no children who could support them during their 'third' and probably very brief 'fourth' age. They were the ones who had to rely on members of the wider family for support, or who ended up depending on public assistance of one kind or another. People were well aware of the nature of life, and how its own particular ledger of credits and debits, of give and take, was only balanced out in the long run. Children were their most important investment, and they knew it.

The creation of a national social security system and its extension to self-employed rural labourers during the middle decades of this century had mo-mentous significance for families in Spain because for the first time the welfare of the aged no longer depended almost exclusively on the family, as had been the case for centuries. This innovation came at a time when declining mortality was leading to substantial increases in the proportion of people's lives lived in retirement, in the 'third' and 'fourth' ages. Even though couples tended to live together longer, and in this sense their situation improved, the increase in their numbers and the years they survived retirement would have probably over-whelmed the ability of the familial welfare system to function effectively. The levels of well-being attained by the aged in Spain over the past 30–40 years would have been unimaginable without the creation of some sort of social security system.

Some people have suggested that by removing welfare from the hands of the family, the very nature of the family was bound to change. In many ways this has happened in Spanish society: families now have fewer children and spend more time rearing them; inheritance has lost a large part of its once crucial importance for young people; and parents no longer have to establish the terms of retirement with their offspring, which guarantee them some measure of independence and comfort. Yet the family continues to be central for the welfare of both young and old in Spanish society. It remains to be seen whether the intervention of the State is in the process of replacing the family as the prime guarantor of welfare or of merely complementing and enhancing it in the light of the social, demographic, and economic forces of change which have transformed society so profoundly in the course of the twentieth century.

Notes

1. For more on the links between marriage and household formation, see Hajnal (1982).
2. '*El que se casa, a su casa*' (If you marry, get your own house) is another aphorism with a similar meaning.
3. The incidence of this type of co-residence was probably considerably greater than the data suggest because the yearly household listings made it possible to track post-marriage residence only at yearly intervals. Thus many stints of co-residence of shorter duration probably went unnoticed.
4. These practices have been documented in extensive interviews of elderly peasants in the rural areas of the province of Cuenca (Reher, 1988: 223–7).
5. In regions around the Pyrenees where the stem family prevailed, since children not designated heirs often received their entire inheritance at marriage, the dynamics of assistance to newly-weds may have been somewhat different.
6. An example of this might be a case in which headship was retained by a widow, even though she was living with her newly-wed son, his wife, and their infant baby. This household would be classified as an 'old' one, when in fact it would be an example of very recent family formation.
7. See Martínez Carrión (1988: 101), Lanza García (1991: 357), and Mikelarena Peña (1995: 275–6). Results from Cuenca are unpublished and are taken from a data base containing basic information on about 14,000 households and over 50,000 persons between the mid-18th century and 1970. For Navarre the data come from 1786 and refer only to male-headed households. In Cantabria and Murcia the data are taken from the 18th century, and in Cuenca from a large sample of families between 1750 and 1970. In these last cases, both male- and female-headed households are included. For examples from Valencia, see Garrido Arce (1995).
8. The examples Mikelarena Peña takes from other stem-family districts of Navarre are basically similar to the findings shown for Pamplona.
9. For a similar approach to the family life cycle but using more contemporary data see, for example, Requena Diez de Revenga (1990).
10. The levels of female headship shown in Table 4.1 are considerably below those holding in the Portuguese community of Lanheses (28–39 per cent for all age groups), which was affected by intense male emigration, and more similar to those holding in other European contexts. See, for example, Brettell (1988: 49).
11. If only widowed household heads are used, the following percentages of co-resident children by age of head appear:
    Male head aged 50–54: 73.6; 55–59: 66.3; 60–64: 54.2; 65–69: 36.4; 70 and above: 20.2.
    Female head aged 50–54: 77.8; 55–59: 60.3; 60–64: 47.8; 65–69: 33.1; 70 and above: 20.1.

12. The primary difficulty inherent in this sort of estimation is that the data cover local areas and children living outside their parental households did not necessarily come from the same area, and those from that area who were living elsewhere escape detection as well. Even though each of these effects tends to neutralize the other, the extent to which our estimations are accurate is unknown. For more on this subject, see Wall (1978).

13. This situation held in an area in which the nuclear family prevailed. In stem-family regions, the patterns were likely quite different.

14. Again it should be recalled that what is presented here is not a true cohort perspective of individual life cycles, but rather a simple juxtaposition of different age groups taken from numerous household listings. For a discussion of life-course methods, see Elder (1987). For examples of recent imaginative studies of family patterns based on the experience of individuals, see Rabell Romero (1994) and Ruggles (1994*a*, 1994*b*).

15. For an interesting view of women in Portuguese households, see Brettell (1986, 1988: 39–53).

16. Between 1850 and 1970, marriage age for women increased by almost two years and celibacy was fairly constant at about 5 per cent.

17. The mean age of the domestic group grew from 45.3 to 50.2.

18. Mean age of co-resident kin went from 31.6 to 42.9.

19. It is important to remember that the weight of household heads in this age group was in fact quite small, as most youths that age continued to live with their parents.

20. A rough and ready calculation of the mean duration of being a spouse in the absence of female mortality can be derived by taking the sum of the proportions of spouses in different age groups (with the length of the last age group fixed at 10 years) and dividing by the maximum proportion of spouses, which for all three periods was found in the 35–39 age group. This yields an estimate of the mean duration of being a spouse for a women surviving to 80 years of age. According to this estimate, the mean length of being a spouse was 43 years during the first period and 44.1 years for the third, a lengthening that is achieved despite the fact that the proportion of spouses between 20 and 30 years of age was far lower during the middle decades of this century than earlier. If only women after age 30 are considered, the length of shared life for those surviving until 80 increased from 36.5 years during the first period to 39.4 in the last period.

21. For more on inter-generational wealth flows, see Caldwell (1976, 1981, 1982).

22. For more on the demographic implications of risk, see Cain (1981, 1983).

23. An example of this might be a 5–9 year old girl who could be of relatively greater help in a woman's household chores than could a boy of a similar age in the fields.

24. Situations in which the woman was the main bread-winner in the family, much as occurred in certain mining villages in the Basque Country, were extremely rare (Pérez-Fuentes, 1993: 243–77).

25. These households corrrespond to the Laslett–Hammel typology 3c and 3d ('father alone with children' and 'mother alone with children').

26. Those living in complex households were not really vulnerable, mainly because their extended families were central to their welfare. Nevertheless, especially for the very young and for those above, say, 40 or 50 years of age, their situation would have been one of certain deprivation had they not been able to rely on co-residence with other kin.

27. For more details on these behaviour patterns, see Reher (1990*a*: 227–39) and Chapter 3.
28. This was taken from an ethnographic interview of an elderly peasant in the province of Cuenca (Reher, 1988: 227).

5 Death and the Family

The Demography of Spanish Families

The demographic underpinnings for family development, decision-making, living arrangements, economic activity, migration, and kinship networks were an essential part both of the stability of traditional family forms and of the changes which have been especially strong over the course of the twentieth century. Examples of this are not difficult to find. Marriage was probably the single most important variable for the social and demographic reproduction of society and it was linked, among other things, to prevailing levels of life expectancy. The number and age distribution of children at home had enormous economic implications for the family. Bearing, raising, and providing for offspring was, until comparatively recently, the main concern of parents over much of the life course. These and other issues are central to any family analysis.

During the course of the next two chapters, aspects of the demography of Spanish families between the late eighteenth century and around 1970 will be evaluated. My purpose is not to cover Spanish population history in depth, but to outline the basic demographic parameters which conditioned the context within which family development took place. In recent years, the growing field of historical demography in Spain has vastly changed our knowledge of population patterns in the past. I will not and cannot do it justice here. My goal, rather, is to sketch the basic demographic realities in the country and in its regions before, during, and immediately after the demographic transition, with special reference to those aspects directly related to many of the family patterns we have discussed at length in this book.

The period covered is one of immense changes in Spain, changes which led to the demographic, economic, and social modernization of Spanish society. Between the end of the eighteenth century and recent decades, total population increased by nearly four times; a high-pressure demographic regime characterized by high and variable levels of fertility and mortality was replaced by one typical of modern societies; mortality crises disappeared; and millions of Spaniards left their homes bound at first mainly for the Americas, and in particular for Argentina and Brazil, and later for the economic centres of northern Europe and for the nodes of economic renovation which were developing within Spain itself. As recently as 1900 Spain was still mainly a rural country whose inhabitants were dedicated to agricultural activities; but by mid-century rapid urbanization had provoked massive out-migration of rural inhabitants bound for the main urban centres in Spain and abroad. Despite ongoing and often annoying gaps in our knowledge, today a fairly accurate sketch can be made of the basic outlines of these momentous changes.

In these chapters, I shall present a review of our knowledge regarding nuptiality, fertility, and mortality in Spain over the period. Earlier studies will be summarized and new data introduced so as to offer an up-to-date portrayal of basic demographic patterns in the past. Explanations for prevailing levels, regional variability, and change will be evaluated in the light of the data presented. These pages will give a general portrayal of demographic dynamics in Spain over the past two to three centuries which is essential if we are to understand in their proper context many of the family patterns which have arisen earlier and which will be discussed in the rest of this book.

Mortality before the Demographic Transition

It is extremely difficult to assess with any acceptable degree of confidence the basic mortality patterns in Spain before the latter part of the eighteenth century or in some cases even later. Registration of deaths, particularly infant deaths, was inadequate in most areas until at least the eighteenth century. Before the middle of the century, registration of *párvulo* deaths (children aged 0–7) was normally spotty, and even when this changed it is not clear at all that deaths to the very young were fully recorded. Though the quality of registration did generally improve over time, it is uncommon to find age at death data before well into the nineteenth century.[1] This makes delving into mortality patterns before 1800 or even later an often risky adventure in which methodological ingenuity can only partially offset the pitfalls posed by generally inadequate data.

Even so, in recent years a number of studies have greatly enhanced our knowledge of pre-nineteenth century mortality in Spain. Many of them have applied techniques of indirect demographic estimation either to regional or sub-regional samples of time series data or to late-eighteenth century census returns. Our knowledge of infant mortality has also grown as a by-product of the family reconstitution studies which continue to be undertaken in Spain, albeit at a slower pace than a decade or more ago. In all of the cases, however, the reliability of the estimates is only as good as the data they are based on. Any generalizations about mortality patterns during this period will be cautious ones indeed.

An idea of the long-term swings in crude death rates can be derived from a long series based on a sample of parishes from the region of New Castile between the late sixteenth and the late nineteenth centuries. The total number of deaths has been adjusted for estimated under-registration, and the rates themselves have been computed on a most likely population estimate, derived by subjecting time series of births to the mortality schedule holding in late eighteenth-century New Castile.[2] Despite problems involving data and estimation techniques, the series give a fairly accurate view of medium- and long-term changes in mortality, though not of current levels. The results suggest that mortality was high between 1590 and 1610, declined to 1620, then reached relatively high levels until almost 1690 (Figure 5.1). Between then and the late eighteenth century mortality was relatively low, except for 1730–60. Crude death rates during the late eighteenth and early nineteenth centuries were again very high (due to a large extent to the crisis of 1803–5 and the deaths that occurred during the War of Independence, 1808–12). Between 1820 and 1840 death rates were low, but increased slightly thereafter. When these rates have been contrasted with independently established vital statistics, there have not been any serious contradictions. These comparisons, however, refer to data from the nineteenth century, when mortality registration was far better than in earlier periods (Reher, 1991*b*; Livi Bacci and Reher, 1993: 72).

Complementary information on childhood mortality patterns can be derived from the same time series by applying two different methods of estimation, one direct and one indirect. In the first, childhood mortality is estimated from the *párvulo* deaths noted in the parish books of some villages of the sample with high-quality registration.[3] Rates of infant and childhood mortality (ICMR) were calculated by dividing the number of *párvulo* deaths by an

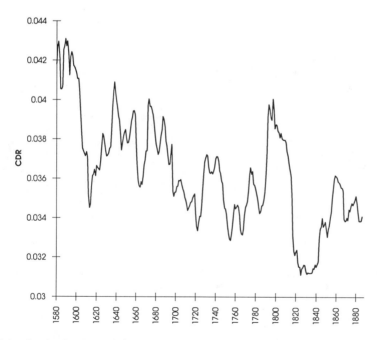

Fig. 5.1 Crude death rate for sample of New Castile, 1580–1888 (25-year moving average)

estimate of the size of the population aged 0–7 years (obtained by applying survival factors to the birth cohorts of the preceding seven years). The resulting data show relatively low infant and child mortality between 1650 and 1760 (with the exception of the rise between 1690 and 1720) (Figure 5.2). The latter half of the eighteenth century was characterized by worsening mortality, which was followed by low levels between 1830 and 1850 and increasing ones thereafter. On the whole there is a notable similarity between the trends of the crude death rates and those of the infant and child mortality rates.

An indirect method for the estimation of childhood mortality which makes no use of the death series was also devised, and serves as a contrast to the previous series. Essentially it is a proxy for survival to marriage and is based on the 'expected' number of marriages which a given birth cohort should give rise to after a certain number of years. The difference between the expected number of marriages and those which actually take place is the result of the level of mortality between birth and marriage (especially during childhood), changes in the age pattern of nuptiality, and changes in the proportion remaining single. Pre-nuptial mortality appears to be by far the most important of these factors.[4] Comparing this index of survival to marriage (ISM) with the one of infant and child mortality (ICMR) suggests that both estimates are basically compatible, since high values of ISM tend to correspond with low values of ICMR.[5] In this way childhood mortality was probably relatively low

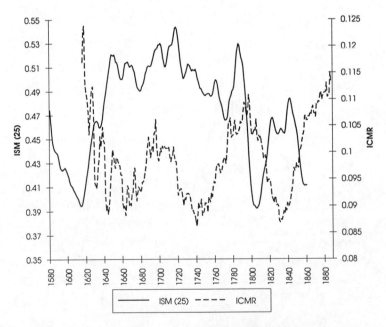

Fig. 5.2 Infant and child mortality rates (ICMR) and index of survivors to marriage (ISM) for sample of New Castile (25-year moving average)

for the mid-seventeenth to the mid-eighteenth century and high at the beginning of the seventeenth and the nineteenth centuries.

The comparison between the crude death rates and both estimates of mortality at young ages may also indicate periods when overall mortality trends differed from those of child mortality. For example, during the middle part of the seventeenth century, and again during the beginning of the eighteenth century, the mid-term trends of adult and of child mortality seem to have been divergent, as opposed to the end of the eighteenth and the beginning of the nineteenth century, when mortality trends were similar everywhere. Extreme caution should be used in interpreting the results derived from this sample of New Castile data, and these observations are more aptly considered as hypotheses for future research, rather than firm conclusions. There is some indication that some of the trends during the eighteenth and the nineteenth century were divergent from those of a sample of Catalan parishes, while other regional samples taken from Valencia and the Canary Islands show no clear trends over the period.[6]

One of the hallmarks of mortality in Spain before the second half of the nineteenth century was the presence of periodic and often exogenous mortality crises which were a key constraint for general mortality levels as well as for population growth rates. Whereas the plague had probably been the single most important determinant of mortality swings before its disappearance from Spain towards the end of the seventeenth century, the frequency and intensity of crisis mortality caused by other types of epidemic continued throughout much of the eighteenth century, especially in areas located in the central part of the country.[7] As recently as the early nineteenth century, important areas located in the central and southern parts of the peninsula suffered through disastrous epidemics of typhus, malaria, and/or yellow fever (Arejula, 1806). Particularly devastating were the effects of the 1803–5 round of epidemics, which in some areas was the most important mortality crisis of the entire Ancien Régime (Pérez Moreda, 1980; Reher, 1990a: 173–87).

After the war of 1808–12, however, the bouts of crisis mortality became increasingly infrequent in most of the country. Much as occurred in the rest of Europe, smallpox, typhus, and malaria were replaced by cholera as the main cause of epidemic disease. Even though cholera was often more virulent than earlier epidemics, its effects were far less widespread. The major ones took place in 1833–5, 1853–6, 1859–60, 1865, and finally in 1885. It is estimated that the most severe of these, in 1853–5, claimed the lives of 236,744 people (about 1.5 per cent of the country's population) (Pérez Moreda, 1985a: 61). As in the rest of Europe, cholera epidemics ended when public health measures designed to guarantee the purity of drinking water became a common practice. It is safe to say that despite the fact that the era of the 'stabilization of mortality' came rather late in many regions of Spain, the nineteenth century witnessed the gradual elimination of the crises which had been an unwanted but inevitable fact of life during the Ancien Régime (Flinn, 1974).

Apart from the periodic mortality crises, themselves often the result of completely exogenous factors, there is an increasing amount of evidence suggesting that economic conditions were an important factor in determining levels of non-crisis mortality. Recent studies in short-run fluctuations of prices and of mortality have shown that in Spain there was a positive and statistically significant contemporary association between price fluctuations and mortality levels, and that over a period of five years price changes resulted in appreciably higher levels of mortality. When this same analysis has been applied in urban areas, poorer areas of towns proved to be much more sensitive to price changes than did the richer districts.[8]

Over the medium and long term, a population's economic well-being may have been influential for its mortality as well. An example of this can be found in the New Castilian series of childhood mortality shown in Figure 5.2. When a 25-year moving average of the childhood mortality rate is plotted together with a detrended real-wage series based on New Castilian and Madrid data, both series appear to maintain a clearly negative relationship. With the exception of 1690–1710, periods of high relative real wages tended to correspond to periods of low mortality, and vice versa (Figure 5.3).[9] The same relation can be seen in a scatter plot with detrended real wages on one axis and ICMRs on the other (Figure 5.4).[10] While these results are not conclusive, they do suggest

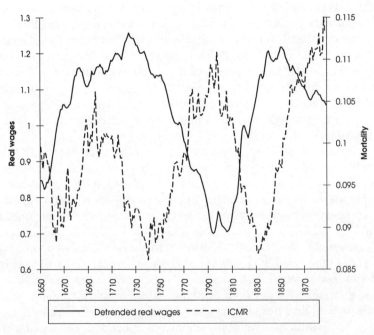

Fig. 5.3 Childhood mortality rates (0–7) and detrended real wages in New Castile, 1650–1888 (25-year moving average)

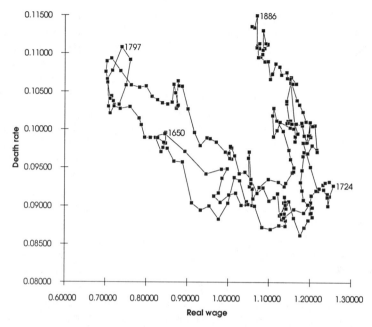

Fig. 5.4   Scatter plot of childhood death rate and detrended real wages, 1650–1888

that in New Castile, both in the short and over the medium and long term, mortality levels seemed to have been very sensitive to economic conditions. The positive check postulated by Malthus was alive and well in pre-industrial Spain.

Mortality during the Epidemiological Transition

While the elimination of the great mortality crises characterized the first part of the nineteenth century in Spain, the secular decline in non-crisis mortality was unquestionably the most spectacular development during the latter stages of the nineteenth and the first decades of the twentieth century. Despite the fact that in some areas of the country there were important increases in life expectancy before 1860, in the country as a whole gains were modest at best and were probably the result of the reduction in crisis mortality more than anything else (e_0 of 28.0 in 1787–97 and 29.8 in 1863–70).[11] Recent studies suggest that only Catalonia and especially the Balearic Islands give indications that mortality was undergoing substantial changes during the first half of the nineteenth century. Elsewhere, the reductions in mortality which had characterized the 1780–1840 period (excepting the great crises at the onset of the century) were reversed entirely during the middle decades of the century.

During the latter decades of the nineteenth century, once again with the exception of Catalonia and of the Balearic Islands, mortality did not seem to have improved much at all, and may well have worsened in several areas. This can be seen in Table 5.1, in which crude death rates show practically no improvement between 1860 and 1900, and life expectancy only modest ones.[12]

The final years of the nineteenth century marks the watershed of the epidemiological transition as there are indications that significant declines in mortality were taking place in almost all areas of the country. Mortality for older children (1–4) was the first to undergo important reductions, followed by infant mortality and finally by deaths among other age groups of the population. By 1900 all age groups were participating in this trend. Life expectancy increased by 7 years between 1900 and 1910 and by another 9 years between 1920 and 1930, crude death rates fell nearly 40 per cent between 1900 and 1930, and infant mortality rates went down by one-third.[13]

In the course of this transition, substantial changes took place in the regional distribution of mortality on the peninsula. The 1887 census provides us with a reliable picture of regional and sub-regional variations in mortality, and suggests that in 1887 Spain had a fairly pronounced interior–periphery dichotomy with respect to mortality (Map 5.1).[15] Areas of relatively low mortality (CDRs < 26 per thousand) clustered along the northern coastal regions, the Pyrenees, in substantial parts of Catalonia, in parts of the Levant, and in the Balearic Islands. The interior and southern parts of the peninsula had high death rates, often exceeding 36 per thousand. It is difficult to know how stable these patterns may have been in the past, though it is quite likely that the entire northern coastal part of the country had traditionally been a low-mortality

Table 5.1 Mortality in spain, 1860–1980

Year	Crude death rate	Infant mortality (q_0)	Male life expectancy at birth (e_0)	Female life expectancy at birth (e_0)
1860	27.4	186	29.8	29.8
1887	31.0			
1900	28.4	204	33.9	35.7
1910	23.2	149	40.9	42.6
1920	23.0	165	40.3	42.1
1930	17.2	124	48.4	51.6
1940	16.1	114	47.1	53.2
1950	10.7	70	59.8	64.3
1960	8.9	44	66.9	71.7
1970	8.5	28	69.7	75.2
1980	7.8	12	71.0	78.0
1990	8.5	8	73.3	79.7

Notes: Life expectancy in 1860 is the same for both sexes, and refers to the 1863–70 period. Life expectancies in 1980 in fact refer to 1982.
   From 1910 to 1980, the IMRs adjusted for deaths during the first 24 hours of life have been used. See Gómez Redondo (1992: 34).

Sources: Instituto Nacional de Estadistica (1952, 1978), Arbelo (1962), Arango (1987), Dopico (1987), Gómez Redondo (1992), and Caselli (1994).

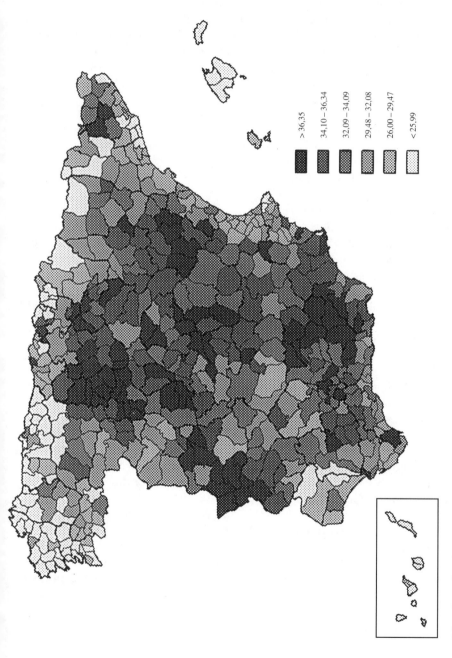

> 36,35

34,10 – 36,34

32,09 – 34,09

29,48 – 32,08

26,00 – 29,47

< 25,99

Map 5.1 Crude death rates by judicial district, 1887

region, as opposed to the Balearic Islands and possibly Catalonia, where recent gains in life expectancy had ended up changing their relative position within the country. By 1930, even though mortality had declined everywhere, the decline had been faster in the north-eastern part of the country, in both the Canary and the Balearic Islands, and in the Basque Country (Map 5.2). The rest of the north no longer had exceptionally low mortality, and the highest levels continued to be located in the central parts of the country.

Traditionally in Spain, mortality in towns had been considerably higher than in adjacent rural areas. During this period, crude death rates were between 10 and 17 per cent higher in towns, and infant mortality between 8 and 11 per cent higher (Reher, 1990*b*: 293). Mortality differentials were far greater for adults than for children; and while this may have been in part the result of the presence of hospitals in urban settings, the differences are large enough to suggest that the unhealthy urban environment was relatively more harmful for higher age groups.[15] Before the onset of mortality transition, the larger towns had higher mortality than the smaller ones. This all changed in the course of the mortality decline as first larger towns and then smaller ones reduced their mortality at a faster rate than in the countryside. By the decade of the 1920s, infant mortality in towns was lower than in the countryside. The urban setting, and in particular large towns, proved to be an ideal setting for the public health and educational measures which were to prove to be so effective in reducing mortality in Spain.

Mortality reductions were only interrupted twice in the course of the present century. The first time was due to the influenza pandemic of 1918 and 1919, which was especially severe in Spain during the autumn of 1918, producing an estimated 260,000 to 270,000 victims (Echeverri Dávila, 1993). The other reversal of mortality trends came during the Spanish Civil War (1936–9) and in the years immediately afterwards. By projecting expected deaths between 1936 and 1942 based on earlier trends and comparing them to actual registered deaths, Juan Díez Nicolás reached the conclusion that 558,000 excess deaths occurred which could be attributed either directly or indirectly to the war itself and its aftermath (Díez Nicolás, 1985).[16]

Despite these reversals, however, the reduction of mortality during the 1887–1940 period was dramatic, and brought life expectancy in Spain from one of the lowest in Europe to a level only slightly below that holding on much of the rest of the continent.[17] After the Civil War, mortality continued its long-term decline. During the 1940s, gains were extremely rapid as life expectancy rose by 12 years in only a decade and were stimulated by the post-war economic recovery, improved health protection, and especially by the increasing use of sulfa drugs and antibiotics.[18] Since then, even though mortality decline has slowed somewhat, it continues to the present. Currently, mortality levels in Spain are fully comparable to those holding in the most advanced nations in the world.[19]

The health transition in Spain can best be conceived as a three-stage pro-

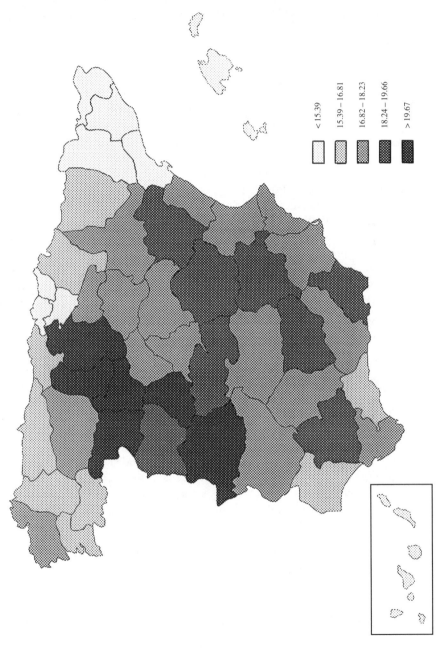

Map 5.2 Crude death rates by province, 1930

cess, each with characteristic causal structures and strategies for reducing mortality.[20] Initially, infectious diseases predominated as the main cause of death, and major inroads against mortality were made thanks to a combination of improved living standards (nutrition) and more efficient public health measures.[21] In Spain, as in other countries of southern Europe, the causal structure of mortality was somewhat different from that holding in England and other northern European countries, with diarrhoea and enteritis being relatively more important and tuberculosis somewhat less (Bernabeu Mestre, 1991: table 1; Caselli, 1991: 74).[22] In these countries infant and childhood disease eradication played a larger role in mortality decline than elsewhere. Emphasis was also on nutrition and public health in Spain, but within this context maternal education regarding child feeding and child care practices was particularly important for reducing mortality levels (Gómez Redondo, 1992).

During the second stage of the health transition, infectious diseases, particularly those of the digestive and respiratory tracts, continued to be the main cause of death, though diseases of the circulatory system and certain degenerative diseases grew rapidly in importance. During this period mortality reduction accelerated primarily as a consequence of new medical discoveries and the increasing efficiency of the health system. Sulfa drugs and antibiotics played a key role in this decline. During the most recent stage in the health transition, mortality patterns tend to be dominated by deaths among the higher age groups of the population caused by degenerative diseases, often related directly to the risks inherent in living in modern industrial society. If mortality levels are to continue to decline it will likely be the product of discoveries by medical science together with changes in people's life-styles.

The implications of this lengthening of life for family development in Spain have been immense. Inheritance practices, family economies, kinship networks, socialization processes, family constraints on marriage, the living arrangements of the elderly and of young adults, the ties between the conjugal family and the larger family group are among those areas of family life directly affected by changing mortality. These and other related themes will be discussed in other chapters of this book. In the rest of this chapter, however, I would like to concentrate on different aspects of childhood mortality which, until recently, was probably the parcel of family life where the implications of mortality were most directly felt by the great majority of the population.

Death in the Early Stages of Life

Earlier we charted long-term trends in childhood mortality for a sample of New Castilian parishes by means of both direct and indirect estimation techniques. The series derived by these methods revealed that mortality was high during the early seventeenth and early nineteenth centuries and relatively low from the mid-seventeenth to the mid-eighteenth centuries. When plotted with long-term swings in real wages, interesting and expected covariations appeared, suggesting that mortality in childhood was sensitive to economic conditions both in the short and in the long run. Mortality was not estimated by means of conventional measures, thus limiting its comparability, and little light has been cast on mortality patterns in other Spanish areas.

Further data regarding childhood mortality can be derived from local studies, which are often based on the method of family reconstitution. While these studies are generally less useful in pinpointing trend changes and the reasons behind them, by estimating mortality with standard probabilities of death (q_x) they give a much more detailed view of mortality during the early stages of life. The results from a number of these can be found in Table 5.2. While certainly not conclusive, the data do suggest the possible existence of certain common patterns. (1) Before the late eighteenth century, infant mortality was high everywhere, with between 200 and 300 infant deaths for every 1,000 live births. (2) In numerous examples, child mortality ($_4q_1$) was as high or higher than infant mortality. This pattern is also visible in 1900, when we have data for the entire country, and suggests that the distinctive structure of childhood mortality which characterized the Mediterranean region may well have been a long-standing one.[23] (3) The only really low mortality in the sample is found in the northern province of Guipúzcoa. It is impossible to know whether or not this indicates generally lower levels of mortality along the northern coast. While in the other rural coastal parish in the region of Santander, infant mortality was only moderate, in the city of Santiago de Compostela it was quite high. (4) In the Catalan examples taken from the nineteenth century, mortality is also very low. This may have been a part of the general reductions in Catalan mortality which seem to have taken place between 1780 and 1850.

Before the onset of the twentieth century, most of our knowledge of infant mortality is necessarily based on local studies such as those just cited. After 1900, however, this situation changes substantially because in that year the Instituto Nacional de Estadística began the publication of yearly volumes of vital statistics which have continued uninterrupted to the present.[24] These data enable us to view not only cross-sectional regional differences in mortality but also the dynamics of change much more closely. In a recent publication, Rosa Gómez Redondo (1992) has combined work of her own and earlier studies by Marcelino Pascua (1934) and A. Arbelo (1962) to generate a complete series of infant mortality rates for Spain as a whole and for each Spanish province between 1901 and 1980. The series traces the basic outlines of infant mortality decline taking place during the present century (Figure 5.5). Between 1900 and 1910 mortality levels fell rapidly. Mortality decline slowed appreciably during World War I and even rose to levels nearing those holding at the turn of the century during the Spanish influenza epidemic of 1918–19. Mortality reduction renewed during the 1920s, but once again the downward trend came to a halt during the early 1930s, probably as a result of the Great Depression and the

Table 5.2   Infant and childhood mortality between the seventeenth and nineteenth centuries

Place	Source	Date,	q_0	$_4q_1$	$_5q_5$	Notes
Santander	a	18th c.–1815	208			4 parishes
		1820–60	171			5 parishes
Santiago de	b	1730–60	252	316	128	family
Compostela (Galicia)		1760–90	201	239	83	reconstitutions,
		1790–1810	225	230	60	average of
						different 10-year
						periods
Guipúzcoa	c	1790–9	127	138		mean of 4 parishes
(Basque Country)		1800–15	145	173		mean of 3 parishes
New and Old Castile	d	18th c.	197			mean values of
		1780–1803	365			several parishes
		1800–39	265			and several
						10-year periods
Otero de Herreros	d	1820–49	185	219	56	mean of several
(Segovia, Old Castile)						decades
	d	1850–99	224	235	71	same
Villacastín (Segovia)	d	1820–39	262	346	90	same
Zaragoza (Aragon)	d	1786–90	210	175	39	mean of 8 parishes
Los Molinos (Madrid)	e	1620–1729 (m)	323	152	93	
(New Castile)		1620–1729 (f)	242	240	62	
		1620–1729 (tot)	282	197	75	
Alameda (Madrid)	e	1652–85	241			
Pozuelo (Madrid)	e	1676–99	293			
Cuenca (town)	f	1842–62	228	240		
(New Castile)						
Valdeolivas (Cuenca)	f	1818–37	305	331		
Penedès (Barcelona)	g	1675–90	219	347		mean of several
(Catalonia)		1784–90	196	312		parishes
		1857–64	178	245		
Palomòs (Girona)	h	1705–51	256	284		
(Catalonia)		1762–99	232	283		
		1810–29	126	186		
Orihuela (general area)	i	1850–70	243			mean of several
(Alicante, Valencia)		1870–1900	240			decades
Yeste (Albacete)	j	1879–1900	224			
(New Castile)						

Sources: *a*: Lanza (1991: 228–42); *b*: Martínez Rodríguez (1992: 54); *c*: Piquero (1991: 163); *d*: Pérez Moreda (1980: 146–67); *e*: Soler Serratosa (1985: 182–4); *f*: Reher (1990: 111); *g*: Muñoz Pradas (1990: 112–24, esp. 113); *h*: Nadal (1956); *i*: Olivares y Vinal (1988: 653); *j*: Martínez Carrión (1983: 259–81).

troubled years of the Second Republic. The Spanish Civil War and its immediate aftermath was once again a period of higher mortality. After 1942, however, decline has been uninterrupted, and was especially fast during the decade of the 1940s.

While these data are quite interesting, they leave a number of very basic questions unanswered. (1) When did infant mortality decline actually begin? What actually occurred during the nineteenth century? (2) Is there reason to believe that other parameters of mortality during the first years of life may

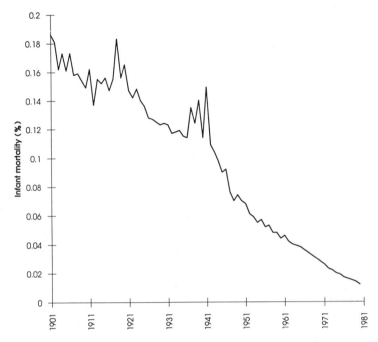

Fig. 5.5   Infant mortality in Spain, 1901–1980

have behaved differently from the standard infant mortality rate, if not in the general downward trend, then in the trend changes or in the intensity of decline? (3) How did mortality by cause change for infant mortality as a whole, and for mortality at other childhood ages? These questions have not been answered by the research of Gómez Redondo, Pascua, or Arbelo, mainly because the requisite data do not appear in published vital statistics. Practically nothing exists before 1900, and after that date it is only possible to distinguish deaths during the first month of life, during the first year, and normally but not always for the 1–4 year age group. Until these questions are addressed, however, it will be impossible to evaluate reliably certain important dimensions of childhood mortality decline in Spain.

As yet preliminary data from an ongoing research project on childhood mortality in Spain may provide answers to some of these questions.[25] Figure 5.6 contains five-year moving averages of three mortality parameters (q_0, $_4q_1$, and $_5q_5$) for a sample of rural villages located in the provinces of Madrid and Toledo between 1800 and 1968.[26] Even though these data are not definitive, they raise a number of interesting points. (1) Mortality was very high at the beginning of the nineteeth century, but declined to fairly low levels during the decade of the 1820s for mortality above one year of life, and the late 1830s for infant mortality. (2) Between 1840 and 1870–90, depending on the parameter

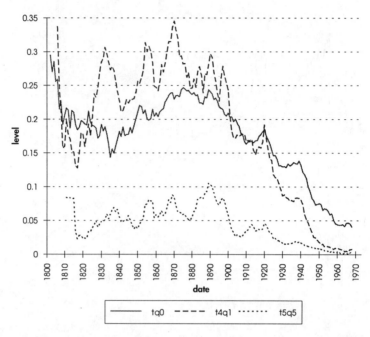

Fig. 5.6 Infant and child mortality (q_0, $_4q_1$, $_5q_5$), Madrid-Toledo, 1800–1968 (5-year moving average)

used, all types of mortality increased by 70 per cent or more. The pattern described in both (1) and (2) also appeared in the mortality indicators plotted in Figure 5.2, which were estimated by different methods.[27] (3) Despite the inherent difficulty in pinpointing trend changes, it would appear that declines in child mortality ($_4q_1$) started around 1870 and preceded those of infant mortality by as much as 20 years. The pace and timing of mortality decline is also apparent if we isolate trends in post-neonatal mortality, q_1, and q_2 (Figure 5.7), and it becomes apparent that the older the age, the earlier and more rapid was mortality decline. (4) Child mortality was consistently higher than infant mortality until around 1900, and was not significantly lower until the early 1920s. (5) Decline of $_4q_1$ was far faster than that of q_0, diminishing to less than 10 per cent of its 1890 levels by 1950, as opposed to infant mortality, which in the same period declined by about 70 per cent.[28] The provisional nature of these data notwithstanding, they point to the heterogeneity of mortality during the first years of life and to the importance of the nineteenth century for the understanding of the crucial initial stages of the mortality epidemiological transition.[29]

Heterogeneity also emerges when looking at mortality levels within different geographic and economic contexts. Not surprisingly, the great regional variation in infant mortality at the turn of the century is the first, most obvious

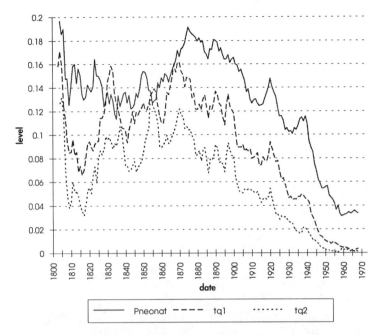

Fig. 5.7   Post-neonatal mortality, q_1 and q_2, Madrid-Toledo, 1800–1968 (5-year moving average)

example of this (Map 5.3). Between 1901 and 1905, while in some provinces infant mortality levels were near or below 120 per thousand, in over one-third of them levels nearly twice that high prevailed. In order to ascertain more precisely the degree of variability in childhood mortality patterns across Spain, we have gathered empirical data on some differing mortality experiences for a number of Spanish regions in 1900 and in 1950.[30] In both cases, the mortality schedules may be considered as a sample of the mortality experience during the early and the later stages of the modern demographic transition in Spain. Data have been grouped by very approximate regions which reflect the differing social, economic, and climatological structures existing in Spain during the first half of this century.[31]

In order to assess strictly structural aspects of infant and child mortality, in the top half of Table 5.3 mortality levels have been held equal in all populations. In 1900 the weight of neonatal mortality was highest in the northern areas, and lowest in the south, while the percentage of deaths taking place for children under 1 year of age ranged from 50 per cent in the northeast to 57 per cent in the north. The similarities, however, are more striking than the differences. Everywhere in Spain in 1900, the weight of death among older children was relatively high, especially if we compare it to other European populations for the same period. For example, in Spain 54.9 per cent of all

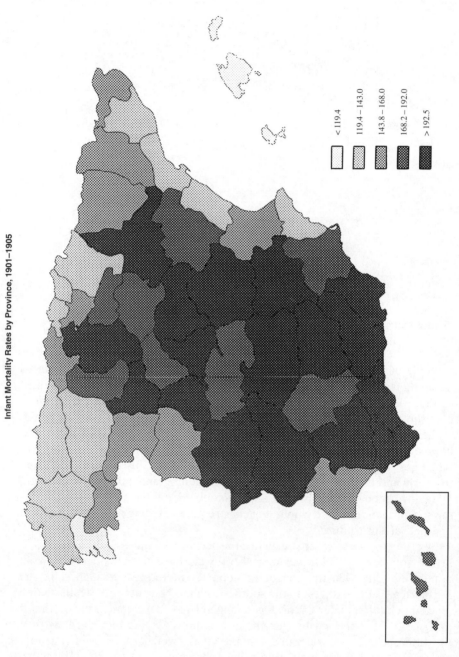

Infant Mortality Rates by Province, 1901–1905

< 119.4
119.4 – 143.0
143.8 – 168.0
168.2 – 192.0
> 192.5

Map 5.3   Infant mortality rates by provinces, 1901–1905

Mortality structures

Table 5.3 Structures and levels of infant and child mortality in selected regional populations

Proportion of infant and child deaths at	1900							1950					
	SPAIN	North coastal	North central	South central	South	Northeast	Prov. capitals	SPAIN	North coastal	North central	South central	South	Northeast
0 months	0.141	0.179	0.135	0.135	0.126	0.148	0.124	0.185	0.203	0.206	0.180	0.161	0.202
1–2 months	0.103	0.109	0.104	0.109	0.109	0.080	0.106	0.146	0.162	0.161	0.150	0.129	0.141
3–5 months	0.107	0.093	0.105	0.126	0.115	0.086	0.106	0.178	0.169	0.212	0.188	0.157	0.176
6–8 months*	0.096	0.088	0.095	0.104	0.102	0.082	0.098	0.187	0.178	0.194	0.182	0.192	0.185
9–11 months	0.102	0.102	0.106	0.096	0.103	0.105	0.093						
1 year	0.240	0.213	0.231	0.238	0.257	0.255	0.239	0.144	0.126	0.116	0.144	0.171	0.133
2 years	0.111	0.108	0.124	0.102	0.104	0.126	0.117	0.084	0.075	0.053	0.088	0.105	0.077
3–4 years	0.098	0.110	0.101	0.090	0.085	0.119	0.118	0.077	0.086	0.058	0.068	0.086	0.087
<1 year	0.549	0.570	0.545	0.570	0.554	0.501	0.526	0.696	0.713	0.772	0.701	0.638	0.703
1–4 years	0.451	0.430	0.455	0.430	0.446	0.499	0.474	0.304	0.287	0.228	0.299	0.362	0.297
Total	1.000	1.000	1.000	1.000	1.000	1.000	1.000	1.000	1.000	1.000	1.000	1.000	1.000
Average age at death (months) for child dying <5	13.77	13.67	14.08	13.15	13.25	15.15	14.74	10.80	10.65	8.94	10.47	12.11	10.93

Table 5.3 (cont.)

Mortality levels

Probability of infant and child death at	1900						1950						
	SPAIN	North coastal	North central	South central	South	Northeast	Prov. capitals	SPAIN	North coastal	North central	South central	South	Northeast
0 months	0.052	0.051	0.054	0.057	0.054	0.047	0.049	0.017	0.016	0.021	0.019	0.017	0.013
1–2 months	0.038	0.031	0.042	0.046	0.046	0.026	0.042	0.013	0.013	0.016	0.016	0.013	0.009
3–5 months	0.040	0.026	0.042	0.053	0.049	0.028	0.042	0.016	0.014	0.022	0.020	0.016	0.011
6–8 months*	0.036	0.025	0.038	0.044	0.043	0.026	0.039	0.017	0.014	0.020	0.019	0.020	0.012
9–11 months	0.038	0.029	0.043	0.040	0.044	0.034	0.037						
$_1q_0$	0.204	0.161	0.219	0.240	0.235	0.161	0.209	0.064	0.057	0.079	0.073	0.066	0.044
$_1q_1$	0.112	0.072	0.118	0.132	0.143	0.098	0.120	0.014	0.011	0.013	0.016	0.019	0.009
$_1q_2$	0.059	0.039	0.072	0.065	0.068	0.053	0.067	0.008	0.065	0.006	0.010	0.012	0.005
$_1q_3$**	0.055	0.042	0.063	0.062	0.059	0.053	0.073	0.005	0.004	0.004	0.005	0.006	0.003
$_1q_4$							0.003	0.003	0.003	0.003	0.004	0.003	
$_4q_1$	0.211	0.145	0.233	0.238	0.248	0.191	0.238	0.030	0.024	0.025	0.034	0.040	0.019
$_5q_0$	0.372	0.283	0.401	0.421	0.425	0.321	0.397	0.092	0.080	0.103	0.104	0.104	0.063

Notes: The probability of dying at different months of age is calculated by dividing deaths by total births. q_x values are life table probabilities of death. The average age at death for infants and children dying before the age of 5 is based on the proportions dying by month of age during the first year of life, and by year of age thereafter. The following lengths of life are assumed for each age group: 0 months = 0.25 month; 1–2 months = 1.9 months; 3–5 months = 4.2 months; 6–8 months = 7.2 months; 9–11 months = 10.3 months; 1 year = 15 months; 2 years = 28 months; 3 years = 41 months; 4 years = 54 months.
For definitions of regions, see text.
National IMRs for 1950 do not coincide exactly with those in Table 5.1 because totals have not been adjusted for infant deaths in the first 24 hours of life.

* In 1950, deaths to infants between 6 and 11 months of age are grouped together.
** In 1900, deaths to children 3 and 4 years of age are grouped together.

childhood deaths happened to children under 1 year of age, as opposed to France, where it was 73 per cent, Prussia 77 per cent, England 64 per cent, and Finland 58 per cent. Compared to central and northern European mortality patterns, childhood death in Spain was relatively late, being especially high for children between 9 and 23 months of age. Only in the humid north was this different, but only modestly so. By 1950, changes in mortality structures had been substantial. Everywhere age at death was significantly earlier, and the per centage of children dying before 1 year of age had increased to between 64 and 77 per cent in all areas. Inter-regional differences, however, had increased.

In 1900 levels of infant and child mortality differed far more than structures. Whereas neonatal mortality was relatively even across the sample, other parameters showed sharp contrasts. Mortality was highest by far in the central and southern parts of the peninsula, and lowest in the northern areas. Mortality in the north-east was situated someplace in between, thanks largely to the fact that by 1900, infant and child mortality was declining rapidly, especially in the Balearic Islands and in Catalonia. Everywhere, however, mortality was high by central and northern European standards, though comparable to levels holding in the Mediterranean region. In most of Spain, nearly 4 in 10 children born in 1900 did not survive beyond the age of 5. By 1950 changes in mortality had been dramatic. Neonatal mortality rates had been reduced to about a third their 1900 levels, while reductions in higher age groups were significantly greater, at times as much as 75–90 per cent. By 1950 the relative advantage of the low-mortality regions of the north and the east was much greater than in 1900.

The variety of the Spanish mortality experience should be clear from the few examples we have put forth. In 1900 and 1950 more than one distinct mortality regime can be located on the peninsula. The origin of these patterns is difficult to pinpoint, though some of the data presented earlier suggest that certain regions had traditionally had lower childhood mortality than others. Over time we can expect structures to have changed, though probably not so much as to obscure a basic pattern of childhood mortality in which deaths to children above 9 months of age were dominant in much of the country. In most areas decisive structural change only began to take place as a by-product of the demographic transition. Figure 5.8, which is based on the local childhood mortality experience of 15 rural villages in central Spain between 1800 and 1969, illustrates both the long-standing nature of basic mortality structures before the beginning of this century, and the changes taking place thereafter. Before the onset of the mortality transition, both the levels and the internal structures of childhood mortality underwent important changes, though no long-term trend can be seen. Once the epidemiological transition set in, however, lower levels of mortality invariably were accompanied by a much younger age distribution of death. Gains in the mortality of children aged 6 months to 4 years were not matched by decreases in neonatal mortality, especially during the first decades of the transition. This reality is forcefully visible in the 1900 and 1950 examples contained in Table 5.3.

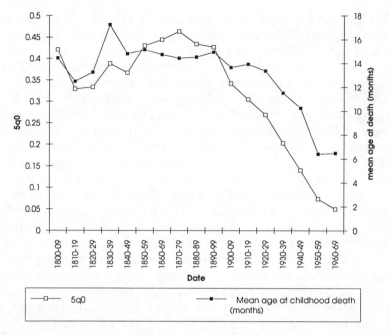

Fig. 5.8   Childhood mortality ($_5q_0$) and mean age at childhood death (months) for a sample of villages from central Spain, 1800–1969

Mortality patterns were determined by a complex web of social, economic, cultural, demographic, epidemiological, and environmental factors. Culturally influenced infant feeding practices, including breast-feeding, supplementary feeding, and weaning, were of key importance, as were general hygienic and living conditions, summer (or winter) temperatures, the water supply, etc. (Knodel, 1988: 74; Lee, 1988: 11–14). Mortality structures were directly related to the intensity of post-neonatal mortality, especially that occurring between 9 and 23 months of age. This was the period in which a child was teething and showed the greatest susceptibility to diseases of the digestive tract. In those areas in which weaning took place outside of the season of greatest risk, or where infant feeding and hygiene received special care, mortality at these ages was relatively lower. Where this took place at a relatively late age, children dying did so relatively late. These were the societies afflicted both by high levels and by unfavourable structures of infant and child mortality.

A closer look at local variations in childhood mortality patterns will bring a number of these issues into sharper focus. A recent study on mortality in the province of Cuenca has revealed the existence of substantial sub-regional and local disparities in mortality patterns (Reher, 1988: 96–114). Here a fairly sizeable sample of infant and childhood mortality was taken from the parishes and civil registers of the three districts into which the province has traditionally been divided: the Sierra (a fairly low mountain range situated in the north-eastern part of the province), the Alcarria (rolling hills to the north-west), and La Mancha (flat country to the south). Throughout much of the 1850–1930 period studied, infant and child mortality was significantly lower in the Sierra, and higher in La Mancha, though indications do exist that change was more intense in La Mancha than in the other districts.[32]

Deaths to young children were concentrated during the summer months, though this seasonal concentration was greatest for children dying above 1 year of age. Significant differences appeared when mortality during the first year of life was decomposed into its exogenous and endogenous components.[33] Once again mortality in the Sierra was lowest on both counts. More interest-ing, perhaps, is the fact that the cumulative totals of deaths by month of age plotted on the scale stipulated by Bourgeois Pichat configured a straight line for infant deaths in the Sierra sample, but not in the Alcarria and La Mancha, where there was an unexpected increase in deaths after 3 months of age (Figures 5.9 and 5.10). Exploring the reasons for these disparities brings the subject of infant feeding practices to the forefront of our discussion of mor-tality patterns. Could infant feeding practices, especially breast-feeding and weaning, have been different enough in these Cuenca districts so as to provoke the disparities in mortality levels and the peculiar hebaviour of deaths after 3 or 4 months of age in two of them?[34]

Breast-feeding and weaning practices were key factors in the ability of

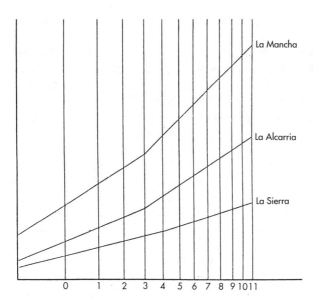

Fig. 5.9 Cumulative infant deaths by month of age (plotted on Bourgeois Pichat scale) for Cuenca districts, 1860–1900

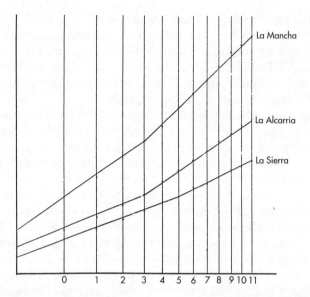

Fig. 5.10 Cumulative infant deaths by month of age (plotted on Bourgeois Pichat scale) for Cuenca districts, 1900–1930

children to survive infancy.[35] In the province of Cuenca, and probably in most of Spain, breast-feeding was given considerable social importance and was considered essential for the protection of the health of the child.[36] As long as a woman's milk was 'good', in Cuenca the child was breast-fed until a very advanced age, often more than a year.[37] If there was some problem with a mother's milk, families tried to find a wet-nurse.[38] While estimating the mean duration of breast-feeding is enormously difficult, the interviews have suggested that in the absence of death or pregnancy, between 12 and 18 months was probably the most common duration.

The effectiveness of breast-feeding in minimizing the risk of infant death was based, to a large extent, on both the salubrious effects of the mother's milk and the fact that a breast-fed child was less susceptible to the dangers of other types of food (Fildes, 1987: 213–19). In the case of Cuenca, however, this protection was almost never complete due to the practice of supplementing maternal milk at a very young age, often between 2 and 6 months according to most people interviewed. Children were normally given '*gachas*' (porridge), '*migas*' (bread crumbs), or '*puches*' made of toasted flour, olive oil, water, and honey or sugar.[39] At around 1 year of age, even though the child continued to nurse, he began to receive supplementary salted foods.[40] According to the people interviewed, mothers prepared food for children without any special care, normally not boiling the water and often touching the food for the baby with their hands or mouths.[41] In fact, general hygiene was extremely low.[42] This is why the summer season was so important; the heat helped spoil food and lower the quality of the water the people drank, and children tended to die of diarrhoea and from the dehydration that came with it.[43] This is why the mountainous part of the province had certain advantages with respect to raising young children. Hygiene and education there were no higher than elsewhere, but summers in the mountains were not as rigorous as in the lower districts like the Alcarria or La Mancha, and mountain water tended to be of higher quality. The result was that the summer diarrhoeas were not nearly as common in that part of the province.

From the preceding paragraphs it is clear that as children grew, successive changes in their feeding practices posed potential risks to their health. Once the dangers directly related to childbirth and birth defects had been overcome, the child entered a period lasting between 3 and 6 months in which he received more or less full protection from his mother's milk. This period of maternal protection might be shorter, especially if the mother had problems with her milk, but seldom lasted longer. From that time on, breast-feeding was supplemented with other types of nourishment, which typically were prepared with minimum attention to hygiene. This was a moment of great potential risks to the child's health. Another period of potential danger was the onset of teething, often accompanied by intestinal problems, which began between 6 and 10 months of age and continued to be a source of real discomfort for the child until he was more than 2 years old. Finally, weaning the child, normally between 12 and 18 months of age, was yet another crucial moment because changes in the child's feeding practices often led to severe gastrointestinal problems.[44] At issue here are the health problems related to feeding practices, and particularly to the digestive tract. These were the ones which were most sensitive to the summer season, and were the main cause of death among young children.[45]

With infant and child mortality patterns so closely linked to feeding practices and to the summer season, it is plausible to think that the moment at which children reached their first summers, and therefore the seasonality of their birth, might have had a decisive influence on their probabilities of survival.[46] This can be seen in eloquent results coming from two villages.[47] In Figure 5.11, where deaths by month of age during the first 24 months of life are plotted, the effects of the summer months are evident. For children born between November and February, once the initial effects of mortality related to childbirth was overcome, the risk of death declined sharply until between the third and sixth months of life. At that stage these children had to face their first summer at an age at which their mother's milk had already been supplemented, and between 7 and 10 months of age the probability of death rose sharply. Once the summer had passed, the incidence of death declined until the children were around 1.5 years of age, when mortality rose once again during their second summer.

Children born between March and June also suffered through two summers, but differently from those born between November and February. When they

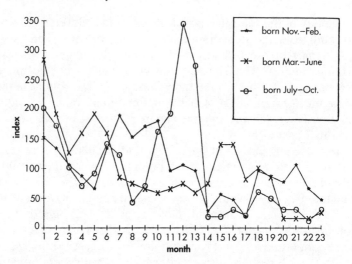

Fig. 5.11 Index of deaths during first 23 months of life, by season of birth, for the Cuenca villages, 1878–1922)

went through their first summer, they were very young and most of them were still nursing and had the protection of their mother's milk. The effects of this first summer were quite moderate among them. From the time they were 7 months of age until their first birthday, mortality levels were relatively low and constant. Only during their second summer, when they were teething and probably no longer nursing, were seasonal effects clearer. Finally, children born during the summer months showed few effects from their first summer, as almost all of them enjoyed the protection of their mother's milk. A year later (between 10 and 13 months of age), however, their second summer had devastating effects on their chances of survival. This summer season came at the worst possible age. Many were in the process of being weaned; and even those who continued to nurse were receiving abundant supplementary nourishment. Moreover, their second summer came during their first bout with teething, which only helped increase the risk of gastrointestinal infections. These were the children who suffered most during the summer, though it is also true that they are the only group which experienced the pernicious effects of only one summer.

The seasonal patterns of childhood development had net effects on their survival probabilities. Children born between March and June had a 25 per cent better chance of surviving to 2 years of age than those born in other periods of the year.[48] As expected, the key to this difference is centred on summer mortality, which for these children was 21 per cent below that of children born between November and February (2 summers), and 11 per cent below those born between July and October (1 summer). At least some of those children born during the spring still enjoyed the protection of their mother's milk and had not yet begun to teethe during their first summer, as opposed to other groups, who confronted their first real summer either weaned or with mixed feeding, and while they were teething. During the second year of life, however, season of birth seemed to have little effect on survival since the basic differences had already been established during the first year of life.[49]

The ever-present reality of season of birth and climate has emerged from these data. These factors have underscored the differences in mortality which were observed earlier in the different districts of the province of Cuenca. In this sense, the Sierra enjoyed a clear, though shrinking, advantage over the other areas. Summer was milder there and water tended to be more abundant and pure than in the lower-lying Alcarria and Mancha, thus providing for more healthful feeding practices and a lower incidence of infectious diseases. It is interesting to note that in the *Diccionario* of Pascual Madoz, compiled during the 1830s and 1840s, summer diarrhoeas were hardly mentioned in the entries for villages located in the Sierra, but were commonplace in other parts of the province.

Despite this, it would not be correct to say that heat itself caused childhood death, but rather the inability of society to compensate for a situation created by climate. Given the fact that during the early part of the twentieth century few doctors lived in isolated rural areas of a province which had long since been left behind by the train of economic development in Spain, the key to the initial decline of infant and childhood mortality was necessarily cultural. The care people took when caring for and feeding the very young was not dependent on doctors or on wealth, but rather on education in these matters. Awareness of the need to give young children food in good conditions was a decisive step on the road to reducing mortality, especially the initial reductions from very high to moderate levels. The central government was aware of this during the early decades of this century. The creation of the '*gotas de leche*' and centres for mothers breast-feeding their infants are examples of governmental attempts to improve the hygiene of infant feeding practices.[50] Since these centres were located in towns, and especially in large towns, they probably contributed to the fact that infant mortality decline was faster there.

In rural areas, however, attitudes were slower to change and mortality continued to be high for longer. The way the new ideas were accepted by the people remains a mystery and is as yet an unexplored chapter of Spanish history. Yet eventually people's attitudes did change. Proof of this is that chances of survival began to increase even in the most backward areas of the country, often as early as the last third of the nineteenth century. Childhood mortality was the first to decline, and was followed soon after by mortality during the first year of life. As this happened the value of children to their parents increased, and this in turn stimulated greater efforts on the part of parents to protect the children they already had.[51] In that sense, mortality reduction became a self-fulfilling prophecy, as improvements tended to beget further improvements in children's probability of surviving the fateful years.[52]

Notes

1. Even though in some parishes and in some areas registration was better than in others, generally speaking quality was low.
2. The inverse projection method pioneered by Ronald Lee (1974, 1985, 1993) was not used to estimate total population because its accuracy depends on complete registration of deaths, and this is not the case with our New Castile sample. Total population counts have proved to be fairly reliable when contrasted with existing 18th- and 19th-century estimates, though the method used does not account for major changes in population totals due precisely to short- and medium-term swings in mortality. For a more complete explanation of the method of estimation, see Reher (1991*b*).
3. Unfortunately the sample is very small. By 1700 there are only 4 useful parishes, and by 1800 this number has increased to 11.
4. When controlling for trends in celibacy, the basic patterns remained the same. For a more complete explanation of the method used, see Livi Bacci (1977*b*) and Livi Bacci and Reher (1993: 78–81, 83).
5. Since ISM is based on marriage cohorts, its values have been plotted 25 years earlier.
6. In all three cases the authors have used inverse projection techniques on samples of rural parishes. See Ardit (1991: 39–40), Macías Hernández (1991: 62), Muñoz Pradas (1991: 80–1).
7. For the classic study on crisis mortality in Spain, see Pérez Moreda (1980).
8. For results on rural Spain, see Pérez Moreda (1988), and on urban Spain, Reher (1990*a*: 143–8). See also Lanza García (1991: 333–44).
9. Since at the end of the 17th century the sample of infant and child mortality is based on data from only 4 parishes, the results for the years between 1690 and 1710 may be spurious. Real-wage data can be found in Reher and Ballesteros (1993).
10. Over the entire period, the bivariate correlation coefficient between both series is −0.361.
11. These estimates of life expectancy at birth are taken from Dopico (1987*b*) and Dopico and Rowland (1990). For the first date they were estimated based on census age structures in 1787 and 1797, and in 1863–70 they make use of census age distribution and the first published vital statistics (based on parish registration data) with deaths by age, adjusted for under-registration. Generally speaking these estimates of overall life expectancy seem fairly reliable, though the concrete regional and provincial values in some cases are open to question and have been contradicted in part by other studies making use of different material. The most noticeable of these apparent contradictions comes from Catalonia, where the census-based estimates reveal no gains in life expectancy over the period, as opposed to other studies which suggest that there were substantial gains of between 4 and 6 years. On this, see Muñoz Pradas (1991). For an alternative

census-based estimate of life expectancy for the late 18th century, see Cachinero Sánchez (1985).

12. Even a modest 5-year gain in life expectancy over the 40-year period would seem unwarranted given the stable death rates, and may suggest that the 1860 e_0 is slightly underestimated.
13. For an overview of mortality in Europe before and during the demographic transition, see Vallin (1991).
14. Only crude death rates can be estimated from the available census and vital registration data, but they are available for the 476 judicial districts making up the country at that time.
15. Elsewhere it has been shown, using urban and rural data from 1900 and 1910, that urban/rural ratios for infant and child mortality (q_0, $_4q_1$) were between 109 and 114, as opposed to adult age groups (30–5, 40–5, 50–5), in which the ratios were between 135 and 157. See Reher (1990*b*: 297).
16. Of these, 344,000 took place during the war itself, and another 214,000 in the 3 years immediately afterwards. Needless to say, these estimates are only approximations.
17. In 1910, life expectancy at birth was below the European average (excluding European territories which later because part of the USSR) by 5.8 years for men, and 7.1 for women. By 1930 the gap had been reduced to 5.2 years for men and 5.4 for women and in 1950 it was 3.1 years for men and 2.9 for women. See Caselli (1994).
18. The 1945–52 period was remarkable for its mortality declines the world over (Dyson and Murphy, 1991).
19. In 1990, life expectancy at birth was higher in Spain than on average in Europe (excluding the European territories of the ex-USSR) by 2.3 years for men and 2.1 years for women. See Caselli (1994).
20. For more on this, see Omran (1971). In outlining this three-stage process we are following closely the ideas of Casselli (1994).
21. For a discussion of these issues, see Schofield and Reher (1991). For differing emphases on the role played by nutrition and public health measures in this process, see, for example, McKeown (1976) and Preston (1976).
22. See also Preston *et al.* (1972).
23. This pattern is reflected in the 'South' model life tables published by Coale and Demeny (1966 [1986]).
24. These are normally called the *Movimiento Natural de la Población.*
25. This project first received funding from the regional governments of Madrid and of Valencia, and subsequently from the Dirección General para Investigacion en Ciencia y Tecnología (DIGICYT).
26. The number of villages included in the sample varies with the date. For the first 20 years of the 19th century there is only one large village (about 5,000 inhabitants), by 1860 there are 7, and by 1900 there are 15. For further details on the data base and the methods used, see Reher *et al.* (1994).
27. The mid-century rise in mortality has also appeared in data from other countries. While a part of the increase might have been due to improved registration, the high levels already holding in our sample suggest that the trend itself cannot be explained by the quality of registration alone.
28. If these Madrid-Toledo patterns are compared to another sample of villages taken

from the eastern coastal province of Alicante, a number of disparities arise, mainly concerning prevailing levels (lower in Alicante) and the starting point and pace of decline. Results from this sample have not been included because as yet the sample size is still very small.

29. For the case of England, see Woods *et al.* (1988–9).
30. These are the only two dates during the first half of this century for which the Spanish *Movimiento Natural de la Población* subdivides deaths taking place under 1 year of age by monthly groups, and deaths between 1 and 4 by exact year of age.
31. In the interests of simplicity, we have adopted a very approximate regionalization of Spanish mortality patterns which retains five general regions: one encompasses the entire northern coastal area, from the Basque Country to Galicia; another includes an entire strip of Spain just south of the northern regions (Old Castile, Leon, and Aragon); a third includes the regions of Extremadura and New Castile located south of the Guadarrama-Gredos mountain ranges; a fourth region the entire southern quarter of the peninsula (Andalucia, Murcia), plus the Canary Islands; and the fifth region groups together the eastern and north-eastern areas of the peninsula (Catalonia, Valencia, and the Balearic Islands).
32. Before 1920, infant mortality (q_0) was between 3–23% higher in the 'Sierra' than in other districts of Cuenca and child mortality ($_4q_1$) was between 13–17% higher! Between 1920–35, both indicators were 10–30% lower in the 'Mancha'. See Reher (1988: 98–9).
33. This was done by means of the method devised by Jean Bourgeois Pichat (1951).
34. On this subject, see Knodel and Kintner (1977), Kintner (1985).
35. This key subject has not received the attention it deserves from Spanish scholars and as yet we know very little about practices existing in Spain before and during the epidemiological transition. For an overview of the subject, see Fildes (1987).
36. It is interesting to note that in the in-depth interviews used in the study of Cuenca, elderly peasants never mentioned the fertility-inhibiting effects of breast-feeding, but only its implications for the child's health. Some examples of this social attitude can be seen in the following excerpts from the interviews: 'People did not know that breast-feeding made it more difficult to become pregnant. They did it to protect their children.' 'They used to breast-feed them for a long time because people thought that weaning them was going to make them die. Even if it was harmful to the mother's health, they kept on breast-feeding the children.' 'Some people did associate breast-feeding with pregnancy, but others didn't know any-thing about it.' For more on the interview process, see Reher (1988: 253–9).
37. 'My mother nursed me until I was 22 months old, and that is how it was for most kids, for the simple reason that none of the economic and scientific techniques available today existed in those days.' 'Breast-feeding lasted until 2 years of age, between 18 and 24 months.' 'For some children breast-feeding lasted until they were 3 years old. Unless something happened to the mother, they were given their mother's milk as long as possible.' 'Kids who were 2 or 3 years old would say "mommy give me tit" (*mamá dame teta*).'
38. 'Women with no milk got somebody else to do it. A wet-nurse.' 'I was born in 1922. My mother had to raise us on tinned milk and also with other women. First my mother's milk, then another woman's, then tinned milk. I even once had an ass's milk. These women did not charge; it was done out of friendship.'

39. 'Mothers' milk was supplemented when the child was under a year of age, normally about 6 months. They were given toasted flour and honey, the *gachas de miel* (honey porridge).' 'Normally when they were 4 or 5 months of age they were given a porridge made of toasted flour, olive oil, and sugar.' 'They were given *puches*, or sweet breadcrumbs when they were 4–5 months old.' 'The mother's milk began to be supplemented when the child was 15 days old. In the morning it was porridge, and later on her own milk. The child also received water with sugar or with anisette.'

40. 'First the *puches* or the sweet crumbs (*migas dulces*), then potatoes, noodles with garlic.' 'From 7–8 months of age they received *migas* with toasted flour. Once they were a year old, they began to receive food with salt: a boiled potato or some *gazpacho*.'

41. 'The *gachas* (porridge) were made with water from the fountain, and nobody knew if it was good or bad.' 'Children died in August, even those breast-feeding. They drank unboiled water and many died of diarrhoea.' 'When they were a few days or weeks old, they began to have their mother's milk supplemented. Since they had no teeth to chew the food with, their mothers chewed it for them and then gave it to them.' 'Water was never boiled. My father only gave me boiled water when I had a cold; it was a type of medicine.'

42. 'Children were never bathed.' 'They had no idea of hygiene. When a baby was born they used to put him in a blanket and nappies and seldom ever changed them. People had no idea of hygiene.'

43. 'Water wasn't boiled. Children died of diarrhoea and malnutrition. The summer heat affected them greatly.' 'People used to say "August makes them sick and September takes them away."'

44. For more on this subject, see Bernabeu Mestre (1994).

45. Other diseases like measles or smallpox were also of considerable importance for young children, but were not directly related to feeding practices and were less centred on the summer months.

46. For more on this subject, within the context of other European countries, see Vilquin (1978), Breschi and Livi Bacci (1986*a*, 1986*b*, 1994).

47. These are Cañamares (1878–90, 1900–22) and La Almarcha (1840–9, 1886–95, and 1900–9), both of which are located in the province of Cuenca. For the sake of simplicity, three groups of births have been used: November–February, March–June, and July–October.

48. These data are based on Civil Registration material taken from the villages of Cañamares and La Almarcha in Cuenca.

49. This pattern was found in another study of a Spanish parish, as children born in spring tended to have better chances of survival than those born in other seasons. As the demographic transition took hold (1938–72), this advantage became minimal and the distinctive seasonal pattern of death practically disappeared. See Giri Brown *et al.* (1985).

50. On this see Pascua (1934), Gómez Redondo (1992).

51. For more on this, see Reher (1995).

52. See Preston and Haines (1991).

6 Marriage, Reproduction, and the Family

Marriage Patterns in Spain

Nuptiality has long occupied a central place in demographic theory. For Malthus it was the prime determinant of fertility levels and the key to the preventive check to excess population growth. The sensitivity of nuptiality to prevailing and expected living standards was the key to its effectiveness, though ultimately Malthus viewed delayed marriage as much a matter of 'moral restraint' as one of economic determinism. For him, this 'moral restraint' could be found in abundance in the 'different states of modern Europe', but much less so in other parts of the world.

More recently John Hajnal has built upon many of Malthus's original ideas regarding nuptiality. The most influential contribution of his seminal article, published in 1965, was to articulate a clear-cut geographical description of differing marriage patterns in Europe: late and restricted nuptiality west of the Leningrad–Trieste line, as opposed to early and intense nuptiality east of that line. He felt that this distinctive European marriage pattern had originated some time between the sixteenth and seventeenth centuries. While demographic realities contributed to this pattern, Hajnal emphasized the critical importance of economic and cultural factors. Since 'the establishment of an economic basis for the life of the couple and their children' was a necessary requirement for marriage, couples were willing to put off marriage until that had been achieved. In this way, 'the marriage pattern is tied very intimately with the performance of the economy as a whole' (Hajnal, 1965: 132–3). Delayed marriage also had a very positive influence on the economic system since it allowed for greater savings, higher living standards, and consequently higher levels of consumption.[1]

Hajnal's work vindicates Malthus's original intuitions, and goes beyond them by building a framework for understanding the origins and implications of marriage patterns based on economic and social factors. In the words of Richard Smith (1981: 618–19), at least in England, 'the critical ideological variable that provided the society with a capacity for demographic self-control was the notion that each social group or stratum placed great weight upon a basic minimum living standard below which individuals were loath to descend when marrying and forming new households.' This he called 'a culturally determined moral economy'.[2] E. A. Wrigley and R. Schofield (1981) and others have demonstrated how nuptiality was the key to high- and low-pressure demographic regimes and how each of them had definite economic implications.[3] All of these authors, from Malthus to Wrigley, have suggested either directly or indirectly that the distinctive marriage pattern holding in Europe contributed to the higher living standards in that part of the world.

In more recent work, Hajnal (1982) has suggested that it is impossible fully to understand marriage patterns unless we see them within the context of prevailing family systems. In most societies marriage led to the dissolution of some households and to the creation of others. It was a key element in definitions of prevailing family living arrangements. He suggested that early marriage could only take place in those societies in which a certain degree of economic independence was not a prerequisite for marriage. Thus areas of very early and intense marriage would tend to be those in which complex household structures prevailed, as opposed to later marriage ages in societies in which marriage led to more or less immediate household formation. Exploring concrete local contexts in Europe has shown that reality can be far richer and more complex than theory. Nevertheless, it is difficult not to be in full agreement with Hajnal when he insists on placing marriage within the context of family formation systems.

More than a formal theory of nuptiality, Hajnal's work is actually an empirical description of marriage patterns, together with a very loose framework for understanding the links between marriage behaviour and society as a whole. His formulation is only economically deterministic in a very approximate way, and perhaps his major contribution to our understanding of behaviour in past societies has been to get historians to significantly broaden their perspective on marriage. His interpretation of marriage patterns is most useful when making general comparisons between north-western European and non-European populations, and it raises a number of questions concerning the origins of these patterns, their causes, and their implications for European society. Unfortunately, as often happens, southern Europe, where regional and even local variability could be very high, was only marginal to Hajnal's original formulation.

Regional and Temporal Dimensions of Nuptiality

Spanish data provide an excellent context in which to discuss the implications of a number of Hajnal's basic ideas. Much like many other Mediterranean countries, vital behaviour often showed distinct regional or sub-regional patterns and was characterized by a degree of variability which would surprise most students of northern Europe. Speaking of Spanish national characteristics in the pre-modern era is often a gross misrepresentation of the complexity of the social fabric in the country. Assessing this degree of regional, local, and even temporal variability is one of the key challenges facing students of nuptiality in Spain.

Before the Census of Floridablanca (1787), the only reliable data on marriage patterns come from local family reconstitutions or by applying indirect population reconstruction techniques to samples of parish data. Over the past 20 years a number of family reconstitution studies have been carried out in Spain which enable us to get a glimpse at prevailing patterns of age at marriage. Regional coverage is very uneven and, as tends to occur with these sorts of studies, generalization can be perilous. Generally younger age at marriage (21–23 for women) than in most of north-western Europe, older ages at marriage in the northern and the north-western parts of the country (especially Galicia), and a very slight indication that in certain areas age at marriage might have increased between the late sixteenth and the late eighteenth centuries are among the most salient but tentative conclusions which we can draw from the existing data.[4]

A different perspective on marriage patterns can be obtained by using techniques of population reconstruction based on time series taken from samples of local parish registers. This sort of approach enables us to view nuptiality as a dynamic process, although the indicators derived are generally quite crude. To date the largest sample used for this sort of purpose is based on 26 parishes taken from the region of New Castile, near and to the south and east of Madrid. Marriage rates taken from this sample and computed on the basis of the 'most likely' population estimates can be seen in Figure 6.1.[5] The results dispel for ever the idea that nuptiality was more or less stable in pre-modern populations, and mirror those found by Wrigley and Schofield for England. Marriage rates were high and increasing during the third quarter of

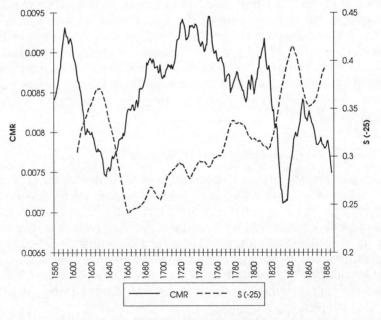

Fig. 6.1 Crude marriage rate (CMR) and estimated index of those remaining single (S) for sample of New Castile (25-year moving average)

the sixteenth century, but began a steep decline after 1590 which lasted until near 1640. During that period, marriage rates declined by nearly 20 per cent. From the low levels holding in the mid-seventeenth century, marriage rates then gradually increased, and reached a relatively high plateau between 1720 and 1740. The ensuing downturn lasted until the early years of the nineteenth century, and was followed by a sharp but short-lived recovery coinciding with the termination of the Peninsular War in 1812. The decline of nuptiality between 1820 and 1840 may be a product of faulty data.[6] After the mid-1840s, the declining levels of nuptiality shown by the time series presented here are confirmed by other sources.

While the method of estimating most likely population, as well as the representativeness of the sample, might be called into doubt, when the rates calculated in this way have been compared to independently estimated crude marriage rates (for 1787, 1860, and 1887), the fit has been fairly close. Proposing a complementary method for estimating a proxy indicator for permanent celibacy, Livi Bacci and Reher (1993: 73–4) found that for the most part periods of declining marriage rates tended to coincide with periods of increasing celibacy (Figure 6.1).

Throughout the Early Modern period and lasting into the early years of this century, medium- and long-term variations in nuptiality appeared to be a key factor in determining prevailing levels of fertility. A good example of this can be seen in Figure 6.2, where for the sample of parishes from New Castile, fertility varied in consonance with nuptiality throughout the Early Modern period and during much of the nineteenth century.[7] Noteworthy is the fact that trend changes in fertility tended to follow trend changes in nuptiality after a very short lag of about 3–5 years.[8] There can be little doubt that, much as is implicit in Malthus's formulations, pronounced long-term swings in nuptiality played an essential role in determining fertility levels in central Spain throughout the period.

Data derived by methods of indirect estimation and from family reconstitutions can give us a useful, though partial and basically local, idea of marriage patterns. Not until adequate census data appear can a more complete, though somewhat more static, picture of nuptiality for the entire country be outlined. The first census with the requisite data is the Census of Floridablanca (1787), though classification by sex, age, and marital status did not become a standard part of modern Spanish censuses until a century later. This gap of 100 years makes it hazardous to generalize about Spanish marriage patterns over the course of most of the nineteenth century.

Judging from the data on marriage age and celibacy contained in Table 6.1, however, it would seem that throughout the nineteenth century, marriage timing and intensity followed an apparently contradictory pattern, with age increasing and celibacy declining.[9] A rise in age at marriage is not surprising within a context of increasing population densities in rural areas, lack of decisive economic transformations in most of the country, and a gradual

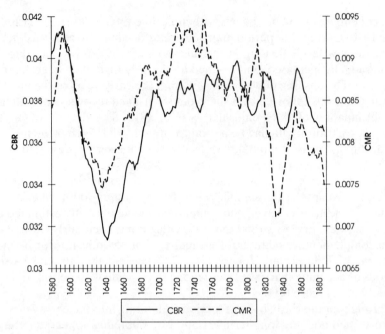

Fig. 6.2   Crude marriage rate and crude birth rate for sample of New Castile (25-year moving average)

Table 6.1   Marriage patterns in Spain, 1797–1970

Year[c]	Mean age at marriage (SMAM)[a]		Permanent celibacy[b]	
	men	women	men	women
1787/97	24.5	23.2	17.4	17.2
1887	27.0	24.2	7.3	10.9
1900	27.4	24.4	6.4	10.2
1910	27.8	25.1	6.6	10.2
1920	27.9	25.7	7.5	11.7
1930	28.2	25.8	7.6	13.7
1940	29.4	26.7	9.2	13.7
1950	29.0	26.4	9.6	15.2
1970	27.5	23.7	8.6	12.3

[a] Singulate mean age at marriage, based on census distribution by age, sex, and marital status.
[b] For 1787/97, permanent celibacy is based on the mean percentage of never-married for the 40–49 and 50–59 age groups. Between 1887 and 1940 it is based on the 46–50 age group, and after 1950 on the 45–49 age group.
[c] Average of estimates for 1787 and 1797.

Sources: for 1787/97, Pérez Moreda (1985*a*); for other dates, Cachinero Sánchez (1982: 87).

reduction in mortality levels. The apparent decline in celibacy, however, is somewhat more puzzling, though the defrocking of much of the regular clergy during the middle years of the nineteenth century, some of whom likely married, probably contributed to this trend. After 1900 trends of both marriage parameters are roughly parallel, with marriage becoming ever later and more restricted. This is somewhat different from what took place in many other European countries, where female nuptiality gradually intensified after the onset of the demographic transition. Intensification of marriage is not visible in Spain until after 1950.

At the end of the eighteenth century Spanish marriage patterns were squarely within what John Hajnal (1965) called the 'European marriage pattern' in so far as celibacy was concerned, but age at marriage was still relatively young. A century later both timing and intensity of female nuptiality were typical of north-western European marriage patterns. This led to birth rates which were sharply lower than a century earlier, despite the fact that marital fertility had only begun to decline in a small part of the country.

Throughout the period, Spain showed itself to be a country of great contrasts. In 1787 age at female marriage ranged from 21.9 to 26.4 years, and permanent celibacy varied from 3.2 per cent to 20.6 per cent. Male patterns showed similar levels of variation, with age at marriage ranging from 23.6 to 27.6, and celibacy between 4.5 to 19.8 per cent. A century later the 1887 census, for which we have a much larger sample (476 judicial districts), yields similar results: female age at marriage ranged from 20.96 to 28.93, while men's age at marriage varied from 24.18 to 30.29. Permanent celibacy for women ranged from 0.78 to 41.13 per cent, and from 1.37 to 28.7 per cent for men (Reher *et al.*, 1993). A small sample of national variability of I_m for different European countries shows that it was greatest in Spain, followed by Portugal and France (Table 6.2).[10]

High levels of variability can also be seen in marriage behaviour at a more local level. An example of this is the historical region of the Basque Country and Navarre, where we can find a great variety of marriage patterns co-existing at the end of the nineteenth century in a very small area (four provinces, 815,000 inhabitants in 1887, and 6,824 square miles; 3.5 per cent of Spain). In 1887 district-level I_m values ranged from 0.452 to 0.728 in the Basque Country. Social group also had considerable importance for marriage patterns, with marriage being more restricted in the well-to-do sectors of rural society. Finally, nuptiality in urban areas was consistently more restricted than in rural areas (Reher, 1989, 1990*b*).[11] Spain, perhaps more than any other European country, tends to elude Hajnal's basic definition of the geographical distribution of marriage patterns. Until well into the twentieth century, in certain parts of the country, such as the northern coastal areas and the Canary Islands, both male and female nuptiality were as restricted as in north-western Europe (I_m values well below 0.500, and often below 0.400), while in others nuptiality was quite intense (10 per cent of the districts with I_m values greater than 0.799).

Table 6.2   Variability of female nuptiality (I_m) in several European nations

Nation	Year	n	Average I_m	Standard deviation	Coefficient of variation
England and Wales	1891	46	0.471	0.039	0.082
France	1896	86	0.555	0.069	0.124
Belgium	1890	49	0.416	0.048	0.115
Germany	1890	72	0.497	0.045	0.091
Italy	1881	89	0.549	0.046	0.084
Portugal	1890	21	0.462	0.060	0.130
Ireland	1891	31	0.329	0.025	0.075
Spain[a]	1887	49	0.588	0.080	0.136
Spain[b]	1887	476	0.608	0.097	0.160

[a] Spanish provincial data.
[b] Judicial district data.
Source: Coale and Watkins (1986: appendix A, 80–152). For Spanish judicial districts, see Reher *et al.* (1993).
Note: All data refer to values of I_m.

Despite the very low levels of nuptiality in some districts, in more general terms towards the end of the nineteenth century age at marriage in Spain was similar to that holding in other areas of Europe (26.8 for men and 23.9 for women) and permanent celibacy for the most part was considerably lower. In fact, male celibacy was only above 10 per cent in 6 of the 49 provinces and for women in only 12 of them. In most provinces it was quite low, ranging between 4 and 6 per cent. If we use I_m as an indicator of female nuptiality, in Spain levels were considerably higher than the European average until at least 1930. Around 1887, I_m was 0.591 in Spain and 0.500 in all of Europe; in 1900, it was 0.573 as opposed to 0.504. Only in 1930 did it dip below levels holding on the continent as a whole (0.513 as opposed to 0.523) (Coale and Watkins, 1986: 51).

We have attempted to include both timing and intensity in a series of maps designed to portray the regional distribution of nuptiality patterns in Spain in 1887, 1920, and 1960.[12] The results of our basic cartography can be seen in Maps 6.1–6.12, and show that low levels of female marriage were typical of the north-western part of the peninsula, as well in parts of the south-west. Male marriage patterns were not dissimilar to female ones, with the principal exception of the entire area of the Pyrenees, where for females nuptiality was intense and young, but for males it was late and restricted. This situation was evidently related to the fact that in the entire Pyrenean area, inheritance was basically impartible and normally given to the male heir. Elsewhere differences are located in and around Madrid, where male nuptiality levels are low, and the south-west, where relative levels for men are still lower than for women. The similarity in male and female marriage patterns is brought out by the bivariate correlation coefficients between each of the four nuptiality indicators, all of which are positive and significant at the <0.001 level.

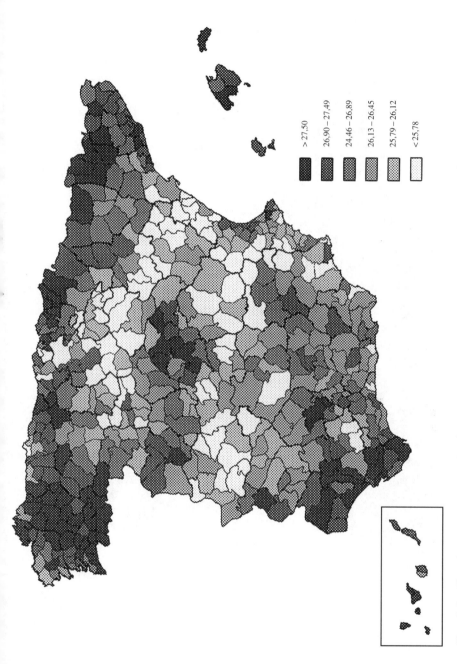

Map 6.1 Singulate mean age at marriage males by judicial district, 1887

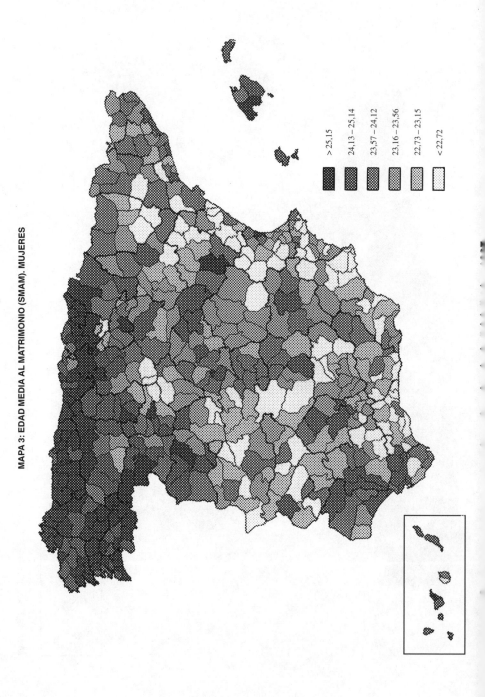

MAPA 3: EDAD MEDIA AL MATRIMONIO (SMAM). MUJERES

> 25,15

24,13 – 25,14

23,57 – 24,12

23,16 – 23,56

22,73 – 23,15

< 22,72

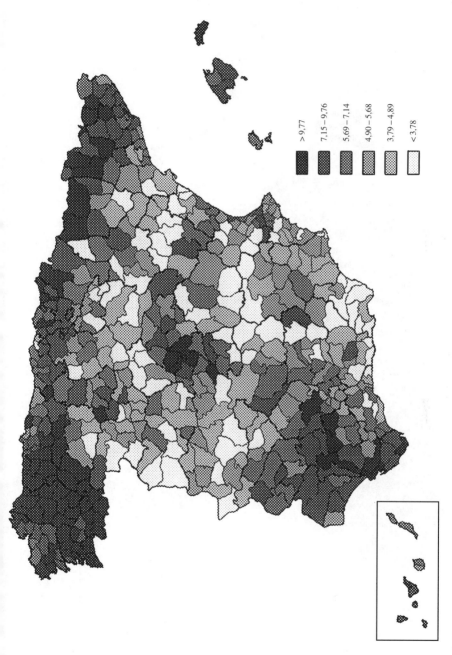

Map 6.3   Permanent celibacy, males, by judicial district, 1887

> 9,77
7,15 – 9,76
5,69 – 7,14
4,90 – 5,68
3,79 – 4,89
< 3,78

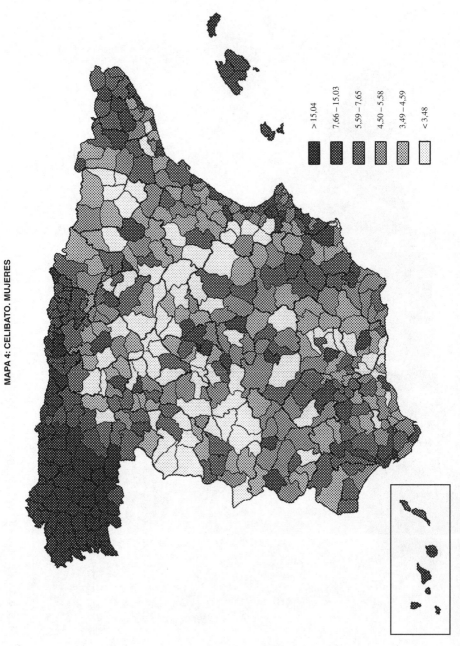

MAPA 4: CELIBATO. MUJERES

> 15,04

7,66 – 15,03

5,59 – 7,65

4,50 – 5,58

3,49 – 4,59

< 3,48

Map 6.4. Permanent celibacy, females, by judicial district, 1887

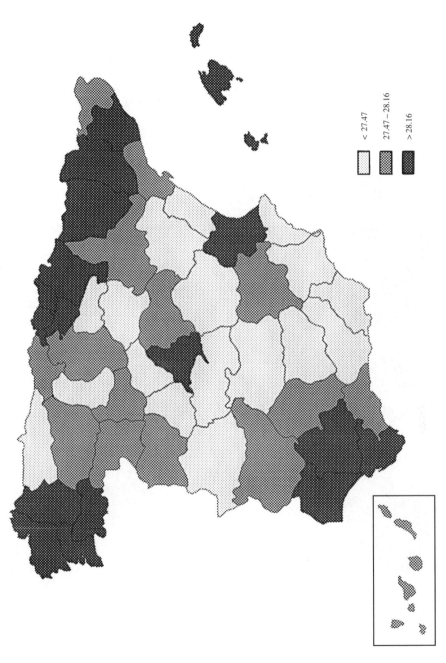

< 27.47

27.47 – 28.16

> 28.16

Map 6.5   Singulate mean age at marriage, males, by province, 1920

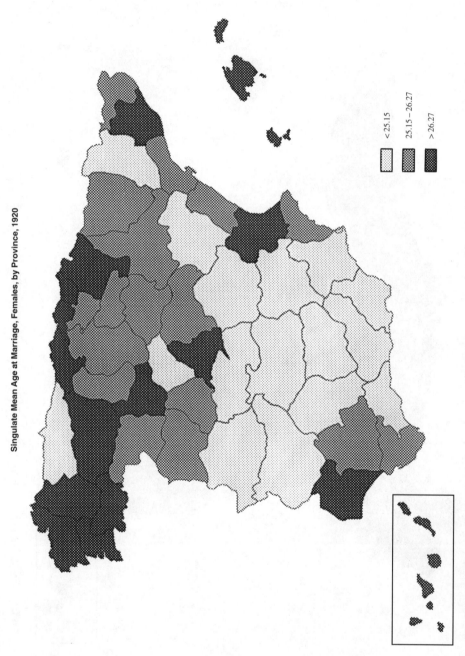

Map 6.6 Singulate mean age at marriage, females, by province, 1920

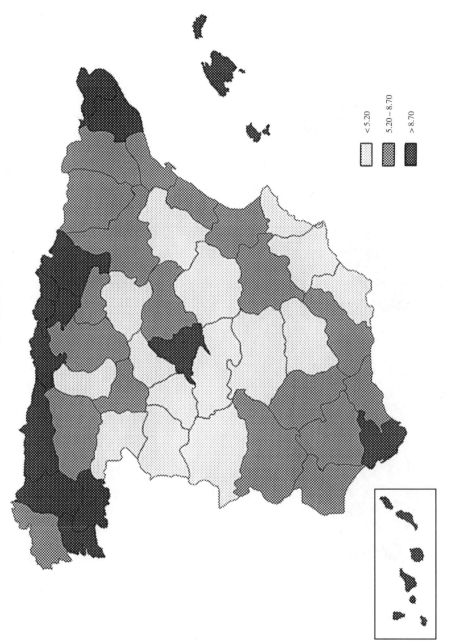

Map 6.7 Permanent celibacy, males, by province, 1920

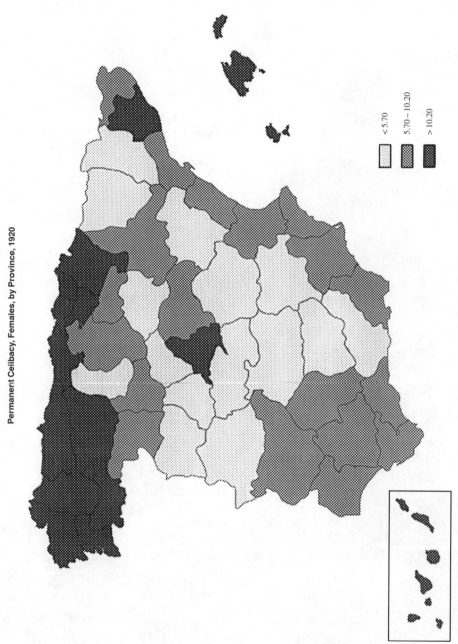

Permanent Celibacy, Females, by Province, 1920

<5.70

5.70 – 10.20

> 10.20

Map 6.8 Permanent celibacy, females, by province, 1920

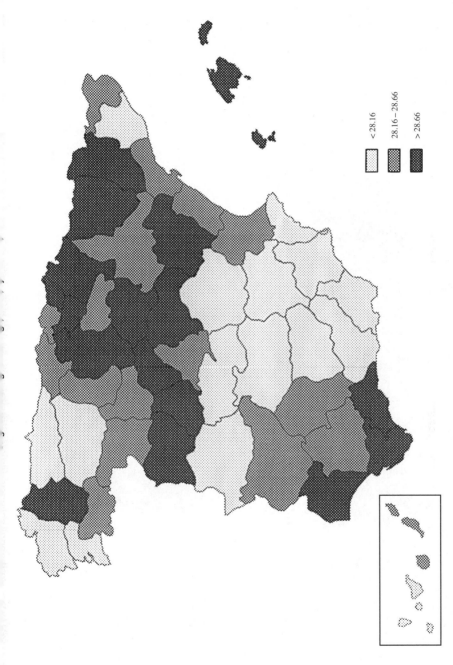

Map 6.9   Singulate mean age at marriage, males, by province, 1960

< 28.16

28.16 – 28.66

> 28.66

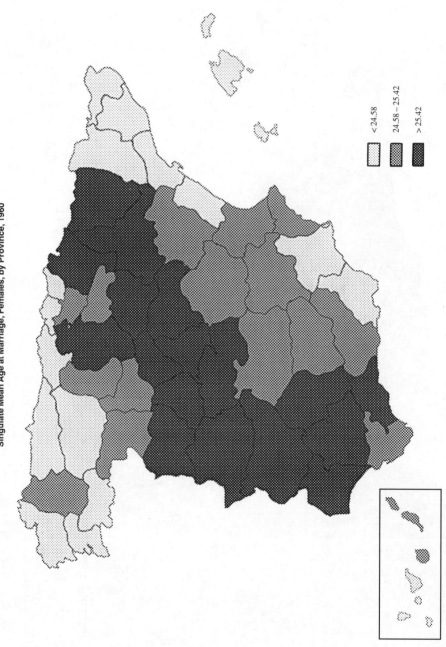

Map 6.10 Singulate mean age at marriage, females, by province, 1960

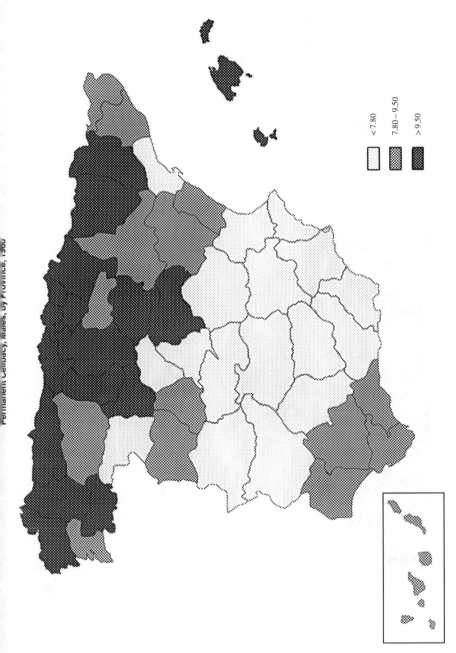

Map 6.11 Permanent celibacy, males, by province, 1960

< 7.80

7.80 – 9.50

> 9.50

Map 6.12. Permanent celibacy, females, by province, 1960

An important aspect of Spanish marriage patterns has been their relative stability over time. In a recent article, Robert Rowland (1988: 101–8) has convincingly demonstrated that female marriage patterns in 1887 were fundamentally similar to those existing a century earlier, and that the key element of stability was age at marriage. This also seems to have been the case between 1887 and 1930, as can be seen in the maps presented in this chapter, and is corroborated by the consistently significant bivariate correlation coefficients during that period (Table 6.3). It is worth noting that the observed pattern of stability is stronger for women than for men, and is more noticeable for

Table 6.3 Bivariate correlation coefficients for nuptiality indices at various dates

SMAM (males)

	1887	1900	1910	1920	1930
1887	1.000	0.782**	0.764**	0.809**	0.667**
1900		1.000	0.832**	0.729**	0.613**
1910			1.000	0.727**	0.714**
1920				1.000	0.854**
1930					1.000

SMAM (females)

	1887	1900	1910	1920	1930
1887	1.000	0.862**	0.817**	0.723**	0.792**
1900		1.000	0.891**	0.742**	0.786**
1910			1.000	0.817**	0.866*
1920				1.000	0.775*
1930					1.000

Celibacy (males)

	1887	1900	1910	1920	1930
1887	1.000	0.947**	0.851**	0.874**	0.886**
1900		1.000	0.885**	0.875**	0.880**
1910			1.000	0.915**	0.897**
1920				1.000	0.935**
1930					1.000

Celibacy (females)

	1887	1900	1910	1920	1930
1887	1.000	0.985**	0.957**	0.936**	0.924**
1900		1.000	0.969**	0.971**	0.960**
1910			1.000	0.957**	0.959**
1920				1.000	0.985**
1930					1.000

** Significance of <0.001.

marriage intensity than it is for timing. Stable regional marriage patterns are firmly anchored in Spain's past.

If we delve still further into Spain's history, what little we know of marriage patterns suggests that the same situation likely existed earlier. During the seventeenth century, age at marriage was a bit younger everywhere, but the regional patterns still emerge. In Galicia female marriage was much later than it was in the southern half of the peninsula (25 years as opposed to 21). Sparse evidence for the case of Castile also exists for the sixteenth century and indicates that age at marriage for women ranged from 19 to 21 years. In other words, there is some indirect empirical evidence to suggest that the basic regional distribution of marriage patterns had been in place by at least the seventeenth century and, if we are to judge from existing data on birth rates, probably from a good deal earlier. Signs of a disintegration of traditional marriage patterns in Spain only begin to become visible in 1940; and by 1960 or 1970 totally different patterns begin to emerge.

A Framework for Understanding Marriage Patterns in Spain

An intriguing question is why marriage was early and intense in some areas, and late and restricted in others; or why marriage rates fluctuated so significantly over time. Hajnal suggested that the uniqueness of the European marriage pattern stemmed from the fact that marriage and household formation were closely linked and that economic factors were an essential part of the decision to marry. For him, however, the economics of marriage was really what might be called a proximate determinant of nuptiality because it too was subject to certain demographic (mortality), economic (structures and cycles), and cultural (family formation patterns) constraints (Hajnal, 1965: 128–35). In a subsequent article, he related the predominance of simple family households to restricted marriage patterns, much as occurs in England, and early and intense marriage to more complex household forms (Hajnal, 1982). In the final analysis, for Hajnal basic marriage patterns are a consequence of cultural norms which end up being implemented by means of economic realities. It is very difficult not to agree with his basic viewpoint as to the importance of a couple's economic expectations when determining just when to get married.

In matters of detail, however, this general argument often proves to be inadequate. There is no reason to believe that the same sort of 'minimum basic living standard', spoken of by Richard Smith (1981, 1983), was not everywhere an essential prerequisite for marriage. Different cultural and economic contexts might dictate different acceptable standards, but economic causality was always present. Yet the relation between the two would not be simple. Abundant evidence exists for Europe suggesting that the wealthy tended to get married less and later than other groups in society. Moreover the relation between marriage and household formation postulated by Hajnal is not clearcut either. In Spain, the areas of most intense nuptiality (the centre and the south) were precisely those in which marriage and household formation were nearly simultaneous events, and where simple households were most prevalent. This seems to have been the case as early as the seventeenth century and perhaps earlier, when women's age at marriage in the southern and central parts of the country was near 20 and Spanish marriage patterns were markedly different from those of much of the rest of north-western Europe. These were modes of behaviour in seeming contradiction with Hajnal's 'two kinds of household formation system. . . .' However, on this point Spain can only be considered a partial exception to the norms postulated by Hajnal because nowhere did marriage age and intensity approximate those levels holding in eastern Europe. Clearly in Spain, much as in those countries clearly within the 'European marriage pattern', a basic minimum living standard was necessary for marriage to take place, but it was itself conditioned by a whole host of other variables, some quantifiable, and others less so.

In a recent article, Robert Woods and P. Hinde (1985: 125–7) have attempted to tackle the problem by proposing a twofold structure of causality within an ecological model.[13] They hypothesize that the timing and intensity of marriage are influenced by the 'supply' of eligible partners, and by the 'opportunity' to marry. Within their basically Malthusian model, supply is reflected mainly by the sex ratio during the marrying ages, and opportunity is mostly a consequence of economic structures. By introducing the supply variable within a coherent theory of nuptiality they have made an important contribution to Hajnal's original explanation because they have made it an autonomous variable, independent of demographic factors or elements of economically motivated choice. Yet despite its advantages, the Woods–Hinde theoretical construct is excessively simplistic because it too leaves out a number of key factors conditioning the marriage patterns of men and women.

The timing and incidence of marriage can be viewed as the result of availability and ability: the availability of a mate, and the economic and social ability to get married. Availability refers mainly to the marriage market, itself subject to constraints implied by sex-specific migration and the barriers imposed by space, social pressure, and personal taste. The working of this marriage market is very complex, and most variables chosen as proxies hardly do justice to the complex interplay of constraints. The economic and social ability to get married, which very nearly corresponds to Hajnal's original postulates, refers to the ability of young people to establish their own home, a key factor where neo-local household formation rules were prevalent, or to support themselves and their offspring. These basic constraints are, in turn, a product of the demographic, economic and socio-cultural context holding in different societies.

The importance of the demographic context of nuptiality should not be underestimated. Demographic factors influence nuptiality in two ways. When prevailing levels of mortality are high, ecological niches open earlier, facilitating access to inheritance and thus to the attainment of the necessary income to get married.[14] Furthermore, since the demographic purpose of marriage is to assure the reproduction of society, areas of high mortality tend to put considerable pressure on women's nuptiality. In other words, the demographic context, and more specifically mortality, works at two levels, one of which is linked to the economic and social aspects of marriage, and the other to the demographic reproduction of society as a whole.

Economic and social structures should also have a very important influence on marriage. The relative availability of land, the dependence or not of young couples on inheritance and land for income, the importance of employment for delaying or enhancing marriage, etc. are all a part of this context. Conversely, economic conjunctures should also affect marriage patterns, though here the causal mechanisms have yet to be fully explained. Finally, social and cultural aspects also play an important role in conditioning marriage patterns. The acceptability or not of marriage between different age groups or social classes can be a key aspect of the relative flexibility of the marriage market. Inheritance patterns should also play a key role, especially in those areas where access to land is important and depends primarily on inheritance.

All of these are mutually interdependent and, taken together, bring pressure to bear either on the availability of a mate, the ability to get married, or both. This can be schematically presented in our theoretical framework Figure 6.3. It retains many of the original ideas of both Hajnal and of Malthus, but it goes beyond their intuitions because of the systematic relation postulated between demographic and cultural factors and nuptiality itself. We have used a path structure in order to convey the fact that when getting married people only reacted indirectly to these contextual factors. They got married because they were able to marry the 'right' person, yet their choices were strongly influenced by factors which were well beyond their control. This type of situation was not formally a part of either Hajnal's or Malthus's explanation of marriage, though both clearly intuited it.

In attempting to explain the basic regional patterns of nuptiality in Spain

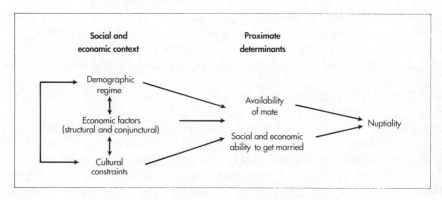

Fig. 6.3 Social and economic influences on nuptiality: a model

other authors have used a similar explanatory framework, based on the original postulates of Hajnal, but with differing emphases. For Vicente Pérez-Moreda (1986) adult mortality, inheritance systems, and peasant economies provide the key to explaining the fact that during the eighteenth century, age at marriage in the central part of Spain was far lower than in the northern areas, where mortality levels had traditionally been considerably lower. His emphasis on the role of mortality contrasts with Robert Rowland's insistence on inserting 'marriage systems' on the Iberian Peninsula within the context of the prevailing 'family systems', much along the lines taken by Hajnal in his 1982 paper. Access to marriage was strictly dependent on prevailing household formation dynamics, parental authority, and inheritance practices. For Rowland more than for Pérez Moreda, cultural factors played a key role in determining whether, when, and who young people married. It is interesting to note that the emphasis on demographic constraints by Pérez Moreda, and on culture by Rowland, places their explanations of marriage patterns at odds, at least apparently, with Malthus, for whom specifically economic factors such as access to land, population densities, and living standards were the key to the preventive check.

The only attempt to test empirically the validity of the explanatory frameworks mentioned above was carried out on census data by means of ecological models designed to explain variation in provincial or district-level male and female marriage patterns in Spain between 1887 and 1930 (Reher, 1991a). Indicators of both marriage timing (SMAM) and intensity (permanent celibacy) were used as dependent variables in two different multiple regression analyses, one based on the 476 provincial districts contained in the 1887 census, and the other pooling data for provinces over five census periods. For these models attempts were made to compile indicators for the different economic, cultural, and demographic constraints which were mentioned earlier.[15] The availability of partners (marriage market) was represented by the sex ratio at marriageable ages. The performance of the models was acceptable, suggesting that despite evident flaws the models are pertinent: levels of variance explained were fairly high and the independent variables often had a statistically significant and expected effect on marriage parameters.[16]

On the whole, they tend to confirm a number of the traditional theories regarding nuptiality. The existence of economic constraints on marriage has received very strong support from the Spanish data, suggesting that economic structures were of singular importance in determining when and how often young people got married. These, however, were only one of the social constraints which conditioned what young couples likely felt was their own personal decision. Cultural and demographic realities, as well as the sheer weight of numbers, were just as important for marriage, if not more.

The ideal scenario for intense nuptiality was a high-pressure demographic regime (high mortality), partible inheritance practices, a balanced marriage market, moderate levels of out-migration affecting both sexes, low levels of adult population density, and an active population which contained high proportions of professions which facilitated marriage. Many of these traits were characteristic of parts of the central meseta and of the eastern coastal regions of Spain, and these had the highest levels of nuptiality. Restricted patterns occurred where inheritance was not fully partible, mortality was low, and where there were high levels of male out-migration and women did not migrate. All of these were prototypical of northern Spain. Within our original theoretical formulation of the question, all of these factors acted upon the availability of a mate or on people's social and economic 'ability' to get married. In other words, they are only indirect determinants of nuptiality levels.

Of considerable interest is the fact that the proposed model proved to be more valuable within some contexts than others. It was more convincing for women than for men, and more accurate when explaining celibacy than age at marriage. The very nature of the model helps explain some of these differences. The framework used in Reher (1991a) picked up a number of structural indicators fairly well, but it was singularly lacking in conjunctural variables and in estimates of living standards. The fact that nuptiality was responsive to economic constraints unrelated to structures is an essential part of both Malthus's and Hajnal's theories of nuptiality. Equally important were people's economic expectations for marriage, especially when they are understood within the general context of prevailing living standards. None of the indicators used in models has been able to express these constraints.

In the long run, ecological models always end up being somewhat dissatisfying. Basically there are two reasons for this. For one, finding adequate indicators to represent the real forces affecting marriage choice is fraught with difficulties. The demographic constraints we spoke of are not adequately summarized in the crude death rate; the world of economic factors is far more than the presence of female servants; cultural norms are only very distantly mirrored in modes of inheritance; and the flexibility and complexity of the marriage market is only poorly represented by the sex ratio. The second reason for this is that change is absent from most cross-sectional models; and even when some indicator for change is included, these sorts of models are never able to reflect adequately the dynamics of nuptiality change.

What about those medium- and long-term swings in nuptiality which probably characterized nuptiality everywhere? Explaining them was essential for Malthus, who considered the preventive check to be the linchpin of demographic regulation in those areas characterized by 'moral restraint'. He felt that swings in nuptiality were closely tied to economic conditions: when they were good people married more and earlier, and when they were bad marriage was delayed or even forgone. Is there any way to marshal empirical proof of these patterns in historic Spain?

In recent years, the problem has been approached from two different angles. Studies in short-term fluctuations of prices and vital events in Spain and in the rest of Europe have shown that detrended fluctuations in marriages and prices were negatively and normally significantly correlated at lag 0 and, somewhat less so, at lag 1.[17] The pattern observed was fundamentally the same when using regional rural samples (Pérez Moreda, 1988: 98) or urban ones (Reher, 1990a: 137–43). These short-term economic fluctuations probably influenced timing almost exclusively, as people tended to delay their marriage in times of economic difficulties.

Earlier we presented data based on a sample of parishes from New Castile in which the long-term swings in nuptiality could be followed for nearly 300 years. Graphing this series alongside an estimate of real wages for the region over the same period suggests that the ties between nuptiality and economic conditions postulated by Malthus were a reality in pre-industrial Castile (Figure 6.4).[18] Before the second decade of the nineteenth century, the consonance between both series is evident: times of rising real wages tended to be accompanied by rising marriage rates, and vice versa. Between 1810 and 1845, the opposite seems to hold true, though this may be due to the doubtful reliability of the data mentioned earlier. After 1845, however, similar trends in both series are once again noteworthy. The positive relationship between nuptiality and real wages is also visible in the scatter plot in Figure 6.5. The correlation between both series is a robust 0.555. While the fit between both series is not perfect, the similarity is striking.

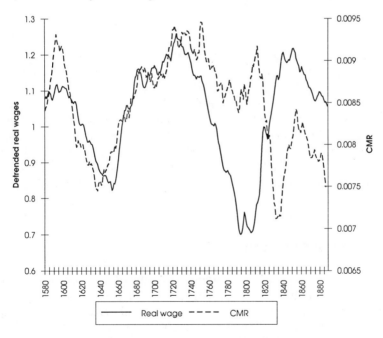

Fig. 6.4 Nuptiality and detrended real wages in New Castile, 1580–1810 (25-year moving average)

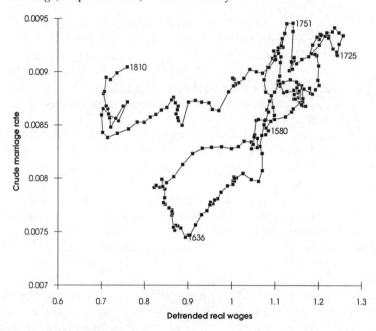

Fig. 6.5 Scatter plot of CMR and detrended real wages in sample of New Castile, 1580–1810 (25-year moving average)

Making generalizations from these sorts of data is always dangerous, though it is difficult not to make a case for the preventive check existing in New Castile throughout much of the pre-industrial period. Real wages, themselves tied to relative levels of population density, seemed to condition marriage swings which, in turn, have been shown to have a decided effect on birth rates. Emphasizing the long-term flexibility of nuptiality, its sensitivity to economic conditions, and its ability to dictate overall fertility levels within a southern European context, characterized by fairly low living standards and high levels of nuptiality, is not a common practice.[19] Perhaps the time has come to recognize that Malthus's preventive check was alive, well, and remarkably effective in pre-industrial Spain.

Reproduction and Reproductive Behaviour

Until very recently assuring demographic reproduction was one of the central functions of all families. The time and effort dedicated to this depended on prevailing levels of fertility and mortality. When both were high, women spent a good part of their lives bearing and rearing children. Since having children was central to the strategies of all families, it was of vital importance to assure reproduction even if this was done so at the expense of other activities. One of the most important by-products of the demographic transition was that the number of childbirths necessary to meet family and societal expectations, as well as the time spent having them, diminished sharply. Before the onset of irreversible fertility and mortality decline, however, there is no reason to expect that levels of fertility and mortality remained stable, or that the relative position of one to the other remained the same.

Delving into some of the questions surrounding fertility before, during, and after the demographic transition is the central theme of this section. Results stemming from local studies and estimates taken from vital registration and census material will be used in an effort to reconstruct the timing and intensity of fertility change over the past three centuries. Explanatory frameworks of fertility transition in Spain will be evaluated, as will some of the implications of more recent changes in childbearing over the past 30 years. What will emerge is a pattern familiar to European historical demographers, sociologists, and economists, in which families, and women, were able to achieve reproductive goals with decreasing amounts of time and energy, thus freeing them for other types of activity. Evaluating the timing and intensity of these changes is central to our study of the family in Spain.

Fertility Before and During the Demographic Transition

Earlier in this chapter, we presented the crude birth rate for a sizeable sample of parishes from New Castile based on a best estimate of population derived by projecting series of births subjected to certain levels and age patterns of mortality. The results suggested that birth rates were high in the late sixteenth century (near 44 per thousand), declined sharply and reached a low point around 1640 (35 per thousand), then gradually increased over the rest of the century (Figures 6.2 and 6.6). This trend continued but at a slower pace throughout much of the eighteenth century. Levels of fertility were fairly high (above 40 per thousand) but showed no long-term trends over the first half of the nineteenth century, after which they seem to decline. Three other studies make use of regional samples of time series and attempt to estimate long-term fertility trends by applying the method of inverse projection to vital series.[20] The one whose results are most directly comparable to our own was carried out for a sample of Valencian parishes and suggests that birth rates there were slightly higher than in New Castile, but that long-term trends were not dissimilar, with fertility being lower in the seventeenth than it was in the eighteenth or the first half of the nineteenth centuries (Ardit, 1991: 39–40). The estimates derived from these methods afford a useful, albeit approximate, assessment of long-term swings in crude birth rates. At present it is impossible to know whether or not these trends in overall fertility witnessed in New Castile and Valencia were also experienced in other areas of the peninsula.

Following trends in marital fertility once again makes the use of indirect estimation techniques inevitable.[21] In a recent paper, Livi Bacci and Reher

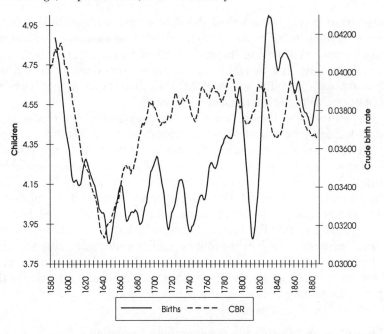

Fig. 6.6 Crude birth rate and estimate of mean number of children per marriage for sample of New Castile (25-year moving average)

have proposed a method based on long series of vital statistics which basically estimates the mean number of children per marriage by applying a standard marital fertility schedule to the marriages likely to result in a birth in a given year (i.e. marriages celebrated in that year and in the 24 preceding years), and then relating this number of 'hypothetical' births to actual births.[22] The results can be found in Figure 6.6 suggest the following general conclusions: (1) The long-range trend in marital fertility reaches a level near 4.75 children per marriage during the sixteenth century and again during the nineteenth, as opposed to periods of low fertility between 1640 and 1750. (2) These estimates of fertility are roughly in line with those found in other studies using family reconstitution methods and based on parishes in New Castile.[23] (3) The long-term trends and the medium-term fluctuations of both crude birth rates and children per marriage are closely related (notice the coincidence of most peaks and troughs in both series). (4) The periods of discrepancy observed in the two series (especially between 1715 and 1750 and again between 1825 and 1850), as well as the pronounced rise in marital fertility at the end of the eighteenth century, help explain those imperfect fits between crude marriage and crude birth rates which appeared in Figure 6.2 earlier in the chapter. A considerable part of the observed variance in the crude birth rates can be explained by fluctuations in nuptiality and in marital fertility.[24]

Some years ago, Massimo Livi Bacci (1968) identified the probable existence of an incipient but modest decline in marital fertility in most of the peninsula between 1787 and 1860. While his hypothesis has received support in some monographs, especially those centred on the north-eastern part of Spain, in most parts of the country we know very little about fertility trends during that period. During the second half of the nineteenth century, when census and vital registration information enable us to estimate some standard indicators of marital fertility (I_g, for example), available data suggest that with the exception of Catalonia,[25] the trend toward lower fertility identified by Livi Bacci for the earlier period came to a halt and was even reversed in some areas of the country (Table 6.4).[26] This period of stability proved to be the threshold of the demographic transition in much of Spain, and by 1910 marital fertility levels were declining in most of the country (Arango, 1980; Pérez Moreda, 1985a, 1985b; Livi Bacci 1988). Overall fertility (crude birth rates or I_f) followed a somewhat different course. After 1860, there was a perceptible decline which accelerated after 1900. Before the early part of this century, the continuing decline in nuptiality explains reductions in birth rates despite stable or even rising levels of marital fertility. After 1900–10, however, both trends in nuptiality and in marital fertility teamed up to accelerate reductions in birth rates.

Much as occurred with nuptiality, on the eve of the demographic transition there was marked regional variation in marital fertility. In 1787 the areas of highest fertility were those located in the northern 'meseta' (Old Castile, León) extending all the way to the northern coastal areas (with the exception of Galicia), together with Catalonia (Livi Bacci, 1968: 228). The limited number of studies based on family reconstitution suggest that at least in certain regions these fertility differences may have been long-standing.[27] This

Table 6.4 Fertility levels in Spain, 1860–1980

Year	Crude birth rate	I_f	I_g
1860	38.6	0.396	0.654*
1887	37.2	0.391	0.650
1900	36.4	0.383	0.653
1910	32.9	0.356	0.623
1920	30.4	0.314	0.586
1930	27.9	0.291	0.540
1940	22.4	0.208	0.464
1950	21.2	0.203	0.419
1960	21.4	0.228	0.403
1970	19.4	0.229	0.365
1980	15.2	0.177	0.282

* The sex, age, and marital status missing in the 1860 census has been estimated by simple interpolation.

Source: Coale and Watkins (1986: 144); Spanish census and vital registration material.

regional pattern, however, changed substantially during the course of the nineteenth century. In 1887, while the northern areas of the peninsula (with the exception of Galicia) continued to be characterized by high levels of marital fertility, Catalonia was now the area with lowest fertility, followed at a considerable distance by the Balearic Islands and Andalusia (Map 6.13). As late as 1930, the northern part of the peninsula continued to be one of relatively high levels of marital fertility, with low levels being concentrated in eastern and, to a lesser extent, southern parts of the country and the area surrounding Madrid (Arango, 1987: 214–16).

The reason for these changing patterns lies in the varied chronology and intensity of the demographic transition on the peninsula. These patterns are eloquently expressed in Map 6.14, where the date of the onset of irreversible fertility decline in Spanish provinces is charted.[28] Catalonia led the way towards fertility control in Spain. There are numerous indications that gradual declines in fertility were already being experienced by the central decades of the nineteenth century. By 1900 these rates of decline had increased sharply, though by that date other provinces in the eastern part of the country together with Madrid were following Catalonia's lead. Quite the contrary occurred in the provinces of the northern plains and coastal areas, which had also undergone some modest fertility decline between 1787 and 1860. The 1880–1910 period was characterized by unchanging or rising levels of marital fertility. For many of these areas fertility transition did not set in until after 1920 or, in some cases, even after the Civil War (1936–9). Since these had been high-fertility areas in 1887, by 1930 provincial disparities in marital fertility were greater than they ever had been before. Only after that date did fertility behaviour tend to become more uniform throughout the country, much as occurred in most of Europe during this period (Watkins, 1991).

The regional distribution of overall fertility in Spain was substantially different from that of marital fertility (Map 6.15). In 1887, areas of low birth rates were centred in the northern parts of the peninsula, while they were high in the central and southern areas. In the north-eastern parts of the country this appears to have been the result of incipient fertility transition. Elsewhere these regional configurations were basically caused by the prevailing marriage patterns. In fact the map of overall fertility is much more similar to that of female nuptiality than it is to that of marital fertility. This only began to change after 1920 or 1930, when the traditional role of nuptiality as the great regulator of reproduction began to weaken.[29]

All attempts to identify the correlates of marital fertility and its decline have ended up emphasizing the fact that any explanatory framework for fertility behaviour must necessarily account for the great social, economic, and cultural variety existing in Spain.[30] Many of the traditional cultural, economic, or ecological variables which have been proposed within general models of the demographic transition as key factors for fertility decline in Spain, when confronted with empirical data, have tended to leave much to be desired. Only

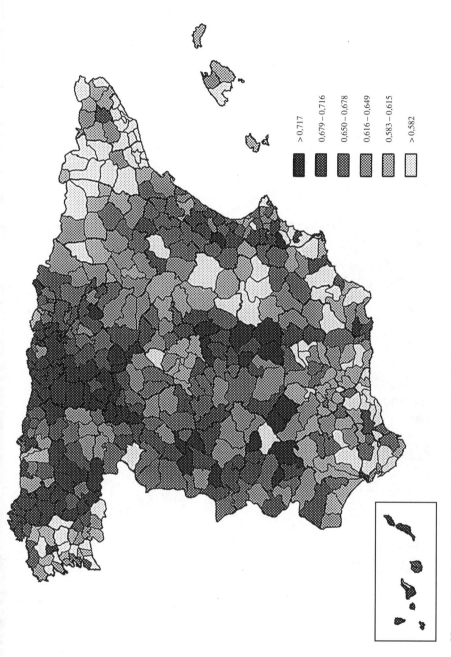

Map 6.13   Marital fertility (I_g) by judicial district, 1887

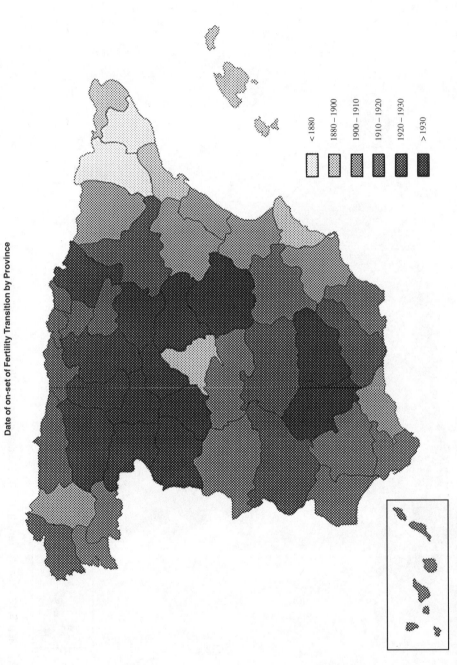

Date of on-set of Fertility Transition by Province

< 1880

1880 – 1900

1900 – 1910

1910 – 1920

1920 – 1930

> 1930

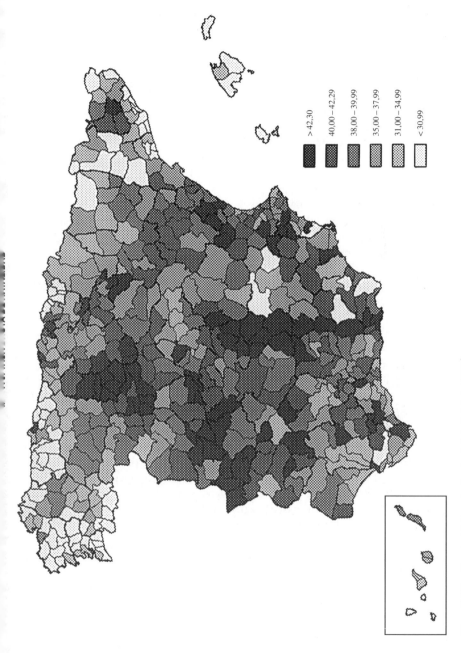

Map 6.15   Crude birth rate by judicial district, 1887

> 42,30
40,00 – 42,29
38,00 – 39,99
35,00 – 37,99
31,00 – 34,99
< 30,99

the influence of mortality has ended up being fully validated by the historical record: nowhere in Spain did fertility decline take place without there being a prior or at least a simultaneous decline in mortality. In most regions, significant mortality improvement, especially during the early stages of life, pre-dated the initial stages of fertility decline by several years.[31] Nuptiality as well seems to have had a statistically significant relationship with levels and change of marital fertility. Areas of low fertility and of rapid fertility decline were those in which mortality was low and falling, and female nuptiality was intense. Within these contexts, fertility control within marriage was used earlier and more extensively than in other areas.

Economic and cultural variables have fared rather more poorly. Multiple regression analysis has revealed that the effect of literacy on fertility was counter-intuitive: even controlling for several other variables, fertility levels tended to be higher and decline later in those areas in which literacy was highest (Reher and Iriso Napal, 1989: 417–25). This was probably due to the fact that during the initial stages of the demographic transition, literacy levels were more a proxy for traditional values (strong numerical presence of the clergy, small settlements and small farms, and traditional resistance to 'liberal' ideas) than they were a sign of modernization.[32] Urbanization and different variables representing economic structures have also proved to be ineffective in explaining fertility.

With the possible exception of Barcelona, it is noteworthy that fertility did not seem to decline in towns at an earlier or a faster pace than in their adjacent rural areas. Between 1860 and 1930 urban marital fertility was consistently between 8 and 10 per cent below levels holding in rural areas; and the urban/rural divergence in crude birth rates was still greater (22 per cent) due to the influence of more reduced nuptiality in urban areas (Reher, 1990b: 289; 1993: 40). If only towns of 30,000 inhabitants or more are used, the urban/rural differences in marital fertility increase to 13 per cent (Livi Bacci, 1988: 151). This pattern is not unlike that which has been observed in other countries of southern Europe, especially Portugal and Italy during the same period (Livi Bacci, 1971, 1977). Yet between 1887 and 1920 fertility decline was about the same in both contexts. It has been suggested that the role played by rural–urban migration flows was essential for this because the ever-greater numbers of people from high-fertility and increasingly distant rural environments in urban settings might well have ended up slowing the pace of aggregate fertility change in towns (Iriso Napal and Reher, 1987: 90–1, 94–5). Nevertheless the available evidence suggests that the traditional pioneering role attributed to towns during the demographic transition may not be entirely warranted in the case of Spain. Once fertility decline had begun in both areas, however, it did appear to fall faster in towns in their adjacent rural areas (Arango, 1980; Sharlin, 1986: 257–60; Reher and Iriso Napal, 1989: 425).

Despite our inability to reach satisfactory explanations of fertility decline in Spain, the demographic transition did occur. We can only suggest the potential influence of some key factors in attempting to explain this key historical event. Mortality reduction was unquestionably essential for fertility decline, as was the influence of Barcelona, the most economically dynamic and open city in the entire country. Some years ago Joaquin Arango (1980) proposed an explanatory framework for the demographic transition which emphasized the great importance of Barcelona as a catalyst for both economic development and the diffusion of the new ideas which sanctioned fertility control within marriage. Within this context, it is probably not surprising that fertility decline seems to have occurred first in Barcelona and its immediate area, then spread to the rest of Catalonia, and from there to the other regions along the eastern part of the country. Despite the fact that it does not do justice to the complexity of the process of demographic transition, his explanation is attractive because it tracks well the spread of fertility control practices in Spain.

Recent Trends in Fertility: Towards a Second Demographic Transition

Since the Civil War, Spanish fertility has followed a relatively straightforward pattern. Sharp declines in the 1930s, culminating in the drastic drop during the war, were followed by unstable levels during the 1940s, relatively high fertility between 1955 and 1975, and a pronounced decline in recent years (Figure 6.7).[33] During the decade of the 1920s and especially up until 1936 the pace of

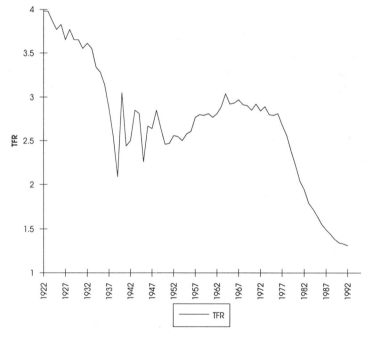

Fig. 6.7 Total fertility rate in Spain, 1922–1992

fertility decline was accelerating sharply mainly because some measure of fertility limitation was now being practised almost everywhere. During the Civil War itself spousal separation, economic deprivation, and war-induced suffering teamed up to reduce fertility to a level which was not to be reached again for over 40 years. Immediately after the war, despite economic and political hardship, fertility rebounded substantially as families were once again united. It is difficult to pinpoint a trend during the decade of the 1940s, but by the early part of the 1950s fertility was at its lowest non-wartime level ever. The traditional cycle of the demographic transition which had begun in the late nineteenth century seems to have drawn to a close during those years.

Depending on the indicator used, during the 15–20 year period after 1955 there was either an increase or a levelling off of fertility.[34] In either case, however, the reversal of the trend is in itself very significant. Between 1950 and 1967, total fertility rates increased by almost 20 per cent, and even in 1975, when fertility had begun to decline once again, total fertility rates (TFR) were still 12.5 per cent above what they had been 25 years earlier (Table 6.4). Since there does not seem to have been much increase in marital fertility over the period, these changes were probably due almost entirely to increases in nuptiality. Cumulative age-specific marriage rates in 1967 were 17.8 per cent above the levels holding during the early part of the 1950s (Muñoz Pérez, 1987: 940). By 1975, however, despite the fact that marriage rates continued to accelerate (26.8 per cent above 1950 levels), overall fertility had begun to decline, thus indicating that declines in marital fertility were instrumental in ending the boom in Spanish fertility. Even though the changes in fertility during the 1950s and 1960s in Spain were not as great as those occurring in the United States or some other European countries, the change in long-term trends is striking and warrants further research. The role played by improving living standards, especially during the 1960s, was probably essential for stimulating nuptiality and ultimately fertility, within the context of a Spanish society which was still largely traditional.

Much as occurred in most of Europe, the Spanish baby boom came to a shattering and sudden close. After 1975 fertility declined at a far faster rate than had ever been experienced during the demographic transition, with the result that by the most recent tabulation, Spain now has one of the lowest fertility rates in the world. Total fertility rates, which during the mid-1970s had been around 2.8, were at 2.0 in 1981 and by the most recent estimation (1992) hover around 1.31. If cohort fertility is estimated, it becomes clear that until now no cohort in Spain has ever experienced below-replacement fertility (Fernández Cordón, 1987). Nevertheless should this trend in period fertility (TFR) continue, in the near future extremely low fertility and negative population growth rates will be a commonplace experience in Spain.

During this second demographic transition, both nuptiality and marital fertility made decisive contributions to declining fertility. The marriage boom of the 1950s and 1960s turned into the marriage bust after 1975, as cumulative marriage rates declined by 39 per cent in 10 years (Muñoz Pérez, 1987: 940). Fertility within marriage also underwent severe reductions as desired family size declined substantially (Hicks and Martínez-Aguado, 1987). An important aspect of this transition has been that the age pattern of fertility has changed substantially. During the early years of this century, the greatest declines in fertility took place in higher age groups as parity-specific fertility measures were implemented. The increases in fertility so characteristic of the 1950s and 1960s were most visible in the prime childbearing ages, and especially between 20 and 29 years of age. The recent decline in fertility originally affected all age groups, but after 1980 has concentrated its effects among the 20–29 year old women. According to the most recent available data, fertility decline in women over 30 has halted and in some areas it has even been reversed, whereas it continues among the younger women. The result of this is that right now there is clear evidence that the average age of childbearing in Spain is increasing as women who have postponed marriage and reproduction until a later period in life begin to have children.

A period of political and social transformation coupled with the ever-increasing presence of women on the labour market paved the way for a reduction in fertility whose relative intensity is unparallelled in Spanish history. Is it a 'second demographic transition' as some have suggested? It might be more useful to consider it another stage of an original demographic transition of Spanish society which began over 100 years ago, has been characterized by periods of decline and recovery, and which certainly does not seem to have concluded. Just how long fertility decline will continue is only a matter of speculation, but the fact that presently fertility is stable or even rising among certain groups in the population may well be an indication that the recent period of declining fertility is drawing to a close (Cabré and Pujadas, 1987).

Demographic Change and the Family

It is difficult to overestimate the importance for families and for domestic co-residential units of the demographic patterns discussed in these past few chapters. They had implications for kin networks, patterns of socialization, the number and age distribution of kin living in the household, inheritance and other forms of property devolution, and family economies. Over the period under study, this key constraint on family development underwent momentous changes which ended up altering the institution of the family itself. One of the central themes of this book is precisely to chart this relationship during the nineteenth and twentieth centuries in Spain. In ending these chapters on family demography, however, I would like to give one very straightforward example of the effects of demographic transformation on the co-residential domestic unit which will help sum up many of the points contained in them.

From the standpoint of the family development cycle, especially in its key reproductive function, nuptiality, fertility, and mortality levels had very direct implications for the number and age distribution of the children present in the household. In order to show this, I have estimated the mean number of children living in two-parent households in which the mother was between 30 and 34 years of age. This age group was chosen because at that age it is unlikely that many of the children had left their parental household via migration. Thus, the example brings out the net demographic effects more clearly: those offspring present were exclusively the product of the age at which the union had begun (marriage), the number of childbirths, and the survival probabilities of young children born.[35]

The results for differing periods stretching from the eighteenth century to 1970 can be seen in Figure 6.8. The mean number of children present in the household was low before 1900. Afterwards the number of children present was much higher until 1940, and dropped sharply in the subsequent decades. In 1970 it was by far the lowest of the entire period. This example brings out the implications of the demographic transition quite clearly. During the pre-transitional period, despite fairly high fertility, the total number of children present was fairly low due mainly to very high levels of infant and childhood mortality. As the nineteenth century progressed, infant and child-

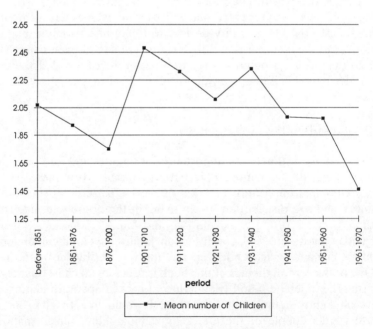

Fig. 6.8 Mean number of children (<15) in two-parent households with mother 30–34, Cuenca

hood mortality levels worsened, fertility was stable, and age at marriage increased, the number of children present in the household declined to its lowest point.

This entire situation underwent a dramatic change during the final years of the nineteenth century and the initial years of the twentieth as infant and childhood mortality began its decisive transition toward lower levels. In New Castile mortality began to decline toward the latter part of the nineteenth century, with childhood mortality leading the way and infant mortality following shortly thereafter. From the standpoint of the family, continuing restrictions on nuptiality within a context in which fertility was still high, and mortality falling, led to greater numbers of young children present within the household.[36] After that point, the number of children present gradually declined, though it remained high until after the Civil War. Continuing increases in age at marriage and small reductions in fertility were gradually beginning to reverse the effects of declining mortality. Only after 1940, however, did the number of children present in the household return to low levels, and a sharp break with the past is only visible in 1970, when the mean number of children was by far the lowest of the entire period.[37] Despite accelerating nuptiality, by the 1950s and 1960s low fertility was leading to reduced numbers of children at home.

This example has been drawn from my Cuenca data set, where fertility decline was modest and relatively late (after 1930–40). However, the same model could have been applied anyplace else in Spain and the results would have been similar, though the timing might be substantially different. During the pre-transitional period, high mortality kept numbers of children at home relatively low. Since the demographic transition was normally a two-part process, with mortality declining earlier and more sharply than fertility, it had a two-step effect on families. For a more or less prolonged period, the number of young children at home increased sharply. These were not necessarily good times for rural families as the number of dependent children grew within a context of increasing population densities and diminishing economic opportunities. Families normally used out-migration as a compensatory mechanism during these periods of adjustment, which may have been more or less prolonged in different areas of the country depending on the timing of fertility and mortality decline. When the children were young, however, this was normally not an option. The effect for family economies of increases of up to one-third of young people at home was probably substantial.[38]

Ultimately, however, fertility did decline as fast or faster than mortality and the number of young children at home declined as well. The drastic reduction visible in 1970 has undoubtedly continued to the present, as fertility decline accelerated in the course of its second transition in Spain. The result has been that the duration of women's reproductive period has been shortened and the number of young children at home has diminished, as has the time parents spend in households with young children. The economic and social repercussions of this have been enormous, every bit as important as those of the original demographic transition.

Notes

1. For more on this, see Wrigley and Schofield (1981: 459–60).
2. Here Smith's line of argument follows the innovative work of Ron Lesthaeghe (1980) in its tendency to understand demographic phenomena in a holistic fashion within given social and cultural contexts.
3. See also Pérez Moreda and Reher (1985). Wrigley (1981) felt that the study of nuptiality was one of the key tasks for historical demography during the present decade. Now, in the mid-1990s, it is difficult to be optimistic about the success with which this challenge has been met within our discipline.
4. The most comprehensive summary of these studies can be found in Rowland (1988: 90–4). See also Pérez Moreda (1986) and Valero Lobo (1984).
5. For a complete description of the data base and of the method used in calculating the 'most likely' population, which differs substantially from the inverse projection method pioneered by Lee (1974, 1985, 1993) and currently popularized thanks to a PC software program designed by McCaa and Pérez Brignoli (1985) and McCaa (1993), see Reher (1991*b*) and Livi Bacci and Reher (1993: 66–70).
6. The period between 1820 and 1840 is puzzling because I have not been able to corroborate the drastic decline in marriages, which is concentrated in a very few years between 1824 and 1834, by any independent means. I suspect that during these years there may be problems with the data, as marriages may not have been fully registered in parishes during a time of great political and social upheaval. The results for these years, then, are subject to considerable doubt.
7. When there is some discrepancy between the two series it can either be explained by fluctuations in marital fertility (Livi Bacci and Reher, 1993: 76) or may be the result of possible data deficiencies (1825–1845). The correlation between both series is 0.580.
8. The agreement between both series is still closer than it is in England (Wrigley and Schofield, 1981).
9. All estimates of age at marriage used in this article refer to the Singulate Mean Age at Marriage (SMAM), which is based on census distributions by sex, age, and marital status. The original formulation of SMAM can be found in Hajnal (1953).
10. This can also be seen in Watkins (1986: 320–1). I_m is a census-based index of marital intensity among women which originally was designed by Ansley Coale within the context of the Princeton European Fertility Project. By controlling for the age structure of natural fertility among Hutterite women, I_m measures the potential contribution of nuptiality to overall fertility. For a discussion of I_m, see Coale and Treadway (1986: 33–5). For the importance of a regionalization of marriage patterns in Europe, see Watkins (1986, 1991).
11. I_m values in towns were between 14 and 23 per cent below those holding in their surrounding rural areas, and permanent celibacy tended to be nearly twice as high (Reher, 1989; 1990*b*: 286–7). Differences in the intensity of marriage were far greater than in its timing: celibacy was often twice as high in towns as in their rural hinterlands, while age at marriage tended to be only slightly higher.

12. For the purpose of the maps, and for our subsequent statistical analysis, celibacy has been measured as the percentage of celibates between 46 and 50 years of age, while timing has been taken to be the singulate mean age of marriage (SMAM).
13. See also Poppel (1992: 209–74).
14. Livi Bacci (1978) has suggested that life expectancy and nuptiality were linked and that over the long course of European history, age at marriage probably ended up adjusting to the levels of life expectancy at the mean age of parenthood.
15. As often happens in these sorts of models, our success at this was only partial. Percentage of female servants and population density, prevailing inheritance practices, and the crude death rate served as proxies for economic, cultural, and demographic constraints.
16. R square was near or above 0.5 in most cases.
17. On this point see Galloway (1988: appendix, table 1) and Weir (1984: 38, 42, 45–7). The bibliography on the links between yearly fluctuations in marriages and economic conditions is now quite formidable. On this point, see, for example: Lee (1981) for England; Weir (1984) and Galloway (1986) for France; Pérez Moreda (1988), Reher (1990a: 143–8), and Lanza (1991) for Spain; Bengtsson (1984) for Sweden; and Reher (1992) for Mexico. For overviews of all of Europe, see Galloway (1988, 1992, 1993). Concerning the long-term links between economic conditions and nuptiality see, especially, Wrigley and Schofield (1981).
18. The real-wage series is based on an adaptation of E. Hamilton's (1934, 1947) original data, together with new data taken from the archives of Madrid (Reher and Ballesteros-Doncel, 1993). These data have been detrended by dividing the 25-year moving average by its secular trend line.
19. This view is quite different from the one I held some years ago. See, for example, Pérez Moreda and Reher (1985: 321–2).
20. All of these are contained in a single issue of the Boletín de la Asociación de Demografía Histórica. See Ardit (1991), Macías-Hernández (1991), Muñoz Pradas (1991). On this same subject, see also Del Panta (1991).
21. Despite the wealth of data regarding marital fertility provided by family reconstitutions, small sample sizes and their corollary of extended time periods used in most of the existing studies make it notoriously difficult to pinpoint the timing of long-term trend changes with them.
22. For further details of this technique, see Livi Bacci and Reher (1993: 76–7, 83). See also Livi Bacci (1977b).
23. For family reconstitution studies based in New Castile, see Soler Serratosa (1985) (Los Molinos); Reher (1990a: 90–8) (Cuenca); and Gómez-Cabrero Ortiz and Fernández de la Iglesia (1991: 75–80) (Mocejón).
24. A multiple regression exercise using crude birth rates as the dependent variable, and crude marriage rates and our estimate of marital fertility as independent variables, yields very significant regression coefficients for both variables and high levels of explained variance.
25. Two excellent recent studies have approached the early decline of marital fertility in Catalonia from different but complementary perspectives. See Muñoz Pradas (1990) and Torrents (1993). See also Cabré and Torrents (1991).
26. Some scholars feel that the rise in marital fertility may well have been the product of improving registration rather than of increased marital fertility. In my opinion,

the widespread nature of this pattern, visible in other European nations as well, suggests that the rise, or at least the stability, of marital fertility was real.

27. If we use the total marital fertility ratio for women married between 20 and 24 years of age as an indicator (based on cumulative fertility multiplied by 5 for the 25–49 age group), general levels for a small sample of studies suggest that fertility in Galicia (TMFR = 4.9) was somewhat lower than in New Castile (TMFR = 5.7) or Valencia (5.6), which in turn were slightly lower than in Extremadura (6.1), Old Castile (above 6.0), and 18th-century Catalonia (6.2). Considering the small number of family reconstitutions which have actually been carried out, inferring too much from these data can be very misleading. See Nadal and Sáez (1972: 109); Barreiro Mallón (1973: 196); Pérez García (1979: table 4.19); Rodríguez Cancho (1981: 216); Poza Martín (1985: 43–4); Soler Serratosa (1985); Reher (1990a: 96); Sánchis Avalos and Madril Muñoz (1990: 78); and Gómez-Cabrero Ortiz and Fernández de la Iglesia (1991).

28. These data are taken from the Princeton Fertility Project, as is the definition of 'irreversible decline': a decline of over 10 per cent in I_g over a 10-year period, with no subsequent increase in fertility. See Coale and Watkins (1986: map 2.1).

29. If we carry out cross-sectional regression analyses with crude birth rates or I_f as a dependent variable and marital fertility (I_g) and female nuptiality (I_m) as independent variables, before 1920 the standardized regression coefficients and their significance are markedly higher for I_m than for I_g. If, however, the same analysis is done on the judicial districts of Catalonia in 1887, the results are just the opposite: marital fertility explains district-level variation in overall fertility more than does female nuptiality.

30. Among the most relevant of these attempts, see Leasure (1963), Díez Nicolás (1971), Arango (1980), Livi Bacci (1988), and Reher and Iriso (1989). See also Cabré (1989), Nicolau Nos (1991).

31. This was the case in Catalonia, where recent studies have suggested that there were reductions in non-crisis mortality which were visible during much of the second half of the 18th century and became especially strong between 1817 and mid-century (Muñoz Pradas, 1991: 80–4).

32. In 1887, the district-level distribution of settlement size and numerical presence of the clergy is very similar to that of literacy (Reher, 1993: 57–63).

33. Tracking fertility trends in recent years is greatly facilitated by the fact that in 1922 the Spanish vital registration statistics begin to include childbirths by age of mother. This enables us to estimate age-specific fertility rates which are considerably more useful than ones available for earlier periods (crude birth rates, I_g, and I_f). Unfortunately, similar improvements do not occur with marital fertility registration, since until very recently births were not classified by age and marital status of the mother. For this reason, most of what we can say about recent fertility trends is based on overall rather than on marital fertility. For sources of data used in Figure 6.7, see Arango (1987: 219–21), Muñoz Pérez (1987: 940), and Fernández Cordón (1994a).

34. The total fertility rates and I_f increase, as opposed to crude birth rates and I_g, which remain mostly the same.

35. By including only two-parent households in the example, the effects of changes in adult mortality on the conjugal unit will not appear.

36. The mean age of these children living in conjugal family units with mothers between 30 and 34 years of age was approximately 6 years.
37. Had we been able to prolong our sample until 1980, this number would certainly have neared 1.0.
38. This is what has occurred in many less-developed countries over the past 40 years, except that the declines in mortality for them were far faster than in Europe, and the lag in fertility response has been every bit as long or even longer. The result was significant declines in living standards in many of these countries, especially during the 1970s and 1980s.

7 Dimensions of the Marriage Market on the Eve of Modernization

Chance and Design on the Marriage Market

'*Matrimonio y mortaja, del cielo bajan*'[1] is a traditional Spanish proverb which underscores the fact that marriage, much like death, is not so much a question of design as it is one of chance. It is a popular response to the perceived vagaries of spousal selection in a world in which most marriages were not the product of pacts between families, but rather the result of the free interplay of young adults in search of what they and their families perceived to be the appropriate person. Yet we might suspect that even though a considerable degree of luck was always present, there were an abundance of social norms which tended to limit the rule of chance as much as possible. A well-functioning marriage market was the key to social and demographic reproduction as well as to the personal happiness of those directly involved; it was too important to be left simply to chance.

Yet the element of chance was also there, and playing the market was a matter of the utmost importance for both the individual and society. People were in competition with one another, especially those of the same sex, to choose and to be chosen by the desirable person. Playing the market began when the 'marriageable' ages began, when it became socially acceptable to find a spouse, and only ended either with marriage, entry into the clergy, or when the person ceased having any realistic chance of success. In addition, adult mortality led to multiple re-entries onto the market, as widows and widowers vied for a chance to marry once again. Failure meant that undesirable unions were formed or, much worse, a person was unable to marry. This last reality was a real possibility and for the most part it was an unwanted outcome for those affected.

Men and women brought with them to the market different expectations which affected the manner in which they played. Some wanted later marriage, others wanted to marry relatively earlier; some preferred locally found spouses, others did not; some had property and others did not. Competing was never simple, and it is not surprising that a successful outcome must have been viewed by all to entail a certain amount of luck. The fact that questions of supply and demand eventually came to terms with each other, and permanent celibacy was never very significant outside of certain very specific regions, is a tribute to the efficiency of the marriage market in most of Spain.

Understanding how it worked in historic contexts is notoriously difficult mainly because the available data are not normally adequate for the task. Yet it is arguably one of the more important proximate constraints on fertility and nuptiality in historical societies. Along with establishing a person's economic position, it was certainly the most important activity undertaken by most people during a significant and unique period of their lives. Despite inherent difficulties, it warrants further consideration. In this chapter I will attempt to evaluate some of the ways in which the marriage market worked in historic Spain, making use of both macro- and micro-level data. This effort will afford no more than a glimpse at certain aspects of how the market worked, but a useful glimpse none the less.

Sex Ratios and the Marriage Market

Sex ratios at marriageable ages are often used as a proxy for the marriage market. They represent the presence or absence of a given sex and, therefore, concentrate on the supply of available mates. Defined in this way and used as an explanatory variable for regional variations in marriage patterns, the sex ratio has proved to be quite useful. In those areas in which the market was severely imbalanced, due normally, but not always, to sex-specific migration flows, lack of one sex led to diminished marriage opportunities for the other. When used in regression equations the coefficients assigned to this variable are often significant.

Little work has been done in Spain on this aspect of the marriage market. Looking at census data spanning the 1887–1940 period, certain regularities can be seen. The most noticeable is that throughout the period there is a characteristic dearth of men at marriageable ages. Sex ratios of 94 in 1887 and 1900, 91 in 1920, 96 in 1930, and 88 in 1940 attest to a market dictated to a large extent by lack of men. Apart from levels in 1940, due probably to deaths and exile resulting from the Civil War, over the rest of the period overseas migration of Spanish males was the reason for their absence from these age groups.

Regional patterns of migration also explain the great range of sex ratios which can be found at any one time in Spain.[2] A close look at Map 7.1, based on the 476 judicial districts existing in 1887, gives fitting testimony of the diversity existing in the country (Reher *et al.*, 1993). This map is a proxy for what we know of several different and often conflicting migration patterns. The influence of sex-selective long-distance migration trends, which were especially intense in the 21–30 age group, is the most visible of them. There was a strong deficit of men along the entire northern coast, in the Canary Islands, and in the eastern part of Andalucia. These were areas in which male migration towards America and northern Africa was strongest.

A balanced sex ratio or an abundance of males might have been the result of limited out-migration for both sexes, male in-migration, or female out-

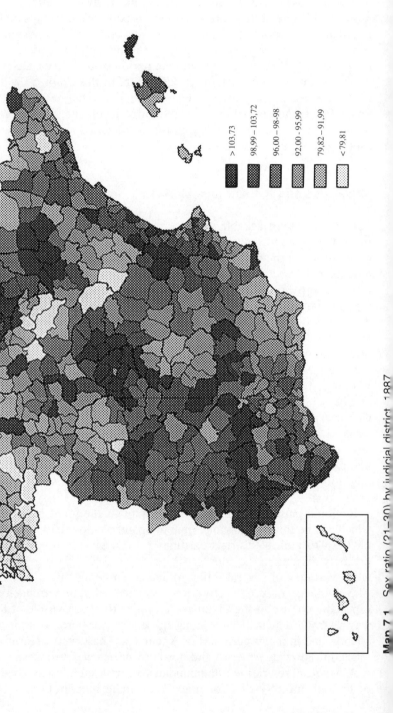

MAPA 14: MERCADO MATRIMONIAL

> 103,73

98,99 – 103,72

96,00 – 98,98

92,00 – 95,99

79,82 – 91,99

< 79,81

Map 7.1   Sex ratio (21–30) by judicial district, 1887

Table 7.1 Matrix of correlation coefficients for the marriage market in Spain, 1887–1940

	1887	1900	1920	1930	1940
1887	1.000	0.914**	0.777**	0.686**	0.287
1900		1.000	0.807**	0.766**	0.291
1920			1.000	0.751**	0.472**
1930				1.000	0.414*
1940					1.000

Note: marriage market = sex ratio between 21 and 30 (20–29 in 1940).
Significance: * < 0.01; * < 0.001.

migration. In these cases short-distance migration, often affecting both sexes, was a central factor. Examples of this can be seen in Map 7.1. Whereas the relative abundance of males around Cadiz was due to the strong presence of the military there, around Madrid it was not the presence of men but the absence of women which determined high sex ratios: the young women had left for domestic service in the capital city. In the general area around the dynamic industrial city of Barcelona, on the other hand, the intense negative net migration rates which characterized most districts affected both sexes almost equally, leaving the marriage market fairly balanced as a result.

The basic regional distribution of sex ratios changed gradually over the course of modernization in Spain (Table 7.1). Up until 1920, the areas of missing males were basically the same as they had been in 1887. This is once again related to the dynamics of overseas migration, which in Spain began in earnest during the decade of the 1880s and reached its peak just prior to World War I. Decreases in emigration and a growth in the numbers of returning migrants after that period gradually altered the regional make-up of the sex ratio in Spain. In 1940 the Civil War helped create quite a different regional pattern. Before then, however, thanks largely to relatively stable patterns of migration in most Spanish regions, the map of sex ratios remained fundamentally unaltered.

Not surprisingly, the areas in which males were in absence were also ones of restricted marriage opportunities for women. Some extreme examples from the 1887 census illustrate this point well. In four judicial districts of Galicia, between 21 and 30 years of age there were an average of 44 men for every 100 women, as opposed to three other districts taken from the central part of the country where sex ratios stood at or near 100. Where the marriage market was imbalanced, female celibacy was near 32 per cent and where it was balanced celibacy was a very low 4 per cent.[3] Similar results have been found in multiple regression equations in which low sex ratios (indicating a relative dearth of men) have been shown to increase both female age at marriage and permanent celibacy (Reher, 1991a: 21–2).

A Closer Look at the Mating Game

Ultimately, using the sex ratio to explain marriage patterns is convenient because it is easy to measure and works well as an independent variable. As a way of understanding the marriage market itself, however, it is somewhat less adequate. The presence or absence of a given sex on the marriage market is, arguably, a rather simplistic way of approaching a very complex phenomenon. The overall supply of a given sex constitutes the bottom line for any marriage market, but it only appears to be statistically relevant for nuptiality when sex ratios are severely imbalanced.[4] Otherwise the heterogeneity of supply had to satisfy an equally heterogeneous demand if the market was to function smoothly. It was not just a question of finding a mate; it was one of finding the right mate.

Under normal circumstances, the marriage market was segmented because demand, and supply, were segmented. Every player came to the market with his or her own hierarchy of priorities which had to be met before he or she was willing to marry. This situation did not differ significantly where the players' families influenced their decisions because they too had priorities and attempted to implement them as effectively as possible. Priorities might differ by social group, by sex, by residential status, by parity, by economic status, by cultural concerns, and by personal tastes. Naturally, in the long run women ended up marrying men and the basic availability of men was essential. However, for a young woman her ideal man, say, had to have land or be in line for an inheritance, live in or near the village, be between one and three years older, and, maybe, be tall and have dark eyes. Otherwise she was not interested, at least for the moment. If there were men who fulfilled those requirements, and if they proved to be compatible, then marriage was a distinct possibility. Supply of available mates enters the picture, but only when filtered through demand. There might be an abundance of young landless day labourers, or farmers who were much younger than she was, or someone ethnically different, but if they did not meet the requirements of this young lady and thus were not potential partners, she would not get married. Each sex, social and economic group, and person or family had a specific set of expectations.

Demand was, however, elastic, and people's requirements could and did change. Ultimately people were interested in a marriage, and so a less than ideal match might be deemed acceptable under certain circumstances. I believe that these 'circumstances' were basically a function of the position of each person on the marriage market, and this was determined to a large extent by age. Every society, and every social group, had its own set of ages at which most people got married. Before reaching that age, the possibility of marriage might not even enter people's considerations. Later, as marriage became an acceptable option, young people would compete on the market knowing that they had a number of years to find a mate. It was then that they could be most demanding, and when marriages were closest to the 'ideal'. People also knew, however, that past a certain age marriage was an increasingly difficult option. This was especially true for women, but affected men as well. As people grew older, they became more willing to make their requirements for marriage more flexible.

Certain dimensions of the marriage market can be identified within the context of rural, pre-industrial Spain. Some of them directly influenced the types of choice people made, and others constrained the market as a whole. In a society in which the principal reason for marriage was to guarantee demographic and social reproduction, and mortality levels were high, the age range at which women were considered desirable was far more restricted than for men. If a woman was to have, say, five or six childbirths, it was imperative that she get married at a relatively young age. Despite the fact that a woman's beauty or wealth might be far greater when she was 30 or 35 years of age, from a reproductive standpoint she was of little use. In high-pressure demographic regimes, it is almost impossible to find significant numbers of never-wed women marrying after 30 years of age. The upper limits of the marriageable ages for women only began to be pushed back somewhat when mortality began to decline and fertility limitation became widespread. For men, on the other hand, the biological clock was not nearly so restrictive and probably had little directly to do with the age at which they married. For many of these same reasons, widows were valued far less on the market than widowers, except when they were either very young or enjoyed a comfortable economic position (Pérez Moreda, 1986).

Age difference at marriage was another factor which tended to underlie the apparent comparative advantage which men seemed to enjoy on the market. Since cultural norms dictated that men should be somewhat older than women, adult mortality led, *ceteris paribus*, to male cohort sizes being somewhat smaller than women's, thus creating a relative 'abundance' of women, and leaving men a greater chance to choose partners they wanted. At a local level, however, this 'advantage' was in fact quite small because there were many ways of circumventing its effects. At a larger regional or national level, however, especially in times of rapid demographic change, cohort size might have had a significant effect on marriage possibilities.[5] The demographically and culturally induced dearth of men at marriageable ages was further complicated by the overall lack of men in Spain at the time due to the prevailing migration patterns in most regions.

It has been said that in England one of the key norms governing nuptiality was that a basic minimum living standard was considered by everybody to be essential for marriage (R. Smith, 1981). There is no reason to believe that in Spain much the same did not hold. This minimum living standard, however, was probably culturally specific and varied by country or region. More pertinent to our argument here is that it also varied by people's economic position in society. For a day labourer whose living standard depended to a large extent on his physical strength, the marriageable ages need not necessarily be the same as for peasant farmers awaiting an inheritance, or for artisans who needed to establish themselves in the non-agricultural sector. For each group, the minimum living standard necessary for marriage might well have varied and was achieved at a different point of their life cycle. It is only reasonable to suppose that their marriage patterns differed as well.

Personal choice and people's position on the market were also mediated by the family group. In many cases marriages were arranged between families, and parental consent was a necessary prerequisite for any union.[6] Even when people were free to choose the mates they desired, family strategies imposed constraints on choice. These constraints existed everywhere, but were much stronger among more well-to-do families and in areas of the country in which more or less impartible systems of inheritance prevailed. Within this context, parity, sex, and the inheritance due each member of the family group had clear repercussions on their ability to marry, and to marry within their own social group.

The marriage market also had certain geographic dimensions which are important to consider. As Louis Henry pointed out some years ago in a simple and elegant article, even in very isolated rural contexts the marriage market was never truly place-specific and always included people from surrounding villages and often areas further afield (Henry, 1981: 191–3). He also pointed out, however, that marriages with people from outside the village were always fewer than might be expected, and that nearby villages were preferable to those located further away.

There were good social and economic reasons for this. The social networks of the young, so essential for courtship and marriage, were basically local. Boys grew up meeting girls from the same village and, to a lesser extent, those from the surrounding areas with whom they came into contact at village fiestas, at the market, through family ties, etc. For most young people, there was little chance to meet young people living further away. People tended to prefer marrying those whom they had known when they were growing up, and with whom they shared a certain cultural and social affinity. This has been shown to affect spousal choice, even when the marriage took place far away. In the town of Cuenca during the eighteenth and nineteenth centuries, there was a statistically significant tendency for people to choose partners who came from their same district of origin, even if it was located a great distance away from the town where the wedding actually took place (Reher, 1990a: 270–4).

Economic considerations were also important, especially in contexts in which young couples inherited property from more than one family and where land markets were not fully developed, as was the case in much of Spain. Having property in different, often distant, villages made little economic sense, and marrying someone from far away was always a potential problem. For those who had no land, however, these local constraints might be different. Nevertheless, even in social groups where property considerations were minimal, the geographical constraints of the market would also be important, mainly because their networks of social contact probably did not transcend the local area. If, however, by reason of education or occupation, young people came into contact with people from further away, the geographical limits of their marriage market might well be somewhat greater. For these reasons, it is plausible to expect the geographical dimensions of the marriage market to differ by social group, as well as by age and prior marital status, even though specifically local marriages were probably always preferable.

Certain options were always less desirable. Great age differences between spouses, marriages involving older women, widowers or widows, or migrants, as well as marrying across social or ethnic lines, are among these.[7] People would only make use of these when their position on the market was relatively disadvantageous. In other words, we would not expect never-wed women of 23 to be marrying 35-year-old migrant widowers, unless they happened to be very rich. They had better options. Parity may also have been a factor, especially in areas in which impartible inheritance customs prevailed, benefiting the designated heir—often, but not always, the first-born male—and making marriage opportunities more difficult for other siblings.[8] Its importance, if any, in the areas of impartible inheritance prevalent in most of Spain is unclear. Examples such as these could be multiplied as the dimensions of individual choice are explored further.

The interplay of market opportunities took place within a context in which certain constraints influenced the choice of all potential partners. The availability of land, housing, and work, all of which were a function of population density, or the prevailing level of mortality, all helped define the scope of marriage possibilities for the entire society. These are the classic variables so central to the ideas of Malthus and of John Hajnal (1965, 1982), the ones which helped give rise to the European marriage pattern of relatively late and restricted marriage. When population density approached the limits of available resources, economic opportunities contracted and people ended up marrying later; times of economic growth coincided with earlier and more widespread marriage. This relationship has been shown to be a significant one in a number of studies covering both short-run and long-term perspectives. Areas of high mortality were also invariably ones of intense nuptiality, and where it was low, marriage opportunities suffered (Livi Bacci, 1978: 76–7; Wrigley and Schofield, 1981; Pérez Moreda and Reher, 1985). As I showed earlier, in Spain and elsewhere the Malthusian preventive check worked quite effectively to keep marriage, and therefore fertility, in consonance with the economic capabilities of society.

These constraints defined the limits of the interplay of personal and group expectations on the marriage market. They affected all players, but not necessarily in the same way. They provided the backdrop for the individual hopes and expectations which we have outlined above. The result was a heterogeneous marriage market in which segmented demand grappled with existing supply to chart basic marriage patterns. Success led to marriage, and failure to celibacy. The market normally ended up sorting itself out with fairly high success rates, mainly because demand tended to be elastic and people were willing to settle for an adequate, though not perfect, mate. Pinpointing when and how this happened is a matter of considerable interest if we are to understand just how marriage unions were established in historic Spain.

Some Historical Case Studies

Testing the validity of these hypotheses with empirical data is very difficult, mainly because it is practically impossible to have source material which enables us to perceive the way the market functioned in view of people's expectations. Making use of micro-level marriage data, however, it is possible to observe certain regularities in the marriage behaviour of certain segments of society which reflect differing market realities and aspirations for each group. In this section I will attempt to ferret out some of those regularities.

For the most part our data will be taken from the marriage registers of two small towns from central Spain. In both cases, they are located in a part of the country in which partible inheritance prevails and where household structures are rigorously simple. Both towns were moderately important sub-regional economic and administrative centres. There are, however, important differences between them.[9] Belmonte is located in the province of Cuenca on the northern part of the flat La Mancha region. During the decade of the 1840s its economy was almost completely agricultural and was centred on the production of cereals, with olive groves and vineyards as complementary economic activities. Apart from some weaving, there was little economic production outside of the agricultural sector. In the area of Belmonte, farms tended to be fairly large, and generally landless day labourers (*jornaleros*) outnumbered peasant farmers (*labradores*). It is located in a part of Spain in which population centres were fairly large and relatively dispersed. Between 1840 and 1920, Belmonte's population was practically stagnant, oscillating around 2,500 inhabitants.

Piedrahita is located in the western part of the province of Avila near the foothills of the Gredos mountain range. It was an area of small farms producing cereals, potatoes, and onions. Its most important economic activity, however, was cattle raising. Unlike Belmonte, Piedrahita always had a fairly vibrant non-agricultural sector which produced hats in the 1840s and candles, chocolate, tiles, etc. during the early part of this century. Since it was an area of small farms and fairly widespread access to land, the weight of landless day labourers was much lower than in Belmonte. Artisans and merchants were also numerous. In both towns, the services sector was fairly important, due mainly to the specific role they played in the civil administration of the region.[10] Unlike Belmonte, the second half of the nineteenth century was a period of important growth for Piedrahita, which went from a population of less than 1,000 in the 1840s to one of nearly 3,000 in 1920. Surrounding villages were smaller, more numerous, and closer to Piedrahita than was the case with Belmonte.

Data were compiled on 1,122 marriages in Belmonte between 1863 and 1930, and on another 780 in Piedrahita between 1871 and 1911. Information was gathered on age at marriage, prior marital status, sex, place of residence, and, where possible, occupation. Registration was complete, except for occupational data, which presented some serious problems. In Belmonte only 135 of the more than 1,100 marriage records contained the man's occupation, while in Piedrahita registration was complete on this count. In both towns, registration of the bride's occupational category, or that of her father, was scant and basically unusable for our analysis. All data were organized by marriage rather than by individual spouse. This technique affords a sharper analytical perspective because it facilitates an evaluation of, say, the marital attributes of women in terms of those of the men they married. The quality of the data appear to be quite high.

The results reveal that marriage patterns were quite divergent between and within the towns used in the sample. Table 7.2 contains basic marriage data for both towns. For women, marriage was younger and remarriage was far less frequent than it was for men. Their marriageable ages were quite different than they were for men. These patterns are apparent in Figures 7.1, 7.2, 7.3, and 7.4, which contain the age distribution for all marriages and for first marriages by sex in both towns.[11] For women the marriageable ages began by 17 or 18 and peaked by 23 in both towns. After that they declined very quickly and by the age of 27 or 28 the possibility of a first marriage for a woman was quite low. For men, things were somewhat different. Before 20 or 21 there were practically no marriages at all, though frequencies increased very quickly after that age. Even at 29 or 30 years of age, first-marriage intensities were significant for men. In Belmonte after 31 and in Piedrahita after 34–35 there were practically no first marriages for either sex. Thus for women the marriageable ages started between 18 and 20 and lasted until about 27, while

Table 7.2 Basic marriage data for two rural populations, 1850–1920

	Belmonte (Cuenca)	Piedrahita (Avila)
Age at marriage	26.6 (5.3)	24.0 (5.0)
Age difference	2.63 (4.1)	2.92 (5.23)
Per cent marriages:		
never married–never-married	89.5	87.0
never married–widow	1.2	2.5
widower–never-married	6.1	7.8
widower–widow	3.2	2.6
Per cent local marriages	74.0	50.8
n	1,083	755

Note: All data are based on marriages of persons under 50 years of age.

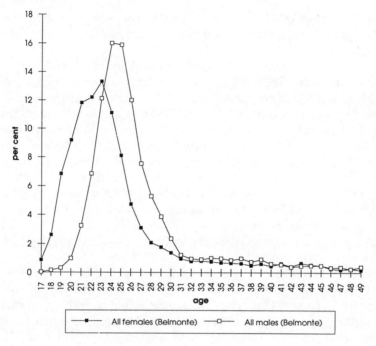

Fig. 7.1 Marriage patterns in Belmonte, all marriages

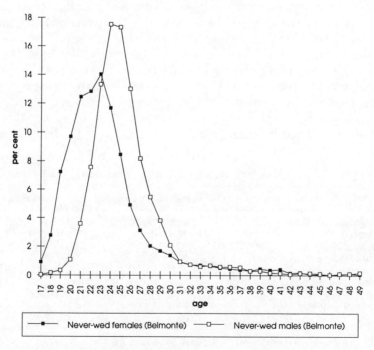

Fig. 7.2 First-marriage patterns in Belmonte

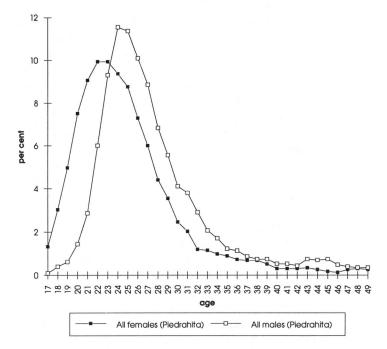

Fig. 7.3   Marriage patterns in Piedrahita, all marriages

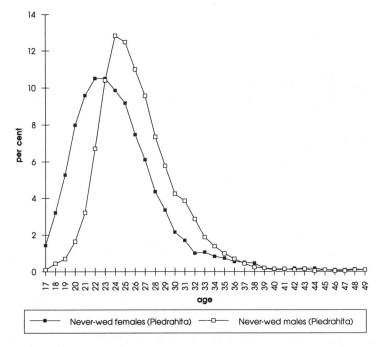

Fig. 7.4   First-marriage patterns in Piedrahita

for men they started later (20–21) but lasted considerably longer. A never-married man at 30 still had a fairly good chance of getting married; a woman did not. In a society in which women were expected to have several childbirths, by the time they were 25 or 26 their value on the marriage market had begun to diminish sharply. Reproduction was a prime factor on the marriage market.

A comparison of marriage patterns between both samples is also instructive. Marriage was later (for both sexes), more spread out, and less local in Piedrahita than it was in Belmonte. These differences are forcefully brought out in Figures 7.5 and 7.6, where first-marriage frequencies for each sex are directly compared. In both cases, in Piedrahita at very young ages frequencies were slightly higher, and peaked either at the same age or earlier. Age at marriage was higher there than in Belmonte due to the ages past the modal age at marriage. In Belmonte marriage frequencies declined very quickly, as opposed to Piedrahita, where decline was much more gradual. For women at 29 years of age marriage frequencies in Piedrahita were twice those of Belmonte, and for men at 31 years of age they were almost four times higher in Piedrahita. Clearly getting married was a possibility in Piedrahita far longer than it was in Belmonte. This difference seems to carry over to remarriages as well, because in Piedrahita nearly 13 per cent of all marriages were a re-marriage for at least one of the spouses, as opposed to the 10.5 per cent in Belmonte. Finally, the greater incidence of non-local marriages attests to a

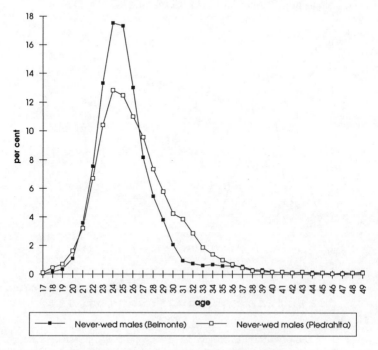

Fig. 7.5   Male first-marriage patterns, Belmonte and Piedrahita

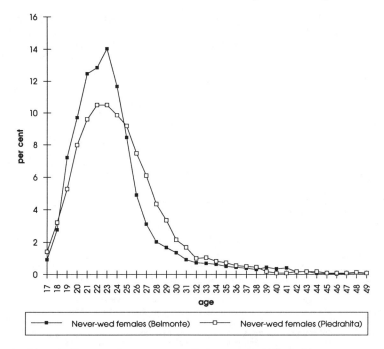

Fig. 7.6 Female first-marriage patterns, Belmonte and Piedrahita

market which in Piedrahita involved people of younger and especially older ages, widows and widowers, and people from outside the town far more than in Belmonte.[12] Despite the fact that marriage was nearly universal in both towns, their marriage markets functioned according to different norms.[13]

Looking at nuptiality by occupational category, further heterogeneity emerges.[14] In the interests of simplicity, a very rough occupational classification has been used which divides the population by economic activity and, within the primary sector, by access to land.[15] Marriage age only differed slightly by occupational category for women, but significantly for men (Table 7.3). It was highest among the privileged groups in society, and lowest among the artisans. If only first-marriage data are used, farmers emerge as those marrying latest, followed closely by those in the services sector. Patterns of later marriage among farmers and especially among members of the services and privileged sectors of society have appeared in other urban and rural contexts, and suggest an important and possibly generalized positive relationship between wealth and age at marriage (Reher, 1988: 87–9).

These differences can be seen still more clearly in Figures 7.7 and 7.8, which show marriage frequencies for males by occupational category.[16] Looking first at all marriages, three or four distinct patterns can be seen. No group showed significant frequencies before 20 years of age, though they were slightly higher among the services occupations. After 20 years of age, artisans, followed by

Table 7.3 General marriage data by occupational category, Piedrahita

	Farmers	Day labourers	Artisans/ employees	Services/ privileged
All marriages				
Age of male	27.9 (5.3)	27.2 (5.0)	26.5 (5.2)	29.4 (7.0)
Age of female	24.9 (4.8)	24.8 (4.4)	24.3 (4.7)	24.7 (6.0)
Age difference	3.1 (5.2)	2.4 (4.9)	2.2 (4.7)	4.7 (6.1)
First marriages				
Age of male	27.1 (4.2)	26.1 (3.7)	25.4 (3.7)	26.8 (4.3)
Age of female	24.1 (4.0)	24.2 (3.8)	23.4 (3.7)	23.2 (4.6)
Age difference	3.0	2.0	2.0	3.6
Per cent marriages				
never married–never married	91	88	88	78
never married–widow	2	2	3	4
widower–never married	6	7	8	14
widower–widow	2	4	2	4
Per cent local marriages	45.5	37.0	62.0	48.8
Total marriages:	200	200	226	129

Notes: Occupation categories represent the following groups of men. 'Farmers' are all men either owning or renting land. 'Day labourers' are men who work other people's land (including shepherds). It also includes rural servants, most of whom were dedicated to agricultural activities. 'Artisans/employees' refers to men who work in the secondary sector (either as wage or self-employed labourers). It includes occupations like cobblers, weavers, mechanics, etc. The final rather heterogeneous category, called 'services/privileged' (for want of a better name), represents all people who either work in occupations requiring some formal education, with implications for local commercial activities, or refers to men belonging to the local landowning elite. It includes policemen, merchants, shop owners, school teachers, civil servants, and the wealthy.
Only marriages of people 50 years of age and younger are included.
Standard deviation in parentheses.

day labourers, reached the highest marriage intensities earliest, with a modal age at marriage of 24 for artisans and 25 for day labourers. Afterwards, frequencies fell quickly, but more rapidly for artisans. The rise in marriage frequencies was much slower for farmers and for the services sector, with modal age at marriage only being reached at 27 years of age. Perhaps more importantly, the ages of most intense marriage lasted five or more years, as opposed to artisans and day labourers, where they lasted only three. The decline in intensity in these two groups was also much more gradual. At 34 years of age, for example, frequencies for farmers and the services sector were double what they were for the other groups. It is interesting to note that after 36 years of age, the services sector and the privileged groups in society emerge as having by far the greatest marriage frequencies. If, however, only first marriages are used, many of these differences between the services sector and farmers all but disappear. For both groups, the optimal marrying ages span almost 10 years (22–32) as opposed to artisans, where they span from about 21 to 29 years of age. Relatively high and very late first marriage frequencies among the privileged (35–39) are also worth noting.

Age differences for both first and all marriages were also much higher among the farmers and those working in the services sector. If all marriages are included, age difference in marriages involving men in the services sector

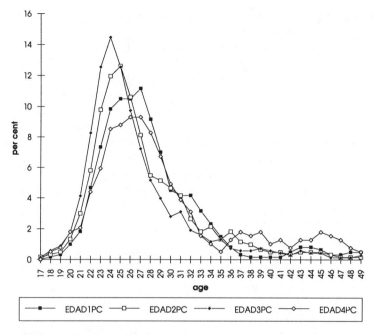

Fig. 7.7   Male marriage patterns by occupational category in Piedrahita, all marriages

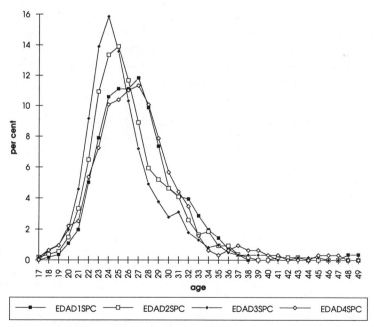

Fig. 7.8   Male marriage patterns by occupational category in Piedrahita, first marriages

was more than twice as great as for artisans or day labourers. One of the keys to these differences is the prevalence of remarriage, especially in the services sector, where the incidence of remarriage among both males and females was much higher. Since it is unlikely that this group had higher adult mortality, remarriage prevalence indicates that for them value on the marriage market was not so closely linked to reproductive matters as it was in other social groups. The lower incidence of remarriage among farmers also suggests a possible link between land and reproduction on the marriage market.

If place of residence is introduced into the discussion, some interesting regularities emerge which tend to confirm much of what was hypothesized earlier. Age at first marriage was somewhat higher in non-local marriages in both Piedrahita and in Belmonte, and age difference between spouses was greater (Table 7.4). This, however, was not equally true for all occupational categories. For farmers, age at first marriage was lower for both sexes in non-local marriages, whereas for the services sector ages for both sexes were sharply higher. In fact, if we only use local first marriages, farmers had by far the highest age at marriage for both men and women, and for the services sector, age at marriage for women was youngest. Age differences were always greatest in this last occupational group, whether they be local or non-local first marriages.

In Belmonte nearly three-fourths of all marriages were specifically local unions, as opposed to only about 50 per cent in Piedrahita. When the propensity to local marriages is estimated for occupational groups, surprisingly, those related to agricultural production show the lowest incidence of local marriage. Men from those occupational categories, however, tended to find their spouses nearby, normally in the surrounding villages (Table 7.5). Artisan non-local marriages involved people somewhat further afield, while the members of the services sector had a marriage market which extended far beyond that of any

Table 7.4 Age at marriage at first marriages (both persons) by occupational status and local/non-local marriages, Piedrahita

	Belmonte	Piedrahita				
	Total	Total	Farmers	Day labourers	Artisans/ employees	Services/ privileged
Local marriages						
age of male	25.2 (3.1)	26.0 (4.1)	27.8 (5.2)	25.5 (3.7)	25.2 (3.2)	25.7 (3.7)
age of female	22.9 (3.3)	23.7 (4.1)	24.7 (4.1)	24.1 (4.2)	23.3 (3.8)	22.6 (4.5)
age differences	2.3	2.3	3.1	1.4	1.9	3.1
Non-local marriages						
age of male	26.1 (4.0)	26.5 (3.8)	26.4 (3.1)	26.5 (3.6)	25.6 (4.3)	27.9 (4.6)
age of female	23.2 (3.9)	23.8 (3.8)	23.6 (3.8)	24.2 (3.5)	23.6 (3.6)	23.8 (4.7)
age difference	2.9	2.7	2.8	2.3	2.0	4.1

Notes: Includes only first marriages for both partners.
Only marriages of people 50 years of age and younger are included.
Standard deviation in parentheses.

Table 7.5 Distance separating spouses' residences in non-local marriages by occupational category

	Distance (km)			
	mean	s. d.	median	n
Piedrahita				
total	38.0	113.3	7	387
farmers	12.2	43.1	5	109
day labourers	12.4	28.5	5	126
artisans/employees	32.5	62.8	9.5	86
services/privileged	136.6	232.7	53.5	66
Belmonte				
total	55.3	72.4	30	277

Notes: All non-local marriages of spouses 50 years of age or younger. In the case of Belmonte, we have not included the four cases in which the distance exceeded 600 km. The maximum distance was over 3,000 km.

other social group. For people related to the land, keeping property manageable meant that even when non-local unions took place they had to involve people who lived close by. This made good economic and social sense. Artisans, however, had greater professional mobility since they basically sold their personal skills and not the product of the land they worked. The services sector was very heterogeneous and included both the local elite and members of the public administration like policemen, schoolteachers, notaries, etc. The data suggest that this group had at least two different types of marriage behaviour: one local and young, and the other much older and ranging much further afield.

In Tables 7.6 and 7.7 I have attempted to show how people's age, and therefore their position on the marriage market, affected the type of marital unions which they formed. In order to approximate different positions on the market, those marrying under 50 years of age have been divided into three approximately equal groups. Those in the first one married young by the standards of the time, and those in the last one married relatively old. The extent to which people played the market differently according to their relative position on it should appear in the marriage patterns of these three groups. The results are striking. As men grew older the average age of their spouses rose, but so did the age difference separating them. For women it was just the opposite. Age difference was greatest when they were very young, and very small among those who married relatively late. The market worked in such a way that while all people became less attractive as they aged, women did so at a faster rate. Men were able to dip into the pool of women at prime ages for a longer time than women, who, if they married late, had to do so with men, who were also marrying late.

As a rule, men married women two to three years younger than they were. The only time this differed was when men were relatively young or women

Table 7.6   Marriage pattern by position in the marriage market, Piedrahita

	Age of male		
	<25	25–27	28–50
Age of male	22.9 (1.3)	25.9 (0.8)	33.1 (5.7)
Age of female	22.7 (3.5)	23.8 (3.6)	27.1 (6.1)
Age difference	0.14	2.07	6.0
Per cent first marriages	100.0	97.4	73.7
Per cent local marriages	55.3	46.3	44.8
Distance in non-local marriages			
mean	37.3 (87.5)	27.0 (88.5)	47.0 (142)
median	6.5	6.0	7.0
Per cent woman older than man	36.6	17.9	10.3
age difference	3.2	3.6	4.1
n	246	229	281

	Age of female		
	<22	22–25	26–50
Age of male	25.1 (3.5)	27.0 (5.5)	31.9 (9.0)
Age of female	19.8 (1.3)	23.4 (1.1)	30.4 (5.3)
Age difference	5.3	3.6	1.5
Per cent first marriages	100.0	99.0	84.4
Per cent local marriages	51.7	47.8	47.0
Distance in non-local marriages			
mean	38.3 (94.1)	25.1 (56.2)	50.3 (158.3)
median	7	7	7
Per cent woman older than man	1.5	14.5	41.9
age difference	1.0	1.8	4.1
n	205	297	270

were relatively old. During the prime ages at marriage for both sexes, men were invariably older than women. In all cases the weight of remarriages grew as people became older, but for relatively older women first marriages were more important than for men. This suggests that widows had far fewer opportunities on the marriage market than widowers, and their chances of marrying were inversely related to their age.

Earlier it was suggested that finding a spouse locally was more desirable than finding her elsewhere, and that people's ability to choose the most desirable match was at least in part a function of their position on the market. As people lost their comparative advantage with age, they were forced to find their spouses further afield, if indeed they were going to get married at all. Judging from the data presented, for the most part this seems to have been the case. In both towns, the weight of local marriages diminished with age and, in the case of Piedrahita, the distance separating spousal residence in non-local marriages was lowest for those marriages taking place during the prime ages, and greatest for those who were relatively older.[17] Even though further research on this question is necessary, the data shown here suggest that as people

Table 7.7 Marriage pattern by position in the marriage market, Belmonte

	Age of male		
	<25	25–26	27–50
Age of male	23.8 (1.1)	25.4 (0.5)	32.5 (6.3)
Age of female	22.0 (3.4)	23.3 (3.2)	27.6 (7.2)
Age difference	1.1	2.1	4.8
Per cent first marriages	99.5	98.5	71.4
Per cent local marriages	81.1	74.6	64.3
Distance in non-local marriages			
mean	44.5 (55.2)	68.1 (95.6)	52.9 (62.3)
median	30	30	30
Per cent woman older than man	13.8	10.5	12.8
age difference	4.1	3.6	4.3
n	428	323	336

	Age of female		
	<22	22–25	26–50
Age of male	24.4 (2.7)	25.4 (3.5)	32.7 (9.7)
Age of female	19.9 (1.0)	23.0 (0.8)	30.7 (6.5)
Age difference	4.5	2.4	2.0
Per cent first marriages	100.0	99.8	82.8
Per cent local marriages	73.7	78.5	66.8
Distance in non-local marriages			
mean	62.1 (34.6)	56.7 (72.4)	51.9 (61.6)
median	30	30	30
Per cent woman older than man	0.0	5.7	32.3
age difference	0.0	1.8	4.0
n	334	442	331

Note: In the case of Belmonte, we have not included the four cases in which the distance exceeded 600 km. The maximum distance was over 3,000 km.

Figures in parentheses are standard deviations.

became less attractive locally, they tended to look for and find their spouses in other villages.

Even though marriage frequencies were generally low for women above 29–30 years of age and for men above 33–34, marriages did take place to people who were older, perhaps considerably more than we might suspect. In order to pinpoint the marriage behaviour of this group more clearly, only data for people marrying above 40 years of age are presented in Tables 7.8 and 7.9.[18] For this age group, the demographic function of marriage no longer existed for women and was minimal for men. Economic considerations were still important, especially when the person marrying was well-off, as were those relating to the regrouping of families from earlier marriages. It is reasonable to expect very few of these marriages to involve never-wed persons.

Data gathered from both towns suggest that a number of these ideas are inaccurate (Tables 7.8 and 7.9). Marriages to older people were considerably more numerous than had been suspected. In both Belmonte and in Piedrahita,

Table 7.8   Old-age marriage, Piedrahita

	Age		
	male > 40	female > 40	both > 40
Per cent total marriages	8.7	3.7	3.3
Age of male	49.2 (7.7)	50.1 (10.9)	52.3 (8.3)
Age of female	36.2 (10.8)	47.5 (5.9)	47.9 (6.1)
Age difference	12.9 (9.9)	2.6 (9.0)	4.7 (6.6)
Per cent woman older than man	5.9	24.1	15.4
age difference	2.5	8.2	2.5
Per cent local marriages	44.0	41.0	38.5
Distance in non-local marriages			
mean	61 (119.0)	43 (81.8)	45 (84.0)
median	12	13	12.5
Per cent first marriages			
male	11.8	13.8	3.8
female	63.2	38.0	34.6
both	10.3	10.3	3.8
Per cent of marriages			
farmers	9.1		
day labourers	6.8		
artisans/employees	6.9		
services/privileged	14.5		
Per cent of total marriages over 50			
male	3.2		
female	1.0		
both	0.9		

Figures in parentheses are standard deviations.

Table 7.9   Old-age marriage, Belmonte

	Age		
	male > 40	female > 40	both > 40
Per cent total marriages	8.0	5.8	4.7
Age of male	49.4 (7.2)	48.0 (10.5)	51.8 (7.0)
Age of female	40.3 (9.7)	46.5 (6.3)	46.8 (6.2)
Age difference	9.1 (8.9)	1.5 (10.9)	5.0 (7.0)
Per cent woman older than man	12.2	35.4	20.8
age difference	3.6	9.0	3.6
Per cent local marriages	57.8	60.0	58.5
Distance in non-local marriages			
mean	30.0 (32.0)	78.5 (38.0)	38.0 (39.8)
median	20	30	30
Per cent first marriages			
male	20.0	24.6	17.0
female	46.7	33.8	30.2
both	13.3	12.3	1.9
Per cent of total marriages over 50			
male	3.7		
female	1.3		
both	1.2		

8–9 per cent of all marriages involved men over 40 years of age, and between 3 and 6 per cent involved women. In an additional 3–5 per cent of all marriages, both spouses were above 40 years of age. A noteworthy 3–4 per cent of all marriages involved men above 50 years of age. Evidently, marriages of relatively elderly persons was not an infrequent experience in the parish churches of Belmonte and Piedrahita.

Once again there is evidence that the market benefited men more than women. To begin with, they were better positioned than women to find partners in more 'desirable' age groups. Female spouses of males over 40 were between 36 and 40 years of age, and age differences were normally in excess of 10 years.[19] Very few men of this age married females older than them. For older women, on the other hand, age differences were small and almost a quarter of the women were older than their male spouses. Elderly men were still able to wed relatively high proportions of never-wed women; but for women, marrying a widower was far more likely. In those marriages in which both partners were over 40, however, rarely was it a first marriage for both of them. One's ability to marry late also differed sharply by occupation and probably by economic standing. The incidence of old-age marriage was more than twice as high among those men in the services-privileged sector than it was among day labourers and artisans.

Remarriage played an important demographic, social, and economic role in rural society, and was instrumental in making the marriage market more flexible and in facilitating marriage for those who had been victims of the demographic lottery imposed by adult mortality.[20] Access to the remarriage market was far more restricted for women than it was for men, mainly because never-married women tended to be available on the market because there were not enough older men to marry them (Corsini, 1981). Single women were invariably deemed preferable to widows, whose remarriage opportunities were few. In all age groups and social categories never-wed females seemed to be more attractive to their potential suitors. It is true that except under exceptional circumstances widowers were also less attractive than bachelors, but they fared relatively better than widows. Thus higher male mortality and an adverse marriage market for women led to a society in which more widows than widowers were present in higher age groups.

Remarriage affected the marriage market for unmarried people because a significant proportion of remarriages involved widowers and never-wed females. It has been said that at certain ages widowers actually competed with never-married men for the available women (Le Bras, 1981). In fact, any competition was probably more apparent than real because all first marriages tended to involve never-married women around 23 years of age, whereas mean age at marriage for never-wed spouses of widowers was considerably higher (28.5 in both towns). This suggests that never-wed women only married widowers as a second choice, and only as their position on the market had begun to weaken. At 27 or 28 years of age, a young woman could no longer wait many years for a suitable mate who would give her a family, and so a match with a widower was better than none at all. Had it not been for marriages to widowers, rates of permanent celibacy for women in both villages would have been sharply higher. Never-wed males marrying widows were also considerably older than those marrying never-wed females, but the incidence of this type of match was very low and probably had little effect overall on male celibacy.

It should be pointed out that the remarriage market worked the way it did largely due to the cross-cohort patterns of first marriages, which implied that men tended to marry women two to three years younger than they were. This meant that under normal demographic conditions, there were not enough men to marry all the available women. This situation was further complicated by the fact that in most areas male out-migration led to marriage markets in which females generally outnumbered males. Both factors enabled widowers to find second wives among the older women who had never married, facilitating lower levels of celibacy and higher rates of family formation. A by-product of this was that cross-cohort patterns of mating were accentuated, because age differences of marriages between widowers and never-wed women were far higher (between 6.5 and 8.5 years in our sample) than marriages of never-wed persons. Had remarriage not worked in this way, the marriage market would have been far more dysfunctional than it was. The only losers were the ones who had lost the demographic lottery and were unable to regroup their households. Widows and older people were particularly vulnerable on this count.

Discussion

Using differential marriage data to infer aspects of how marriage markets worked is fraught with problems, though here it has yielded some useful insights. While some aspects might be specific to Belmonte or to Piedrahita, the complexity of the market was probably common to pre-industrial society. Supply met demand on the market, but both were heterogeneous. Marriage markets had the distinctive quality that each player was both supply and demand in the marriage equation. People's expectations, as well as their value, varied by age, sex, marital status, and origin. Since the goal for everyone was to get married and since a person's value on the market was not constant over his life-span, people were encouraged, or rather obliged, to be flexible in their expectations. This enabled the market to be fairly efficient, and relatively few people were left out.

The market was subject to constraints beyond those affected by individual decision-making. The overall supply of one sex or the other was of key importance. During the period under study, in much of Spain this generally meant that there was a dearth of men.[21] There were also demographic constraints, especially where the chief purpose of marriage was to guarantee the demographic reproduction of society, and where high levels of mortality made high fertility the only reasonable option. The social and economic make-up of a given area, whether or not neo-local household formation systems were the norm, and partible or impartible inheritance practices were also factors of great importance. Finally, cultural considerations constrained the market as a whole. The fact that in Belmonte and Piedrahita men had to be older than the women they married was, at least in part, a normative pattern rooted in cultural beliefs regarding the appropriate ages for marriage. Young people knew when the courting ages (the marriage market) began and ended, and that marriage involved older men and younger women. There were, of course, exceptions to this, but for the great majority of couples this was the way marriage had to be.

The marriage market had two built-in mechanisms which made it far more flexible than some of its structural constraints might have otherwise allowed. The fairly common practice of remarriage was one of them. It enabled widowers to dip into the still-available pool of never-wed women, and allowed an appreciable number of people to put families back together which had been broken up by adult mortality and which otherwise would have been victims of what has been described in the 'nuclear hardship' hypothesis (Laslett, 1988; Smith, 1988). Had it not been for remarriage, fertility would have been lower, permanent celibacy higher, and the number of people living alone much greater.

The other element of flexibility was spatial and hinged on the fact that the marriage market was not restricted to the local town or village. The exact geographic extension of the market differed by age, by sex, and by social status, but existed for everyone. In situations in which finding a spouse outside of a given village or town was readily accessible, it was easier for supply to match demand. As a result, the market worked much more smoothly. For everyone, finding a local spouse was preferable but not always possible. For certain social groups the dimensions of the market were far broader than for others, but transcending local choice was an alternative strategy available to everyone.

Over and over again men have appeared to enjoy a predominant position on the market. Wherever matters of choice have emerged, it has seemed as though men were positioned more advantageously than women. Men, for example, were able to remarry more easily, widowers were able to marry never-wed women, and men's marriageable ages were more liberal than women's. Basically this was due to two factors. For one, prevailing levels of male out-migration in most of Spain left fewer men on the market. Even when the shortfall was only moderate, such as in the villages we have seen here, it was a factor to be reckoned with. Moreover, the existence of cross-cohort marriage patterns dictated that men take younger brides. In a society in which reproduction was the key to survival, women beyond a certain age were no longer considered to be desirable mates. Men, on the other hand, were not fit for marriage until they had established themselves economically, and this took place at a later age. In other words, women were ready for marriage demographically before men were ready economically. The result of both migration and age differences at marriage was that women were relatively more abundant on the market than men; supply of women outstripped demand for them. Fortunately for all, at least in the case of the two towns studied here, compensatory mechanisms ended up facilitating access to marriage for practically everyone, and so any disadvantage women may have had was not detrimental to their eventual success in marrying. This, however, was not the case in other markets, especially those constrained by a severe dearth of one sex.

Age loomed large as a key determinant of a person's position on the marriage market. At very young ages, people could afford to be picky, and settled for high-value spouses found locally. As they grew older and became less attractive for marriage, strategies became more flexible: age differences changed and potential spouses in less than ideal age ranges were chosen, they were sought elsewhere at an ever-greater distance, and often they were widows or widowers. Yet this did not keep people from marrying. The high levels of remarriage and the significant proportions of people marrying above 40 and even 50 years of age attest to the fact that marriage was possible and desirable far beyond the age when it might have been considered demographically viable. The oldest couple married in our sample was made up of a 76-year-old 'property owning' widower from La Nava de Béjar in Salamanca who married a never-wed woman of 48 from Piedrahita. Marriages to elderly people, however, were exceptional and generally the possibility of marriage diminished sharply with age for everyone, though much faster for women than for men.

Economic factors were a central part of segmented marriage markets. Each social and economic group had its own agenda for marriage and played the market according to its own expectations. As a result, surprisingly diverse marriage patterns held within a single cultural context. The two groups in society for which property and inheritance were relatively less important, and whose productive peak was reached relatively early, were also those who married earliest. Farmers, for whom the inheritance of land was essential and whose economic position did not tend to decline with age, ended up marrying later and a greater proportion of them married past 40 years of age. People who worked the land had the lowest proportion of local spouses, but invariably found them nearby. Artisans were more mobile by definition and found their spouses much further afield than did farmers or day labourers. The most divergent behaviour was that of those we have classified as 'services/privileged'. This heterogeneous group was made up of people who had some sort of education or people who were considered to be the local economic elite. They were moderately late in marrying for the first time, had the greatest proportions of remarriage for both sexes, sought their spouses furthest afield, and had by far the highest percentage of old-age marriage.

In all of these cases, the economic attractiveness of a given group determined the dimensions of its particular marriage market. For those whose economic peak began early and possibly ended early, marriage came early, and it seldom came late. For those like the farmers and especially the well-to-do, however, who could command positions of certain economic and social privilege, marriage came later because their rise to acceptability on the market was subject to the reception of an inheritance and to achieving a social position which required a period of preparation which was basically incompatible with marriage. For them the marriageable ages began later; but they lasted much longer than for anyone else. When a man or a woman was past 35 years of age, there was little he or she could do to be attractive on the marriage market, unless of course he or she had wealth and prestige. In that case, everyone seemed to agree that age mattered somewhat less.

Notes

1. 'Marriage and the shroud are sent from heaven.'
2. In 1887 provincial sex ratios between 21 and 30 years of age ranged from 57 to 116, in 1900 from 57 to 113, in 1920 from 58 to 133, in 1930 from 73 to 122, and in 1940 from 75 to 119.
3. The judicial districts used are the following, with sex ratio and percentage of female celibacy in parentheses: Corcubión, La Coruña (50, 33%); Padrón, La Coruña (47, 30%); Puentearas, Pontevedra (44, 31%); Puente-Caldelas, Pontevedra (33, 34%); Tudela, Navarra (99, 6%); Torrelaguna, Madrid (101, 4%); Huete, Cuenca (101, 3%).
4. If, for example, we use only provinces with sex ratios between 90 and 103, which represent the mainstream of Spanish experience for the period of the demographic transition, all ties between the sex ratio on the marriage market and celibacy or age at marriage disappear.
5. On this point some of the ideas of Anna Cabré regarding the marriage market in contemporary Spain have been very useful for my own work. See, for example, Cabré (1993, 1994).
6. Marriage without parental consent was grounds for disinheritance.
7. In the town of Cuenca, age at marriage was higher for male migrants than it was for males born locally (Reher, 1990a: 82).
8. An example of this is given by Llorenç Ferrer i Alòs for wealthy families in 18th- and 19th-century rural Catalonia, where the prevailing system of impartible inheritance led to sharply differing marriage opportunities for the heir, his sisters, and especially younger male siblings, who often had to choose between emigration or celibacy. See Ferrer i Alòs (1993).
9. Social and economic data on these towns has been taken from the Census of Floridablanca (1787), the *Diccionario geográfico* of Pascual Madoz (1845–50), the Census of 1887, and the *Enciclopedia universal ilustrada* (1907–30).
10. In 1887, both were capitals of judicial districts (Reher *et al.*, 1993).
11. It should be noted here that these are not cohort marriage frequencies, which

would have been ideal, because they have been taken from a number of years, and may reflect a number of different period effects. On this point, see Coale (1971:193–9). The frequencies are the result of estimating a 3-year moving average for marriage ages between 16 and 50. It would have been far more desirable to have been able to generate age-specific marriage rates. Lack of census data by age structure and marital status, together with the fact that the marriages occurred over a prolonged period of time, has made this impossible.

12. A local marriage is one in which both spouses are from the town in which they were married. All marriages involving at least one spouse from outside town are considered non-local unions.

13. Permament celibacy as estimated for the judicial districts of Piedrahita and of Belmonte for 1887 yields the following values: Piedrahita, 4.0 men, 2.6 women; Belmonte, 4.4 men, 4.9 women. In the towns themselves, levels were probably quite similar.

14. Here we are obliged to use only the occupational data for male spouses from Piedrahita.

15. See Table 7.3 for an explanation of this classification.

16. Since there is no way of knowing the occupational categories of their spouses, female frequencies have not been included in the figures.

17. This last point, however, does not seem to be the case in Belmonte.

18. The 50-year-old age limit for marriage which was used on all earlier tables has been eliminated.

19. For a comparison with 19th-century Britain, see Drake (1981).

20. For more on the fertility replacement effect of remarriage, see J. Smith (1981), Schofield and Wrigley (1981). For examples of the incidence of remarriage in other European societies, see Akerman (1981), Cabourdin (1981), Imhof (1981), and Livi Bacci (1981).

21. In the villages studied here, there was a moderate surplus of women. In 1887 sex ratios at the marriageable ages in their respective judicial districts were 87 in Piedrahita and 93 in Belmonte (Reher *et al.*, 1993).

8 Family Economies

In this chapter, certain aspects of family economies within a Spanish historical context will be discussed in the light of some case studies which have appeared in recent publications.[1] While some of the points raised are specific to Spain, many of them are applicable in different pre-industrial and early-industrial historical contexts. The family unit can be seen as a rational decision-making group whose economic options and activities were conditioned by the property it possessed and by the availability of labour within the household. Household economies were organized so as to secure the maximum benefit for the family group, defined in both economic and social terms. All members of the household were involved in this process, though the contribution of each varied by age and sex.

A necessary point of departure for any discussion of pre-industrial peasant economies is the work of A. V. Chayanov, who affirmed that the relative well-being of the Russian peasant varied significantly over the family life cycle, mainly because of the changing balance between producers and consumers existing within the household itself. For Chayanov, the economic rationality of peasants did not always aim at optimizing profits.[2] When the ratio of producers to consumers was most favourable, the peasant economy did not necessarily make use of all its potential labour power. In moments of great need, when the ratio of producers to consumers was low, the peasant made full use of the potential productive capacity of the household, even within a context of diminishing returns. From a formalist perspective, this type of behaviour can be interpreted as a strategy of peasants to maximize the average long-run product of their labour in the absence of alternative technologies and where high demographic densities prevailed. From a substantivist perspective, the type of behaviour observed by Chayanov can be seen as a situation in which peasants only worked in order to meet the family needs considered to be materially and socially necessary, with no aim at maximizing earnings.[3] In this way, a type of cyclical stability became more vital to the peasant than the possibility of accumulating wealth.[4]

For Chayanov there were three characteristics which marked the life course for any domestic unit. On the one hand, when peasant families were young and had many young children the amount of land they held tended to increase through rental, leasing, purchase, or even through donations. Later, as the number of net consumers decreased, families tended to get rid of a part of their property. Within the context of much of rural Spain, recourse to the market place, implied by Chayanov's ideas, was also complemented by a gradual access to inheritance, either in usufruct or as real property, followed at a later stage by property devolution in favour of the next generation. During periods in which the needs of consumers were greater than the productive capacity of the land owned by the peasant farmer, members of the domestic group sought work in trades not related to agricultural production, even though they normally remained at home. Finally, a characteristic of these peasant economies was that the employment of non-family labour was practically non-existent.[5] Thus, Chayanov's clearly anti-materialist analysis portrays a situation in which the peasant economy adapted to the needs of the moment; and household demographics was the principal determinant of these needs. It was a situation in which the accumulation of wealth was singularly absent. Within this context, the peasant economy, and therefore social mobility, was fundamentally cyclical in nature (R. Smith, 1984: 6–14).

Chayanov's postulates are attractive, especially because they tend to explain the often surprising social and economic stability over time which can be observed in numerous rural societies in pre-industrial Europe. The extent to which his ideas are applicable to other social and economic contexts, such as those existing in the industrializing urban areas of Spain, is a question which warrants further consideration.[6]

A Comparative Perspective of Family Economies

There are only two published studies of the Spanish past which have attempted to make a formal empirical assessment of the economic implications of the demographic life cycle for family economies, and in both cases the ideas of Chayanov have received strong support.[7] Even though some of their basic hypotheses differ, their results are quite comparable. In my study of the family in rural areas of the province of Cuenca, I applied certain production and consumption indices derived by Richard Smith (1984: 68–71) to empirical demographic data for several periods of the nineteenth and twentieth centuries. In her study on the economies of factory workers in the industrial town of Sabadell located close to Barcelona, Enriqueta Camps-Cura (1990*a*: 349–66) used demographic data, company payrolls, and some contemporary estimates of family expenses in order to reconstruct family budgets in 1890.

The results in both cases are quite similar (Tables 8.1 and 8.2). The period immediately following marriage was one of relative economic well-being, which gradually disappeared as children arrived. The most difficult moment of the family life cycle occurred when the household head was between 35 and 44 years of age, a period in which his children were still not productive. After 45 years of age the economic situation changed since some of the children had already left the parental household and, more importantly, others had begun to be economically productive and started to contribute to the overall family

Table 8.1 A model of family production and consumption, Cuenca

Age of household head	Date				
	18th c.	1851–75	1920–5	1946–55	1966–70
20–29	0.29	0.27	0.24	0.28	0.23
30–39	−0.10	0.04	−0.15	0.03	−0.03
40–49	0.01	0.18	−0.01	0.05	0.17
50–59	0.45	0.39	0.44	0.67	0.56
>60	−0.02	−0.18	−0.07	0.09	0.02
Total	0.63	0.70	0.45	1.12	0.95

Note: All data refer to households with children. The values in the table are the result of summing a series of indices which vary according to the sex and age distribution of the members of the domestic group. We have used a series of production/consumption indices ranging from −0.43 to 0.32 for women, and from −0.36 to 0.97. For men, which were based on others derived by Richard Smith (1984: 68–71). The values of the indices vary according to age, and tend to be lowest for children under 10 and persons over 60. Negative values of the global index do not necessarily mean that consumption was greater than production, but rather that these were more difficult moments of the economic life cycle of the family. For further explanation on the method followed, see Reher (1988: 191–4, 269–71).

Table 8.2 Family Budgets in Sabadell, 1890

	Age of household head								
	20–24	25–29	30–34	35–39	40–44	45–49	50–54	55–59	>60
Family size	3.1	3.97	4.26	4.72	5.26	5.00	5.35	5.16	4.38
Producers/consumers*	2.5	1.33	0.85	0.82	0.97	1.68	1.83	2.26	0.87
Per capita income**	7.92	6.85	5.48	5.32	5.12	6.35	6.59	7.28	4.65
Income/expenses***	4.28	3.68	1.08	−1.01	−2.45	0.66	1.46	4.67	−5.35

* The number of producers/number of consumers living within the household.
** Total household income/number of persons living within the household. Expressed in *reales* per day.
*** Total household income/household expenses according to contemporary estimates. Expressed in *reales* per day. When estimating actual income we have discounted 53 non-working days per year.

Source: Camps-Cura (1990*a*: 350–66; 1995).

economy. Within the context of the models used, the third age would seem once again to have been very negative from an economic standpoint.[8]

Household structures were slightly different in Sabadell and in Cuenca. In rural Cuenca, simple household structures were overwhelming, whereas in Sabadell the prevailing practice of impartible inheritance led to somewhat higher proportions of complex households (near or below 20 per cent). In situations such as these, and possibly in other quite different ones, strictly demographic factors related to the reproductive cycle had a critical impact on the household economy, especially when the incidence of complex living arrangements was only moderate, as is the case in the examples used here. From this vantage point, then, the model of Chayanov is a basically demographic model and is, at least partially, a self-fulfilling prophecy: its results are known beforehand.

This cyclical nature of dependency can also be seen from the perspective of the individual life course. Figure 8.1 charts dependency over the life course for rural areas of the province of Cuenca.[9] The results are not dissimilar to those coming from Tables 8.1 and 8.2, though the vantage point is slightly different. Dependency within the domestic group is high during the early years of life, between 30 and 44 years of age, and during old age. The effects of demographic change on these patterns do not appear to have been significant. Basically, over a person's life he could expect to live through two periods of economic well-being and another three of economic difficulties. Reproductive cycles, generational length, and co-residential patterns determined the range of the fluctuations and the length of the periods. It constituted the basic common denominator of all family economies.

The life cycle of any co-residential domestic unit can be expected to follow a comparable course in a context in which simple household structures, neo-local household formation rules, relatively low celibacy, and only moderately high marriage ages are the norm. If any of these variables differed, the form of the model might alter, but its basic structure would not. Should a married son reside in his parental household for a prolonged period of time, as was possible wherever the stem family household was prominent, the model would be different from the one I have just described, though it would still be tied to the life cycle of its component members. In the period immediately following the marriage of the chosen heir of the younger generation, the economic situation

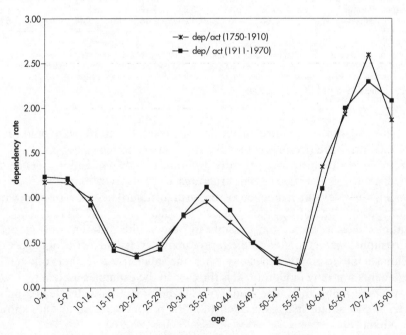

Fig. 8.1 Dependency over the life course by period, Cuenca

of the domestic group would be relatively better off since more productive persons would be resident. This situation would change quickly as the relative advantage became a disadvantage, once these complex households had more consumers both in the younger generation (children) and in the older one (aged parents, in-laws, etc.). Despite these changes, however, the basic life-cycle effect would persist. This could only be altered fundamentally in those societies where multi-generational and polynuclear households predominated. This sort of situation was typical of some areas of the Balkan Peninsula and Russia (Czap, 1983) but is nowhere to be found in the Iberian Peninsula, where only modest variants of the stem family existed.

Another of Chayanov's ideas which is much more difficult to verify with Spanish data is his affirmation that peasant families made little effort to save during the more benign moments of their economic cycle. Underlying this is the hypothesis either that saving was not possible or, more likely, that during the negative moments bare subsistence minimums were seldom reached. It is most difficult to control empirically for the validity of this affirmation, mainly because sufficiently detailed family budgets are rare. Some do exist for nine-teenth-century peasant families (Le Play, 1990), but none of them show the effects on the family economies caused by the differing age and sex composi-tion of the domestic group.[10] Normally model budgets are used, and this makes it impossible to capture the flexibility which no doubt characterized the pro-duction and consumption patterns of families.

Despite these problems, isolated data suggest that some of Chayanov's affirmations on this subject warrant a critical reappraisal. In her recent study of working-class families in Sabadell, E. Camps-Cura was able to identify some periods in which factory workers did not make enough money to meet house-hold expenses (Table 8.2). This result seems plausible and had already been noted by contemporary observers.[11] Similar situations have been observed in other parts of historic Europe when the families of workers fell below the threshold of poverty at the same stage of the life cycle as in Sabadell. Both in industrial Lancashire (Anderson, 1974) and in early nineteenth-century Flor-ence (Woolf, 1986), the moment when the household head was between 35 and 45 years of age was critical for the family economy, and many household heads were forced to rely on the help of charitable institutions during that period.

Insufficient family incomes forced people to take full advantage of all the human resources present in their family households. Within this context, some sort of saving during the good times must have been possible. In Sabadell, for example, families were able to save on average 463.55 *reales* per year, suffi-cient to enable them to cover expenses for 20 non-working days of the family each year, apart from holidays. Le Play (1990: 97, 151) also observed the same sort of pattern among the families of the northern coastal region which he studied. The importance of savings and the extent to which they were used to enhance productive capacity are still unclear.

In towns, wage labour functioned as the cornerstone of the family economy. For those households prevalent in industrial areas, the implications for the domestic economy of employing one more person were perfectly clear, especially since age and sex-specific salary levels were well defined.[12] While the salaries of men increased according to the time they had been working in the company, women were basically excluded from all opportunities for internal promotion. Their salaries were similar to those of a 15-year-old adolescent and did not increase with age. Considering the *de facto* salary caps on female labour, from the point of view of a working-class family it was probably more advantageous for families to substitute adolescent labour for female labour. These, along with the accumulation of domestic activities, were the reasons why married women generally left the labour market.

Peasant economies were significantly different from those of the inhabitants of towns. Here the implications of occupying an additional person in wage-earning activities were not nearly so clear-cut as in urban areas, especially within a context of variable harvests and as long as the population density was not so high as to reduce the marginal productivity of labour to zero. Even here, available data suggest that economic production increased with age. At the beginning of the twentieth century in Cuenca, global family incomes tended to increase over the life course (Reher, 1988: 188). While in the higher age groups this might have been the result of the contribution of children to the family economy, it also occurred at younger ages. For example, the income of households headed by men aged 30–39 was slightly higher than of households where the head was aged 20–29.[13] Similar results have been found for the rural areas of Mallorcan society during the same period (Schurer and Moll-Blanes, 1990). Increased income was mainly the result of the efforts of the peasant families themselves. Within a rural context dominated by partible inheritance, as was the case in Cuenca, increases in household income were also stimulated by the gradual access to inheritance as the older generation died. It was not exceptional for household heads who worked as 'day labourers' when they were young to appear as 'farmers' a few years later. In fact, the trend towards growth in the amount of land held by a family, as observed by Chayanov among Russian peasants, was parallelled in much of rural Spain both by access to inheritance together and the acquisition of property on the market.[14] This process tended to mitigate, at least partially, the negative economic effects of having several very young children in the household.

The role of inheritance transfers was quite different in industrial Catalonia, where impartibility was a key factor contributing to the social decline of those sons and daughters not destined to inherit. The dowries and legal portions of inheritance to which they were entitled might help them establish new households, but were not normally enough to consolidate new property (Camps-Cura, 1990a: 198–223). That is why the influence of inheritance practices on the family economies of factory workers must have been minimal. Consolidating the formation of structurally complex families with access to rural property around the designated heir was one way of multiplying the number of nuclear families (of younger siblings) subject to out-migration or to a potential reduction of their economic and social position in society. For many years the rural areas of Catalonia were able to absorb a growing population, although by 1860–87 in most districts this was no longer a viable option. From that moment on, out-migration toward Barcelona or abroad characterized those nuclear families not destined to inherit family property.[15] This flow of people toward industrial areas played a key role in the transformation of the Catalan economy.

Despite the observed differences, both in industrial Catalonia and rural Cuenca the implacable logic of family demography dictated that families had to diversify their sources of income. Although this need was more pressing during the poorer parts of the family life cycle, it was probably always present. Here families had a certain amount of flexibility, especially when one or more offspring were old enough to work, although the manner in which this resource was implemented differed between town and country. Whereas in the industrial urban world the primacy of wage labour was unquestioned, in rural areas this was not the case. In industrial towns the principal manner of supplementing incomes was by entering the labour market; but in rural areas there were many options of employment either on land belonging to the family or to other people, in cottage industries where they existed, or as apprentices in craft occupations especially in larger villages. In rural Castile, by the age of 7 young boys were sent out to tend flocks and to help at harvest time, and by 10 they were used to transport goods. Generally family labour was preferred to non-family labour. 'It was always better to have children. No matter how cheap shepherds might be, they were always more expensive than children,' proclaimed an aged farmer from the mountainous areas of Cuenca (Reher, 1988: 62). A similar situation seems to have existed in other areas of Spain where children made a decisive contribution to the family economy.[16]

In towns, on the other hand, this resource was less accessible since children entered the process of industrial production at a later age than in rural areas, and seldom contributed economically to their families before the age of ten. Even at that age the wages they earned were extremely low. In rural areas, a young boy could be considered fully productive by 14 or 15 years of age, whereas in towns it was at that age that industrial apprenticeships began.[17] It was from that moment that his wages began to increase, although not before reaching 20 years of age did he begin to earn an adult's salary. The integration of children into the production process was slower and later in factories than on farms.

Even though the examples we have used in this section refer to different economic contexts, they retain certain common features. This is because family formation processes and the effects of the life course on family economies were similar in both worlds. The transition to the factory system, however, did have certain implications for the way in which families mobilized their human resources, obliging them to make full use of potential household labour at all times. In rural areas, on the other hand, the availability of home-produced consumer goods, the seasonality of labour, and the flexibility in the use of household labour suggest that despite generally lower rural wages, peasant families with access to land had greater flexibility than urban wage-earning families.[18] In both cases, family economies seem to have had a moderate capacity for saving.

Migration and Family Economies

Migration was essential to the diversification of family incomes. The classical scenario in which a continual flow of young adults took up more or less permanent residence in major urban centres existed in Spain, although perhaps was less pervasive than might be imagined. Before 1920–40 this type of in-migration was only important in rapidly industrializing areas such as Catalonia or the Basque Country, or in Madrid, which offered a ready source of employment in the services sector. Otherwise the ability of towns to attract vast numbers of migrants was somewhat limited.

There were other types of migration which, both numerically and economically, were probably more important. Data from a middle-sized Catalan industrial town like Sabadell or from the pre-industrial town of Cuenca suggest that in-migration was intense and often involved entire families. Almost 20 per cent of in-migrants to Sabadell were above 40 years of age, and in the town of Cuenca in any given year between 1842 and 1847 nearly 10 per cent of persons in each age group above 40 entered or left the town. Most of these people, as well as children below the age of 10 or 15, moved as members of a family. In Sabadell, the typical migrant family was made up of four or five persons, some of whom were children below the age of 14 (Camps-Cura, 1990a: 161–83). Many of these migrant families were immersed in the downward part of the household economic life cycle, thus suggesting that the temporary imbalance between income and expenses tended to stimulate migratory tendencies by making families more sensitive to fluctuations in the labour market.

Both in pre-industrial Cuenca and in industrial Sabadell there seems to have existed a strong current of out-migration affecting all age groups. In Sabadell between 1874 and 1890, for every 100 persons officially listed as in-migrants on the city lists, another 74 were registered as out-migrants. The age distribution of these out-migrants was very similar to that of in-migrants, mainly because many of the same persons were involved. Around 80 per cent of out-migrants from Sabadell had been there less than five years. Sabadell was not normally their first destination since 61 per cent of all in-migrants had already resided in at least one municipality other than their place of birth before arriving in Sabadell. In the town of Cuenca between 1843 and 1847, our measure of annual migration flows suggests a still more striking situation, because in-migration levels involving nearly 15 per cent of the population of a given year were matched by out-migration flows (Reher, 1990*a*: 249–53). As in Sabadell, the age structure of out-migration was almost identical to that of in-migration.[19]

These data seem to indicate the existence of migration patterns affecting unmarried individuals as well as entire families. For many persons the stay in town was quite short, almost seasonal, while for others it might last somewhat longer, although permanent residence was not necessarily established. In the case of Cuenca, where the intensity of the flows was clearly greater than in the industrial centre of Sabadell, a high proportion of the migrants may have remained there only temporarily. This is not surprising because a declining and economically lacklustre centre such as Cuenca had much less to offer in terms of long-term economic opportunities than a dynamic town like Sabadell. Despite the demographic similarities in the migratory flows affecting both towns, their basic nature and the role they played in the local economy seem to have been somewhat different.

The existence of significant levels of return migration is fairly clear, at least in the case of the town of Cuenca; but the destination of these urban out-migrants is not. In Sabadell the majority of them probably went to Barcelona and, to a lesser extent, to other industrial towns. Only among urban peasants was return migration to their places of origin important, affecting 29 per cent of all out-migrants of that socio-economic group (Camps-Cura, 1990*a*: 157).[20] Among other social groups, out-migration to other towns seems to have been more important. While in Cuenca the majority of the mobility observed can be explained by the seasonal and complementary nature of rural and urban jobs, in Sabadell its causes must be found in the effects that the transition to industrial capitalism had for artisan and wage-earning families.

In industrializing towns, the growth of the factory system succeeded in generating a floating population, composed to a large extent of families ladened with unproductive members, who no longer were able to return to their places of origin. In fact, their native villages were often situated in areas whose local cottage industry had been partially or totally destroyed by the mechanizing forces inherent to the process of industrialization. These families played a key role in the creation of the urban system of Catalonia, and were an essential factor in the industrialization of Catalan society. The formation of this floating population is testimony to the fact that during the initial stages of industrialization the dependence of proto-industrial workers on the changing demand for labour increased. Out-migration, then, seems to have been an adaptive strategy for workers faced with the experience of a fluctuating labour market. The circulation of industrial families through the urban network also suggests that for these workers serious housing problems and deficit family economies were ever-present realities.[21]

The return migration of peasants which has been observed in Cuenca, and to a lesser extent in Sabadell as well, can be adequately interpreted in terms of the ties which existed between the rural and urban worlds. These ties were stronger in the sleepy pre-industrial Castilian town than in industrial Catalonia; but they existed everywhere. Wherever rural–urban relations were fluid, at least in so far as people were concerned, family economies bridged both worlds. In other words the migratory flows of peasants can be explained, at least in part, by family interests spanning both urban and rural worlds and by the need of peasants to make use of resources in both in order to supplement family incomes.

In rural areas, towns were a preferred migration destination for young servants who, after a brief urban stay, tended to return home. As one Cuenca peasant stated, 'Girls here between 16 and 18 years of age went to Barcelona as servants. All of them' (Reher, 1988: 61). In 1887 the excess female population around 25 years of age was evident in almost all Spanish towns, as it was, for example, in the industrial or semi-industrial judicial districts of Catalonia such as Mataró, Sabadell, Arenys de Mar, Terrassa, Granollers, and Igualada (Reher *et al.*, 1993: map 14). These women were the young domestic servants and industrial wage-earners so prevalent in urban areas. For many the stay in town was only temporary. In Cuenca, for example, the degree of servant mobility was extremely high. Nearly 40 per cent of all servants entered or left the town in any given year, and 3 of every 10 female migrants were servants. [22]

The routes followed by young men from agrarian rural areas coming into the towns to seek work as unskilled day labourers were not unlike those of female servants. Stable work was difficult to find straightaway in industrial centres. Available data suggest that full integration into the industrial world only took place after a generation of urban residence had passed (Camps-Cura, 1990*a*: 198–214).[23] This did not keep peasants from migrating to towns, because urban areas offered a relatively wide range of work opportunities. Ultimately, however, both men and women migrated to towns, in order to supplement family incomes and to save for marriage, without necessarily having any intention of staying there permanently. The decision to remain in town was made later, and was a function of the job and marriage opportunities offered by the urban environment.

For peasant families the harvest was fundamental. It was then that the human resources of the household were mobilized more than at any other time of the year. Apart from the harvest on family land, household members would help with other harvests both in neighbouring areas and in districts somewhat further away. Entire families might be involved in seasonal migrations, though it was more typical for the male members of the household to move. Interviews with aged peasants of the province of Cuenca have brought to light that most of them participated in the grape harvest in La Mancha and in the olive harvest in Andalusia. Once their own harvests had been concluded, farmers from the Alcarria district of the province of Cuenca often went to parts of Aragon where they participated in the grain harvest, which took place there at a later date than in the Alcarria. This type of seasonal migration was common across much of Spain and at times involved an important proportion of the population. For the peasant farmers from the northern coastal regions studied by Le Play (1990), earnings from temporary migration to Castile or even to Andalusia constituted a sizeable part of their family budgets.

At times the nature of the work undertaken meant that the period spent away from the family household might last considerably longer. This happened when the work undertaken involved more than the harvest, including mining, public works, forestry projects, the tending of transhumant flocks, and even temporary work in towns. Normally only some of the male members of the household were absent for extended periods. In those cases, the economic ties with the parental household continued, much as occurred with the Castilian in-migrants in the Basque mining districts who periodically sent remittances to their villages of origin (Pérez-Fuentes, 1993).

It is not clear just what percentage of the income earned by younger household members in seasonal or temporary work ended up in the parental household. Adolescent workers still residing at home probably gave almost all of their earnings to their families. As they grew older, and especially as their workplace and place of residence moved further away from their original home and as the possibility of marriage loomed, the percentage of income sent home must have decreased substantially. Even when no earnings went to the parental budget, migration away from home was always beneficial because it reduced the number of household consumers. Unfortunately there is little concrete empirical evidence which might enable us to understand how this process worked more clearly.

The recourse to migration as a way of supplementing family economies meant that an important part of household income was generated from outside the co-resident domestic group itself. This has important implications for the study of peasant family economies because it implies that the domestic group cannot be analysed as though it was simply an autonomous unit of production and consumption. What is more, household income was not obtained simply from productive household members living away from home. Other sources of non-household income were also important. The progressive accumulation of property through inheritance mentioned earlier was one way in which income and wages could be generated independently of the co-resident domestic group. During old age and in times of need, the economic and material help of other kin, unrelated to the original domestic group, was also a source of income. Negotiating informal debts with other kin was one such formula used by some urban wage earners when faced with economic hardship.[24] Conversely, there were many occasions in which a part of the household income ended up outside the domestic unit. The payment of a rent by tenant farmers, dowries, advances on inheritance in favour of children, help given to newly-weds, the payment of debts, etc. are all examples of this process.

From a methodological standpoint, therefore, it would be mistaken to see the domestic group as a unit of production and consumption immune to foreign influences. This is why the majority of the empirical models developed to test Chayanov's theories are relatively disappointing. They normally are unable to cover more than the product of the labour of resident members of the domestic group, minimizing or even completely omitting larger aspects of family economies based not only on the mobilization of human resources present in the household, but also on those of people absent but in one way or another linked to it. Which of the two facets was more important? There are no empirical data which might enable us to answer this question, but it would seem reasonable to suppose that the relative weight to be attached to foreign elements in the household economy varied over the life course of the household head and of his wife. Within the context of Cuenca, once the initial dependence of young newly-weds on parental assistance had ended, the moments of greatest economic self-sufficiency characterized the first years of marriage, before the children were old enough to migrate and before gradual access to inheritance had begun. In other words, it was during the moments of greatest economic difficulty that households were most likely to struggle on their own, though during this period families may well have incurred some debts. Subsequently the importance of income and expenses from sources outside the household probably tended to increase. In the case of Sabadell, the entry of money into the domestic group began during the economically negative moments of the life course by means of informal debt arrangements, and continued later in the form of contributions to the family economy by members living away from home. Contrary to what happened in rural areas, inheritance was of little importance for wage-earning factory workers.

Household Decision-Making: Kin and Servants over the Life Course

In certain contexts and at given moments of the household life cycle, families might find it advantageous to secure additional labour to work the family farm, to help around the house, or to care for some member of the family. Often this type of labour was found locally, and this did not imply any co-residence. At times, however, it might prove necessary to have additional live-in help. Kin, servants, and, in exceptional cases, lodgers made up the potential supply of non-household labour available to families. Earlier we saw that in most of Spain co-resident kin were not numerically relevant, though their importance in households did vary substantially according to the family life cycle. In stem-family areas there were far more kin present at home, though they were mostly there for matters immediately related to succession.

Servants and lodgers were never very important in most areas of Spain, and Cuenca was no exception.[25] Between the eighteenth and the twentieth centuries, moreover, the importance of servants declined to practically zero.[26]

This decline in importance was accompanied by the progressive feminization of domestic service, as the ratio of three men for every woman during the eighteenth century turned into one in which men were almost completely absent (Reher, 1988: 154, 172–6). At first servants tended to be occupied in agricultural activities, though this type of servant was never very numerous because small farms basically were able to rely on family labour. The disappearance of servants was a by-product of the gradual demographic modernization of society, which led to increasing numbers of working-age children at home or present in the village. With an abundance of family labour, or readily accessible non-family labour, there was no need to hire live-in servants. What remained were female servants, who were involved in domestic chores, and who were much more numerous in the well-to-do families.

Whereas children arrived as a result of fertility, kin and servants in the family household were the product of the decision-making of the household head and his spouse, even in those areas where they were not numerically important. In some cases, kin might have been present as a function of family solidarity and their contribution to the household would have been materialized either in terms of the help they gave in raising and socializing younger children or in the satisfaction they afforded families who knew that by caring for them they were fulfilling their obligations as members of an extended family. Other times, however, it is not unreasonable to suspect that at least some kin, and all servants, fulfilled a specifically economic function, and that the decision to have them present or not in the family household was made in terms of the economic needs of the household itself. Servants and kin tended to be more prevalent in households headed by landholders and by the privileged sectors of society, and the presence of both was positively correlated with family income.[27] Few studies, however, have attempted to specify the conditions under which non-family labour entered households. The Cuenca data base yields some interesting insights on this point.

It can be postulated that to a certain extent family members and kin or servants of working age were interchangeable, and that the presence of one was at least in part the consequence of the absence of the other. In other words, families with no children or families with very young children would tend to have more servants and kin of working age than those families in which there was an abundance of human capital. In this case, the presence of kin, and especially of servants, can be considered as a compensatory mechanism designed to neutralize a shortage of family labour. Moreover, it is not unreasonable to suspect that by and large men and women were not interchangeable, and that women tended to substitute for women and men for men.[28] I have implemented these hypotheses in a very direct way by estimating the number of male and female members of the family household of working age (from 15 to 60), as well as those kin of the same ages.[29] All servants have been considered working population, independent of their age. Households were classified by the total number of dependent members and of active members, and by the net

Table 8.3   Family and non-family labour: a bivariate correlation matrix

All households

Non-family labour	Dependent family members			Active family members			Net active family members (act – dep)		
	males	females	total	males	females	total	males	females	total
Servants (male)	0.051**			−0.067**			−0.076**		
Servants (female)		−0.030**			−0.073**			−0.026*	
Servants (total)			0.033**			−0.088**			−0.076**
Active kin (male)	−0.035**			0.007			0.028**		
Active kin (female)		−0.66**			−0.050**			−0.012	
Active non-family (m)	0.025**			−0.053**			−0.050**		
Active non-family (f)		−0.065**			−0.087**			0.012	
Active non-family (tot)			−0.022*			−0.077**			−0.037**

Note: Active = all persons 15–60 years of age; Dependent = all persons older or younger. Non-family = kin + servants. Net active = total active − total dependent.
Number of cases: 14,060.

Significance: * < 0.01; ** < 0.001.

Table 8.3   (cont.)

Peasant farmer and professional households

Non-family labour	Dependent family members			Active family members			Net active family members (act − dep)		
	male	female	total	male	females	total	male	female	total
Servants (male)	0.066**			−0.101**			−0.106**		
Servants (female)		−0.033			−0.106**			−0.047**	
Servants (total)			0.050**			−0.131**			−0.116**
Active kin (male)	−0.037*			0.008			0.028**		
Active kin (female)		−0.080**			−0.074**			0.043**	
Active non-family (m)	0.046**			−0.089**			−0.085**		
Active non-family (f)		−0.072**			−0.128**			−0.035**	
Active non-family (tot)			0.000			−0.125**			−0.082**

Note: Active = all persons 13–60 years of age; dependent = all persons older or younger. Non-family = kin + servants. Net active = total active − total dependent. Number of cases in total sample size: 14,060; peasant farmer and professional households: 6,021.

Significance: * < 0.01; ** < 0.001.

active population they contained (active minus dependent). A simple bivariate correlation analysis of these variables yields striking results (Table 8.3).[30]

Only servants showed a significant and expected relationship with the presence of working-age population in households. While male servants showed the expected link with respect to all three variables, the presence of female servants in the household was always negatively related to the presence of women, independent of their age. This suggests that the decision to have female servants in the household was negatively related to the total number of women at home, probably because the type of work women did was accessible to a wider age range of people than was male labour. With kin the situation was very different. The presence of female kin was always negatively related to that of women in the household, independent of their age. With males, while the negative relationship with the presence of dependent family members in the household was much the same as with women, the correlations with active population were not significant at all. With kin it is difficult to detect any economic reasons whatsoever for their presence in the household.

These results suggest that the functions that kin of both sexes and female servants carried out in Cuenca households were loosely spread out over most ages, while male servants were more likely to be incorporated as a function of the existing household labour supply. Female servants were basically involved in domestic household chores which could be carried out by women of almost any age, though they were more frequent in households in which the net active female presence was lower. Kin of both sexes, however, fulfilled a far wider range of functions than might be suggested by a simple household/non-household labour model. They helped raise and socialize the children of the household, they assisted with household chores, or they were retired parents who were staying temporarily with the family. In all of these cases, unlike male servants, they were not sources of substitute labour. Families had other, more important reasons for having kin in their homes.

Female Employment, Reproduction, and Family Life Course

The nature of the contribution of women to the family economy raises certain questions. It is important to start from the basic understanding that at all times the labour of women was considered absolutely necessary for the well-being of the family, even though their contribution was not always of a monetary kind or even directly related to household production and income. The nature of female work varied substantially between urban and rural contexts. Where factory labour predominated, women received salaries on more or less the same basis as men. This was not the case in rural areas, where female economic activity was often spent in temporary or part-time jobs. A classic example of the former was the harvest, when all available family labour was mobilized. Cottage industries or tending to the family vegetable garden were examples of part-time work. In order to understand adequately the economic activity of women in the rural world we must bear in mind that they were simultaneously involved in economic production and in other activities which produced no immediate income. As opposed to an industrial context, where their contribution can be measured, in rural areas this is practically impossible. Even so, peasant families were well aware of the importance of women's labour, and considered it fundamental to the economy.[31] For the families studied by Le Play (1990: 92, 146), women contributed between 18 and 24 per cent of the total family income, not including their household labour. In Sabadell in 1890, during the early stages of household formation, income derived from women's work represented about 25 per cent of the total family income (Camps-Cura, 1990*a*: 356).

In towns, and probably in rural areas as well, the labour of women was not as well paid as that of men. As pointed out earlier, within a Catalan context men's wages increased with their age and the years spent in a factory, whereas women's salaries showed little sign of increasing over time. Women's employment rates were higher before they were 20, and tended to diminish later, especially after they were 30 years of age (Camps-Cura, 1985). The mechanisms whereby adolescent labour was gradually substituted for female labour tend to explain the extremely low employment rates of women over the age of 30. Not even during the critical moments of the family life course did women show signs of returning to salaried labour. Something similar also occurred in rural areas, where the period of greatest economic activity of women gradually gave way after marriage to another, more intermittent participation in economic production.

It is important, then, to bear in mind that both in urban and in rural areas the productive capabilities of adult women were normally not maximized.[32] While criteria of economic rationality would seem to dictate other ways of taking advantage of potential family labour, especially during the difficult moments of the life cycle, women simply stayed at home and worked at income-generating activities only intermittently. It would be erroneous, however, to construe this dynamic as an indication of a lack of economic rationality. It is unquestionable that in Spanish society economic rationality was a basic principle adhered to by all, and all available measures necessary to attain the values families perceived as essential were taken. Yet women fulfilled other functions which were considered more important than simply making a monetary contribution to the household economy.[33] Most important, women were the cornerstone of the reproductive process. Having children who survived to adult ages was considered a good without equal; and, given the prevailing demographic regime, this meant that high marital fertility was necessary. The existence of heirs, the eventual contribution of offspring to the family economy, the security for old age represented by children, and the need for personal family relationships were essential and were perceived as such by everyone.

Despite the early onset of the demographic transition in some parts of north-eastern Spain, during the second half of the nineteenth century the process of demographic reproduction still demanded considerable time and effort. For at least 20 or 25 years of a woman's life, it was her main job. Women were essential for family life, educating and caring for the children, cooking meals, maintaining order in the household, cleaning, etc. In this way, their strictly reproductive period was prolonged still further. Family life, which revolved around the mother, was perceived as a complement to her reproductive capacity. She was the key to the socialization of the younger generation and was essential for the well-being of the family. The young were aware of this and were educated in the importance of the gender-specific nature of many household activities. They, in turn, assumed it as normative behaviour when they became adults. The holistic nature of the role of women was quite incompatible with any full-time dedication to wage earning; and yet in broader economic terms it was fundamental. When tentative attempts have been made to quantify the monetary value of a woman's work at home, her contribution to the family economy measured at market prices has proved to be greater than that of her husband, at least among poorer social groups (Pérez-Fuentes, 1993).

A woman's strictly economic activity differed between town and countryside, even when it was located in the household. In rural areas, even though the intensity varied over the life course, her dedication to productive activities was an ongoing complement to her reproductive role. Within an urban context, however, the possibility of fulfilling both roles simultaneously was severely limited due, at least in part, to the physical separation of home and workplace. The organization of factory labour created further difficulties for part-time female wage earning, thus shortening her 'economically active' life. Despite exceptions, it seems clear that by and large the productive capacity of women was less consistent and extended in towns than it was in rural areas.

The contribution of women to the household economy, therefore, was essentially complementary to that of the other members of the household. It was a system which worked adequately as long as the conjugal unit had children and remained intact. When this did not happen, as in the case of a death of one of the spouses, the implications were serious, especially when younger children still resided at home. When it was the woman who was widowed, unless she had land and the sons or other kin to work it, her ability to compensate for the loss of earning power resulting from her husband's death was severely limited because her work was not paid nearly so well as that of men. As happened in rural Cuenca during the early part of this century,[34] in Mallorca per capita incomes in female-headed households were nearly 25 per cent lower than those of male-headed households (Schurer and Moll-Blanes, 1990). This pattern probably prevailed everywhere. Even though widowers would also be adversely affected by the absence of their wives, in strictly economic terms they were likely much better off than widows. Moreover, economic and demographic reasons gave males a distinct advantage on the marriage market, and it was nearly always easier for a man to regroup a family unit through remarriage than it was for a woman. Female-headed households were prime candidates for an appearance on the lists of the poor. The limits of vulnerability charted in Chapter 4 of this book are eloquent testimony to the economic disadvantages of being a woman trapped in the vagaries of the demographic lottery.

The demographic transition fundamentally altered the role of women within the family. As fertility and mortality declined, the amount of time parents, and especially women, invested in the reproductive aspects of family life diminished sharply. This process started at the beginning of this century, and has continued with increasing intensity until today. At first the net effects on women's activities were modest because despite decreasing fertility, the number of children at home actually increased as mortality declined faster than fertility and as age at marriage rose steadily. During the middle decades of this century, however, the net number of children at home began to decline. The implications for women have been momentous. For one, fewer surviving children have ended up receiving more attention from their parents and from society, thus driving up per capita investment in the 'quality' of children. Since institutions outside the household, especially those involved in education, have played an important role in this investment in child quality, the implications for women's time have been only modest. But they have been substantial for household economies. Partly in response to the increasing economic demands placed on the family and partly because reproduction was no longer a full-time activity, increasing numbers of mothers have ended up combining their reproductive role within the family with an active participation in the labour force. This participation has had extremely salubrious economic effects both for family economies and for the society as a whole, as economic modernization has opened up increasing numbers of jobs in the services sector. Unquestionably, women at work away from home have become the sign of the times during the final decades of the twentieth century.

The Aged

This brings us to the key subject of the aged in society. Normally the third age has been considered a period of physical and economic decline for persons who well might spend the final years of their lives in an extremely precarious economic situation. Is this idea borne out by empirical evidence, or does it require some modification? Family production and consumption models leave little doubt that old age is the period of life with the most negative economic implications. It could not be otherwise. After 60 years of age, an individual's productivity began to diminish ever more rapidly. And even though there were no longer any fully dependent people from the younger generation in the family household, those offspring who remained were few in number. Furthermore, many of the elderly lived alone. A life-cycle model along these lines serves to reinforce the stereotype we have of the aged: poor and alone.

There are, however, data which suggest that it might be necessary to change or at least to modify this standard interpretation of the third age. First of all, the models presented are based on income and expenses generated directly from within households. They do not take into account the possibility of saving over the life course which, as pointed out earlier, might well have existed. In my study of the rural areas of Cuenca, I was able to make use of certain municipal listings at the beginning of the twentieth century which contained estimates of total family income.[35] When controlling for the age of the household head and for the number of persons residing in the domestic group, the basic results of the Chayanovian production/consumption model were corroborated, except for one age group: those above 60 years of age (Table 8.4). According to these data, despite an overall decrease in income (17 per cent lower than that of the 50–59 age group), smaller household size meant that these persons experienced an increase rather than a decrease of disposable income.

The explanation of these results is fairly clear in the light of what was said earlier. Within the age group above 60 there are people who continue to be economically active. It would be a grave error to confuse the 'third' with the 'fourth' age. Elderly persons usually continued to control the ownership of their property, since the title to land was normally not transferred before death. This does not mean that the usufruct of the property was not placed in the hands of their heirs; the process of devolution began much earlier and accelerated as the fourth age approached. This, however, was only done in return for economic and social compensations promised by children. Retirement contracts were not common in Spain, and these arrangements were normally specified in informal agreements. It is impossible to understand adequately the economic position of the elderly without keeping in mind the importance of undocumented transfers of income from outside the household,

Table 8.4 Household income by age of household head, Cuenca, 1910–1930

Age of household head	Nuclear households			All households		
	Total income	Mean household size	Per capita income	Total income	Mean household size	Per capita income
20–29	2,694	3.01	895	2,896	2.90	999
30–39	2,763	3.21	656	2,949	4.11	718
40–49	3,198	5.10	627	3,219	4.83	666
50–59	3,555	4.63	768	3,469	4.18	830
>60	3,017	3.25	928	2,917	2.56	1,139

Note: 'Nuclear households' include only two-partent families. All monetary values expressed in pesetas.
Source: Reher (1988: 198).

or by pooling assets through the co-residence of both generations. In areas of stem-family systems, the role of children in the care of the aged was material-ized by legally mandated co-residence. The net effect, however, was similar: the well-being of the elderly was a family matter.

The true situation of the elderly probably lies somewhere between the 'pessimism' of the production/consumption model and the 'optimism' of the early twentieth-century Cuenca data. It is unquestionable that the family played a key role in the economic, social, and personal care of the aged, by bringing them into the households of the younger generation or by helping them when they lived alone. The number of the aged obliged to reside in hospitals and other charitable institutions in Spain is surprisingly low. These were only used as a last resort, and under normal circumstances it was the family which handled the basic needs of the elderly. Families were well aware that children, although initially a burden, offered a guarantee of security later in life, at least in the historical context at issue here. The existence of this reality is unquestionable. The concrete form it took was conditioned by other factors such as family relations, inheritance practices, and the social standing of the families concerned (factory workers, day labourers, etc.). Defining the distinct patterns of social welfare is a challenge for future research.

In the course of this century, the role of the family in the welfare of the aged has undergone huge changes. The demographic and economic modernization of society has led to longer periods of spousal union, increasing parts of people's lives spent as elderly persons, the ability of persons to save for their own retirement, and a substantial growth of demographic, social, economic, and political importance of the elderly within the society as a whole. It has also led to a significant increase in the role played by public institutions in the welfare of the aged. Retirement plans, state-run social security, and public health care are all examples of this. Today the family is no longer basically alone in providing for the well-being of its own elderly members.

Conclusions

In this chapter I have discussed some of the more salient aspects of family economies. An analytical framework was proposed which emphasizes their dynamic aspects in both industrial and pre-industrial urban and rural contexts. As with Chayanov, the age distribution of the human resources within the household has emerged as a key factor for the family's economic well-being. The family group, however, has shown itself to be quite flexible, able to adapt to new situations arising from concrete demographic and economic realities.

This does not mean that the household was able to rise above the constraints of its own life cycle or that economic survival was a simple matter. Abundant data underscore the importance of these life-cycle constraints, and the flexibility we have discussed is best interpreted as an ongoing attempt to neutralize the ill effects of the low points in the economic cycle or the negative effects of the 'demographic lottery'. The presence of servants or kin in the household, or the temporary out-migration of the members of the domestic group, were the results of economic decision-making. During the latter part of the last century and the first decades of this one, in the rural areas of the province of Cuenca, the logical consequence of an increase in the number of children present in the household, a by-product of the initial stages of the demographic transition, was the virtual disappearance of servants (Reher, 1988: 65, 172–4).

Migratory processes, whether temporary or permanent, marriage strategies, and the age and sex-specific use of child and kin labour were the component parts of this flexible and dynamic situation, which operated within a frame-work conditioned by economic structures and demographic realities. The fact that over the life course there were continual flows of income entering or leaving the household was also governed by the same basic constraints men-tioned above. It is impossible to appreciate adequately the complexity of family economies if we centre our analysis exclusively on the household.

Domestic economies of the inhabitants of the towns differed from those of their rural counterparts mainly due to the timing and intensity of the economic contribution of their members. In rural areas, the contribution of women to the family economy was ongoing though variable over their lives, as opposed to the situation in the towns, where marriage often meant the end of a woman's participation in the labour market. In rural areas children became productive at a much earlier age than in town, though this advantage was neutralized to a large extent by higher urban incomes. It would seem, however, that the weight of the family economy tended to fall more directly on the male household head in urban areas than it did in the countryside, where the burden was more evenly distributed among the other members of the household. Does this imply that rural areas enjoyed higher living standards than rapidly industrializing towns? Scant and often contradictory data make it extremely risky to venture a clear-cut opinion on this matter. Nevertheless, during the first stages of the process of industrialization, and especially among urban in-migrants, it is not at all clear that the process of urbanization brought an improvement in their living standards or in the quality of life.

The demographic and economic modernization of Spanish society taking place over the past century has had profound effects on the way in which family economies have come to grips with the question of survival and well-being. The rise in the costs related to rearing children together with their insignificant contribution to the family economy while at home, the entry of women into the job market, the increased role of public institutions both for children and for the aged, and the ability, modest at times, of parents to save for their leisure time and their own old age are all hallmarks of these changes.

Notes

1. Parts of this chapter were originally published in a paper I wrote together with Enriqueta Camps-Cura. See Reher and Camps-Cura (forthcoming).
2. See Chayanov (1925 [1966]). A most thoughtful consideration of Chayanov's ideas can be found in Richard Smith (1984).
3. On this subject, see Sahlins (1972).
4. For a critical appraisal of Chayanov, see Harrison (1977: 331; 1981).
5. The postulates of Chayanov are especially applicable to societies where access to land is common, but considerably less so when analysing societies in which day labourers, salaried labour, and large farms predominate, as occurs in much of the southern part of Spain.
6. Chayanov's theories have been discussed within the context of proto-industrial household economies, as well as within that of industrial factory workers' economies. On the first point, see Dewerpe (1985); on the second, see Strumingher (1977), Tilly and Scott (1978), Tilly (1979).
7. There are also other projects dealing with this type of perspective, but as of yet firm results have not appeared. See especially Schurer and Moll-Blanes (1990).
8. These results are not substantially different from those presented for areas of Mallorca during the same period. See Schurer and Moll-Blanes (1990).
9. Instead of the weighted consumer/producer index used in Table 8.1, Figure 8.1 tracks the more traditional dependency ratio (persons under 15 and over 60 divided by persons 15–59) of the co-resident domestic group by age of the individual.
10. A recent attempt to establish family budgets from local sources can be found in Pérez-Fuentes (1993: 243–76). Her study does not show the life-cycle effects under discussion here.
11. See, for example Cerdà (1867) or Sallares i Pla (1892).
12. See, for example, Camps-Cura (1990*a*, 1990*b*, 1995).
13. The fact the increase is so small (2–4 per cent) is not surprising if we bear in mind that the dynamism of the rural economy is not comparable to that of urban centres. In addition, peasant economies do not reflect production destined to be consumed at home, and therefore real wages in rural areas could not oscillate to the same extent as they did in towns.
14. For the Italian case, see Delille (1990).
15. Recent studies have suggested that the immigrant population in medium-sized industrial towns such as Igualada, Manresa, Mataró, Terrassa, and Sabadell did not originate in the agrarian districts of Catalonia, but rather in districts with decaying rural cottage industries (Camps-Cura, 1990*a*). Barcelona increased its share of internal Catalan migration from 65–75 per cent before 1877 to 95 per cent toward the end of the century. On this point, see Camps-Cura (1990*c*, 1995). The origin of those Catalan emigrants leaving Spain has yet to be documented. In England, Sidney Pollard (1978) considered that the main source of English emigration was the families expropriated during the 19th century. On this same subject, see also Baines (1985).
16. In one family from Santander, Le Play (1990: 92) found that an 8-year-old son provided 8 per cent of the total days worked per year, and 1.5 per cent of the annual family income.

17. In pre-industrial times, apprenticeship often meant an additional expense for the apprentice's family. During the period of industrialization, this does not seem to have been the case.
18. Industrial wages were higher than rural wages. In rural areas wages were higher in the economically dynamic districts. On this subject, see Camps-Cura (1990*d*, 1995) and Garrabou *et al.* (1991).
19. It should be pointed out that the data from Sabadell and those from Cuenca are not strictly comparable, because they do not measure the same types of flows. In Sabadell migration data are based on municipal lists registering people as official in-migrants or out-migrants. For this reason, the data tend to reflect the arrival (or departure) of persons who for one reason or another wanted their formal residence to be established in the town (or elsewhere). Thus the type of migratory pattern revealed by these data was fundamentally a stable one. On the other hand, the flows visible in the pre-industrial town of Cuenca refer to the *de facto* presence or absence of persons in the town. In other words, they also identify those people who would have remained in town for only short periods of time, or who had no intention of establishing an official residence there. These transient people are, by definition, absent in the data from Sabadell. This is one of the reasons why the migratory flows as measured for Cuenca are so much higher than those of Sabadell.
20. Had we been able to capture the migratory flows of the truly transient population, no doubt levels of return migration would have seemed greater.
21. A similar perspective using Italian evidence can be found in Pullan and Woolf (1978); Woolf (1986).
22. The extreme mobility of this group is evidenced by the fact that another 16–17 per cent changed households within town in any given year. In other words between 50 and 60 per cent of servants moved at least once every year (Reher, 1990*a*: 296).
23. This contradicts the rather widely accepted idea that peasants were the ideal source of labour for industrial societies. In Catalonia, as in other regions of Europe, a large population of the factory workforce had proto-industrial rather than agricultural origins, and had already lived in a town for a relatively long time. The transfers of population between different sectors of economic activity were quite rigid, due mostly to the use of a system of apprenticeship before the age of 20 to regulate access to industrial employment, and to prevailing inheritance practices (Camps-Cura, 1990*a*: 215–23).
24. This type of indebtedness is extremely difficult to document since normally it was not legally registered. Debts do appear sometimes in post-mortem inventories, but these only reflect the situation of a small and relatively privileged sector of the population.
25. In 1887, 1.7 per cent of men between 21 and 40 were servants and 4.8 per cent of women. Since most of these servants were concentrated in the 21–25 age group, the weight of servants at that age was probably around 5 per cent for men and slightly over 10 per cent for women (Reher *et al.*, 1993: 233). Naturally, this distribution varies sharply by region, with the Canary Islands, the Basque Country, and Madrid having the highest values. In the rural areas of Cuenca, less than 2 per cent of the households had servants, and they represented between 1.1 and 3.6 per cent of the population of the household (Reher, 1988: 172–6).
26. During the 18th century, servants made up 5 per cent of the mean household size

in Cuenca, 3.6 per cent between 1800 and 1850, 1.1 per cent between 1850 and 1875, and 0.0 per cent in 1970.

27. In 19th century Cuenca, for example, 6.5 per cent of all households with a yearly income below 500 *reales* per year had co-resident kin, as opposed to an average of about 15 per cent for those whose income exceeded 2,500 *reales*. For these income categories, the percentage of households with servants ranged from 5.3 to nearly 35.0 (Reher, 1988: 181).

28. Here I am following some ideas noted by Laurel Cornell in a recent paper (1994).

29. I suppose that younger and older kin could not possibly have fulfilled an economic function in the household, and must have been present for reasons of family solidarity.

30. The data presented in the top part of the table are based on all Cuenca households between the 18th century and 1970. In the lower half of the table they are based only on the landed groups in society or on those groups with professional or economic status, who were the ones most likely to have both servants and kin in their households. In this case, the correlation coefficients are higher, but the direction of the relationships is the same.

31. Oral testimony to the importance of women's work is abundant. Here are a few examples taken from interviews with elderly peasants in Cuenca: 'The wife worked as much as the husband. In the morning she cooked the meal in the oven, watched over the irrigated garden, and made sure things were transported properly; and in the afternoon she gathered wood. In this village, during the month of August women worked more than men.' 'Women worked at home and in the fields, especially the garden. They also gathered wood, participated in the harvest, especially of olives. All of them participated.' 'Women weeded and harvested grapes and olives for a wage. They paid them 1.5 pesetas a day. They also all worked at home. The only ones who didn't work were those with a lot of children, or when they were breast-feeding' (Reher, 1988: 60–1).

32. The case of the mining community of San Salvador del Valle in the province of Vizcaya, in which many of the local women had in-migrant miners boarding in their homes, is exceptional (Pérez-Fuentes, 1993).

33. Here our position is not unlike that of Sahlins (1972) when he speaks of the important role of institutions in determining the 'needs' of society.

34. Income of households headed by widows was one-third lower than in households headed by widowers. See Table 4.3.

35. The original model presented earlier made use of estimated levels of production and consumption which were applied to a variety of populations and historical contexts.

9 Changing Dimensions of Kinship Networks During the Twentieth Century

Throughout this book, the family in Spain has been approached from a number of different vantage points. It has been both subject and object of my analysis, both independent and dependent variable. It has been viewed as an institution subject to economic, demographic, social, and cultural constraints, as well as the context within which social, demographic, economic, and even cultural reproduction was assured. The importance of demographic patterns and demographic change for the family itself has received considerable emphasis, and in many ways demographic modernization has been shown to be the key source of change for many aspects of family formation and family life. The nature of the data used has meant that much of my analysis has often been confined to the co-residential domestic group, despite the importance of family links stretching beyond the household itself, and has stopped by and large in 1970, just when the second demographic transition was getting under way.

In Chapter 4 and elsewhere, household analysis was taken about as far as the existing data allow. Interesting results emerged regarding the life course of both the household and the individual, and key transition periods in people's lives were identified. Throughout, however, it has proved to be impossible to take this analysis satisfactorily beyond the household and to evaluate many of the implications the extended family had for people's socialization or welfare. Apart from scattered ethnographic data, and a good deal of common-sense speculation, this larger subject has been left untouched for the most part. Household-level data can be a rich source of information when analysing the co-residential domestic group, but are notoriously poor when it comes to ascertaining other aspects of family realities. Other approaches must be tried.

In the course of this chapter the use of microsimulation techniques will enable us to get beyond some of these limitations and bring our picture of the family in Spain up into the realm of the present and future. Microsimulation can yield the number of kin by differing degrees of kinship over the life course of the individual; but it says nothing of the relations holding within the extended family. In other words, it gives us information on the dimensions of the kin group, but not on how that group functions. Simulation results are not empirical results, and only give a general idea of how families actually developed. Considering that there are little or no empirical data on the dimensions of kinship in Spain, simulated estimates can prove to be extremely valuable because they afford us a type of understanding of the family that otherwise would be impossible to obtain. Many of the results stemming from this analysis will bring us face to face with some of the most serious issues and challenges affecting the present and the future of the family in Spanish society.

Microsimulation of Kinship

If we wanted to assess the total number of kin a person had, simply asking him would be sufficient, as long as he had a good memory and we were not asking about very distant relatives. His reply regarding his parents, siblings, and children would likely be quite accurate, though the reliability of his memory would be somewhat lower if we asked him about people further removed within his extended family, such as first or second cousins or aunts and uncles. Surveys like this do not exist for historical populations, and even today are infrequent. Moreover, their accuracy and reliability would be suspect because people's memories might falter and, more important, any survey of this kind would necessarily be small and its representativeness of society as a whole questionable. Family reconstitution is another technique which could yield information about kin groups, though here too problems would arise, mainly because family reconstitution only gathers data about the biological process of reproduction and there would be no way to control for the present status of members who had moved out of the reconstituted parish. Where more or less complete ascending or descending genealogies were available, the dimensions of kin networks could be more readily ascertained. Since these documents normally only refer to individual families, however, the degree to which they represent the experience of society as a whole is probably quite low. In all of these examples I have just mentioned, generalizing from the experience of a very small sample of the population to society as a whole would be very risky to say the least.

Microsimulation is a different way of approaching the question of kinship networks, and can be used to approximate the dimensions of kinship. Even though microsimulation has many constraints and limitations which will be discussed in the following paragraphs, it yields kin counts by age of the individual which are based on empirical data representing the experience of the entire society. It is an entirely different approach from the other methods just mentioned. Unlike the hypothetical survey which approaches kinship from the standpoint of existing families and through the perspective of the individual, microsimulation reconstructs the individual life course itself directly from the requisite demographic data.[1] In going from demographic events to families, the approach is not unlike that of family reconstitutions or genealogies. These however make use of individual-level data on births, marriages, and deaths, while microsimulation starts with demographic rates and then simulates individual demographic events. In so doing, the computer program ends up portraying a population of individuals that would exist with the prevailing demographic characteristics inputted into the program. As this population is being created, the simulation can keep track of the kinship relations existing between the simulated individuals to as great an ascending, descending, or lateral depth as is desired (Smith and Oeppen, 1993: 281–2).

For years family demographers and anthropologists have been aware of the need to use indirect methods of this kind in order to evaluate certain characteristics of families which had proved to be inaccessible when using most types of available data.[2] More recently a number of microsimulation models have been developed. These models vary in many of the input parameters they require, the assumptions they use, and the output they yield, but all use computer-generated microsimulations for some aspect of kinship within a historical perspective. CAMSIM and SOCSIM are perhaps the best known of these models, though others exist as well.[3] The major differences between these two models lie in some of their basic simulating assumptions, in the number of assumptions they use, in the complexity of the different input parameters required, and in their ability to handle changing demographic rates and other input variables such as migration. Both of them generate kin counts for individuals at different stages of their lives, as well as other related kinship and demographic statistics.[4]

All simulation models make simplifying assumptions about demographic reality. This is done for both reasons of data and of interpretation. Normally, the available information can only be used for the simplest assumptions. While data on marriage, mortality, and fertility rates can be readily generated in most twentieth-century contexts, information on the incidence of remarriage and the delay between death or divorce and remarriage by age and sex, for example, are more difficult to find.[5] The output derived from relatively simple input parameters gives a general picture of the population emerging from given fertility, mortality, and marriage rates, but falls short of reflecting the actual complexity of empirical reality. Simplifying assumptions can be useful because they make these models more readily interpretable, though perhaps somewhat less precise. If there were data for all the most complex assumptions, the output generated would no longer be a simulation, but rather an empirical portrait of society. In those cases, simulation would not be necessary. Moreover, as Nathan Keyfitz (1987) has wisely suggested, should that happen it would be necessary to 'start from the beginning to make simpler models in order to draw understandable conclusions'. Simplifying assumptions are both necessary and useful, but care and historical common sense must be used in interpreting the results.

For the purposes of this study of the family in Spain, I have used the CAMSIM microsimulation model because it is the least complicated of the major models, is relatively 'benevolent' with the input data requirements, and yields the desired results in a simple and straightforward way.[6] CAMSIM generates kin sets of all individuals who occupy specified kinship positions related to a sample individual. Various degrees of kinship can be used, though in the applications we have run seven generations of linear kinship (ego, children, parents, grandparents, great-grandparents, grandchildren, and great-grandchildren) and one level of non-linear kinship (nephews, nieces, aunts, and uncles) has been included. While it would have been possible to define kinship further afield, it is unlikely that beyond this degree of kinship the extended family functioned as such in any sort of useful fashion, especially as a source of socialization of the young and of welfare for people at many ages.

CAMSIM produces one kin set for each simulated ego which contains a life history of each member of the kin set. Egos are all given the same birth date and constitute a birth cohort, and thus the results can be considered as a sample of individuals from a birth cohort.[7] CAMSIM applies the same demographic parameters to each simulated ego and to all the individuals in the ego's kin set. It is an open model with regard to marriage. This means that when an ego is going to marry, his or her spouse is created just for that marriage, and thus has no kinship history of his or her own.[8] Ascending kin can also be simulated by situating the ego as the child of a kinship group which consists of his or her parents and siblings.[9] While CAMSIM simulations can be run either for a male or a female ego, the results presented here will refer only to female egos. In any given run, the number of life histories simulated can be made to vary, and the smoothness of the parameters derived depends to a certain extent on the number of simulations run. In the case of our Spanish data, 500 egos and their kin sets have been modelled for each set of input data. CAMSIM also generates a set of demographic rates corresponding to the stable population it creates, and these can be compared to the input rates to check for the internal consistency of the simulation.

A major constraint of CAMSIM is that it must use constant demographic rates.[10] This means that the sample populations generated are stable populations in which the basic fertility and mortality inputs remain constant. This of course was not the case at any period in history, especially not during the twentieth century, which is when the Spanish simulations have been run. The simulations, then, do not reflect empirical realities for two key reasons. Not only are many simplifying assumptions used in constructing the model, but the input rates themselves do not change. The results of a microsimulation would be the same as those found in the 'real world' only if the basic assumptions held in reality and if a given population experienced the same set of demographic rates over a prolonged period of time spanning several generations. This is unrealistic, and so great caution must be used when interpreting results. The simulations do, however, give us a sample of plausible kin sets and kin counts holding under different demographic conditions. This provides us with a very useful yardstick with which to measure the approximate dimensions of kinship at any given period of time. Moreover, when they are run with different input parameters, the results enable us to see how empirical demographic change influenced the structure of kinship. Often the changes occurring between two sets of data from two different periods are more instructive than the actual number counts themselves. It is in this spirit that the results from Spain will be presented and interpreted in this chapter.

Basically CAMSIM is a demographic model of the individual life course which requires demographic inputs. At birth, each individual is assigned an age at death according the life-table distribution of ages at death, and then is simulated forward in time with events such as marriage and fertility occurring at the appropriate time. In order to fix age at death, life-table death probabilities (q_x) must be known, and these are then converted to a corresponding death-age distribution. When the requisite q_x values are not available, model life-tables for corresponding life expectancies at birth (e_0) are used. Cohort age distributions of marriage are derived from data on mean, minimum, and maximum first-marriage age by means of the marriage frequencies set out by Coale and McNeill (1972). Divorce and separation are not included in the CAMSIM model, though in the case of Spain divorce was not an important factor in Spanish family life until just a few years ago, when it was legalized. CAMSIM models only marital fertility and requires as standard input birth-interval distributions for the first birth as well as parity progression ratios for second and higher birth orders.

Generating these data for Spain was not always an easy or direct task. Before the twentieth century, almost none of the requisite data exist. Even after 1900, in numerous instances the relevant data regarding, say, marital fertility had to be gleaned from related indices such as age-specific marital fertility rates. Since more or less adequate data are available from 1900 on, the microsimulations have been run with demographic inputs taken from 1900, 1930, 1960, and 1985–90. As has been outlined in earlier chapters, this century has been one of momentous demographic change and the microsimulations will give us a fairly clear idea of the implications for kinship of these changes. Table 9.1 contains the demographic characteristics of the populations used in the four microsimulations.[11] Tables containing the complete simulation results for each date can be found in the Appendix.

Extreme caution should be used in interpreting the results because microsimulation recreates stable populations, and populations were not stable in Spain during this century, or at any other moment in the past. The simulations give us an idea of the possible dimensions of kinship and the intensity and direction of changes in kinship. In many ways, the 1985–90 microsimulation gives us an idea not so much of the present situation, but of the future of kinship during the rest of this century and into the next one. Should the current demographic rates remain the same, it tells us what kinship will increasingly be like as the future becomes the present, and the present the past. The simulations are indicators, not maps. Even so, the contours of the landscape of kinship they portray are of immense importance for the present and the future of the family in Spain.

Table 9.1   Demographic parameters of stable populations (generated by CAMSIM microsimulation, Spain

Demographic parameters	Data circa			
	1900	1930	1960	1985–90
Life expectancy (e_0), women	35.7 (35.6)	51.6 (51.7)	71.7 (70.1)	78.8 (76.3)
Age at marriage, women	24.5	25.8	25.5	24.9
Permanent celibacy, women	0.102	0.107	0.138	0.079
Gross reproduction rate	2.23	1.83	1.31	0.76
Net reproduction rate	1.15	1.33	1.23	0.75
Mean age at maternity	31.72	30.97	31.60	29.18
Probable survival to mean age at maternity	0.515	0.727	0.940	0.982
Parity progression ratios				
0	0.92	0.90	0.90	0.82
1	0.94	0.88	0.85	0.66
2	0.91	0.85	0.80	0.50
3	0.88	0.82	0.70	0.34
4	0.85	0.79	0.65	
5	0.83	0.76	0.60	
Intrinsic growth rate	0.004	0.009	0.007	−0.010

Note: Life expectancy, age at marriage, celibacy, and parity progression ratios have been based on the input empirical estimates. Simulated life expectancy at birth for women is in parentheses. Other parameters have been estimated from the stable populations simulated. See text for details on adjustments.

Kinship Patterns over the Life Course

The number, category, and age structure of kin changed over a person's life course. When he was young, most kin were ascending, and as he grew older his age relative to that of his kin also increased. The total number of his kin was highest when he was middle-aged, and lowest at the beginning and towards the end of his life. These patterns are clearly visible in Figure 9.1, which is based on the experience of women. The simulations were done with demographic data taken from 1900, a moment at which the demographic transition was just getting under way in most of Spain. It is the closest we can come to replicating what might have been a pre-transitional population in Spain, since mortality and fertility were still very high. Nevertheless, this is only an approximation because had a simulation been possible at an earlier date, mortality and most likely fertility would have been substantially higher.

Figure 9.1 only contains the closest of kin, those who came from the nuclear family itself. At birth, a female ego had on average two siblings and two parents. As she grew older, the number of her siblings increased, reaching its highest point between 10 and 24 years of age and declining gradually thereafter. The number of parents decreased continually over her life course, and by the time she was 30, on average only one of her parents was still living. After 20, the number of living children she had began to increase rapidly and reached its highest point when she was 45 years of age, just as she was ending her reproductive period. It was also at that age that for the first time the total

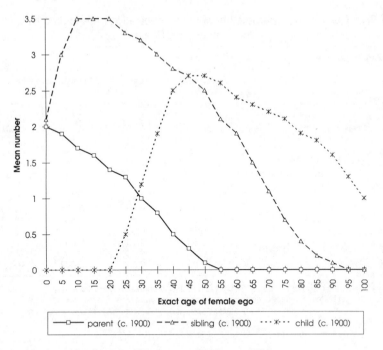

Fig. 9.1 Nuclear kin over the life course, Spain, c. 1900

number of children she had outnumbered her siblings. After 60, children had become by far the most prevalent of her nuclear kin.

By the latter part of this century, many of the basic kin relationships had changed profoundly (Figure 9.2). A female ego had more parents at a higher age than before, the peak number of siblings came later, and the moment when her children outnumbered her siblings came earlier in life. The most important change, however, was in the number of direct kin she had. For example, with the 1900 simulation, at 30 years of age a female ego would have had on average 1 parent, 3.2 siblings, and 1.2 children, whereas in the 1985–90 simulation the number of parents had risen considerably to 1.7, but the number of siblings had been reduced by more than half, and that of children by one-third.

These changes can be seen more clearly in Figures 9.3, 9.4, and 9.5, which contain the results for all four microsimulations. In the demographic regime holding during the early part of this century, only at birth could people count on having both their parents. As they grew older the mean number of parents per child dropped rapidly. In this way, say at 10 years of age, a female child would have 1.7 living parents, and 15 per cent of female children would have lost their fathers as opposed to 11 per cent who would have lost their mothers. By the time they married, at about 25 years of age, 14 per cent of young brides had no living parents and over 40 per cent had lost their fathers; and, by the time they were 50, 88 per cent had no living parents at all. As the century has

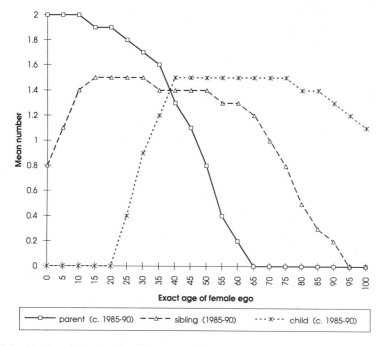

Fig. 9.2 Nuclear kin over the life course, Spain, 1985–1990

progressed, this picture has changed substantially as more egos have had more living parents at later and later ages. For example, the percentage of 40-year-old females with at least one living parent more than doubled in the course of the four simulations (from 43 to 90 per cent). At the beginning of the twentieth century, many children had lost at least one of their parents by the time they reached adolescence, and at marriage the most normal situation was that only one parent was alive. By century's end, this pattern had been completely reversed. Increases in adult life expectancy were responsible for all of these changes.

The trends observed in the mean number of living siblings in the course of this century are not uniform (Figure 9.4). The greatest abundance of siblings was found in the 1930 microsimulation, due mainly to the fact that between the first and second simulations, mortality had dropped more than fertility, with the end result being an increase in siblings. By 1960 the continued decline in fertility led to fewer siblings at the start of life, though rapidly improving mortality meant that this shortfall was only temporary, as the number of living siblings in the third simulation (1960) surpassed those of the female egos in the first simulation after 20 years of age, and in the second simulation (1930) after 65 years of age. With the fourth and last simulation, the basic pattern is similar, though this time the drastic reduction in fertility creates a pronounced short-fall in living siblings which is only fully compensated by improving mortality

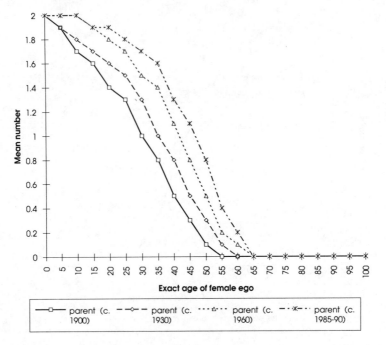

Fig. 9.3   Mean number of living parents, Spain

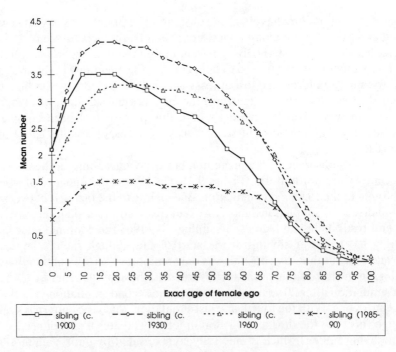

Fig. 9.4   Mean number of living siblings, Spain

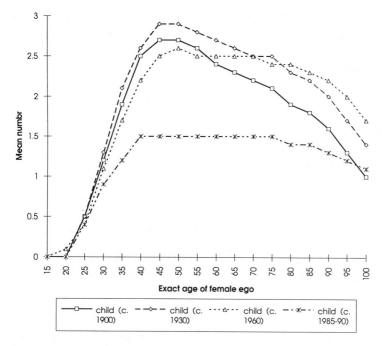

Fig. 9.5 Mean number of living children, Spain

past 70–80 years of age.[12] Living siblings for adult females were most prevalent during the middle years of this century, and were much less numerous during the pre-transitional demographic regime due to high mortality, and in the current one due to extremely low fertility.

The number of living children an ego has follows a pattern which is not dissimilar to the number of living siblings (Figure 9.5). Early in this century, the maximum number of living children was reached when a woman was between 40 and 49 and dropped rapidly thereafter. As happened with siblings, children were generally more abundant in the second simulation mainly because the decrease in fertility was more than compensated by declines in mortality. In the third simulation with data from 1960 the situation is somewhat different as children are considerably less numerous at earlier ages, but more numerous at higher age groups, as the effect of decreased adult mortality made itself felt as a female ego aged. By the time a woman reached 60 years of age, she had more living children than she would have had in 1900 and when she reached 80, she had more living children than in any other simulation. With more contemporary data, the total number of children is far lower than in any other simulation, though by the time a woman reaches old age the practically negligible effects of mortality among her children lead to a significant reduction in the shortfall of living children. It was during the first half of this century that living children were most numerous for adult women. For elderly women, on the other hand, it was during the middle decades of this century that living children were most abundant. The fourth simulation indicates that the demographic characteristics of modern-day Spain are in the process of creating a veritable dearth of children over most of the life course.

If the microsimulation is enlarged to include the next level of kinship (aunts, uncles, grandparents, etc.), we can get a reasonable idea of the general dimensions of kinship for the extended family. Figures 9.6 and 9.7 contain the total number of all kin within these limits for the first (1900) and the fourth (1985–90) simulations. They give an accurate indication of the development of the extended family as seen from the perspective of a woman throughout her life course. In 1900 when she was still an infant, the number of lateral kin (siblings, cousins) was about the same as that of ascending kin. By 20 years of age, kin of the preceding generation had been reduced by nearly 40 per cent, and those of the same generation had increased by nearly two-thirds. By 50 years of age, only 64 per cent of female egos had one or more ascending kin remaining, and the number of lateral kin had declined by one-third. These declines were compensated in part by the rise in the number of descending kin, itself the product of the fertility of the ego and that of other females of her generation and family.

In the fourth simulation, the dimensions of kinship are markedly different. The most noteworthy change is that, with the partial exception of ascending kin, the total number of kin is far lower than in the first simulation. At 10 years

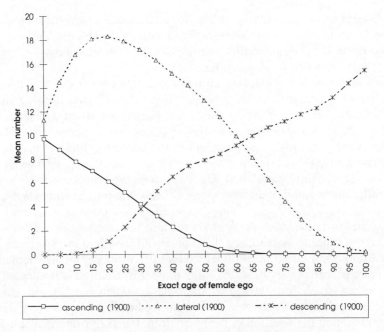

Fig. 9.6 Total number of ascending, lateral, and descending kin, Spain, ca. 1900

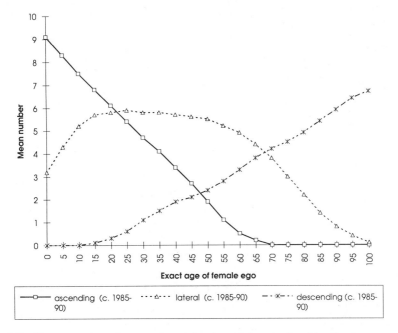

Fig. 9.7 Mean number of ascending, lateral, and descending kin, Spain, ca. 1985–1990

of age, in 1900 a female ego had over 16 lateral kin as opposed to slightly over five in 1985–90. At 60, she had around nine lateral kin and another nine descending kin, as opposed to less than five lateral and only about three descending kin in the last simulation. These patterns can be seen more clearly in Figure 9.8, in which the total number of kin within the kinship boundaries we have used are shown over the life course of a female ego for all four simulations. Over much of this century, the patterns by age remained the same: an increase in the total number of kin during the first years of life, a subsequent decrease until an ego was 80–90 years of age, and then a small rebound. This pattern is explained by mortality at all ages, and the reproductive cycle of the female's cohort as well as that of their mothers. The peak age for kin, however, is somewhat different in the different simulations, being earlier in the first and last simulations, and later in the middle two. The most noteworthy change in these simulations concerns the total number of kin, which was highest during the middle years of this century, and especially in the second simulation (1930), and lowest in the high mortality/high fertility context of 1900 and in the extremely low fertility/low mortality context of the last simulation.

These patterns suggest that the net effect of the demographic transition on the dimensions of kinship in Spanish society was a changing one. At first high

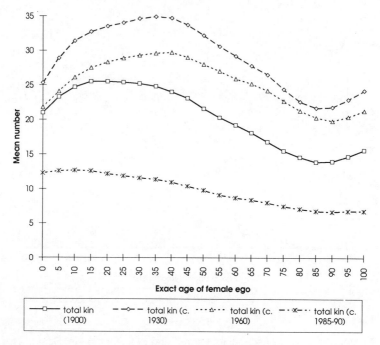

Fig. 9.8   Total number of kin by age of female ego, Spain

fertility and mortality kept the dimensions of kinship relatively reduced. As fertility and mortality declined, however, the number of available kin increased, especially after a female ego had reached full adulthood. At that point, the kin-enhancing implications of declining mortality were outstripping the kin-reducing effects of declining fertility. Eventually, however, this situation proved to be a transitory one, as fertility decline began to dictate the basic structure of kinship. In Spain during the first half of this century, the number of kin a person could count on having tended to rise, though that trend was reversed during the second half, slowly at first and ever more rapidly thereafter. The deepening dearth of kin is one of the most salient characteristics of family life in present-day Spain. It is quite likely that today the dimensions of kinship are lower than at any time in Spanish history. At an empirical level, this present-day dearth is much more visible among the younger age groups of the population, but it affects everyone.

Kinship and the Family in Spain

The microsimulation models used in this chapter are demographically driven, and thus their results are basically demographic. Yet the implications of these trends for family systems, inheritance, socialization of the young, and the ability of the family to act as a provider of welfare are enormous. There can be little doubt but that the demographic factors underying kinship structures were essential to the way in which the family developed over time in Spain. Many of the key changes affecting family life during the past three centuries, and particularly the accelerated pace of change during the twentieth century, can be traced directly or indirectly to demographic patterns. When these patterns were relatively stable, kinship and the family tended to be stable as well, at least in many of their visible characteristics. In times of great demographic change, especially when it was very rapid, the family could not help but be profoundly affected.

This has been the case in the twentieth century. As fertility and mortality underwent the throes of a demographic transition, the dimensions and structures of kinship changed accordingly, first increasing the number of living relatives and then decreasing them drastically. Family life was profoundly affected in the process. Cultural factors may have been instrumental in the origin of different family forms in Spain, and often served to mitigate the forces of change, but they have been unable to resist the momentous changes in family life that have been the hallmark of this century. The modernization of economic activity together with the growth of the State, both of which have also undergone profound transformations over the past 100 years, were the essential fellow travellers of demographic change. Together they have led to a family in Spain today which bears little resemblance to that which had characterized Spanish society for so long.

One of the most important implications of these changes has been that the very nature and meaning of generation and generational length is undergoing a profound transformation. In the past, the stages of life and their duration were pretty clear to people. Infancy and childhood did not last long, mainly because children became economically important to their household at a young age, and by 10–12 they were in fact young adults in traditional Spanish society. Mature and fully productive adult life began with marriage, began to wane with the termination of people's reproductive period, and definitively ended when the last of the children had left the household via marriage. The age of retirement was normally short-lived because health failed quickly, and the 'fourth age', if there was one, was very, very brief. This was in the demographic nature of things because many people were born and few lived beyond the age of 60. It was a bottom-heavy population pyramid, in which transitions from one stage of life to another were reasonably clear-cut. Now this is no longer the case. The reduction in fertility and especially the lengthening of life has profoundly altered this panorama: childhood lasts much longer, the young spend far more years being economically unproductive, reproduction occupies less time, and the time spent in retirement is longer and affects more people than ever before. These changes can be seen clearly in the results of the microsimulations we have run.

The conditions of marriage and inheritance have been changed by these processes. In pre-transitional contexts, when a young couple got married most likely at least one of the four conjugal parents would have died, and within the first 10–15 years of marriage, all of the members of the parental generation would have disappeared. This can be seen in the first microsimulation, carried out with data from 1900, at which over 10 per cent of female egos of marrying age (20–29) had no living parent at all, and by the time they had finished their reproductive period some 15–20 years later, two-thirds of them had no living parents.[13] Had earlier demographic data been available, at a time when in most areas of Spain mortality was considerably more severe than it was in 1900, the death of one or more of the parents would have come much earlier in life. By the third simulation in 1960, however, the percentage of women with no living parent had declined to 1.5 per cent during her marriageable ages, and to 32 per cent towards the end of her reproductive period; and by the last simulation these percentages had declined to 1 per cent and to 15 per cent respectively. This means that should the demographic rates informing the last simulation persist into the future, the majority of women will have lost both parents only when they reach 55 years of age, 15 years later than for the first simulation, and many will have living parents well into their own years of retirement.

In traditional Spanish society, death in one generation was the key to marriage in another, mainly because inheritance devolved upon the younger generation at the death of the older one. In the first simulation, most couples had inherited from at least one parent by the time they married, and the transmission of the complete patrimony in most cases had taken place soon thereafter. This is no longer a realistic possibility in a context such as the one holding in the 1960 or in the 1985–90 simulations, in which married couples continued to have most of their parents living well past the end of their reproductive years. In the new context, inheritance can no longer play its traditional role as the key to inter-generational property transmission. The importance of the potential increase in the share of inheritance which younger generations might have expected thanks to smaller sibsize and numbers of heirs sharing the family estate has been more than offset by the amount of time people must wait to inherit. In Spanish society today, except among the very rich, it is evident that inheritance is no longer considered to be much of an asset by the younger generations, mainly because by the time they can enjoy it they no longer need it to establish their own economic base. In many ways, if inheritance were to skip a generation and go directly from grandparents to grandchildren, its economic and social importance would probably be far higher than it is today. This is yet another irony of contemporary life![14]

The alteration of the traditional duration of the stages of life also tends to undermine the importance of the inheritance offspring stand to receive from their parents in another way. In recent years more and more people have been using a part of their life's savings to face longer and longer periods of retirement with the greatest possible security, and this is frequently done at the expense of the estate they will eventually bequeath to their heirs. This trend is only just beginning to be visible in Spain, though its importance will invariably increase as the duration of retirement increases.

The economic changes taking place in Spanish society during this century have played a key complementary role in the patterns I have just discussed, mainly because the primacy of wage labour, which was firmly established in most of the country by the middle years of this century, as well as the progressive entry of women into the job market characteristic of these past two to three decades, has enabled people to continue to marry and to live reasonably well without the benefit of inheritance. Yet by minimizing the importance of inheritance, one of the essential elements of traditional forms of family cohesion has also been removed. It remains to be seen just how this will affect family development in Spain in the future, but I think that fundamental changes will occur and are occurring which will affect how the family functions and how it is viewed in society as a whole. The removal of one of its basic functions cannot help but profoundly alter its cohesiveness, and potentially its importance as well.

In stem-family areas, the increasingly prolonged survivorship in the parental generation is threatening to undo the basic family system altogether. In addition to the fact that recent economic and demographic changes have sharply reduced the importance of inheritance and therefore of succession in stem-family systems, a by-product of demographic change has been the prolongation of the period of co-residence which all heirs are required to spend with their parents. Within the context of the demographic rates holding in 1900, by 40–45 years of age a man could reasonably expect to have lost at least his father and probably his mother as well. Nowadays, the period of co-residence has been prolonged by as much as 20 years, and includes not only the heir and his children, but also the generation of his parents and that of his grandparents. Throughout this century, the demographic and economic changes taking place in Spain have teamed up to make the position of the chosen heir profoundly undesirable, and have rendered the stem family in Spain practically meaningless in social and economic terms, little more than an antiquated but cherished relic of the past.

Kinship networks were also essential for the way in which children were socialized because it was through contact with kin that young people learned the meaning of the family, of its importance and of norms of social behaviour. It was the first and often the most meaningful contact a child had with the outside world, and thus a key link between the individual and the society as a whole. It was the nuclear family which was most instrumental in the socialization of children and young adults, though the extended family also participated in this process. Demographically induced changes in the dimensions of kinship networks have had important implications for the way in which the young have been socialized in Spanish society, though these effects have been at least apparently contradictory. On the one hand, the total number of both conjugal kin (siblings, parents) and kin further removed first increased, then decreased substantially over the century. The total kin pool available to 10-year-old girls, for example, comprised about 25 persons in the first simulation (circa 1900), jumped to more than 31 in the second (circa 1930), then declined to 25 in the third simulation and just above 12 in the last one. It is easy to corroborate the importance of this decline over the past 50 years by just asking people from different generations about the number of cousins or siblings they had at any given age. The answers consistently underscore the fact that the decline is general for all sectors of Spanish society.

Just as the kin pool available for the socialization of the young has shrunk, the number of elderly available precisely for this task has increased substantially thanks to the improved regimen of mortality. The number of children who have a chance to get to know their grandparents or even their great-grandparents has increased enormously during the course of this century (Figures 9.9 and 9.10). In 1900, for example, only about half of young girls aged 10 had at least one living grandparent, as opposed to the more than 95 per cent in the last simulation. Grandparents were not only more numerous, they lived longer as well. At age 30, almost no female egos continued to have any living grandparents in the first simulation, as opposed to nearly 15 per cent in 1960 and almost one-third in the last simulation. Families spanning four generations were practically unknown at the beginning of this century, but the proportion

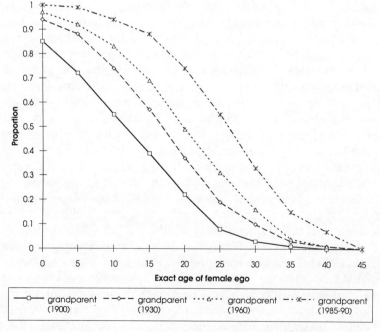

Fig. 9.9 Proportion of female egos with at least one living grandparent

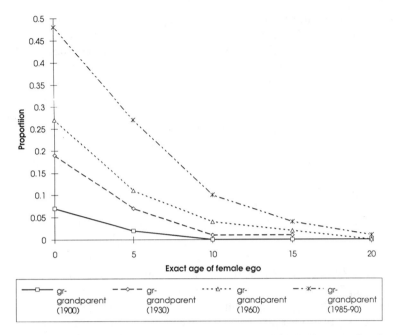

Fig. 9.10 Proportion of female egos with at least one living great-grandparent

of young girls who are able to get to know their great-grandparents has increased steadily. The microsimulations we have run suggest that at present, between 5 and 8 per cent of all 10-year-olds continue to have at least one living great-grandparent, and if the demographic conditions of low mortality persist, this percentage will increase sharply in the future.

These patterns suggest that the type of kin available for the socialization of children is changing. Whereas in the past, parents were able to rely on the support of siblings and of the relatively abundant kin pool made up of cousins, aunts, and uncles for support in the socialization of their children, as the century has progressed both of these sources of kin support have diminished sharply. The burden of socialization falls increasingly to the parents themselves, and to their own parents and grandparents. Moreover, with the progressive increase of families in which both parents work outside the household, the role of grandparents will likely grow in the near future.

In this way, the family education of the young has become increasingly vertical and multi-generational. The transformation from the multi-directional nature of family support so characteristic of traditional society, to the fundamentally vertical one prevalent today, not only indicates a shift in the sources of family support, but also probably has important implications for the way in which young children are socialized and the priorities consonant to their familial education. The process of socialization in which siblings, cousins, and aunts and uncles are central can never be the same as one which relies on parents and especially grandparents. Social constraints and values, for example, will never be filtered through parents and grandparents the way they are through siblings and cousins. A potential implication of this could be that family-based socialization processes might be grounded on the traditional values and attitudes typical of the older generations in the family more than they ever were in the past. Should this be the case, family education will tend to become increasingly at odds with the education children receive through their friends, their teachers, and the television.

Elsewhere in this book the key role the family played for the welfare of its members was discussed at length. Before the twentieth century, and in the absence of Poor Laws and most other civil sources of welfare, the family provided the first social safety net for those who were most vulnerable in society: young children, single-parent families, and especially the elderly. The advent of a national social security system during the central decades of this century proved to be an important departure from the past in that a number of people's needs could be covered by non-family means of support. Despite these changes, however, in Spain and in other parts of the developed world, the family continues to be essential for the welfare of its members, because affording complete care for people, especially those who are ill, is far beyond the economic capacity of any contemporary society. Moreover, the family provides other types of company, comfort, and support which institutions cannot deliver no matter how good and efficient they might be.

Kinship networks are an integral part of familial-support systems mainly because it is within them that vulnerability arises and risk must be managed. Just as the ability of society to meet adequately the needs of its own vulnerable members depends on the age structure of dependency, much the same occurs within the kin group. If the family is laden with dependent kin, it will not be able to care for them as well as when the relation between dependent and active kin is more positive. Since these relations are strictly subject to demographic constraints, they will not remain stable either through the lifetime of a person or over historical time. Here microsimulation can be very useful because it enables us to view the relationship of dependence within the kin group under the demographic conditions resembling those found in society itself.

One of the CAMSIM routines tabulates the mean number of dependent kin in various categories and the proportion of egos who have dependent kin, all classified by age of ego. Dependency is strictly determined by age, and people below 15 and above 65 are considered dependent regardless of whether or not they are economically active. While this type of classification may present problems when a fine-tuned analysis is desired, it is perfectly adequate when we want to ascertain the overall ability of the family group to meet the needs of those who are dependent and potentially vulnerable. I have used these data to establish two summary measures of dependence within the kin group. One is the standard dependency ratio (dependent kin/active kin), and the other is the net number of active kin (active kin minus dependent kin). Both these measures are highly correlated, and depict dependency and vulnerability within the kin group in a complementary fashion. The female egos have not been included in either of these measures and, even if they had, the basic patterns observed would not have changed. Since the presentation of the results is by the exact age of a female ego, they can be most aptly interpreted as the actual relations of dependence as defined by the age distribution of the kin group at different times of a female ego's life, and its potential ability to care for her needs at that age.

The microsimulations suggest sharply fluctuating relations of dependency over a female ego's lifetime (Figures 9.11 and 9.12). When she was young, dependency was high, began to decline at about 10 years of age, and reached a low point at 25. At that time, her parents, aunts, and uncles were still fairly young and active, her lateral kin were just reaching their maturity, and there were few descending kin left in the family. An increase in dependency can be observed between 25 and 40, followed by a decrease to another low point between 50 and 59 years of age.[15] This process can best be explained by the fact that before 40, the birth of dependent children occurred more quickly than the disappearance of dependent parents, though later just the opposite holds true. After 55–60, however, both indicators of dependency increase sharply

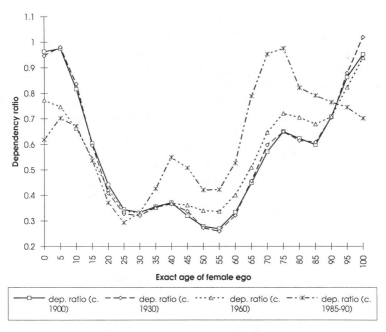

Fig. 9.11 Dependency ratio in kin group by age of ego (not including ego)

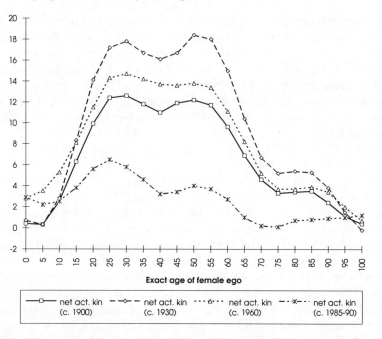

Fig. 9.12 Net number of active kin in kin group by age of female ego (not including ego)

throughout much of the rest of the female ego's lifetime.[16] This pattern suggests that the moment at which levels of dependency within the family group were highest was precisely when a female ego was least able to fend for herself, and the moment when the age distribution of the kin group was most favourable was precisely when she was a net provider.[17] It is also true, however, that when women were in their most productive years (25–50) and were the least likely to need family support, they were active in supporting other members of the kin group who did need help to manage vulnerability more successfully.

The first two simulations done with data from the early part of the present century suggest that the dependency ratio within the family hardly varied, though the net number of active kin increased considerably during the most productive periods of a woman's life cycle. In the third simulation (data circa 1960), a decrease in dependency at younger ages together with an important increase after 45 can be observed. This pattern can be more or less directly attributed to the fact that female egos had fewer young siblings when they were young, and fewer siblings and grown children when they were older. In 1960, the net number of active kin shows a substantial decrease with respect to levels holding in 1930. The trends observed between the second and the third simulations accelerate with the fourth and last simulation, based on data from 1985–90. Here levels of dependency increase dramatically with respect to the other simulations, and the net number of active kin declines to near zero at many ages, indicating that at key moments of the life course there were almost as many dependent members in the family group as there were active ones.

The extremely low fertility and mortality of this last simulation creates a situation in which the size of the kin group is greatly reduced and its mean age grows. Even though a stable population of this kind does not yet exist in Spain, the observed results suggest that, barring an important reversal in demographic trends, it is only a matter of time before these types of patterns become commonplace. It is a society in which a young married couple may have very few if any children of their own, but they still have three of four parents in their sixties and perhaps one or two grandparents in their nineties. The care for those grandparents may fall in part to retired offspring who themselves are entering into a period of vulnerability and dependency. Complicating this is the fact that care of the aged is more expensive and can be more time-consuming for society as a whole and for the family itself than, say, care for the very young, whose health needs are generally fairly low.

In the light of these results, it is evident that the family in Spain will increasingly find itself short-handed when attempting to meet the needs of its elderly members. An example of this is an aged person who needs ongoing personal and medical monitoring. The options the younger members of his or her kin group are facing are either to place the parent or grandparent in the home of a family member or in a rest home where he will receive professional care. At home, the costs to the younger generation are both personal and economic. In a rest home, the costs are basically economic, but are far greater than with the first option. At present in Spain the social security system does have some rest homes, and these are free of cost for people pensioned under this system. However, should families forgo having the elderly at home with them, the system would be swamped immediately; and in the future it will probably be swamped regardless of what individual families decide to do. The only other option, in that case, would be to make use of private rest homes, so ubiquitous in other countries like the United States.

The point here is that a considerable part of the costs related to this care, be they personal or economic, are normally borne by the family either directly, or out of the savings of the elderly which would have eventually devolved upon the younger generation. Even if widespread private retirement insurance did exist in Spain, costs relating to the care of the aged would still be considerable.[18] When it comes to bearing these costs, it is an entirely different matter for a family of, say, a 70-year-old woman, which in 1930 had a total net number of active living kin of almost 7 and almost 2.5 living children, than it is for a family shown in the last simulation, where there are as many dependent as there are active kin and where there is only one surviving child. The objective 'costs' for the care of this person will likely be similar, unless, of course, they are able to enjoy higher levels of general health, but the number of kin handling those costs has decreased dramatically.

In Chapter 4, I showed how an increasing percentage of these elderly persons were able to continue to live longer with their spouses, and the microsimulations suggest the same pattern exists and will continue into the future.[19] This is unquestionably a source of great comfort for elderly women and, from the standpoint of the family group as a whole, it lessens the immediate need to find suitable living conditions for her. The husband, however, is also dependent and potentially vulnerable, and in the long run one of the spouses will end up being alone. At that point, however, *ir por meses*, the age-old custom of spending short periods of time in the household of each child, will not be a shared task because there will only be one child left to shoulder the responsibility.

The demographic changes taking place in Spanish society during the second half of this century have jeopardized the ability of the family group to adequately fulfil its traditional task of being the key source of support for its own members. The issue of ageing, dependence, and economic and physical vulnerability could just as easily have been couched in terms of society as a whole, though here the use of microsimulation makes it especially appropriate within the context of the kin group. Ultimately, however, any adequate response to the challenge must necessarily end up implicating both the family and society.[20] The progressive ageing of the Spanish family and of Spanish society is unquestionably one of the crucial emerging issues facing Spain at this juncture of its history. It remains to be seen whether or not the response given will be adequate.

In the final analysis, the data derived from the simulations we have run do not yield strictly empirical results because the Spanish population is not a stable one. Nevertheless, the trends shown in the dimensions of kinship are unmistakable. Better than any other analytical method, these simulations give us an idea of the general outlines of the future of the family in Spain. The results suggest that profound changes are occurring and these will affect and are affecting many of the basic tasks the family has traditionally performed. Its ability to meet these challenges, however, remains to be seen. Even though some of the constraints which are beginning to affect family life are visible, the future of the family has yet to be written.

Notes

1. The major difference between macrosimulation and microsimulation is that the first approach uses a group as its basic point of reference, whereas microsimulation is based on the individual. For a useful overview of microsimulation, see Wachter (1987). See also Ruggles (1990).
2. The paper by Kunstadter *et al.* (1963) was among the first to make use of this type of approach.
3. CAMSIM was designed at the Cambridge Group for the History of Population and Social Structure and SOCSIM at the University of California at Berkeley. Other

approaches such as BACKPOP and MOMSIM also exist. See, for example, Le Bras (1973) and Ruggles (1987). For more on other family-related types of simulation, see, for example, Bongaarts (1987), Pullum (1987), and Le Bras (1993).

4. For literature on SOCSIM, see Wachter *et al.* (1978), Reeves (1987), and Hammel *et al.* (1990). For applications of this model see, for example, Wachter *et al.* (1978), Hammel *et al.* (1979), Hammel *et al.* (1991), and Hammel and Mason (1993). For methodological introductions to CAMSIM, see Smith (1987) and Smith and Oeppen (1993).

5. At earlier dates, many of even the basic input parameters are difficult to find.

6. The Cambridge Group for History of Population and Social Structure graciously allowed me to make use of their CAMSIM program. I am grateful to James Smith and Jim Oeppen (Cambridge Group) and particularly to Zhongwei Zhao (Cambridge Group and East–West Center) for their help in adjusting the Spanish input data to suit the requirements of the program and in running the simulations themselves.

7. In these paragraphs I am following the ideas of James Smith (1987: 250–60) and of James Smith and Jim Oeppen (1993: 283–92).

8. This can become a limitation especially if the incidence of a spouse's earlier history of fertility is important for analytical reasons, as in the case of simulating half-siblings or step-children. Since CAMSIM uses this type of open population for marriage, it cannot be used in simulating the way marriage markets work.

9. James Smith (1987: 252) has described the CAMSIM algorithm for simulating a group of kinship positions for a female ego as a four-stage process: '1) creating a female at birth, 2) simulating her life course forward in time from her birth, 3) creating a spouse of the appropriate age whenever the female is scheduled to marry, and 4) creating a child at each point where the female is scheduled to give birth. This yields a completed life history for the female, a partial life history for each of her spouses (marriage date, marriage age), and a partial life history of each of her children (birth dates).'

10. Even if using changing demographic rates were a feature of the program, it would be extraordinarily difficult to generate a complete set of rates over any sort of prolonged historical period.

11. At any one point in time, some of the requisite input data were likely to be missing. When this occurred, best estimates based on related indicators were used. This was the case, for example, with the parity progression ratios. Original values were only available on the retrospective fertility histories contained in the 1930 census, but corresponding to women 41–45 who had lived much of their reproductive period closer to 1900–10 than to 1930. Otherwise, these ratios have been derived from empirical estimates of marital fertility rates and other related demographic indices. Since the simulated results refer to a stable population, the values sometimes differ a little from those based on cross-sectional empirical data.

12. For example, in the last simulation the number of siblings a 10-year-old female ego had was 77 per cent below the number of siblings she would have had at the beginning of the century, 79 per cent below those in the second simulation, and 72 per cent below those in 1960. At 70 years of age, the differences were much smaller, as women of the fourth simulation had only 9 per cent fewer siblings than at the beginning of the century, 64 per cent fewer than in 1930, and 66 per cent fewer than in 1960.

13. Between 20 and 29, 38 per cent no longer had a living father, and 27 per cent no living mother. Between 40 and 49, 83 per cent had no living father and 76 per cent no living mother.
14. Should this suggestion ever be implemented, the first generation which is effectively skipped in the line of inheritance would no doubt feel slighted!
15. The actual levels of kin included in the simulation can alter in part the patterns observed. For example, cousins have been included, but children of cousins have not. This tends to decrease the dependency ratio when egos are in their middle years and increase them when they are older. On the other hand, had, say, grand-aunts and granduncles or the cousins of aunts and uncles or their children been included, the net effect would have been just the contrary.
16. The basic similarities between these patterns and the cycles of dependency observed in the co-residential group in 19th- and 20th-century Cuenca, which were discussed in the preceding chapter, are striking: dependency was high among the young and during old age, and relatively low for young adults and persons in their 50s. The relatively higher levels of dependency among 30–45 year old adults were much more visible among households than in the microsimulations.
17. Had the female egos been included in the measure, the moments of relatively high dependency within the family would have been higher, and those of low dependency lower.
18. In fact, this type of insurance is still quite uncommon in Spain.
19. At 70 years of age, 29 per cent in the first simulation, and 54 per cent in the fourth, continue to have a living spouse.
20. For a very useful and typically insightful approach to the issue of public and familial support of the elderly within the context of British society, see Laslett (1989: 122–39).

10 Present and Future Perspectives for the Family in Spain

During the course of this book, I have raised a number of issues directly affecting family life in Spain. My discussion for the most part has been historical and little empirical evidence from present-day Spain has been used. Within this context, family systems, co-residential patterns, the life-cycle limits of vulnerability, family economies, marriage markets, and different aspects of family demography have all been evaluated. I have attempted to focus on structural changes taking place over the long run and have paid considerably less attention to more immediate or less lasting patterns of change. In this analysis, the continuity of family forms and behaviour patterns has prevailed over their instability. This long-term perspective has been used because stability and gradual transformation have been central to the development of the family in Spain for the last three centuries. Key changes affecting family life have been numerous but for the most part their effects have been gradual, often only making themselves felt in medium- and long-term contexts.

By the same token, any analysis of the family which emphasizes stability and continuity as this one does would end up being partial and misleading if it did not trace family patterns up until the very present. Recent years have witnessed momentous demographic, social, and economic changes taking place in Spain. Whether or not these changes have altered family life so much as to make it almost unrecognizable by historical standards is an important question which merits an answer. In the preceding chapter, the use of microsimulation techniques helped sharpen the focus on certain aspects of past, present, and possibly future patterns of family life. As in any simulation, the results are constrained by the validity of the input data and the extent to which these data hold in future contexts. For the people living in Spain during much of the twentieth century, there can be little doubt but that the patterns emerging from the simulations are accurate in general terms. This, however, is not necessarily the case for the last simulation, which used rigorously contemporary data to unveil some of the potential contours of future kinship networks in Spain. The results suggest that profound changes have been taking place in the course of this century and that the pace of change seems to have been accelerating in recent years.

What of other aspects of family life? Are changes there going to be as pervasive as they seem to be for the dimensions of kin groups? Is there going to be nothing left of the traditional Spanish family? Will it be the victim of the latest wave of economic and social modernization? While it is never possible to have more than a hazy and very imprecise idea of the future, sociological and anthropological research in Spain has done a great deal to shed light on some of the main characteristics of the contemporary Spanish family.[1] In this concluding chapter I will briefly outline some of the major contemporary issues affecting the family, especially those relating to some of the themes raised earlier in this book. Despite the intensity of change, links to the past will be shown to be strong both in terms of people's behaviour and their attitudes towards the family. It is a chapter designed to link past and present family forms, while timidly opening a peephole towards the future.

Decades of Change

The political, economic, and social transformations taking place in Spain in recent decades have been astounding. A visitor to Spain in 1995 who had not been there since 1960 would scarcely be able to recognize it as the same country. In 1960 Spain was poor by European standards, politically conservative, and socially traditional and Catholic. It was a country which in many ways seemed to have tiptoed only hesitantly and often unwillingly into an era of modernization. In many areas wheat continued to be threshed by hand, widows invariably dressed in black, the occasional female tourists wearing short pants were liable to be stoned, and levels of urbanization and educational attainment were modest at best. Economic backwardness and the political and social scars of a Civil War were central to the lethargic pace of Spanish modernization. It is not that important changes had not taken place in the preceding decades. They had, but in many ways the dynamics of change had slowed almost to a crawl, especially in the aftermath of the Civil War. The social and economic distance separating Spain from its European neighbours, especially those to the north, was likely greater in 1960 than it had been in 1920 or in 1930. Yet by the final decade of this century all of this was different. Spain and Spaniards were rich as they had never been before, they were highly educated, urban and urbane, dedicated consumers and, at least apparently, far less traditional. The distance separating them from their neighbours was far less than it had been in 1960, or in 1930 for that matter.

During these past three decades, profound change has affected all areas of national life. Within the realm of politics, this period witnessed the end of one regime and its replacement by another. The dictatorship of Francisco Franco, which had remained in place since the end of the Civil War, crumbled with his death in 1975 and was replaced by a parliamentary monarchy. Censorship gave way to free speech; and political organization in Spain became democratic and stable for the first time in its history. This change was accompanied by the entry of Spain into NATO (1979) and into the European Economic Community (1986), symbolic of the first full acceptance of Spain by the international community since before the Civil War. For Spaniards it symbolized the linking of their collective destiny to that of the rich nations of western Europe. At home, the political changes brought with them an outburst of political enthusiasm, as the dynamics of the democratic political process were learned and mastered. Today, despite numerous and persistent problems, democracy in Spain is admired abroad and accepted at home by increasingly important segments of the population as the best or perhaps only viable way to address the often thorny issues confronting the country. It is within this context of political transition and renovation that recent developments in the family must be understood.

From an economic standpoint changes have been no less dramatic. After the Civil War, Spanish economic growth practically came to a standstill for nearly 15 years. The depletion of human and economic resources during the war, an autarkic and protectionist economic policy designed to cut Spain off from outside influences, and the political isolation it was subjected to by most other nations contributed to this lacklustre economic performance. The entire economic panorama changed sometime between 1955 and 1965 thanks to the increasing acceptance of the Franco regime by other nations and especially to the opening up of the Spanish economy to foreign investment and trade, symbolized by the Law of Economic Stabilization of 1959.[2] The economic turnabout was momentous; and a period of extremely rapid economic growth ensued which was going to have long-ranging effects on Spanish society. It was a period in which the Spanish economy grew at a rate only exceeded by Japan's among the developed countries of the world. Uninterrupted growth lasted until 1973–4, was followed by an important recession lasting until 1983, and then another spate of growth until 1991. Taking the period as a whole, however, the changes have been immense. Between 1930 and 1960 per capita gross domestic product increased by less than 25 per cent, as opposed to between 1960 and 1990 when growth was nearly 12 times as fast.[3] As a result, the gap separating Spanish per capita domestic product from that of other industrial nations diminished substantially.[4]

The economic take-off in Spain, especially during the initial years before 1974, was arguably the most important event of the twentieth century because it transformed the nature of Spanish economic activity and altered the underpinnings of Spanish society itself. Since living standards grew as a result, social stability was assured and the basis was laid for the consumer society that exists today. It also made the ensuing political transition possible. In 1960 Spanish society might well have been symbolized by the sleepy village of La Mancha portrayed in the film *Bienvenido Mr. Marshall* directed by Luis García Berlanga. There, dreams were the key to all expectations: one person dreamed of being a conquistador, another of being a sheriff in the American West, and yet another of tractors being parachuted to him somewhere from heaven. All were living a dream; in many ways Spain seemed to be living a dream as well. By 1990 credit cards, holidays abroad, conspicuous consumption, political moderation, and high social and economic expectations have become much apter symbols of a transformed society.

Women, Work, and Reproduction in Times of Change

It is hardly likely that Spanish families could have remained untouched during times of such intense social, economic, and political transformations. They were, though some aspects of family life were more affected than others. The changing role of women in Spanish society was a key link between families and social, economic, and political change. The importance of the role played by women for the family cannot be underestimated: the entire family life cycle was predicated on their reproductive process, their contribution to the household budget was fundamental, and their role in the education and socialization of children made them essential for the entire process of social reproduction. More than any other member of the family, mothers were the chief source of cohesion within the family and their importance was recognized by all. Yet women were more directly affected by the transformations rocking Spanish society than any other member of the family.

In very general terms, prior to the central decades of this century, the role of the vast majority of women in society was clearly set out. Often active in the work-force at young ages, women normally abandoned salaried labour when they married. The most productive years of their lives were spent bearing and raising children, as well as playing a complementary role in household economic activities. Given the demographic constraints of the period, however, this meant that a woman's role as mother and educator was not really finished until she was well into her fifties, when the youngest of her children had grown up and abandoned the family household. In other words, a woman's role in the process of social reproduction took up most of the productive years of her life.

All of this changed in recent years. A necessary prerequisite for these changes was a reduction in the amount of time which women had to spend bearing and rearing their families. This reduction was a by-product of the demographic transition which took place in Spain during the first half of this century. Whereas in 1900 as many as six childbirths might have been necessary to assure the demographic reproduction of the family, by the middle of the century slightly more than three would suffice.[5] Once this demographic threshold had been reached, social and economic forces became central for the definition of women's role in society. Their educational attainment and their increasing participation at all ages in the labour market, both directly linked to the profound modernization of Spanish society over the past three decades, are the most enduring symbols of this change.

For centuries literacy and educational attainment in Spain were considerably lower than in other European nations. Thanks to an increased emphasis on education both during the final period of the Franco regime and under the current democratic governments, in recent years much has been done to close an annoying gap which was traditionally an important obstacle to social progress. Between 1970 and 1992, levels of illiteracy were reduced by more than half, and now stand at 4.6 per cent of the population, still higher than in most other countries of Europe. Since the General Education Law of 1970–71, considerable government efforts have been dedicated to enlarging the coverage and improving the quality of the public educational system in Spain.[6] An example of this can been seen in the enrolment ratios for higher education, which increased more than threefold from 8.91 per cent in 1970 to 31.5 per cent in 1987,[7] bringing Spain fairly close to the average for western Europe as a whole.[8] Even though progress everywhere has been noteworthy, it has been with women's educational attainment that the strides have been greatest. Between 1975 and 1987, for example, enrolment ratios in higher education went from 26.2 to 30.7 per cent for men, but jumped from 14.6 to 32.2 per cent for women (Figure 10.1). In only 13 years, women's participation in higher education more than doubled, and today the presence of women in Spanish universities is greater than that of men.[9]

The unprecedented entry of women into the labour market went hand in hand with the gains in their educational attainment. Together they have revolutionized the role of women in Spanish society. The economic modernization of the country was in the process of producing huge amounts of jobs in the services sector at a time when families were finding it increasingly difficult to maintain the living standards they desired with only one wage. For some a second wage was the vehicle for improving their economic position, while for

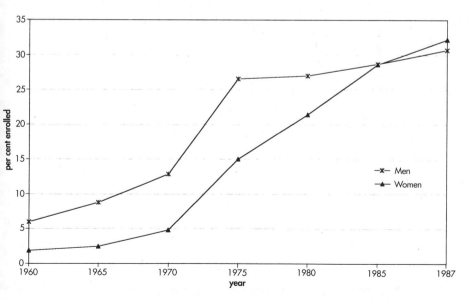

Fig. 10.1 School enrolment ratios for higher education in Spain by sex and date

others it became a valuable resource to fend off economic insecurity or to consolidate gains in living standards achieved earlier. In all cases, families and women began to see their role within the family increasingly as both mothers and as bread-winners. And work they did! In recent decades, the rate of increase in female labour-force participation has been astounding and has affected women of all ages (Figure 10.2).[10] For unmarried women (aged 20–24) participation increased steadily after the middle part of the 1950s, though as recently as 1970 it was clear that for most women holding a job was essentially a pre-marital affair as participation rates declined greatly for higher age groups (Delgado Pérez, 1993: 145–7). This all changed during the decade of the 1970s as women's labour-force participation increased dramatically in all age groups. By 1990, it was clear that life-long jobs were becoming common for the majority of the female population. Participation rates have only declined among the younger age groups, and this has been due to the fact that increasing numbers of young women are intent on obtaining a university degree before entering the labour force. Even though labour-force participation of women in Spain continues to be lower than in most northern European countries,[11] the rate of increase, with participation more than tripling in certain age

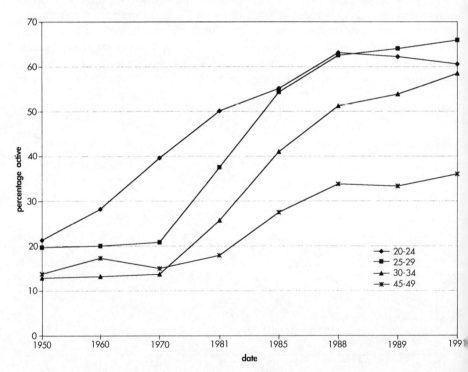

Fig. 10.2 Economically active female population in Spain by age group, different dates

groups, attests to just how intense the change of women's roles in Spain has been.

The implications of these changes for families have been no less dramatic. Combining the dual role of mother and wage earner has not always been easy for women. Adjustment to this new role has been hindered by the resistance to change of society as a whole, and especially of men, who have insisted that women continue to fulfil their traditional role of mothers and homemakers. In many ways, life has become considerably more complicated for women as they have had to continue their responsibilities within the family, even as they have taken on a significant economic role outside the household. Men have often been reticent to increase their participation within the household and have continued to leave the lion's share of the work to women. As is happening elsewhere, eventually this situation will change because sharing the economic burden of a household inevitably will lead to sharing its domestic burden as well. Women will demand, and eventually get, this type of burden-sharing.

Even so, it is also clear that working women cannot possibly continue to play as active a role in the socialization of their children and as homemakers as they did before. Even if they had enough energy, there are not enough hours in the day for that. As a result, public and private institutions have stepped in to take over at least part of the burden. A case in point are kindergartens and day care centres, which hardly existed in Spain 25 years ago, but which now are as ubiquitous as they are essential for working couples. More traditional sources of help such as grandparents continue to be important but they are mainly complements to other forms of child care. Despite these aids for working parents, it is hard to underestimate the role of television and, more recently, of computer games in the education and socialization of children. It is quite likely that the role played by the family in the process of children's education and socialization has diminished both in scope and in quality as a result of the recent changes in Spanish society.

During the early 1970s Spain had one of the highest fertility rates in western Europe, but in less than 20 years it has declined to less than half its earlier values. Spain now has one of the lowest fertility rates in the world, well below those levels holding in most other European nations.[12] The veritable marriage bust taking place in Spain since 1975, with marriage rates declining by nearly 40 per cent in a matter of 10 years, has been accompanied by a drastic reduction in fertility (Muñoz Pérez, 1987: 940; Sardon, 1992: 881; Delgado Pérez, 1993). Both the decline of fertility within marriage and the reduction of marriage rates can be traced, at least in part, to the new role being assumed by women in society. Even though recent trends in fertility and nuptiality have also been the consequence of other factors, not the least of which was the differential economic growth taking place during the 1980s which ended up making household formation far more difficult for younger people, the importance of women in the labour market should not be underestimated. At present there is some indication that the trend toward lower fertility is coming to a halt, and may be about to change direction much as it has in other European nations. In recent years fertility decline has only continued in the younger age groups, while among women of higher age groups, it has either stopped falling or appears to be on the rise.[13] Women who postponed their own reproductive activity until they had achieved some measure of success in their professional careers are behind the trend reversal.

Teenage fertility is slightly below the levels holding in most other European countries, and well below those shown by American teenagers. After rising briefly during the latter part of the 1970s, it declined along with fertility in other age groups throughout the 1980s (Delgado Pérez, 1994: 21, 27). Illegitimacy, on the other hand, which had declined steadily after the Civil War and reached a low point in 1970, began to increase gradually at first and more rapidly later. By 1986, the illegitimacy ratio (illegitimate births as a percentage of all births) was nearly six times what it had been in 1970.[14] While the increase has been substantial, trends were similar to those observed in other European countries and levels reached in Spain cannot be considered exceptional (Muñoz Pérez, 1991: 886–92).

It is impossible to know just when fertility will cease to decline in Spain, and once that happens, just how much it will rise, if at all, in the future. What is clear is that the changes in reproductive behaviour in Spain during the past 20 years have been dramatic, and can be both directly and indirectly linked to the profound transformations taking place in Spanish society. These changes have not been so noticeable with non-traditional modes of reproduction (fertility outside marriage, among teenagers) as they have been with married women. One of the most remarkable aspects of this entire process is how quickly it has taken place. In many ways, this pattern has been common to many traditional countries of southern Europe, which initiated their 'Second Demographic Transition' late, but once under way they went from traditionally high to exceptionally low fertility in a very short amount of time (Muñoz Pérez, 1987: 923–5). These were societies in which traditional modes of behaviour were being undermined by the forces of social and economic modernization much more quickly and completely than elsewhere.

During this same period of time, reductions in mortality have been nearly as spectacular as declines in fertility. By 1960 Spain had already achieved fairly high levels of life expectancy at birth (e_0 = 66.7 for men and 75.2 for women), but still lagged behind its neighbours in western Europe with the exception of Portugal. By 1990, life expectancy was up (73.3 for men and 79.7 for women) and, perhaps more significant, Spain was no longer a relative laggard as life expectancy was 2.2 years higher than the average in Europe.[15] Gains in infant mortality are indicative of this trend. In 1970, infant mortality stood at 28.1 deaths for every thousand live births; but by 1990 it was 7.6 per thousand. During this period Spain's relative position in the world changed drastically. In 1970, 22 developed countries had lower infant mortality rates than Spain; but by 1990, Spain had the 13th lowest infant mortality rate among developed countries, well ahead of nations like the United States, Norway, Belgium, or Italy (Pinnelli *et al.*, 1994: 370–2).[16]

Changes in mortality can also be traced directly to the modernization of Spanish society, which has been so intense in recent decades. A more comprehensive health care system, higher levels of education on health matters, and pre-natal care have all played a role. In so far as infant mortality is concerned, most authors consider that levels holding in a given country are directly related to the relative position of women in that country. In this sense, the increasingly relevant role women have played in Spanish society has undoubtedly been an important factor in improved health during childhood. Advances in medical science have been common in most developed countries and have gone a long way towards improving health and life expectancy. What has made changes more dramatic in Spain has been the rate of social transformation, which has been faster here than in most European nations outside of the southern European region. Once again, what sets Spain aside has not been the changes themselves, but their intensity. From a demographic standpoint, the past 25–30 years in Spain have been little short of revolutionary.

These demographic trends have extremely important implications for Spanish society and, by extension, for Spanish families. Perhaps the most important of these is that Spain is now a rapidly ageing society. Even though a general trend towards ageing has been present since the early part of the twentieth century, in the past 15–20 years its pace has accelerated sharply. In 1971, 14.1 per cent of the entire population was above 60; in 1981 this had risen to 15.4 per cent and today to just over 20 per cent. If current trends continue, population forecasts suggest that this age group will encompass 21.5 per cent of the total population by the turn of the century, 23 per cent in 2011 and 28.3 per cent in 2026 (Fernández Cordón, 1994*b*: 54–77). While there is always a large margin of error in any population forecast, the trend is unmistakable. The challenges posed by these trends will be immense, and will have profound social, economic, and cultural implications for the entire society. Much as the data presented in the preceding chapter suggest, an ageing society will also have a profound effect on families. Traditional forms of familial organization are changing and will change much more in the near future as families will find it increasingly difficult to provide support for their elderly members. The entire issue of ageing and the aged will unquestionably be one of the major challenges facing Spanish society and Spanish families in the years to come.

Recent demographic trends also have other related implications for society. One of particular importance for families has been the progressive reduction both in relative and in absolute terms of the number of young people. Since 1976 the total number of births in Spain has diminished sharply every year, and with it the size of younger cohorts. By 1991 the number of children born was more than 40 per cent below those levels holding towards the end of the decade of the 1970s. There is some indication that the decrease in births may soon end, as women who were born in the years of relatively high fertility and abundant births (1960–75) begin to have children of their own (ibid. 54–5). Yet two decades of declining births is already in the process of reducing the demand for education. Many elementary and some secondary schools have closed. These trends could well have negative implications for the quality of education children receive as local and national governments reorient their spending priorities towards other groups in society.

If present trends continue, as well they might, it is only a matter of time before the Spanish population begins to decline in size. Recent projections have estimated that the onset of negative natural growth rates will take place sometime between the years 2011 and about 2025 (ibid. 57–63). The actual date of absolute decline will be determined by future demographic trends and by the intensity of migratory flows. Whatever these may be, the general direction is unmistakable, as Spain becomes older and, eventually, smaller. The social, political, and economic implications of these trends will be immense and often negative. [17] As I have already pointed out earlier, the seeds of these implications are already present in Spanish society and in Spanish families.

Living Arrangements and Family Formation in a Modern Society

If the co-resident domestic group becomes the focal point of our analysis, the effects of decades of change are less clear. While certain important transformations in co-residential patterns can be seen, none of these seem to be fundamental to the traditional ways in which Spanish families have organized their households. There have been substantial increases in the numbers of persons living alone and some evidence of a growth of certain types of cohabitation, but the normative form of familial organization continues to be the nuclear household which is central to the life course of its members even after they have embarked on their own process of family formation. In this sense, despite changes in the size and age structure of households, and in the timing of the family formation, there is much to be recognized in Spanish households today: they tend to be formed upon marriage, are the basic environment in which children are raised and socialized, and enter a period of decline when the younger generation marries. While the timing and context of each of these events may vary, their importance does not. The basic elements of the family life cycle today are not extraordinarily different from those holding, say, 50 or 100 years ago. In many ways, the differences existing between Spanish and, say, American, Swedish, or even French modes of family and household organization seem to be just as large today as they were 30 years ago.

Between 1970 and 1981, nuclear household organization maintained or increased its importance nearly everywhere in Spain. This increase was more noteworthy in urban areas, but was present everywhere. [18] Recent data covering the city of Madrid suggest that the percentage of nuclear households in

1970 stood at 83.9, at 79.1 in 1986, and at 76.1 in 1991.[19] Despite the slight decline in the weight of nuclear households, with percentages of nuclear families as high as these, it is clear that for the vast majority of the Spanish population marriage and household formation continue to be related events.

Even though single-parent households are generally classified as nuclear, whenever they are not the consequence of a death of one of the parents they may well indicate certain forms of non-traditional behaviour with regard to the family. In Spain between 1970 and 1986 there seems to have been a substantial increase in the weight of this type of household, though its importance remains limited. In Madrid, for example, between 1981 and 1986, the number of single-parent households headed by women nearly doubled, though by 1991 the weight of these types of household appears to have diminished slightly.[20] The majority of these households were headed by widows or widowers, with divorced women accounting for somewhat less than 20 per cent and unmarried parents for a very insignificant proportion of them (Requena, 1990: 74–5). Even though the effects of the 1981 law legalizing divorce can be seen, the number of single-parent households due to divorce in Spain is in fact quite low (Campo, 1991: 120; Delgado Pérez, 1993: 136–7). In France, for example, among female-headed households, 57.4 per cent are headed by divorced or separated women, 23.5 per cent by widows, and 19.1 per cent by unmarried mothers (Lefaucher, 1988: 155). As yet there is little indication that Spain is moving in this direction. Single-parent households headed by men are much less important, accounting for 1.3 per cent of all households in both 1981 and 1991 in the city of Madrid.

The importance of solitary households has also increased substantially. In 1981, in all of Spain 10.3 per cent of all households were made up of only one person, an increase of over 37 per cent from the 1970 census (Flaquer and Soler, 1990: 26–7). By 1991, in the city of Madrid solitary households represented 16.6 per cent of all households, up from 15.3 per cent in 1986, 12.6 in 1981, and 6.9 in 1970. The trend is clear, though these levels of solitary households are by no means exceptional. A sizeable sample of rural Cuenca, for example, suggests that throughout the nineteenth and twentieth centuries the importance of solitary households was similar to that holding in Madrid and in Spain over the past two decades.[21] For a sample of developed countries located outside the southern European region, levels of solitary households were higher than those holding in Spain by as much as 11 percentage points in 1970 and by almost 16 points in 1980.[22] The majority of solitary households are made up of the elderly, almost 63 per cent according to 1991 data (Abellán, 1994: 113). The inroads made by divorce or other solitary living arrangements (especially at young ages) are visible (8.4 per cent of all solitary households were headed by divorced and separated persons in 1991 in Madrid), but as yet they do little to explain trends which are the result to a large degree of both the increase in and the increased disparity by sex of life expectancy among the elderly.[23]

Cohabitation, which has become a major form of non-traditional union in numerous European countries, is just beginning to become relevant in Spain. The retrospective survey carried out together with the census of 1991 gives us our first chance to estimate with any sort of reliability the extent to which it is used as a viable option by couples. The results of the survey suggest that its importance is still very limited (1.7 per cent of all unions are consensual unions), though there is clear indication that the incidence of cohabitation is greater in those unions formed more recently. Of all unions formed between 1981 and 1985, 4.0 per cent were made up of consenting unmarried adults, and among those formed after 1985, 7.8 per cent were the result of cohabitation.[24] In most cases these unions were not first choices for alternative life-styles, but rather were the result of people who had been married earlier.[25] It is impossible to know how important this sort of cohabitation will become in the coming years, though it is likely that non-traditional living arrangements will become somewhat more common, especially as the incidence of divorce grows.

From an historical standpoint, one of the most significant changes in recent years has been the practical disappearance of the stem family. Everywhere in Spain the importance of complex living arrangements has decreased dramatically since 1970, especially in urban areas, where the decline has been nearly five times stronger than in rural areas (Flaquer and Soler, 1990: 131–2).[26] Nowhere, however, has the decrease been more dramatic than in the traditional stem-family areas of Catalonia, the Basque Country, Navarre, and along the Pyrenees. In rural areas between 1970 and 1981, the decline in the incidence of complex households was more than three times stronger than in the country as a whole.[27] Elsewhere I have discussed the demise of an institution which in certain areas of the country came to symbolize rural stability and regional identity. The economic, demographic, and social changes of the second half of this century have rendered it practically meaningless as a viable form of rural family organization.

There is abundant evidence suggesting that over the past 20 years the process of family formation has become much more difficult and has been taking place at later ages. Age at marriage, which continues to be a prerequisite for family formation for the vast majority of Spaniards, has become progressively later since at least 1979–80. Between 1980 and 1987, for example, the percentages of marriages involving persons below 25 years of age decreased by 28 per cent for men and by 18 per cent for women (Miguel, 1992: 205).[28] Age at marriage increased by 2.4 years to 28.6 for men and by 2.6 years to 26.2 for women between 1979 and 1991.[29]

Age at which children leave their parental households in Spain has traditionally been markedly higher than in other European nations outside the Mediterranean region. In 1984, for example, 74 per cent of men and 58 per cent of women aged 22–24 continued to live in their parental households, as opposed to an average of 35 per cent of men and 18 per cent of women in a sample of six European nations.[30] In recent years, however, there are ample indications that the age at which children leave home is increasing. In 1988, for example, 39 per cent of men aged 28–29 continued to live with their parents as opposed to 32 per cent in 1984; and for women the percentages for the same period and age group were 27 and 21 respectively. In the retrospective survey carried out recently by the Instituto Nacional de Estadística, the mean age at leaving home for both sexes was set at 25.7, though if more timely data were used this age would probably be nearer to 26 for women and 27 or 27.5 for men (INE, 1993: 160–2).

Cultural and socio-economic factors help explain both general differences separating Spain from its neighbours to the north and recent trends. Historically the process of household formation was somewhat different in Spain than in many European countries. In the central and north-western parts of the continent, significant percentages of young people spent a more or less prolonged period of time outside their parents' household, normally involved as rural servants or as urban workers.[31] The same did not hold in most areas of Spain, where time spent as servants was normally short-lived and only involved a small part of the population. The implication of this was that in England and in other areas of Europe, young people often left their parental households well before marriage, as opposed to most areas of Spain, where children abandoned their parent's homes permanently at marriage, and seldom before. The reasons for this behaviour were probably both cultural and economic, though the persistence of this practice over time suggests that cultural modes of behaviour prevailed.

The data I have presented for more contemporary Spain suggest that marriage, household formation, and leaving the parental home are events which continue to be linked in a somewhat different way than they are in other European countries. In recent years, young adults have been faced with shrinking marriage opportunities and increasing difficulties in finding housing of their own. The economic growth which characterized most of the 1980s appears to have improved the lot of some, but worsened that of others. People in their twenties have been adversely affected because among them unemployment has been extremely high, housing has become prohibitively expensive and, as a consequence, marriage has been delayed. On this point, once again the family has shown itself to be an enormously flexible institution because these young people have tended to stay at home while they have attempted to find a job, an apartment, or a spouse. The fact that they were able to stay was never questioned because the links between a job, marriage, household formation, and leaving home were and are accepted by all. In other contexts, like in the United States, for example, while remaining at home might be an option for a part of the population, it would never have been nearly as widespread as it has been in Spain because in those countries developing a sense of self-reliance beyond the family, especially in the face of adversity, is considered an essential part of growing up. If the strength of the institution of the family is predicated on its ability and willingness to shelter and care for its members, it is hard to escape the conclusion that in Spain it is very healthy indeed.

Shortages of available housing, insufficient numbers of new jobs, an inflexible labour market, real estate speculation, rent control, high interest rates, and decidedly unfavourable mortgage policies have all contributed to a situation which has left many young people feeling short-changed on the road to modernization. Behind all of these, however, there have been very powerful demographic reasons which have done their fair share to make the situation more difficult. During the past decade, the numbers of young people who are seeking a job, a home, or a marriage have been far more numerous than ever before in Spanish history. They belong to the extremely large cohorts born during the 1960s and they have created an unprecedented increase in the demand for jobs and homes which the economy has been unable to generate.[32] While cohort size by no means explains the entire plight of this generation, it is a variable whose influence is evident (Figure 10.3).[33] At least in so far as the demographic constraints are concerned, this situation is likely to last at least another five or ten years, as the size of the cohorts entering the job market continues to be very large. After that, however, when the effects of the free fall

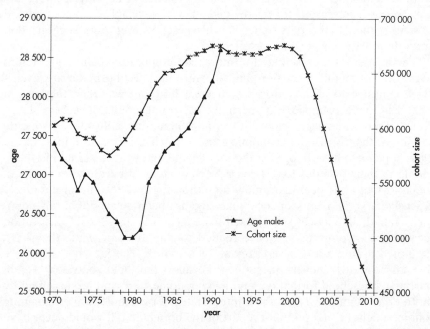

Fig. 10.3 Male age at marriage and cohort size of young adults (5-year moving average of births 25 years earlier), Spain, 1970–2010

in the number of people born after 1977 makes itself felt on the job and the housing markets, the ability of young adults to set themselves up in life is likely to improve substantially. At that juncture, marriage age will likely decline and people will leave home at younger ages than they do today. Until then, however, Spanish families will continue their traditional role as a buffer protecting their members as much as possible from the economic and social forces affecting society as a whole. Were it not for this flexibility, the plight of the generation of Spaniards born between 1955 and 1975, who have grown up with high expectations and few results, would be even darker today than it already is.

A Crystal Ball for the Future of the Family in Spain?

Other than in its most general outlines, the future of the family is not ours to see. Too many variables exist whose present course is difficult to know and where future trends are quite impossible to predict. Even if we could predict most of them, other factors would likely arise which could change the outcome of our prediction altogether. This is not to say that we know nothing about the future course of the family in Spain. We can be fairly sure of some aspects, especially those having to do with people who have already been born. But the amount we know is but a pittance compared to what we do not know or what we would like to know. Despite these limitations, certain aspects of the future of the family can be made out fairly clearly.

Traditional forms of stem-family organization have disappeared, probably for ever. They have been replaced by the unquestioned predominance of the nuclear family nearly everywhere. While certain alternative patterns of co-residence such as cohabitation, single-parent households due to divorce, separation, or choice, and some types of solitary households appear to be on the increase, as yet they can hardly be considered as widespread alternatives to the nuclear family.

Thanks to extremely low fertility and mortality in recent years, the family and the kin group in Spain appear to be embarked on an unmistakable process of reduction in size and extension in generational depth. The numbers of collateral kin of young people today in Spain is lower than it has ever been in the history of this country, save perhaps in moments following extremely severe mortality crises. Conversely, the percentage of people in society with living grandparents and even great-grandparents is higher than it ever was before. This shrinking and elongation of kinship networks will have extremely important implications for the way in which the family fulfils its traditional function of socialization and education of the young, and of care for the elderly. There is every indication that older generations will have to play an increasing role in the education of the young, especially when the parents are working outside the home.

In like manner, it looks as though the family as a whole will find it increasingly difficult to provide the support the elderly have traditionally been able to expect from their kin groups. Growing numbers of senior citizens who live longer and longer will place an extremely heavy burden on decreasing numbers of descendant kin. The concrete situation of the elderly, however, will also depend on their health status and their ability to save for their own retirement. At this time it is impossible to predict either of these variables with any reliability. The role of the State in the care of the elderly and the education of the young will be a key factor, but the ability of society to shoulder satisfactorily the responsibility for the welfare of these social sectors is a matter of serious debate and, at least right now, appears to be unlikely. No matter how public support is materialized, it is clear that acceptable levels of social well-being will not be achieved or maintained without the active intervention of the family, though the extent to which diminishing kinship networks will hinder this role remains to be seen.

Low mortality and low fertility have totally altered the traditional stages of life. One of the implications of this is that inter-generational transfers of property and wealth have lost a great deal of the value they once had. For centuries inheritance was the cornerstone of family systems, of social and economic reproduction, and of family cohesiveness. None of that is true any longer. By the time most parents die and inheritance becomes a realistic possibility, its usefulness for offspring is only marginal because by then the younger generation is probably in their fifties or older and their economic position in society has long since been established. Moreover, since the older generation stands to live much longer than before, they will be forced to use their own savings—the potential inheritance of their children—in order to protect themselves from risks of vulnerability brought on by age. This is not to say that families have ceased to show inter-generational solidarity. They have and they do, but it has tended to take on a different form than it ever did before. Many young people, for example, continue to be economically unproductive due to schooling or to unemployment until a far higher age than was ever possible within historical contexts. These are periods of life in which the wealth flows of the family continue to run from parents to children. In the long run these may more than compensate for diminished inheritances. Even so, it is important to underline the fact that the traditional historic economic links of family solidarity have been undermined by demographic change, and the extent to which this change will make its mark on the institution as a whole is an open question.

In recent years fertility has fallen dramatically and women have assumed a much more relevant role in society outside their households than ever before. It is unlikely that these trends will be reversed, at least not in the near future. At the same time there is a growing social awareness that higher fertility and more births are essential for the well-being of society. Just how the trends in society will be brought into line with the needs of society remains to be seen.

At this level, it is likely that public policy will play an increasingly important role in supporting women who want to have children. Even though some demographers dispute the effectiveness of these policies, it is unlikely that any government can afford not to implement them.[34] Should fertility continue to fall, or even if it remains at its extremely low current levels, there is also a possibility that public policies designed to encourage births by discouraging the economic activity of women or certain alternative life-styles might be enacted. Abortion and divorce are two such policies which only recently have been legalized in Spain. Once again, however, the effectiveness of such policies or people's willingness to accept them is a matter of speculation. What is clear, however, is that as the process of ageing speeds up, public concern and even alarm over its potentially negative implications will become more intense.

The past two or three decades have been ones of momentous changes for Spanish society and for Spanish families. The effects of the social, economic, and political regeneration taking place in the country have had far-reaching effects. Women have entered the labour market and the educational system in great numbers; fertility and mortality have fallen dramatically; the size and make-up of kinship networks have changed, possibly for ever; the elderly have assumed a far more relevant role in society than before, often at the expense of the young; and certain forms of family organization have disappeared, others seem to have held their own, and still others have appeared. Despite the continuities which everywhere are visible, it has been a period of change and transformation of every aspect of Spanish life. Yet now there are many signs that the intensity of change is slowing. Complete political renewal is no longer a matter of pressing concern; the great gains in living standards have slowed to a crawl; the process of urbanization and migration has come to a halt; fertility decline may well be about to bottom out, especially at certain ages; and gains in life expectancy have slowed appreciably. All of these suggest that the period of great, almost revolutionary change in Spanish society which began in the decade of the 1960s may well be coming to a close. The foreseeable future will likely be one of consolidation rather than of change. Instead of enlarging the frontiers of modernity, in the coming years Spaniards will be consolidating the implications of that modernity as they lose the air of *nouveau riche* which has at times characterized them in recent years.

The Spanish family has proved to be remarkably resilient during the years of change. Despite important transformations, the family has continued to fulfil many of its traditional roles. Family solidarity appears to be intact, living arrangements continue to be based on the family nucleus, demographic reproduction takes place within the family, etc. In the years of consolidation which are to come, the rate of change within families should also slow. Given the fact that marked increases in living standards are unlikely in the medium term, the family will have to continue to assume its traditional role in supporting its members. The plight of the young today is an excellent case in point.

The Family, the Future, and the Legacy of History

The family has always attracted more than its share of speculation, theories of social organization, and predictions for the future. It was and is a hot topic for social pundits, social scientists, religious figures, political leaders, and people in the street.[35] The family is never very far from political speeches, religious sermons, or ideas for social reform. This relevance has been present in western society for centuries and stems from the key role the family has always played in society: a basic social building block which in many ways constitutes the ground zero of people's life experience. The family as object of concern and centre of the most varied generalizations can be seen in the press or in scholarly journals, and nearly everyone with any curiosity about society seems to have an interpretation of the family and the role it plays for social order. Spain, of course, is no exception to this love for generalization regarding the family. A brief review of its present and recent past shows that the family was a cornerstone of the social policies of the political regime of Francisco Franco, was and is a key symbol in religious iconography and central to the entire social doctrine of the Catholic Church, the object of concern of governments of both the left and the right in the past 20 years, and, of course, a fitting subject for debate, generalization, and speculation by nearly everyone.

In the concluding pages of this book, I would like to discuss briefly two proposals regarding the present and future of the family, both of which are good examples of this penchant for generalization and prediction regarding the family. One of these is old and the other fairly new; one predicts the demise of the family as we know it and the other stresses the future convergence of family forms in most western societies. Both are informed by the ubiquitous pretension for lavishing generalizations on the family, and both show little sensitivity towards or understanding of the weight of history, of the vastly deep roots of family forms, or of the nature of historical change.

The idea of a breakdown of the family caused by social and economic modernization has a fairly long tradition in certain circles of social scientists and social critics. According to this line of thinking, high divorce rates and marital instability, increases in the number of single-parent homes, declines in fertility and nuptiality, the rise of abortion, the decreasing importance of inheritance, increases in cohabitation and in adolescent pregnancies, and the proliferation of single-sex couples are harbingers of the demise of the family, or at least of a drastic reduction in its importance.[36] For much of the twentieth century, sociologists have been talking of the disintegration of marriage, of the reduction of family life to a simple venue for sexual activity, or of the family's inability to fulfil its most important social and psychological functions.[37] Two writers have even gone so far as to set dates for the extinction of the family: Watson (1928) predicted that marriage would no longer exist by 1977 and Etzioni (1977) felt much the same would happen to the family by 1990. In Spain pessimists regarding the family, or at least those who think that the break with the past has been more or less complete, are not difficult to find either, though it is interesting to note that wide-ranging predictions of the family's demise have never been very numerous.[38]

And yet, despite these predictions, the family has not disappeared nor has the vaunted breakdown occurred in Spain or anywhere else. In many ways, one of the basic points I have attempted to make throughout this book has been the striking resilience of the family during the extended periods of social, economic, and demographic transformation taking place in Spain over the past two centuries. While the implications of changes under way are numerous, and the external indicators of family forms and family organization have undergone significant fluctuations, there is no indication whatsoever of the disappearance or the breakdown of the family. In some ways the importance of the family has never been more evident than it is today. In recent years fertility has undergone drastic reductions, many women no longer spend most of their reproductive years at home, divorce and even cohabitation have modestly increased, and multiple-generation co-residence has declined. Yet these are not the only changes which have occurred to family life over the past two centuries in Spain, and may not even be the most important ones. The reduction in marital fertility from very high levels to moderately low ones; the vast increases in the likelihood of children surviving past infancy and early childhood; the dramatic decline in rural and pre-modern economic activity in favour of urban and industrial life; the major overhaul of the legal basis for succession; the effects of economically or politically induced long-distance migration, which separated kin groups by continents or by great distances; the advent of mandatory education, which took young children out of the family labour force and put them into the schools, are all examples of changes which profoundly affected family life and organization. Yet none of these are specific to the past two or three decades of Spanish history.

There is a tendency to think of the past, especially the more or less distant past, as something uniform, a world in which change, if it did occur, was always less dramatic than the transformations affecting the present and the more recent past. This is a variant of the Whig version of history, one in which the only historical processes worth mentioning are the ones directly affecting the present. Nothing could be further from the truth, especially in so far as the family is concerned, where the changes of the past were every bit as important, perhaps more so, than those of recent years. And yet, the family did not disappear then, nor is it in the process of disappearing now. The ability of Spanish families to compensate for the lack of job opportunities for the young or for the presence of women in gainful employment outside the home is fitting testimony to their resilience and ability to adapt to change.

In the final view, this entire debate involves the wider issue of historical change and the uniqueness of the present. We all want to believe that the present is somehow unique, almost as though history had stopped with us. Yet that opinion, which underlies many interpretations of our society, is grounded in the type of ignorant vanity so prevalent in the world today. Momentous change does indeed occur, but seldom does it do so overnight. Normally, the process of historical change is a gradual one, one which transcends the lives of individuals, who are simply actors at certain points along that process.[39] The family is no exception. It is an institution which in its basic form has been around for well over a millennium, and perhaps even longer; its historical roots are as deep or deeper than those of most other key social institutions. Predicting the demise of this institution, a demise based on a few short decades of history, is daring, risky, and not very sensible. It is unquestionable that the family will change in the coming decades, and it is equally certain that it be around long after all of us have passed away.

Also imbued with the desire to find universal patterns for family development, though considerably more cautious, are the ideas suggesting that the family in much of the developed world is immersed in a process of increasing uniformity, at least in its external configurations. Recently Louis Roussel (1992) proposed a model for the future development of the family in western Europe. For him, there is a process of convergence afoot on the continent which eventually will render the family similar in Germany and in France, in Sweden and in Spain. He feels that in the more 'advanced' nations, the rates of change will slow, while they will continue to be high on the southern flank of the continent. The end result will be a truly 'European' family for the first time. Roussel's idea is attractive, especially because it emphasizes the commonality of European experience. None of the trends in the family which we have mentioned are specific to Spain, and nearly all of them are shared by most European nations and particularly by those in the Mediterranean region. What has set Spain apart from its neighbours to the north has been the rate of change. Contrary to Roussel's prediction, however, now there is every indication that here too the rate of change is slowing, much as it is nearly everywhere else.

Nevertheless, I cannot but disagree with Roussel's admittedly attractive idea, mainly because its underpinnings appear to be basically anti-historical. At the very least they tend to minimize the depth of cultural differences in Europe. Once again it is as though modern society had finally done away with the pernicious effects of history, launching us toward the adventure of the future, unencumbered by the weight of the past. It is a type of neo-modernization discourse in which economic and social change torches all vestiges of cultural and historical difference. This is hardly likely because historical roots run deep indeed. Differences among family systems in Europe are very old and are not likely to disappear in the near future. Take family systems in southern and northern Europe as an example. For as long as there is an historical record to account for it, in much of southern Europe most children abandoned their parental households for good only upon marriage, whereas in other areas of the continent, more or less prolonged stints as servants represented an intermediate phase between childhood and marriage. This was the case during the seventeenth and eighteenth centuries, and it is still the case today. Traditionally in England, for example, the community played a very significant role in caring for the poor and the elderly, whereas in Spain, especially before the advent of national welfare, it was the family which shouldered much of the responsibility. That was true during the sixteenth century, and it continues to be true today. These are but two examples of enduring distinctions between northern and southern European family systems which have nothing to do with levels of social or economic development.

The point here is that these are differences which have characterized European societies for centuries, and it would not be prudent to write their death certificate too hastily. It is unquestionable that in Europe certain external indicators of the family and of family forms seem to be converging: the importance of solitary households is on the rise, the weight of extended families is decreasing, fertility and nuptiality are declining, and the number of children born out of wedlock is on the rise. These are all indisputable signs of recent times. But does that mean that European families are on the path to uniformity, much as Roussel seems to suggest? Perhaps not. For example, despite general moves in the same direction, most of these indicators show no decline in relative variability whatsoever. In other words, while total fertility rates for much of western Europe went from 2.68 to 1.58 between 1960 and 1989, the relative differences among European nations hardly changed.[40] Perhaps more important is to bear in mind that the family is an institution which is far more complex than we might suspect when using straightforward empirical indicators reflecting certain types of behaviour bearing on the family. People's attitudes towards the family, the way they live family life, and the type of influence the family has over the lives of its members are essential to the meaning of the family; and there is no indication whatsoever of any convergence on this count.

My guess is that the outcome will probably be a Spanish family with modern trappings but which is recognizable within a historic context. So far, that modern Spanish family gives every indication of being a traditional one from a European point of view. It is traditional not only in the measurable ways, ranging from low divorce rates to high levels of support for the elderly, but also traditional in the less tangible way in which parental authority and family coherence are maintained. Spaniards continue to care for their dying parents, just as grandparents care for the young offspring of their working children; children continue to be the centre of everyone's attention; Sunday lunch and holidays spent together in family are sacred; parents continue to support their children at home no matter how old they are, as long as they are not married; and children frequently give money to their parents. These are all indications of traditional modes of behaviour, and all of these appear to be very much alive in Spain today. Even though Roussel might be right if we use a very long perspective, for the time being the relative differences between the family in Spain and in other modern nations appear to be as great as they ever were.

Things have changed everywhere, but the disparities between societies continue to loom large. The traditional modes of familial behaviour have very deep roots and offer numerous advantages both for individuals and for societies as a whole. It is not at all clear that these will change or that Spaniards want them to change. Appreciating the strength and resilience of the modern Spanish family continues to be central to any viable understanding of Spain today.

Notes

1. Research on contemporary family issues has been abundant, with demographers and sociologists leading the way. Much though by no means all of this work has been confined to local or regional case studies and quality has been uneven. For a useful overview of these studies, see Iglesias de Ussel and Flaquer (1993). See also Campo Urbano and Navarro (1985), Flaquer (1990), Campo Urbano (1991), Alberdi (1994).

2. The law has been called 'a remedy . . . taken from the recipe book of orthodox capitalism' (Carr and Fusi, 1979).

3. This estimate is based on the new series of Spain's real gross domestic product compiled recently by Leandro Prados de la Escosura (1993: tables D.2 and D.3). For more on the economic situation in Spain during the initial period of economic take-off, see Fraga Iribarne *et al.* (1973).

4. In 1930 Spanish real GDP per capita was 48 per cent that of the United States; in 1950, 27 per cent; in 1960, 34 per cent; and by 1990, 55 per cent (Prados de la Escosura, 1993, table D.3).

5. In 1920 in Spain nearly half of all married women between 35 and 44 years of age had experienced 5 or more childbirths. By 1970 it was 14 per cent, and by 1985, 8 per cent (Miguel, 1992: 63).

6. This law is often referred to as the Law of Villar Palasí, who was the Minister of Education at the time. Basically it stated that all Spaniards had a right to a free public education, and that the State was obliged to find the means to implement this right. Despite fiscal problems in the early going, the law signified the beginning of a long-term commitment to enlarge the educational supply in Spain, and this was continued by democratic governments after Franco's death in 1975. As a result, several new universities were created and enrolment at other ones increased sharply.

7. Enrolment ratios are calculated by dividing the population enrolled in post-secondary school education (universities, technical schools, etc.) by the total population 20–24 years of age. Since participants in these programmes come from other age groups as well, the enrolment ratios yield slightly higher levels of enrolment than would be derived if only students 20–24 were included in the numerator. See UNESCO *Statistical Yearbook* (various years). See also Delgado Pérez (1993: 148).

8. In 1987, for example, higher education enrolment ratios in Sweden stood at 31.5 per cent, at 37.2 per cent in France in the same year, 23.5 per cent in the United Kingdom in 1988, and 33.7 per cent in Germany in 1987. In 1970, enrolment ratios in higher education in Sweden, France, Denmark, Germany, Italy, and other countries were between 2 and 3 times higher than in Spain.

9. Between 1970 and 1991, the percentage of male adults with a higher degree increased by 61 per cent to 8.7, as opposed to women, where it nearly tripled to 6.3 per cent (Miguel, 1992: 554). This gap separating men and women remains, but is closing rapidly.

10. The source for the data in Figure 10.1 is the *Yearbook* of the International Labour Office.

11. In Denmark, for example, 87 per cent of women aged 25–29 were economically active in 1990.

12. The total fertility rate, which stood at 2.21 in 1980, declined by more than 40 per cent to 1.31 in 1991 (Delgado Pérez, 1993: 143).

13. Age-specific total fertility rates between 1987 and 1991 declined for women aged 15–29, increased for those 30–34, and remained stable in higher age groups. Age-specific marital fertility rates declined for married women 15–24, remained practically stable for those 25–29 and 35–44, and rose slightly for women aged 30–34 (INE, *Movimiento natural de la población española*, 1991: 165, 171, 173).

14. The illegitimacy ratio for Spain was 2.42 in 1960, 1.37 in 1970, 2.03 in 1975, 3.93 in 1980, 5.21 in 1983, and 8.01 in 1986. See Muñoz Pérez (1991: 883).

15. The European average does not include the European territories of the ex-Soviet Union. See Caselli (1994).

16. Among European nations, the reduction of infant mortality in Spain by 73.0 per cent between 1970 and 1990 was only surpassed by that of Portugal (80.2 per cent).

17. For a penetrating view on some of the potentially negative political and social implications of low fertility, with particular reference to the quality of education, see Coale (1986: 209–14). The position he takes is not an optimistic one: 'These demographic characteristics imply a social environment radically different from the environment that would be created if fertility were again to rise above the replacement level. In a low-fertility society children grow up with few collateral relatives; a small portion of a typical lifetime is spent in the role of parent of dependent children; the ease of getting a job and the chances of promotion are affected; transfer payments from the employed to the retired are enlarged; and so on. . . . Alfred Sauvy once said that a stationary population is a population of old people ruminating over old ideas in old houses. Such a depiction describes tendencies only, not inevitable characteristics. But such tendencies are even stronger in a population with sustained low fertility than in a stationary population' (ibid. 214).

18. In rural areas 78.6 per cent of all households were nuclear in 1971 and 80.0 per cent in 1981. For urban areas, the percentages were 78.8 in 1971 and 86.1 in 1981. See Flaquer and Soler (1990: 66).

19. For data on 1970 and 1986, see Valero Lobo (1991: 100); and for 1991, see Comunidad de Madrid (1994: vol. v, table 1). Comunidad de Madrid (1992: 248) yields slightly lower percentages of nuclear households.

20. In 1986, 10.5 per cent of all households were headed by women with children, and in 1991 it was 7.6 per cent. These data are taken from Valero Lobo (1991: 100) and from Comunidad de Madrid (1992: 127). See also Almeida and Flaquer (1993).

21. During the first two-thirds of the 19th century, levels just below 10.0 per cent held, then rose to near 11 per cent between 1875 and 1925, declined to around 8 per cent between 1930 and 1950, and finally increased to 13.5 per cent in 1960 and 15.4 per cent in 1960. See Reher (1988: 6).

22. The percentages of solitary households in these countries in 1970 and 1980–2 were: Canada (13 and 20), the United States (17 and 23), Holland (17 and 22), England and Wales (18 and 22), Sweden (25 and 33), Federal Republic of Germany (25 and 30), and Switzerland (20 and 29). See Roussel (1986: 916).
23. See Comunidad de Madrid (1992: tables 12 and 14).
24. INE (1993: 330). See also Delgado Pérez (1993: 132–3).
25. Only 1.1 per cent of first unions were consensual, as opposed to 27.2 per cent of subsequent unions.
26. For the country as a whole, the weight of complex households declined by 26.1 per cent between 1970 and 1981. In the area of Madrid the decline has continued until the present.
27. Galicia is exceptional on this account because between those dates declines in complex living arrangements were very modest.
28. In 1987 it stood at 38 per cent for men and 62 per cent for women.
29. These results are based on all marriages. See INE, *Movimiento* (1991: vol. i, 167). If crude marriage rates are used instead, the results are slightly different. From a high point in 1973 (7.8 per thousand), marriage rates declined to 5.1 per thousand in 1983, then rose to 5.7 in 1989, finally declining to 5.6 in 1991 (ibid. 159). Between 1975 and 1991 the percentage of persons married at 20–24 years of age declined by 39 per cent for men and by 43 per cent for women (Delgado Pérez, 1993: 128–35).
30. The European sample dates from 1982 and includes the United Kingdom, Ireland, Holland, France, the Federal Republic of Germany, and Denmark. In southern Europe the percentages are much closer to those holding in Spain. For more on this, see Vallés (1992: 154–5).
31. Peter Laslett (1983: 526–7) has considered the widespread presence of life-cycle servants in rural households to be an important distinguishing characteristic of domestic group organization in western and central Europe.
32. Between 1977 and 1990 the size of the cohort of young people entering the labour market every year grew by nearly 18 per cent.
33. In the past three decades, the only time in which marriage age appears to have been impervious to cohort size was between 1965 and 1971, precisely during the height of the Spanish economic boom, when yearly growth in real per capita economic output was almost without equal in the developed world.
34. For more on this subject, see Campo Urbano (1974, 1991) and Fernández Cordón (1994c).
35. The love of generalization and grand theories concerning the family is also well established among historians. For different theories of family development in historical contexts see, for example, Ariès (1960), Shorter (1976), Stone (1977).
36. For more on this tradition in sociological thought, see Clayton (1979), Gelles (1995: 486–591).
37. For further examples of this general line of thought, see Sorokin (1937), Moore (1958), Lasch (1977), and Popenoe (1988).
38. For more on this subject within the context of Spain, see, for example, Alberdi (1977, 1982), Alberdi and Alberdi (1982), Campo and Navarro (1985: 5–13); Flaquer (1990: 542–6), Campo (1991: 20–9). See also Alberdi (1994: 9–11, 461–81).
39. Fernand Braudel had an exquisite understanding of the nature of historical change, and much of his work was dedicated precisely to exploring that concept. For his most brilliant example, see Braudel (1966).

40. The coefficient of variation for total fertility rates was 0.150 in 1960 and 0.149 in 1989. Two other indicators showed the same pattern: while total marriage rates declined by around 40 per cent on average between 1965 and 1988, there was no change at all in the coefficient of variation; and births outside of marriage, which more than tripled, actually showed an increase in the coefficient of variation from 0.782 to 0.829 between 1960 and 1988. All of these data are taken from Roussel (1992: 140–3).

APPENDIX

Detailed CAMSIM Microsimulation Results

Note: In all tables, a blank indicates no cases in simulation; 0.0. indicates less than 0.01.

Table 1a   Mean number of living kin, data ca. 1900

Kin	Exact age of ego (years)																				
	0	5	10	15	20	25	30	35	40	45	50	55	60	65	70	75	80	85	90	95	100
husband					0.1	0.4	0.7	0.7	0.7	0.7	0.7	0.6	0.5	0.4	0.3	0.2	0.1	0.0	0.0	0.0	
parent	2.0	1.9	1.7	1.6	1.4	1.3	1.0	0.8	0.5	0.3	0.1	0.0	0.0	0.0							
father	1.0	0.8	0.9	0.8	0.7	0.6	0.5	0.3	0.2	0.1	0.1	0.0	0.0	0.0							
mother	1.0	1.0	0.9	0.8	0.8	0.7	0.6	0.5	0.3	0.2	0.1	0.0	0.0	0.0							
sibling	2.1	3.0	3.5	3.5	3.5	3.3	3.2	3.0	2.8	2.7	2.5	2.1	1.9	1.5	1.1	0.7	0.4	0.2	0.1	0.0	0.0
brother	1.0	1.5	1.7	1.7	1.7	1.6	1.6	1.5	1.4	1.3	1.1	1.0	0.9	0.7	0.5	0.4	0.2	0.1	0.0	0.0	0.0
sister	1.1	1.5	1.8	1.8	1.8	1.7	1.6	1.5	1.4	1.4	1.3	1.1	1.0	0.7	0.6	0.4	0.2	0.1	0.0	0.0	0.0
child					0.0	0.5	1.2	1.9	2.5	2.7	2.7	2.6	2.4	2.3	2.2	2.1	1.9	1.8	1.6	1.3	1.0
son					0.0	0.2	0.6	1.0	1.3	1.4	1.3	1.2	1.2	1.1	1.1	1.0	0.9	0.9	0.8	0.6	0.5
daughter					0.0	0.2	0.6	1.0	1.2	1.3	1.3	1.3	1.2	1.2	1.1	1.1	1.0	0.9	0.8	0.6	0.5
grandparent	1.7	1.2	0.8	0.5	0.3	0.2	0.1	0.0	0.0												
grandfather	0.7	0.5	0.3	0.2	0.1	0.1	0.0	0.0													
grandmother	1.0	0.7	0.5	0.3	0.2	0.2	0.1	0.0	0.0												
grandchild										0.0	0.4	1.0	2.0	3.2	4.2	5.0	5.4	5.4	5.2	5.0	4.8
grandson										0.0	0.2	0.5	1.0	1.5	2.0	2.4	2.6	2.6	2.5	2.5	2.3
granddaughter										0.0	0.2	0.5	1.0	1.7	2.2	2.6	2.8	2.8	2.7	2.6	2.5
gr-grandparent	0.1	0.0	0.0	0.0																	
gr-grandfather	0.0	0.0	0.0																		
gr-grandmother	0.1	0.0	0.0	0.0																	
gr-grandchild															0.0	0.2	0.8	1.9	3.6	5.8	7.9
gr-grandson															0.0	0.1	0.4	0.9	1.8	2.9	3.9
gr-granddaughter															0.0	0.1	0.4	1.0	1.8	2.9	3.9
aunt/uncle	6.0	5.7	5.3	4.9	4.4	3.8	3.1	2.4	1.8	1.2	0.7	0.4	0.2	0.1	0.0	0.0	0.0				
aunt	3.0	2.9	2.7	2.5	2.3	2.0	1.6	1.3	1.0	0.6	0.4	0.2	0.1	0.0	0.0	0.0	0.0				
uncle	3.0	2.8	2.6	2.4	2.1	1.8	1.4	1.1	0.8	0.5	0.3	0.2	0.1	0.0	0.0	0.0	0.0				
first cousin	9.2	11.5	13.4	14.5	14.8	14.6	14.0	13.2	12.4	11.5	10.5	9.3	8.1	6.6	5.1	3.7	2.5	1.5	0.9	0.4	0.2
nephew/niece	0.0	0.0	0.1	0.4	1.1	2.3	3.8	5.3	6.5	7.3	7.5	7.4	7.1	6.7	6.4	5.9	5.5	4.9	4.3	3.5	2.7
nephew	0.0	0.0	0.1	0.2	0.6	1.2	1.9	2.7	3.3	3.6	3.7	3.6	3.5	3.3	3.1	2.9	2.6	2.4	2.0	1.6	1.3
niece	0.0	0.0	0.1	0.2	0.5	1.1	1.9	2.6	3.3	3.7	3.8	3.7	3.6	3.4	3.2	3.0	2.8	2.5	2.3	1.9	1.5
fam. or.	4.1	4.9	5.2	5.1	4.9	4.6	4.2	3.8	3.4	3.0	2.6	2.2	1.9	1.5	1.1	0.7	0.4	0.2	0.1	0.0	0.0
fam. proc.					0.2	0.9	1.8	2.7	3.2	3.4	3.4	3.2	2.9	2.7	2.5	2.2	2.0	1.8	1.6	1.3	1.0
ascending	9.7	8.8	7.8	7.0	6.1	5.2	4.2	3.2	2.3	1.5	0.8	0.4	0.2	0.1	0.0	0.0	0.0				
lateral	11.3	14.5	16.8	18.1	18.3	17.9	17.2	16.3	15.2	14.2	12.9	11.5	9.9	8.1	6.2	4.4	2.9	1.7	0.9	0.4	0.2
descending	0.0				1.1	2.3	3.8	5.0	6.5	7.4	7.9	8.4	9.1	9.9	10.6	11.1	11.7	12.2	13.1	14.3	15.4

Table 1b Proportion having living kin, data ca. 1900

Kin	Exact age of ego (years)																				
	0	5	10	15	20	25	30	35	40	45	50	55	60	65	70	75	80	85	90	95	100
husband					0.11	0.44	0.65	0.72	0.74	0.72	0.68	0.61	0.50	0.38	0.29	0.18	0.10	0.05	0.02	0.01	0.00
parent	1.00	1.00	0.98	0.96	0.93	0.86	0.77	0.61	0.43	0.25	0.12	0.04	0.01	0.00							
father	1.00	0.93	0.85	0.75	0.67	0.57	0.46	0.33	0.22	0.12	0.06	0.02	0.01	0.00							
mother	1.00	0.95	0.89	0.83	0.77	0.69	0.58	0.44	0.31	0.17	0.07	0.02	0.00	0.00							
sibling	0.73	0.90	0.91	0.91	0.91	0.91	0.90	0.89	0.89	0.88	0.87	0.85	0.81	0.73	0.60	0.47	0.30	0.16	0.07	0.03	0.01
brother	0.56	0.72	0.77	0.77	0.77	0.77	0.75	0.74	0.72	0.72	0.68	0.63	0.58	0.50	0.38	0.29	0.18	0.08	0.04	0.02	0.00
sister	0.56	0.74	0.80	0.79	0.78	0.77	0.75	0.74	0.73	0.71	0.69	0.64	0.59	0.49	0.39	0.29	0.17	0.09	0.03	0.01	0.00
child					0.03	0.29	0.53	0.68	0.74	0.75	0.75	0.74	0.74	0.73	0.72	0.71	0.69	0.68	0.65	0.61	0.54
son					0.03	0.19	0.38	0.52	0.61	0.62	0.61	0.60	0.59	0.58	0.56	0.54	0.53	0.51	0.47	0.41	0.35
daughter					0.01	0.17	0.38	0.54	0.63	0.64	0.64	0.62	0.61	0.60	0.58	0.56	0.55	0.52	0.49	0.45	0.37
grandparent	0.85	0.72	0.55	0.39	0.22	0.08	0.03	0.01	0.00												
grandfather	0.58	0.43	0.29	0.19	0.12	0.03	0.01	0.00													
grandmother	0.71	0.58	0.43	0.27	0.15	0.06	0.03	0.01													
grandchild										0.04	0.18	0.34	0.50	0.60	0.65	0.67	0.67	0.68	0.68	0.68	0.67
grandson										0.02	0.12	0.24	0.41	0.50	0.59	0.62	0.63	0.64	0.64	0.64	0.63
granddaughter										0.02	0.12	0.26	0.40	0.53	0.59	0.62	0.63	0.63	0.63	0.62	0.61
gr-grandparent	0.07	0.02	0.00	0.00																	
gr-grandfather	0.03	0.01	0.00																		
gr-grandmother	0.05	0.01	0.00																		
gr-grandchild															0.02	0.11	0.24	0.38	0.49	0.58	0.62
gr-grandson															0.02	0.08	0.17	0.32	0.44	0.54	0.59
gr-granddaughter															0.01	0.07	0.19	0.32	0.42	0.54	0.58
aunt/uncle	0.99	0.99	0.99	0.98	0.97	0.95	0.91	0.83	0.74	0.58	0.40	0.24	0.12	0.05	0.01	0.00					
aunt	0.95	0.95	0.92	0.90	0.86	0.83	0.76	0.65	0.56	0.40	0.27	0.16	0.08	0.03	0.01						
uncle	0.92	0.91	0.90	0.88	0.85	0.81	0.72	0.63	0.50	0.37	0.24	0.12	0.05	0.02	0.01						
first cousin	0.91	0.97	0.98	0.98	0.98	0.98	0.98	0.98	0.98	0.98	0.97	0.96	0.95	0.91	0.88	0.81	0.69	0.54	0.39	0.22	0.11
nephew/niece	0.00	0.01	0.06	0.17	0.34	0.51	0.68	0.79	0.83	0.84	0.85	0.85	0.85	0.85	0.85	0.84	0.84	0.84	0.82	0.79	0.74
nephew	0.00	0.01	0.05	0.13	0.26	0.42	0.58	0.70	0.77	0.79	0.80	0.80	0.80	0.79	0.79	0.77	0.76	0.74	0.72	0.66	0.58
niece	0.00	0.01	0.03	0.12	0.26	0.42	0.58	0.71	0.76	0.79	0.81	0.80	0.80	0.79	0.79	0.77	0.76	0.74	0.72	0.67	0.60
fam. or.	1.00	1.00	1.00	0.99	0.98	0.98	0.96	0.95	0.93	0.91	0.88	0.85	0.82	0.73	0.60	0.47	0.30	0.16	0.07	0.03	0.01
fam. proc.					0.12	0.45	0.68	0.77	0.82	0.83	0.84	0.82	0.81	0.79	0.77	0.74	0.71	0.68	0.66	0.61	0.54
ascending	1.00	1.00	1.00	1.00	0.99	0.99	0.97	0.91	0.83	0.64	0.43	0.26	0.13	0.05	0.01	0.00					
lateral	0.96	1.00	1.00	1.00	1.00	1.00	1.00	1.00	1.00	1.00	0.99	0.99	0.99	0.97	0.94	0.88	0.75	0.60	0.41	0.24	0.11
descending	0.00	0.01	0.06	0.17	0.34	0.51	0.68	0.79	0.83	0.85	0.87	0.90	0.92	0.92	0.93	0.94	0.94	0.94	0.94	0.93	0.91

Table 1c Mean age of living kin, data ca. 1900

Exact age of ego (years)

Kin	0	5	10	15	20	25	30	35	40	45	50	55	60	65	70	75	80	85	90	95	100
husband					26.6	29.2	33.2	37.2	41.6	46.1	50.3	55.1	59.6	63.7	68.4	72.2	76.2	77.3	77.6	74.2	
parent	33.7	38.6	43.6	48.2	52.9	57.4	61.8	65.8	69.6	72.4	76.0	79.2	83.7	86.7							
father	35.1	40.0	44.7	49.2	53.8	58.1	62.5	66.1	69.5	72.7	76.5	80.2	84.0	86.7							
mother	32.3	37.3	42.5	47.3	52.1	56.8	61.3	65.5	69.6	72.2	75.6	78.2	80.3	86.7							
sibling	6.3	8.3	11.3	15.4	19.9	24.8	29.8	34.7	39.6	44.4	49.2	53.8	58.2	62.0	65.9	69.2	72.2	75.2	77.0	78.2	83.3
brother	6.4	8.2	11.3	15.3	19.8	24.7	29.6	34.5	39.3	44.0	48.8	53.4	58.0	62.1	65.9	69.3	72.4	74.7	77.4	78.6	83.1
sister	6.3	8.4	11.4	15.5	20.1	24.9	29.9	34.9	39.9	44.8	49.5	54.1	58.4	62.0	65.9	69.0	71.9	75.6	76.5	77.2	83.4
child					1.1	2.2	3.9	5.8	8.5	12.2	17.0	21.8	26.8	31.8	36.8	41.8	46.7	51.5	56.1	60.5	64.8
son					1.4	2.4	3.9	5.9	8.4	12.1	17.0	21.8	26.7	31.7	36.7	41.6	46.5	51.3	56.0	60.4	64.8
daughter						2.0	3.8	5.8	8.4	12.1	17.0	21.8	26.8	31.9	37.0	42.0	46.9	51.7	56.2	60.6	64.8
grandparent	62.5	66.1	69.1	71.8	75.0	77.3	79.3	80.6	89.5												
grandfather	63.2	66.7	69.6	72.6	76.6	78.4	80.3	76.1													
grandmother	62.0	65.7	68.8	71.2	73.8	76.7	79.0	81.7	89.5												
grandchild										1.2	2.2	3.5	5.0	6.7	9.0	11.7	15.1	19.5	24.1	29.0	33.9
grandson										1.2	2.1	3.6	4.9	6.8	9.1	11.6	15.0	19.2	24.0	28.8	33.8
granddaughter										1.2	2.3	3.5	5.1	6.7	8.9	11.8	15.2	19.7	24.2	29.1	34.0
gr-grandparent	77.2	81.7	84.4	86.2																	
gr-grandfather	76.2	81.3	87.5																		
gr-grandmother	77.7	82.0	81.2	86.2																	
gr-grandchild															1.3	2.0	3.0	4.1	5.4	7.0	8.9
gr-grandson															1.4	1.9	3.0	4.1	5.3	6.8	8.8
gr-granddaughter															1.2	2.1	3.0	4.2	5.5	7.1	9.1
aunt/uncle	32.7	37.5	42.2	46.8	51.1	55.1	58.7	62.2	65.5	68.3	71.2	73.7	76.4	79.1	79.2	83.4					
aunt	32.6	37.5	42.2	46.9	51.3	55.2	58.8	62.3	65.7	68.3	71.5	73.8	76.8	79.5	82.0	83.4					
uncle	32.7	37.6	42.2	46.7	50.9	54.9	58.6	62.1	65.3	68.2	70.9	73.6	75.8	78.7	77.1	83.4					
first cousin	9.2	11.2	13.7	16.7	20.4	24.5		33.7	38.3	42.9	47.2	51.4	55.3	58.9	62.1	65.0	67.6	70.2	72.6	74.7	75.4
nephew/niece	1.8	2.4	2.5	3.3	4.2	5.2	6.6	8.6	11.0	13.9	17.8	22.5	27.2	32.1	36.9	41.7	46.3	50.8	54.9	58.8	62.2
nephew	1.8	4.5	2.6	3.6	4.2	5.3	6.7	8.5	11.1	14.1	18.0	22.2	27.2	32.1	37.1	41.8	46.4	50.8	54.9	58.8	62.0
niece		1.2	2.4	3.0	4.1	5.1	6.6	8.5	10.9	13.8	17.7	22.2	26.9	31.9	36.8	41.6	46.4	50.7	54.9	58.8	62.4
fam. or.	19.6	20.1	22.1	25.5	29.6	33.7	37.6	41.0	44.3	47.2	50.5	54.3	58.4	62.1	65.9	69.2	72.2	75.2	77.0	78.2	83.3
fam. proc.					14.5	15.4	14.5	14.4	16.0	19.2	23.8	28.3	32.4	36.3	40.6	44.3	47.8	51.9	56.2	60.6	64.8
ascending	38.4	41.9	45.4	49.0	52.6	56.0	59.7	63.1	66.5	69.1	72.0	74.3	76.9	79.4	79.2	83.4					
lateral	8.7	10.6	13.2	16.4	20.3	24.5	29.2	33.9	38.5	43.2	47.6	51.8	55.8	59.4	62.8	65.7	68.3	70.8	72.9	74.9	75.7
descending	1.8	2.4	2.5	3.3	4.2	5.2	6.6	8.6	11.0	13.8	17.1	20.0	22.1	23.8	25.7	27.4	28.9	29.7	29.0	27.5	26.2

Table 1d Mean number of dependent kin, data ca. 1900

Kin	Exact age of ego (years)																				
	0	5	10	15	20	25	30	35	40	45	50	55	60	65	70	75	80	85	90	95	100
husband				0.0	0.1	0.2	0.3	0.4	0.4	0.3	0.0	0.0	0.1	0.2	0.2	0.2	0.1	0.0	0.0	0.0	
parent			0.0	0.0	0.0	0.1	0.2	0.2	0.2	0.1	0.1	0.1	0.0	0.0							
father			0.0	0.0	0.0	0.1	0.1	0.1	0.2	0.1	0.1	0.0	0.0	0.0							
mother			0.0	0.0	0.0	0.0	0.1	0.1	0.0	0.0	0.0	0.0	0.0	0.0							
sibling	2.0	2.6	2.4	1.7	1.0	0.4	0.3	0.4	0.4	0.3	0.0	0.0	0.0	0.0							
brother	1.0	1.3	1.2	0.9	0.5	0.2	0.1	0.2	0.2	0.1	0.0	0.0	0.0	0.0							
sister	1.0	1.3	1.2	0.9	0.5	0.2	0.1	0.2	0.2	0.1	0.0	0.0	0.0	0.0							
child					1.0	2.2	3.5	4.4	2.1	1.8											
son				0.5	0.5	1.1	1.8	2.2	1.1	0.9	1.5										
daughter				0.2	0.5	1.1	1.7	2.2	1.1	0.9	1.6										
grandparent	0.6	0.7	0.6	0.5	0.3	0.1															
grandfather	0.3	0.3	0.3	0.2	0.1	0.0															
grandmother	0.3	0.4	0.3	0.2	0.2	0.1															
grandchild										0.0	0.4	1.0	2.0	2.9	3.4	3.4	2.7	1.8	0.9	0.3	0.1
grandson										0.0	0.2	0.5	1.0	1.4	1.6	1.6	1.3	0.9	0.5	0.2	0.0
granddaughter										0.0	0.2	0.5	1.0	1.5	1.8	1.7	1.4	0.9	0.5	0.2	0.0
gr-grandparent	0.1	0.0	0.0	0.0																	
gr-grandfather	0.0	0.0	0.0																		
gr-grandmother	0.1	0.0	0.0	0.0																	
gr-grandchild															0.0	0.2	0.8	1.8	3.5	5.2	6.3
gr-grandson															0.0	0.1	0.4	0.9	1.7	2.6	3.2
gr-granddaughter															0.0	0.1	0.4	1.0	1.8	2.6	3.1
aunt/uncle	0.3	0.1	0.1	0.2	0.3	0.5	0.8	0.9	1.0	0.8	0.6	0.3	0.2	0.1	0.0	0.0					
aunt	0.1	0.1	0.0	0.1	0.2	0.3	0.4	0.5	0.5	0.5	0.3	0.2	0.1	0.0	0.0	0.0					
uncle	0.1	0.0	0.0	0.1	0.1	0.2	0.4	0.4	0.5	0.4	0.3	0.1	0.1	0.0	0.0	0.0					
first cousin	7.3	8.1	7.9	6.8	5.0	3.1	1.6	0.8	0.4	0.3	0.5	0.9	1.4	1.8	2.0	1.9	1.6	1.1	0.7	0.4	0.2
nephew/niece	0.0	0.0	0.1	0.4	0.6	1.1	3.5	4.4	4.7	4.1	3.0	1.8	0.8	0.3	0.0	0.0	0.1	0.3	0.6	0.9	1.0
nephew	0.0	0.0	0.1	0.2	0.5	1.1	1.8	2.2	2.3	2.1	1.5	0.9	0.4	0.1	0.0	0.0	0.1	0.2	0.3	0.5	0.5
niece	0.0	0.0	0.1	0.2	0.5	1.1	1.7	2.2	2.3	2.1	1.6	0.9	0.4	0.1	0.0	0.0	0.1	0.2	0.3	0.5	0.6
fam. or.	2.0	2.0	2.4	1.7	1.0	0.5	0.4	0.4	0.4	0.3	0.2	0.2	0.1	0.2	0.2	0.2	0.4	0.2	0.1	0.0	0.0
fam. proc.																					0.5
ascending	1.0	0.8	0.7	0.6	0.7	0.8	1.1	1.3	1.4	1.1	0.7	0.4	0.2	0.1	0.0	0.0					
lateral	9.3	10.7	10.3	8.6	6.0	3.5	1.7	0.8	0.4	0.3	0.6	1.1	1.8	2.3	2.6	2.5	2.0	1.3	0.8	0.4	0.2
descending	0.0	0.0	0.1	0.4	1.1	2.2	3.5	4.4	4.7	4.2	3.4	2.8	2.8	3.2	3.5	3.6	3.6	3.9	5.0	6.4	7.4

Table 1e Proportion having dependent kin, data ca. 1900

Kin	Exact age of ego (years)																				
---	0	5	10	15	20	25	30	35	40	45	50	55	60	65	70	75	80	85	90	95	100
husband			0.00	0.01	0.05	0.15	0.30	0.34	0.37	0.25	0.01	0.02	0.08	0.19	0.22	0.16	0.07	0.02	0.01	0.00	
parent			0.00	0.01	0.04	0.09	0.16	0.17	0.18	0.12	0.12	0.06	0.01	0.00							
father			0.00	0.01	0.01	0.07	0.17	0.22	0.24	0.17	0.06	0.02	0.01	0.00							
mother							0.04	0.01	0.00		0.07										
sibling	0.72	0.89	0.85	0.68	0.42	0.19	0.07	0.01	0.00	0.01	0.04	0.12	0.27	0.39	0.44	0.43	0.29	0.16	0.07	0.03	0.01
brother	0.56	0.69	0.65	0.49	0.30	0.13	0.04	0.01			0.02	0.06	0.15	0.22	0.24	0.24	0.17	0.08	0.04	0.01	0.00
sister	0.55	0.71	0.69	0.51	0.29	0.13	0.05	0.01			0.02	0.07	0.16	0.21	0.25	0.25	0.15	0.09	0.03	0.01	0.00
child					0.03	0.29	0.53	0.67	0.72	0.65	0.48	0.26	0.06								
son					0.03	0.19	0.38	0.52	0.56	0.51	0.33	0.16	0.04								
daughter					0.01	0.17	0.38	0.54	0.60	0.49	0.34	0.16	0.02								
grandparent	0.48	0.54	0.45	0.36	0.22	0.08	0.03	0.01	0.00												
grandfather	0.28	0.28	0.23	0.18	0.11	0.03	0.01	0.01													
grandmother	0.32	0.37	0.32	0.23	0.14	0.06	0.03	0.00													
grandchild										0.04	0.18	0.34	0.50	0.59	0.64	0.63	0.56	0.46	0.32	0.17	0.05
grandson										0.02	0.12	0.24	0.40	0.49	0.56	0.55	0.48	0.39	0.25	0.11	0.03
granddaughter										0.02	0.12	0.26	0.40	0.53	0.56	0.56	0.49	0.36	0.25	0.12	0.03
gr-grandparent	0.07	0.02	0.00	0.00																	
gr-grandfather	0.03	0.01	0.00																		
gr-grandmother	0.05	0.01	0.00																		
gr-grandchild															0.02	0.11	0.24	0.38	0.49	0.58	0.62
gr-grandson															0.02	0.08	0.17	0.32	0.44	0.54	0.58
gr-granddaughter															0.01	0.07	0.19	0.32	0.42	0.54	0.57
aunt/uncle	0.13	0.08	0.05	0.11	0.22	0.37	0.48	0.58	0.61	0.52	0.37	0.23	0.12	0.05	0.02	0.00					
aunt	0.08	0.05	0.03	0.07	0.15	0.24	0.29	0.34	0.40	0.33	0.25	0.16	0.08	0.03	0.01	0.00					
uncle	0.09	0.04	0.02	0.05	0.11	0.21	0.30	0.27	0.36	0.30	0.21	0.11	0.05	0.02	0.01	0.00					
first cousin	0.89	0.93	0.92	0.84	0.74	0.60	0.41	0.27	0.19	0.21	0.32	0.43	0.62	0.69	0.75	0.73	0.66	0.52	0.38	0.22	0.10
nephew/niece	0.00	0.01	0.06	0.17	0.34	0.51	0.67	0.77	0.79	0.74	0.67	0.52	0.30	0.13	0.05	0.04	0.08	0.21	0.33	0.48	0.51
nephew	0.00	0.01	0.05	0.13	0.26	0.42	0.58	0.69	0.70	0.66	0.56	0.39	0.21	0.09	0.03	0.03	0.05	0.12	0.20	0.29	0.33
niece		0.01	0.03	0.12	0.26	0.42	0.57	0.68	0.71	0.66	0.56	0.40	0.21	0.09	0.02	0.02	0.04	0.13	0.21	0.34	0.37
fam. or.	0.72	0.89	0.85	0.69	0.45	0.34	0.36	0.35	0.37	0.26	0.16	0.16	0.28	0.39	0.44	0.43	0.29	0.16	0.07	0.03	0.01
fam. proc.					0.03	0.29	0.63	0.72	0.73	0.60	0.48	0.28	0.13	0.19	0.22	0.16	0.07	0.03			
ascending	0.61	0.61	0.50	0.46	0.45	0.53	0.63	0.67	0.73	0.60	0.42	0.28	0.13	0.05	0.01	0.00					
lateral	0.96	0.99	0.98	0.92	0.79	0.64	0.43	0.28	0.19	0.21	0.34	0.48	0.71	0.79	0.85	0.84	0.73	0.59	0.40	0.24	0.11
descending	0.00	0.01	0.06	0.17	0.34	0.51	0.67	0.77	0.79	0.76	0.72	0.67	0.63	0.64	0.65	0.65	0.63	0.66	0.74	0.79	0.81

Table 1f   Proportion co-residing with kin, data ca. 1900

Kin	Exact age of ego (years)																				
	0	5	10	15	20	25	30	35	40	45	50	55	60	65	70	75	80	85	90	95	100
husband					0.11	0.44	0.65	0.72	0.74	0.72	0.68	0.61	0.50	0.38	0.29	0.18	0.08	0.03	0.01	0.00	
parent	1.00	0.97	0.94	0.90	0.78	0.45	0.23	0.12	0.07	0.04	0.02	0.01	0.00								
father	0.98	0.91	0.83	0.74	0.60	0.31	0.13	0.07	0.04	0.02	0.01	0.01									
mother	1.00	0.92	0.84	0.78	0.65	0.35	0.19	0.09	0.06	0.03	0.02	0.01									
sibling	0.73	0.88	0.90	0.89	0.75	0.42	0.19	0.11	0.06	0.04	0.02	0.02									
brother	0.56	0.70	0.75	0.74	0.60	0.31	0.15	0.08	0.03	0.02	0.01	0.01									
sister	0.56	0.73	0.79	0.75	0.61	0.31	0.14	0.06	0.03	0.02	0.01	0.01									
child					0.03	0.29	0.53	0.68	0.73	0.73	0.70	0.66	0.58	0.45	0.34	0.26	0.20	0.17	0.15	0.12	
son					0.03	0.19	0.37	0.52	0.60	0.59	0.56	0.52	0.42	0.32	0.21	0.13	0.10	0.09	0.07	0.05	
daughter					0.01	0.17	0.37	0.54	0.62	0.62	0.56	0.50	0.41	0.30	0.21	0.17	0.13	0.10	0.10	0.08	
grandparent	0.01	0.01	0.01	0.01	0.00																
grandfather	0.01	0.01	0.01	0.00	0.00																
grandmother	0.01	0.01	0.01	0.00	0.00																
grandchild											0.00	0.00	0.00	0.00	0.00	0.00	0.00				
grandson											0.00	0.00	0.00	0.00	0.00	0.00	0.00				
granddaughter																					
gr-grandparent																					
gr-grandfather																					
gr-grandmother																					
gr-grandchild																					
gr-grandson																					
gr-granddaughter																					
aunt/uncle	0.01	0.01	0.00																		
aunt	0.00	0.00																			
uncle	0.01	0.01	0.00																		
first cousin						0.00	0.00														
nephew/niece					0.00	0.00	0.00														
nephew																					
niece																					
fam. or.	1.00	0.98	0.98	0.96	0.84	0.50	0.26	0.15	0.09	0.06	0.03	0.02	0.02	0.01	0.01	0.01	0.01	0.00	0.00		
fam. proc.					0.12	0.45	0.68	0.77	0.82	0.83	0.83	0.79	0.73	0.63	0.52	0.39	0.27	0.20	0.16	0.12	
ascending	1.00	0.99	0.95	0.91	0.79	0.45	0.23	0.12	0.07	0.04	0.02	0.01	0.00								
lateral	0.73	0.88	0.90	0.89	0.75	0.42	0.19	0.11	0.06	0.04	0.02	0.02	0.02	0.01	0.01	0.01	0.01				
descending					0.00	0.00	0.00				0.00	0.00	0.00	0.00	0.00	0.00	0.00				

Table 2a   Mean number of living kin, data ca. 1930

Kin	Exact age of ego (years)																				
	0	5	10	15	20	25	30	35	40	45	50	55	60	65	70	75	80	85	90	95	100
husband					0.1	0.4	0.7	0.8	0.8	0.8	0.8	0.7	0.7	0.6	0.4	0.3	0.2	0.1	0.1	0.0	0.0
parent	2.0	1.9	1.8	1.7	1.6	1.5	1.3	1.0	0.8	0.5	0.3	0.1	0.0								
father	1.0	0.9	0.9	0.8	0.8	0.7	0.6	0.5	0.3	0.2	0.1	0.0	0.0								
mother	1.0	1.0	0.9	0.9	0.8	0.8	0.7	0.6	0.5	0.3	0.2	0.1	0.0								
sibling	2.1	3.2	3.9	4.1	4.1	4.0	4.0	3.8	3.7	3.6	3.4	3.1	2.8	2.6	2.5	2.5	2.3	2.2	2.0	1.7	1.4
brother	1.1	1.6	2.0	2.1	2.1	2.0	2.0	1.9	1.9	1.8	1.7	1.6	1.5	1.3	1.3	1.2	1.1	1.0	0.9	0.8	0.6
sister	1.1	1.6	1.9	2.0	2.1	2.0	2.0	1.9	1.9	1.8	1.7	1.6	1.5	1.4	1.3	1.2	1.2	1.1	1.0	0.9	0.8
child					0.0	0.5	1.3	2.1	2.6	2.9	2.9	2.8	2.7	2.6	2.5	2.5	2.3	2.2	2.0	1.7	1.4
son					0.0	0.3	0.7	1.1	1.3	1.4	1.5	1.4	1.4	1.3	1.3	1.2	1.1	1.0	0.9	0.8	0.6
daughter					0.0	0.2	0.6	1.0	1.3	1.4	1.4	1.4	1.3	1.3	1.3	1.2	1.2	1.1	1.0	0.9	0.8
grandparent	2.3	1.8	1.3	0.8	0.5	0.2	0.1	0.0	0.0												
grandfather	1.0	0.7	0.5	0.3	0.2	0.1	0.0														
grandmother	1.3	1.1	0.8	0.5	0.3	0.1	0.1	0.0	0.0												
grandchild									0.0	0.1	0.4	1.2	2.6	4.1	5.6	6.6	7.0	7.1	6.9	6.8	6.5
grandson										0.0	0.2	0.6	1.4	2.1	2.9	3.4	3.6	3.6	3.6	3.5	3.3
granddaughter										0.0	0.2	0.6	1.2	1.9	2.7	3.2	3.4	3.4	3.4	3.3	3.2
gr-grandparent	0.2	0.1	0.0	0.0																	
gr-grandfather	0.1	0.0	0.0	0.0																	
gr-grandmother	0.2	0.1	0.0	0.0																	
gr-grandchild														0.0	0.1	0.4	1.2	2.8	5.4	8.7	11.9
gr-grandson														0.0	0.0	0.2	0.6	1.5	2.9	4.5	6.1
gr-granddaughter														0.0	0.0	0.2	0.6	1.3	2.6	4.2	5.8
aunt/uncle	7.6	7.3	7.0	6.6	6.1	5.6	4.9	4.0	3.0	2.2	1.4	0.8	0.4	0.2	0.1	0.0	0.0	0.0	0.0		
aunt	3.7	3.6	3.5	3.3	3.1	2.8	2.5	2.1	1.6	1.2	0.8	0.5	0.2	0.1	0.0	0.0	0.0	0.0	0.0		
uncle	3.9	3.7	3.6	3.3	3.1	2.7	2.4	1.9	1.4	1.0	0.6	0.4	0.2	0.1	0.1	0.0	0.0	0.0	0.0		
first cousin	11.1	14.5	17.2	19.0	19.8	20.0	19.6	18.9	18.2	17.3	16.2	14.8	13.1	11.2	9.1	6.9	4.8	3.1	1.8	1.0	0.5
nephew/niece	0.0	0.0	0.1	0.4	1.3	2.7	4.8	7.0	8.9	10.0	10.5	10.5	10.3	10.0	9.7	9.3	8.8	8.2	7.4	6.4	5.2
nephew	0.0	0.0	0.0	0.2	0.7	1.4	2.4	3.5	4.5	5.1	5.3	5.3	5.2	5.0	4.9	4.6	4.3	4.0	3.5	3.0	2.4
niece	0.0	0.0	0.0	0.2	0.6	1.4	2.4	3.5	4.4	4.9	5.1	5.2	5.1	5.0	4.8	4.7	4.4	4.2	3.9	3.4	2.8
fam. or.	4.1	5.1	5.7	5.9	5.8	5.5	5.2	4.9	4.5	4.1	3.6	3.2	2.8	2.4	1.9	1.3	0.8	0.4	0.2	0.1	0.0
fam. proc.					0.2	0.9	2.0	2.9	3.9	4.1	4.7	5.2	6.0	7.3	8.6	9.8	10.7	12.2	14.4	17.2	19.8
ascending	12.1	11.2	10.2	9.2	8.2	7.3	6.3	5.1	3.9	2.7	1.7	1.0	0.4	0.2	0.1	0.0	0.0	0.0	0.0	0.0	0.0
lateral	13.2	17.7	21.1	23.1	24.0	24.0	23.5	22.8	21.9	20.9	19.6	17.9	15.9	13.5	11.0	8.2	5.6	3.6	2.0	1.1	0.5
descending	0.0	0.0	0.1	0.4	1.3	2.7	4.8	7.0	8.9	10.1	10.9	11.7	12.9	14.1	15.4	16.2	17.0	18.1	19.8	21.8	23.7

Table 2b Proportion having living kin, data ca. 1930

Kin	Exact age of ego (years)																				
	0	5	10	15	20	25	30	35	40	45	50	55	60	65	70	75	80	85	90	95	100
husband					0.11	0.45	0.69	0.77	0.81	0.78	0.74	0.68	0.58	0.45	0.34	0.22	0.12	0.06	0.02	0.01	0.00
parent	1.00	0.99	0.99	0.98	0.97	0.94	0.87	0.76	0.61	0.44	0.26	0.12	0.03								
father	1.00	0.95	0.90	0.83	0.77	0.68	0.56	0.45	0.34	0.22	0.11	0.04	0.01								
mother	1.00	0.98	0.94	0.90	0.85	0.79	0.72	0.59	0.46	0.32	0.17	0.08	0.02								
sibling	0.73	0.93	0.94	0.94	0.94	0.94	0.94	0.94	0.93	0.93	0.92	0.91	0.90	0.86	0.79	0.67	0.50	0.31	0.18	0.06	0.01
brother	0.58	0.76	0.82	0.82	0.82	0.81	0.81	0.80	0.79	0.79	0.74	0.74	0.69	0.64	0.53	0.41	0.26	0.15	0.07	0.03	0.01
sister	0.54	0.75	0.81	0.82	0.82	0.81	0.81	0.79	0.79	0.78	0.75	0.75	0.74	0.61	0.56	0.50	0.36	0.22	0.12	0.03	0.00
child					0.03	0.29	0.57	0.69	0.77	0.78	0.77	0.75	0.73	0.74	0.73	0.72	0.71	0.69	0.68	0.65	0.59
son					0.02	0.18	0.41	0.55	0.61	0.62	0.61	0.61	0.60	0.60	0.58	0.58	0.56	0.53	0.51	0.47	0.39
daughter					0.02	0.19	0.40	0.53	0.60	0.61	0.61	0.60	0.59	0.58	0.58	0.57	0.56	0.55	0.53	0.49	0.44
grandparent	0.94	0.88	0.74	0.57	0.37	0.19	0.10	0.03	0.01												
grandfather	0.71	0.58	0.45	0.29	0.18	0.08	0.03	0.00													
grandmother	0.87	0.78	0.62	0.45	0.26	0.14	0.08	0.03	0.00												
grandchild									0.00	0.04	0.19	0.39	0.56	0.63	0.67	0.69	0.70	0.70	0.70	0.70	0.70
grandson										0.03	0.13	0.31	0.48	0.57	0.64	0.66	0.67	0.66	0.66	0.65	0.65
granddaughter										0.03	0.13	0.29	0.46	0.55	0.62	0.64	0.65	0.64	0.64	0.64	0.64
gr-grandparent	0.19	0.07	0.01	0.01																	
gr-grandfather	0.08	0.02	0.00	0.00																	
gr-grandmother	0.14	0.05	0.01	0.01																	
gr-grandchild														0.00	0.04	0.14	0.31	0.45	0.58	0.63	0.66
gr-grandson														0.00	0.03	0.09	0.24	0.38	0.53	0.60	0.63
gr-granddaughter														0.00	0.02	0.11	0.24	0.39	0.52	0.59	0.63
aunt/uncle	0.99	0.99	0.99	0.99	0.99	0.99	0.98	0.95	0.88	0.77	0.60	0.45	0.24	0.12	0.05	0.01	0.01	0.00			
aunt	0.96	0.96	0.96	0.95	0.94	0.92	0.91	0.84	0.76	0.63	0.46	0.32	0.17	0.07	0.03	0.01	0.01	0.00			
uncle	0.95	0.95	0.94	0.94	0.92	0.90	0.86	0.80	0.69	0.55	0.40	0.27	0.13	0.07	0.04	0.01	0.01	0.00			
first cousin	0.91	0.96	0.97	0.99	0.99	0.99	0.99	0.99	0.99	0.98	0.98	0.98	0.98	0.98	0.96	0.92	0.83	0.71	0.54	0.37	0.21
nephew/niece	0.00	0.01	0.04	0.17	0.37	0.57	0.79	0.87	0.89	0.90	0.91	0.91	0.91	0.91	0.90	0.90	0.90	0.89	0.89	0.87	0.83
nephew	0.00	0.00	0.02	0.12	0.28	0.46	0.67	0.80	0.84	0.87	0.87	0.87	0.86	0.86	0.86	0.85	0.85	0.83	0.81	0.78	0.73
niece	0.00	0.01	0.03	0.11	0.29	0.48	0.68	0.80	0.85	0.87	0.87	0.87	0.87	0.87	0.87	0.86	0.86	0.84	0.83	0.81	0.76
fam. or.	1.00	1.00	1.00	1.00	0.99	0.99	0.99	0.99	0.98	0.97	0.94	0.92	0.90	0.86	0.79	0.67	0.50	0.31	0.18	0.06	0.01
fam. proc.					0.11	0.46	0.70	0.80	0.85	0.86	0.87	0.87	0.86	0.83	0.81	0.78	0.74	0.72	0.69	0.66	0.59
ascending	1.00	1.00	1.00	1.00	1.00	1.00	1.00	0.98	1.00	1.00	0.66	0.49	0.26	0.12	0.05	0.01	0.01	0.00			
lateral	0.95	0.99	1.00	1.00	1.00	1.00	1.00	1.00	1.00	1.00	0.99	0.99	0.99	0.99	0.99	0.97	0.92	0.79	0.61	0.41	0.22
descending	0.00	0.01	0.04	0.17	0.37	0.57	0.79	0.87	0.89	0.91	0.92	0.95	0.97	0.97	0.97	0.97	0.97	0.97	0.96	0.95	0.95

Table 2c Mean age of living kin, data ca. 1930

Kin	Exact age of ego (years)																				
	0	5	10	15	20	25	30	35	40	45	50	55	60	65	70	75	80	85	90	95	100
husband					25.5	29.4	33.4	38.0	42.3	47.0	51.2	55.9	60.4	64.8	68.8	72.5	74.3	75.2	75.2	77.6	80.9
parent	32.6	37.4	42.3	47.2	52.0	56.6	61.0	65.5	69.6	73.5	76.7	80.3	84.1								
father	33.9	38.7	43.6	48.4	53.0	57.5	61.7	66.0	70.2	73.9	77.2	80.5	84.4								
mother	31.2	36.2	41.1	46.1	51.0	55.8	60.5	65.1	69.1	73.2	76.3	80.3	84.0								
sibling	5.8	7.8	10.8	14.7	19.4	24.4	29.3	34.2	39.2	44.1	48.8	53.7	58.2	62.6	66.8	70.6	73.7	76.7	79.7	82.4	85.2
brother	5.5	7.6	10.6	14.6	19.3	24.3	29.1	34.0	39.0	43.9	48.6	53.5	57.8	62.2	66.6	70.4	73.6	76.5	79.3	81.8	85.6
sister	6.1	8.0	11.0	14.9	19.5	24.5	29.5	34.5	39.4	44.4	49.1	53.9	58.5	62.9	66.9	70.7	73.8	76.8	79.9	82.9	84.6
child					1.1	2.3	4.0	6.3	9.3	13.1	17.8	22.7	27.7	32.6	37.6	42.5	47.4	52.2	56.9	61.5	65.8
son					0.9	2.4	4.2	6.6	9.6	13.5	18.0	23.0	28.0	32.9	37.9	42.8	47.7	52.4	57.1	61.6	65.9
daughter					1.3	2.2	3.7	6.1	9.0	12.7	17.5	22.5	27.4	32.3	37.2	42.2	47.1	51.9	56.7	61.3	65.7
grandparent	61.6	65.2	68.6	72.0	74.8	77.5	80.2	82.0	85.1												
grandfather	62.2	65.5	68.7	72.2	75.1	78.4	80.8	81.5													
grandmother	61.1	65.0	68.5	71.9	74.7	77.0	80.0	82.1													
grandchild									1.8	1.3	2.7	3.8	5.1	7.1	9.3	12.3	16.0	20.2	25.0	29.9	34.8
grandson										0.7	2.5	3.7	5.2	7.1	9.4	12.4	16.1	20.3	25.0	29.9	34.8
granddaughter									1.8	1.7	2.9	3.8	5.1	7.0	9.2	12.2	15.8	20.2	24.9	29.9	34.9
gr-grandparent	78.4	80.6	81.2	83.4																	
gr-grandfather	79.5	83.1	81.1	86.1																	
gr-grandmother	77.9	79.5	81.2	82.5																	
gr-grandchild														2.2	2.2	2.8	3.6	4.6	6.0	7.6	9.6
gr-grandson														2.7	2.1	3.0	3.6	4.5	5.9	7.6	9.6
gr-granddaughter														1.8	2.3	2.7	3.7	4.8	6.0	7.5	9.5
aunt/uncle	31.8	36.6	41.5	46.1	50.7	55.0	59.2	62.9	66.2	69.5	72.2	75.1	76.6	78.1	80.8	78.5	83.8	85.5			
aunt	32.1	36.9	41.8	46.5	51.1	55.5	59.6	63.3	66.6	69.9	72.4	75.6	77.2	78.6	80.4	75.5	81.9	82.7			
uncle	31.6	36.4	41.1	45.8	50.2	54.5	58.8	62.5	65.9	69.0	72.0	74.4	75.9	77.5	81.0	80.2	85.7	88.3			
first cousin	9.1	11.1	13.7	16.8	20.5	24.7	29.3	33.9	38.6	43.2	47.8	52.0	56.1	59.7	63.1	66.1	68.6	71.2	73.3	75.3	77.2
nephew/niece	1.9	2.6	3.1	3.4	3.9	5.1	6.7	8.5	10.9	14.1	18.0	22.4	27.2	32.0	36.9	41.8	46.5	51.1	55.4	59.6	63.5
nephew	2.4	3.2	2.7	3.3	3.9	5.2	6.7	8.5	10.9	14.1	17.9	22.3	27.2	32.0	36.7	41.6	46.3	50.7	54.9	59.1	63.0
niece	1.3	2.3	3.5	3.6	3.9	5.0	6.6	8.5	11.0	14.2	18.1	22.5	27.2	32.1	37.1	42.0	46.7	51.5	55.9	60.1	63.9
fam. or.	18.8	18.9	20.9	24.3	28.5	33.0	37.1	40.9	44.6	48.0	51.0	54.7	58.5	62.6	66.8	70.6	73.7	76.7	79.7	82.4	85.2
fam. proc.					18.1	15.2	14.2	14.9	17.0	20.4	24.6	29.2	33.4	37.3	41.3	45.0	48.7	52.7	57.1		
ascending	38.5	41.7	45.2	48.7	52.3	56.1	60.0	63.6	67.0	70.3	73.0	75.7	77.2	78.1	80.7	78.5	83.8	85.5			
lateral	8.6	10.5	13.1	16.4	20.3	24.6	29.3	34.0	38.7	43.4	47.9	52.3	56.4	60.2	63.7	66.8	69.3	71.9	74.0	75.8	77.4
descending	1.9	2.6	3.1	3.4	3.9	5.1	6.7	8.5	10.9	14.0	17.4	20.5	22.8	24.8	26.7	29.0	30.9	31.8	31.1	29.7	28.4

Table 2d Mean number of dependent kin, data ca. 1930

Kin	Exact age of ego (years)																				
	0	5	10	15	20	25	30	35	40	45	50	55	60	65	70	75	80	85	90	95	100
husband	0.0	0.0	0.0	0.0	0.0	0.2	0.3	0.5	0.6				0.1	0.2	0.3	0.2	0.1	0.0	0.0	0.0	0.0
parent	0.0	0.0	0.0	0.0	0.0	0.1	0.2	0.2	0.3	0.5	0.3	0.1	0.0								
father	0.0	0.0	0.0	0.0	0.0	0.1	0.2	0.3	0.3	0.2	0.1	0.1	0.0								
mother						0.1	0.2	0.3	0.3	0.3	0.2	0.1	0.1								
sibling	2.0	2.8	2.9	2.2	1.2	0.4	0.1	0.0													
brother	1.0	1.5	1.5	1.1	0.6	0.2	0.0	0.0													
sister	1.0	1.4	1.4	1.1	0.6	0.2	0.1	0.0													
child					0.0	0.5	1.3	2.1	2.2	1.7	1.0	0.4	0.1								
son					0.3	0.7	1.1	1.1	0.8	0.5	0.4	0.2	0.1								
daughter					0.2	0.6	1.0	0.9	0.9	0.5	0.5	0.2	0.1								
grandparent	0.8	0.9	0.9	0.7	0.5	0.3	0.1	0.0													
grandfather	0.3	0.4	0.4	0.3	0.2	0.1	0.0	0.0													
grandmother	0.4	0.5	0.5	0.4	0.3	0.1	0.0	0.0													
grandchild														0.0	0.1	0.4	1.2	2.8	5.1	7.6	9.4
grandson	0.2	0.1	0.0	0.0										0.0	0.0	0.2	0.6	1.4	2.7	4.0	4.8
granddaughter	0.1	0.0	0.0	0.0										0.0	0.0	0.2	0.6	1.3	2.4	3.7	4.6
gr-grandparent	0.2	0.1	0.0	0.0																	
gr-grandfather	0.1	0.0	0.0	0.0																	
gr-grandmother	0.2	0.1	0.0	0.0							0.0										
gr-grandchild																					
gr-grandson																					
gr-granddaughter																					
aunt/uncle	0.3	0.1	0.1	0.2	0.4	0.8	1.3	1.6	1.8	1.6	1.2	0.8	0.4	0.2	0.1	0.0	0.0	0.0			
aunt	0.1	0.0	0.0	0.1	0.2	0.5	0.7	0.9	1.0	0.9	0.7	0.4	0.2	0.1	0.0	0.0	0.0	0.0			
uncle	0.2	0.1	0.0	0.1	0.2	0.4	0.6	0.8	0.8	0.7	0.5	0.3	0.2	0.1	0.0	0.0	0.0	0.0			
first cousin	0.9	10.4	10.3	8.8	6.4	4.1	2.2	1.0	0.5	0.6	0.9	1.7	2.7	3.5	4.0	3.9	3.3	2.4	1.6	0.9	0.4
nephew/niece	0.0	0.0	0.0	0.4	1.2	2.7	4.4	5.9	6.4	5.7	4.0	2.3	1.1	0.4	0.1	0.1	0.2	0.6	1.1	1.7	2.3
nephew	0.0	0.0	0.0	0.2	0.6	1.3	2.2	2.9	3.2	2.9	2.1	1.2	0.5	0.2	0.1	0.0	0.1	0.3	0.5	0.7	1.0
niece	0.0	0.0	0.0	0.2	0.6	1.3	2.2	2.9	3.1	2.8	2.0	1.1	0.5	0.2	0.1	0.0	0.1	0.3	0.6	1.0	1.3
fam. or.	2.0	2.8	2.9	2.2	1.2	0.6	0.4	0.5	0.6	1.7	1.0	1.1	0.5	0.8	1.1	1.1	0.8	0.4	0.2	0.1	0.0
fam. proc. ascending	1.3	1.1	1.0	0.9	0.9	1.2	1.7	2.2	2.4	2.1	1.5	0.9	0.4	0.2	0.3	0.2	0.1	0.1	0.2	0.5	0.8
lateral	11.0	13.2	13.2	10.9	7.6	4.5	2.3	1.7	0.5	0.6	1.0	1.9	3.1	4.4	5.1	5.0	4.0	2.9	1.8	1.0	0.4
descending	0.0	0.0	0.1	0.4	1.2	2.7	4.4	5.9	6.4	5.8	4.4	3.5	3.6	4.1	4.7	4.6	4.6	5.3	7.2	9.7	11.8

Table 2e   proportion having dependent kin, data ca. 1930

Kin	\	Exact age of ego (years)																		
	0	5	10	15	20	25	30	35	40	45	50	55	60	65	70	75	80	85	90	95	100
husband	0.00	0.00	0.00	0.01	0.04	0.14	0.29	0.45	0.52	0.00	0.02	0.24	0.13	0.24	0.28	0.18	0.10	0.05	0.02	0.01	0.00
parent	0.00	0.00	0.00	0.01	0.04	0.09	0.16	0.23	0.29	0.44	0.26	0.12	0.03								
father					0.00	0.06	0.18	0.30	0.35	0.22	0.11	0.04	0.01								
mother										0.32	0.17	0.08	0.02								
sibling	0.73	0.93	0.91	0.72	0.46	0.20	0.06	0.00		0.01	0.04	0.13									
brother	0.58	0.75	0.74	0.56	0.35	0.14	0.03	0.00		0.00	0.03	0.07									
sister	0.54	0.74	0.72	0.55	0.32	0.13	0.04	0.00		0.01	0.02	0.09									
child					0.03	0.29	0.57	0.69	0.69	0.59	0.41	0.21	0.30	0.52	0.67	0.64	0.50	0.31	0.18	0.06	
son					0.02	0.18	0.41	0.54	0.56	0.45	0.28	0.13	0.16	0.30	0.39	0.37	0.25	0.15	0.07	0.03	
daughter					0.02	0.19	0.40	0.53	0.55	0.45	0.30	0.13	0.21	0.36	0.46	0.44	0.35	0.22	0.12	0.03	
grandparent	0.50	0.63	0.63	0.54	0.37	0.19	0.19														
grandfather	0.30	0.34	0.36	0.26	0.18	0.08	0.03														
grandmother	0.37	0.47	0.46	0.40	0.25	0.14	0.08														
grandchild								0.03	0.01	0.04	0.19	0.39	0.56	0.62	0.64	0.62	0.54	0.42	0.29	0.15	0.06
grandson								0.00	0.01	0.03	0.13	0.31	0.47	0.56	0.59	0.56	0.48	0.35	0.22	0.11	0.04
granddaughter								0.03	0.00	0.03	0.13	0.29	0.46	0.54	0.59	0.56	0.49	0.36	0.22	0.09	0.03
gr-grandparent	0.19	0.07	0.01	0.01																	
gr-grandfather	0.08	0.02	0.00	0.00																	
gr-grandmother	0.14	0.05	0.01	0.01																	
gr-grandchild														0.00	0.04	0.14	0.31	0.45	0.57	0.63	0.65
gr-grandson															0.03	0.09	0.24	0.38	0.52	0.59	0.62
gr-granddaughter															0.02	0.11	0.24	0.39	0.51	0.57	0.60
aunt/uncle	0.15	0.06	0.06	0.12	0.23	0.43	0.57	0.73	0.79	0.72	0.59	0.44	0.24	0.12	0.05	0.01	0.01	0.00	0.00		
aunt	0.10	0.04	0.04	0.08	0.17	0.30	0.44	0.55	0.61	0.55	0.45	0.32	0.16	0.07	0.03	0.01	0.01	0.00			
uncle	0.11	0.05	0.03	0.06	0.14	0.28	0.39	0.49	0.54	0.47	0.38	0.26	0.13	0.07	0.04	0.01	0.01	0.00			
first cousin	0.91	0.95	0.95	0.91	0.81	0.62	0.45	0.30	0.21	0.26	0.38	0.54	0.72	0.83	0.89	0.89	0.81	0.70	0.54	0.37	0.21
nephew/niece	0.00	0.01	0.04	0.17	0.37	0.57	0.79	0.86	0.87	0.82	0.74	0.54	0.34	0.16	0.06	0.03	0.11	0.28	0.47	0.64	0.72
nephew	0.00	0.00	0.02	0.12	0.28	0.46	0.67	0.78	0.79	0.76	0.65	0.45	0.25	0.11	0.03	0.02	0.07	0.17	0.29	0.42	0.52
niece	0.00	0.01	0.03	0.11	0.29	0.48	0.67	0.78	0.80	0.75	0.63	0.43	0.24	0.11	0.02	0.02	0.07	0.20	0.36	0.51	0.60
fam. or.	0.73	0.93	0.91	0.74	0.49	0.34	0.35	0.45	0.52	0.44	0.30	0.25	0.34	0.52	0.67	0.64	0.50	0.31	0.18	0.06	0.01
fam. proc.					0.03	0.29	0.57	0.69	0.69	0.59	0.42	0.23	0.18	0.24	0.28	0.18	0.10	0.07			
ascending	0.70	0.70	0.69	0.63	0.59	0.61	0.71	0.84	0.89	0.82	0.66	0.48	0.26	0.12	0.05	0.01	0.01	0.00			
lateral	0.95	0.99	1.00	0.96	0.87	0.67	0.47	0.31	0.21	0.26	0.39	0.56	0.76	0.89	0.95	0.96	0.91	0.78	0.61	0.41	0.22
descending	0.00	0.01	0.04	0.17	0.37	0.57	0.79	0.86	0.87	0.83	0.79	0.71	0.71	0.68	0.67	0.65	0.66	0.74	0.80	0.87	0.89

Table 2f Proportion co-residing with kin, data ca. 1930

Kin	Exact age of ego (years)																				
	0	5	10	15	20	25	30	35	40	45	50	55	60	65	70	75	80	85	90	95	100
husband	1.00	0.97	0.97	0.95	0.11	0.45	0.69	0.77	0.81	0.78	0.74	0.68	0.58	0.45	0.34	0.22	0.12	0.05	0.02	0.01	
parent	0.98	0.93	0.88	0.82	0.84	0.49	0.24	0.14	0.09	0.06	0.03	0.01	0.00								
father	1.00	0.95	0.92	0.87	0.68	0.36	0.15	0.09	0.05	0.03	0.01										
mother	1.00	0.91	0.92	0.92	0.72	0.41	0.20	0.11	0.07	0.05	0.02										
sibling	0.73	0.91	0.92	0.92	0.80	0.44	0.19	0.10	0.06	0.04	0.02	0.02	0.02	0.01	0.01	0.01	0.01	0.00			
brother	0.58	0.75	0.80	0.80	0.68	0.35	0.14	0.07	0.04	0.02	0.02	0.01	0.00	0.00	0.00	0.00	0.00	0.00			
sister	0.54	0.74	0.79	0.78	0.64	0.30	0.13	0.07	0.03	0.02	0.02	0.01	0.01	0.01	0.01	0.01	0.01	0.00			
child					0.03	0.29	0.57	0.69	0.74	0.74	0.70	0.64	0.55	0.44	0.33	0.25	0.21	0.19	0.17	0.15	
son					0.02	0.18	0.41	0.55	0.61	0.61	0.57	0.50	0.39	0.28	0.20	0.14	0.11	0.10	0.09	0.07	
daughter					0.02	0.19	0.40	0.53	0.59	0.59	0.53	0.46	0.36	0.27	0.18	0.13	0.11	0.10	0.09	0.08	
grandparent	0.01	0.01	0.01	0.01	0.00																
grandfather	0.01	0.01	0.00	0.00	0.00																
grandmother	0.01	0.01	0.01	0.01	0.00																
grandchild											0.00	0.00	0.00	0.00	0.00						
grandson											0.00	0.00	0.00	0.00	0.00						
granddaughter																					
gr-grandparent																					
gr-grandfather																					
gr-grandmother																					
gr-granchild																					
gr-grandson																					
gr-granddaughter																					
aunt/uncle	0.02	0.01	0.01	0.01	0.01	0.00															
aunt	0.01	0.01	0.00	0.00	0.00																
uncle	0.02	0.01	0.01	0.01	0.00	0.00															
first cousin																					
nephew/niece																					
nephew																					
niece																					
fam. or.	1.00	0.98	0.98	0.98	0.87	0.51	0.26	0.16	0.10	0.08	0.05	0.02	0.02	0.01	0.01	0.01	0.01	0.00			
fam. proc.					0.11	0.46	0.70	0.80	0.85	0.86	0.85	0.82	0.76	0.66	0.54	0.41	0.31	0.24	0.19	0.16	
ascending	1.00	0.99	0.98	0.96	0.85	0.49	0.24	0.14	0.09	0.06	0.03	0.01	0.00								
lateral	0.73	0.91	0.92	0.92	0.80	0.44	0.19	0.10	0.06	0.04	0.02	0.02	0.02	0.01	0.01	0.01	0.01	0.00			
descending					0.03	0.29	0.57	0.69	0.74	0.74	0.70	0.64	0.55	0.44	0.33	0.25	0.21	0.19	0.17	0.15	

Table 3a   Mean number of living kin, data ca. 1960

Kin	Exact age of ego (years)																				
	0	5	10	15	20	25	30	35	40	45	50	55	60	65	70	75	80	85	90	95	100
husband					0.1	0.4	0.7	0.8	0.8	0.8	0.8	0.7	0.7	0.6	0.5	0.3	0.2	0.1	0.0	0.0	0.0
parent	2.0	2.0	2.0	1.9	1.8	1.7	1.5	1.4	1.1	0.8	0.5	0.2	0.1	0.0							
father	1.0	1.0	1.0	0.9	0.9	0.8	0.7	0.6	0.4	0.3	0.2	0.1	0.1	0.0							
mother	1.0	1.0	1.0	1.0	0.9	0.9	0.8	0.8	0.6	0.5	0.3	0.2	0.1	0.0							
sibling	1.7	2.3	2.9	3.2	3.3	3.3	3.3	3.2	3.2	3.1	3.0	2.9	2.6	2.4	2.0	1.5	1.0	0.7	0.3	0.1	0.1
brother	0.8	1.1	1.5	1.6	1.6	1.6	1.6	1.6	1.6	1.5	1.5	1.4	1.2	1.1	0.9	0.7	0.5	0.3	0.1	0.1	0.0
sister	0.9	1.2	1.4	1.6	1.6	1.7	1.6	1.6	1.6	1.6	1.6	1.5	1.4	1.3	1.1	0.8	0.6	0.4	0.2	0.1	0.0
child					0.1	0.4	1.1	1.7	2.2	2.5	2.6	2.5	2.5	2.5	2.5	2.4	2.4	2.3	2.2	2.0	1.7
son					0.0	0.2	0.6	0.9	1.2	1.3	1.3	1.3	1.3	1.3	1.3	1.2	1.2	1.2	1.1	1.0	0.8
daughter					0.0	0.2	0.5	0.8	1.1	1.2	1.2	1.2	1.2	1.2	1.2	1.2	1.2	1.1	1.1	1.0	0.9
grandparent	2.7	2.2	1.7	1.2	0.8	0.4	0.2	0.1	0.0												
grandfather	1.2	1.0	0.7	0.5	0.3	0.1	0.1	0.0	0.0												
grandmother	1.5	1.3	1.0	0.7	0.5	0.3	0.1	0.0	0.0												
grandchild										0.1	0.3	1.0	2.0	3.3	4.5	5.4	5.9	6.1	6.1	6.1	6.0
grandson										0.0	0.2	0.5	1.0	1.7	2.4	2.8	3.1	3.1	3.1	3.1	3.1
granddaughter										0.0	0.2	0.5	1.0	1.6	2.2	2.6	2.9	3.0	3.0	3.0	3.0
gr-grandparent	0.4	0.1	0.1	0.0	0.0																
gr-grandfather	0.1	0.0	0.0	0.0																	
gr-grandmother	0.3	0.1	0.0	0.0	0.0																
gr-grandchild														0.0	0.1	0.3	0.9	2.1	3.9	6.3	9.0
gr-grandson															0.0	0.1	0.4	1.1	1.9	3.2	4.6
gr-granddaughter															0.1	0.2	0.4	1.0	2.0	3.1	4.5
aunt/uncle	6.6	6.5	6.3	6.2	5.9	5.4	4.9	4.2	3.5	2.6	1.9	1.2	0.6	0.3	0.1	0.0	0.0	0.0			
aunt	3.4	3.3	3.2	3.2	3.1	2.8	2.5	2.3	1.9	1.5	1.0	0.7	0.3	0.2	0.1	0.0	0.0	0.0			
uncle	3.2	3.2	3.1	3.0	2.8	2.6	2.3	2.0	1.6	1.2	0.8	0.5	0.3	0.1	0.1	0.0	0.0	0.0			
first cousin	8.4	10.9	13.0	14.6	15.5	16.1	16.2	16.0	15.7	15.2	14.5	13.7	12.5	11.1	9.5	7.6	5.9	4.1	2.7	1.6	0.8
nephew/niece	0.0	0.0	0.1	0.4	1.0	1.9	3.3	4.8	6.2	7.2	7.8	8.1	8.1	8.1	8.0	7.8	7.6	7.3	6.8	6.2	5.4
nephew	0.0	0.0	0.1	0.2	0.5	1.0	1.7	2.5	3.2	3.8	4.1	4.2	4.2	4.2	4.1	4.0	3.9	3.7	3.5	3.1	2.6
niece	0.0	0.0	0.1	0.2	0.5	0.9	1.6	2.3	2.9	3.4	3.7	3.9	3.9	3.9	3.9	3.8	3.7	3.6	3.4	3.1	2.8
fam. or.	3.7	4.3	4.9	5.1	5.1	5.0	4.8	4.6	4.3	3.9	3.5	3.3	2.7	2.4	2.0	1.5	1.0	0.7	0.3	0.1	0.1
fam. proc.					0.2	0.8	1.7	2.5	3.0	3.4	3.5	3.3	3.2	3.1	2.9	2.7	2.5	2.4	2.2	2.0	1.8
ascending	11.7	10.9	10.1	9.3	8.5	7.5	6.6	5.6	4.6	3.4	2.4	1.4	0.7	0.3	0.1	0.0	0.0	0.0	0.0	0.0	0.0
lateral	10.1	13.2	15.9	17.8	18.8	19.4	19.4	19.2	18.9	18.3	17.5	16.6	15.1	13.5	11.5	9.1	6.9	4.8	3.0	1.7	0.9
descending	0.0	0.0	0.1	0.4	1.0	2.0	3.3	4.8	6.2	7.3	8.1	9.0	10.1	11.4	12.6	13.6	14.4	15.5	16.8	18.7	20.4

Table 3b Proportion having living kin, data ca. 1960

Kin	Exact age of ego (years)																				
	0	5	10	15	20	25	30	35	40	45	50	55	60	65	70	75	80	85	90	95	100
husband	1.00	1.00	1.00	1.00	0.12	0.45	0.68	0.76	0.80	0.79	0.78	0.78	0.74	0.56	0.45	0.34	0.19	0.09	0.04	0.02	0.01
parent	1.00	0.98	0.97	0.93	0.99	0.97	0.93	0.88	0.77	0.60	0.41	0.23	0.08	0.02							
father	1.00	1.00	0.98	0.93	0.87	0.82	0.71	0.60	0.44	0.32	0.18	0.06	0.02	0.00							
mother	1.00	1.00	0.98	0.96	0.94	0.89	0.83	0.76	0.64	0.48	0.33	0.18	0.07	0.02							
sibling	0.70	0.85	0.94	0.94	0.94	0.94	0.94	0.94	0.94	0.93	0.93	0.93	0.91	0.88	0.83	0.73	0.59	0.41	0.24	0.11	0.05
brother	0.51	0.66	0.76	0.79	0.79	0.79	0.78	0.78	0.77	0.76	0.75	0.73	0.69	0.64	0.56	0.45	0.34	0.22	0.10	0.05	0.02
sister	0.51	0.64	0.76	0.80	0.80	0.80	0.80	0.80	0.80	0.79	0.77	0.78	0.76	0.72	0.67	0.56	0.43	0.30	0.18	0.08	0.03
child					0.05	0.29	0.55	0.69	0.74	0.76	0.79	0.77	0.76	0.76	0.76	0.75	0.75	0.75	0.73	0.72	0.68
son					0.03	0.20	0.39	0.53	0.60	0.63	0.63	0.63	0.62	0.62	0.62	0.60	0.60	0.60	0.58	0.55	0.49
daughter					0.03	0.15	0.36	0.50	0.57	0.61	0.61	0.61	0.61	0.60	0.60	0.60	0.59	0.59	0.58	0.55	0.52
grandparent	0.97	0.92	0.83	0.69	0.49	0.31	0.16	0.04	0.01												
grandfather	0.83	0.72	0.59	0.42	0.26	0.12	0.06	0.01	0.00												
grandmother	0.91	0.84	0.73	0.58	0.41	0.25	0.12	0.14	0.01												
grandchild					0.00					0.04	0.19	0.36	0.53	0.63	0.68	0.71	0.72	0.72	0.72	0.72	0.72
grandson										0.03	0.11	0.27	0.42	0.55	0.64	0.67	0.68	0.68	0.69	0.69	0.68
granddaughter										0.03	0.13	0.26	0.43	0.54	0.61	0.65	0.66	0.67	0.67	0.67	0.67
gr-grandparent	0.27	0.11	0.04	0.02	0.00																
gr-grandfather	0.12	0.03	0.01	0.00																	
gr-grandmother	0.23	0.09	0.04	0.02																	
gr-grandchild														0.01	0.05	0.15	0.27	0.44	0.56	0.63	0.69
gr-grandson														0.00	0.03	0.10	0.21	0.37	0.50	0.58	0.65
gr-granddaughter														0.00	0.03	0.11	0.20	0.36	0.48	0.59	0.64
aunt/uncle	0.99	0.99	0.99	0.99	0.98	0.98	0.97	0.95	0.93	0.86	0.74	0.56	0.37	0.18	0.10	0.03	0.00	0.00			
aunt	0.96	0.96	0.96	0.95	0.95	0.93	0.91	0.89	0.82	0.71	0.59	0.41	0.24	0.12	0.07	0.02	0.00	0.00			
uncle	0.94	0.94	0.93	0.92	0.91	0.89	0.87	0.81	0.75	0.64	0.48	0.36	0.23	0.11	0.05	0.01	0.00	0.00			
first cousin	0.90	0.96	0.98	0.99	0.99	0.99	0.99	0.99	0.99	0.99	0.99	0.98	0.97	0.97	0.96	0.94	0.88	0.79	0.67	0.50	0.35
nephew/niece	0.00	0.02	0.07	0.18	0.35	0.53	0.71	0.83	0.88	0.89	0.90	0.90	0.89	0.89	0.89	0.89	0.89	0.89	0.88	0.88	0.87
nephew	0.00	0.01	0.04	0.14	0.26	0.41	0.59	0.73	0.81	0.85	0.86	0.86	0.86	0.86	0.86	0.86	0.86	0.85	0.84	0.82	0.80
niece	0.00	0.01	0.04	0.11	0.26	0.42	0.60	0.74	0.83	0.84	0.86	0.86	0.86	0.86	0.86	0.86	0.86	0.85	0.84	0.82	0.80
fam. or.	1.00	1.00	1.00	1.00	1.00	1.00	0.99	0.99	0.99	0.98	0.96	0.94	0.92	0.88	0.83	0.80	0.78	0.77	0.75	0.73	0.69
fam. proc.					0.12	0.45	0.68	0.78	0.83	0.85	0.86	0.86	0.85	0.84	0.82	0.80	0.78	0.77	0.75	0.73	0.69
ascending	1.00	1.00	1.00	1.00	1.00	1.00	1.00	1.00	0.97	0.91	0.80	0.62	0.40	0.19	0.10	0.03	0.00	0.00			
lateral	0.95	0.99	1.00	1.00	1.00	1.00	1.00	1.00	1.00	1.00	1.00	1.00	1.00	1.00	0.99	0.98	0.94	0.84	0.71	0.53	0.38
descending	0.00	0.02	0.07	0.18	0.35	0.53	0.71	0.83	0.88	0.89	0.90	0.93	0.95	0.96	0.96	0.96	0.96	0.96	0.96	0.96	0.96

Table 3c   Mean age of living kin, data ca. 1960

Kin	Exact age of ego (years)																				
	0	5	10	15	20	25	30	35	40	45	50	55	60	65	70	75	80	85	90	95	100
husband					25.6	28.9	33.2	37.7	42.1	46.6	51.3	56.2	60.7	65.0	69.3	73.1	76.4	78.2	78.8	78.8	81.4
parent	33.5	38.4	43.4	48.3	53.0	57.7	62.1	66.3	70.2	74.1	77.8	81.3	83.7	87.1							
father	35.1	40.1	45.0	49.8	54.4	59.0	63.3	67.3	70.8	74.6	78.7	81.8	83.2	86.2							
mother	31.8	36.8	41.8	46.7	51.7	56.4	61.0	65.6	69.8	73.7	77.3	81.1	83.8	87.2							
sibling	7.3	9.6	12.1	15.8	20.2	25.0	30.0	35.0	39.9	44.8	49.7	54.3	58.7	63.1	67.1	70.6	73.6	76.5	79.1	81.2	83.4
brother	7.4	9.5	12.1	15.7	20.2	25.1	30.0	35.0	39.9	44.7	49.6	54.1	58.4	62.7	66.6	70.2	73.4	76.7	78.0	80.6	83.7
sister	7.3	9.6	12.1	15.8	20.2	25.0	30.0	35.0	40.0	44.9	49.7	54.4	59.0	63.4	67.5	70.9	73.8	76.4	79.6	81.5	83.3
child					1.2	2.8	4.4	6.8	9.6	13.2	17.9	22.8	27.8	32.8	37.8	42.7	47.7	52.6	57.4	62.0	66.3
son					1.5	3.0	4.7	7.2	9.7	13.4	18.0	22.9	27.9	32.9	37.9	42.9	47.8	52.6	57.3	61.9	66.0
daughter					0.8	2.5	4.1	6.5	9.5	13.1	17.7	22.7	27.7	32.7	37.7	42.6	47.5	52.6	57.4	62.0	66.5
grandparent	63.1	66.9	70.1	73.1	76.0	78.9	81.6	82.6	83.6												
grandfather	63.6	67.3	70.6	73.5	76.2	79.6	83.3	82.4	88.5												
grandmother	62.6	66.5	69.8	72.8	75.8	78.6	80.8	82.6	81.6												
grandchild									2.2	2.3	3.2	4.2	5.7	7.4	9.6	12.6	16.2	20.6	25.4	30.3	35.2
grandson									1.5	2.3	3.1	4.1	5.6	7.2	9.3	12.5	16.0	20.5	25.3	30.2	35.1
granddaughter									2.8	2.2	3.3	4.3	5.8	7.5	9.8	12.6	16.3	20.7	25.4	30.3	35.3
gr-grandparent	79.7	80.2	81.1	82.8	82.8																
gr-grandfather	80.0	81.1	81.2	81.4																	
gr-grandmother	79.6	79.8	81.1	83.1	82.8																
gr-grandchild														2.6	2.0	3.2	4.1	5.1	6.5	7.9	9.8
gr-grandson														3.2	2.0	3.3	3.9	5.0	6.5	7.8	9.7
gr-granddaughter														1.4	1.9	3.1	4.3	5.2	6.5	8.1	9.8
aunt/uncle	32.9	37.7	42.4	47.1	51.6	55.8	59.7	63.5	67.0	70.0	72.7	75.1	77.3	78.9	81.1	82.7	83.5	85.0			
aunt	33.1	38.0	42.7	47.5	52.0	56.2	60.0	63.9	67.4	70.4	73.1	75.5	77.2	78.6	80.6	82.0	83.5	85.0			
uncle	32.7	37.5	42.1	46.7	51.2	55.4	59.4	63.0	66.4	69.5	72.1	74.7	77.4	79.3	81.8	84.2					
first cousin	11.2	13.1	15.5	18.5	22.0	25.9	30.3	34.9	39.5	44.0	48.4	52.6	56.5	60.2	63.6	66.4	69.3	71.6	73.9	75.8	77.8
nephew/niece	0.7	1.6	2.9	3.7	4.9	6.1	7.6	9.4	11.6	14.5	18.1	22.3	26.8	31.7	36.6	41.4	46.2	50.9	55.3	59.5	63.3
nephew	0.7	2.1	2.9	3.6	5.0	6.2	7.7	9.4	11.6	14.4	18.0	22.3	26.8	31.7	36.6	41.4	46.1	50.7	55.0	59.1	62.8
niece		1.3	2.9	3.9	4.7	6.0	7.5	9.4	11.6	14.6	18.2	22.3	26.9	31.7	36.7	41.5	46.4	51.1	55.6	59.9	63.7
fam. or.	21.5	22.9	24.7	27.8	31.9	36.2	40.3	44.2	47.6	50.8	53.7	56.4	59.5	63.3	67.1	70.6	73.6	76.5	79.1	81.2	83.4
fam. proc.					16.9	16.5	15.6	16.4	18.1	21.2	25.6	30.4	34.7	38.7	42.7	46.5	49.8	53.6	57.8	62.2	66.4
ascending	41.6	44.4	47.6	50.8	54.1	57.5	60.9	64.3	67.8	70.9	73.8	76.2	78.0	79.4	81.1	82.7	83.5	85.0			
lateral	10.6	12.5	14.9	18.0	21.6	25.8	30.3	34.9	39.6	44.2	48.6	52.9	56.9	60.7	64.2	67.1	69.9	72.3	74.5	76.2	78.1
descending	0.7	1.6	2.9	3.7	4.9	6.1	7.6	9.4	11.6	14.4	17.5	20.4	22.7	24.7	26.7	29.1	31.3	32.8	33.2	32.4	31.4

Detailed CAMSIM Microsimulation Results 313

Table 3d Mean number of dependent kin, data ca. 1960

Kin	Exact age of ego (years)																				
	0	5	10	15	20	25	30	35	40	45	50	55	60	65	70	75	80	85	90	95	100
husband			0.0	0.0	0.1	0.3	0.5	0.7	0.0	0.0	0.0	0.1	0.1	0.3	0.4	0.3	0.2	0.1	0.0	0.0	0.0
parent					0.1	0.2	0.3	0.4	0.9	0.8	0.5	0.3	0.1	0.0	0.0	0.0	0.0	0.0	0.0	0.0	0.0
father					0.0	0.1	0.2	0.4	0.4	0.3	0.2	0.1	0.0								
mother					0.1	0.1	0.1	0.0	0.5	0.5	0.3	0.2	0.1	0.0							
sibling	1.6	1.8	1.8	1.5	1.0	0.4	0.1	0.0	0.0	0.0	0.1	0.3	0.5	1.0	1.1	1.2	0.9	0.6	0.3	0.1	0.1
brother	0.8	0.9	0.9	0.8	0.5	0.2	0.1	0.0	0.0	0.0	0.1	0.1	0.2	0.4	0.5	0.5	0.4	0.3	0.1	0.1	0.0
sister	0.8	0.9	0.9	0.7	0.5	0.2	0.1	0.0	0.0	0.0	0.1	0.2	0.3	0.6	0.7	0.7	0.5	0.4	0.2	0.1	0.0
child					0.0	0.4	1.1	1.6	1.9	1.5	0.9	0.3	0.0								
son					0.0	0.2	0.6	0.8	0.9	0.8	0.5	0.2	0.0								
daughter					0.0	0.2	0.5	0.8	0.9	0.7	0.4	0.1	0.0								
grandparent	1.1	1.3	1.3	1.1	0.7	0.4	0.1	0.0													
grandfather	0.5	0.6	0.6	0.4	0.3	0.1	0.0														
grandmother	0.6	0.7	0.7	0.6	0.5	0.3	0.1	0.0													
grandchild									0.0	0.1	0.3	1.0	1.9	2.9	3.6	3.5	2.7	1.6	0.8	0.3	0.1
grandson									0.0	0.0	0.2	0.5	1.0	1.5	1.9	1.8	1.4	0.8	0.4	0.1	0.0
granddaughter									0.0	0.0	0.2	0.5	0.9	1.4	1.7	1.7	1.3	0.8	0.4	0.1	0.0
gr-grandparent	0.4	0.1	0.1	0.0	0.0																
gr-grandfather	0.1	0.0	0.0	0.0	0.0																
gr-grandmother	0.3	0.1	0.0	0.0	0.0																
gr-grandchild														0.0	0.1	0.3	0.9	2.0	3.6	5.5	7.0
gr-grandson														0.0	0.0	0.1	0.4	1.0	1.8	2.8	3.5
gr-granddaughter														0.0	0.0	0.2	0.4	1.0	1.8	2.7	3.5
aunt/uncle	0.4	0.2	0.2	0.3	0.7	1.0	1.5	1.9	2.0	1.9	1.6	1.1	0.6	0.3	0.1	0.0	0.0				
aunt	0.2	0.1	0.1	0.2	0.4	0.6	0.8	1.1	1.1	1.1	0.9	0.6	0.3	0.2	0.0	0.0	0.0				
uncle	0.2	0.1	0.1	0.1	0.3	0.4	0.7	0.8	0.9	0.8	0.7	0.5	0.3	0.1	0.1	0.0	0.0				
first cousin	6.0	6.9	6.9	6.2	4.9	3.4	2.1	1.2	0.8	0.9	1.4	2.2	3.0	3.8	4.4	4.4	4.1	3.2	2.3	1.5	0.8
nephew/niece	0.0	0.0	0.1	0.4	0.5	1.0	1.5	2.0	2.2	2.1	1.6	1.1	0.6	0.5	0.2	0.1	0.2	0.6	1.2	1.8	2.4
nephew	0.0	0.0	0.1	0.2	0.3	0.5	0.7	1.0	1.1	1.0	0.8	0.5	0.3	0.2	0.1	0.0	0.1	0.3	0.5	0.8	1.1
niece	0.0	0.0	0.1	0.2	0.3	0.5	0.8	1.1	1.2	1.1	0.9	0.6	0.3	0.2	0.1	0.1	0.1	0.3	0.6	1.0	1.3
fam. or.	1.6	1.8	1.8	1.6	1.1	0.7	0.6	0.8	0.9	0.8	0.6	0.4	0.2	1.0	1.1	1.2	0.9	0.6	0.3	0.1	0.1
fam. proc.					0.1	0.7	1.6	2.3	1.9	1.5	0.9	0.4	0.1	0.3	0.4	0.3	0.2	0.1	0.0	0.0	0.0
ascending	1.9	1.6	1.6	1.5	1.5	1.7	2.2	2.7	2.9	2.7	2.1	1.3	0.7	0.3	0.1	0.0	0.0	0.0	0.0	0.0	0.0
lateral	7.6	8.7	8.7	7.8	5.9	3.8	2.9	2.7	2.9	2.7	2.5	3.0	3.7	4.8	5.6	5.6	5.0	3.9	2.7	1.6	0.9
descending	0.0	0.0	0.1	0.4	1.0	1.8	2.9	3.8	4.3	4.1	3.5	3.0	3.0	3.4	3.8	3.9	3.8	4.3	5.5	7.6	9.4

Table 3e   Proportion having dependent kin, data ca. 1960

Kin	\	\	\	\	\	Exact age of ego (years)	\	\	\	\	\	\	\	\	\	\	\	\	\	\
	0	5	10	15	20	25	30	35	40	45	50	55	60	65	70	75	80	85	90	95	100
husband									0.00	0.00	0.01	0.06	0.15	0.32	0.36	0.30	0.17	0.08	0.04	0.02	0.01
parent					0.09	0.21	0.38	0.57	0.66	0.59	0.41	0.23	0.08	0.02							
father					0.08	0.16	0.27	0.37	0.38	0.32	0.18	0.06	0.02	0.00							
mother					0.02	0.11	0.22	0.33	0.49	0.47	0.33	0.18	0.06	0.02							
sibling	0.70	0.85	0.83	0.69	0.51	0.25	0.10	0.02	0.00												
brother	0.50	0.60	0.61	0.51	0.35	0.15	0.05	0.00	0.00												
sister	0.50	0.60	0.57	0.48	0.35	0.16	0.06	0.02													
child					0.05	0.29	0.55	0.69	0.70	0.62	0.47	0.24	0.16	0.06							
son					0.03	0.20	0.39	0.53	0.54	0.45	0.33	0.16	0.03								
daughter					0.03	0.15	0.36	0.49	0.53	0.45	0.30	0.14	0.03								
grandparent	0.67	0.75	0.75	0.67	0.49	0.31	0.16	0.04	0.01												
grandfather	0.46	0.49	0.50	0.39	0.25	0.12	0.06	0.01	0.00												
grandmother	0.48	0.57	0.59	0.54	0.39	0.25	0.12	0.04	0.01												
grandchild									0.01	0.04	0.19	0.36	0.52	0.63	0.67	0.67	0.62	0.49	0.35	0.16	0.05
grandson										0.03	0.10	0.27	0.41	0.53	0.61	0.59	0.55	0.37	0.24	0.09	0.03
granddaughter										0.03	0.10	0.26	0.42	0.52	0.59	0.59	0.52	0.41	0.24	0.10	0.03
gr-grandparent	0.27	0.11	0.04	0.02	0.00																
gr-grandfather	0.11	0.03	0.01	0.00																	
gr-grandmother	0.23	0.09	0.04	0.02	0.00																
gr-grandchild													0.00	0.01	0.05	0.15	0.27	0.44	0.55	0.62	0.68
gr-grandson															0.03	0.10	0.21	0.37	0.49	0.57	0.64
gr-granddaughter															0.03	0.11	0.20	0.36	0.48	0.58	0.62
aunt/uncle	0.22	0.13	0.12	0.20	0.37	0.52	0.68	0.79	0.84	0.82	0.73	0.56	0.36	0.18	0.10	0.03	0.00	0.00			
aunt	0.14	0.08	0.08	0.13	0.27	0.39	0.51	0.62	0.67	0.64	0.57	0.40	0.23	0.12	0.07	0.02	0.00	0.00			
uncle	0.16	0.07	0.06	0.12	0.24	0.32	0.44	0.53	0.58	0.56	0.44	0.34	0.23	0.11	0.05	0.01					
first cousin	0.88	0.94	0.93	0.88	0.80	0.69	0.54	0.41	0.34	0.36	0.47	0.59	0.75	0.84	0.89	0.92	0.88	0.78	0.67	0.50	0.35
nephew/niece	0.00	0.02	0.07	0.18	0.35	0.53	0.59	0.82	0.85	0.82	0.72	0.56	0.40	0.23	0.12	0.07	0.13	0.31	0.46	0.64	0.75
nephew	0.00	0.01	0.04	0.14	0.26	0.41	0.59	0.72	0.76	0.72	0.61	0.45	0.29	0.16	0.08	0.05	0.09	0.22	0.35	0.52	0.57
niece		0.01	0.04	0.11	0.26	0.42	0.47	0.58	0.66	0.69	0.61	0.45	0.29	0.16	0.08	0.05	0.17	0.13	0.24	0.11	0.64
fam. or.	0.70	0.85	0.84	0.72	0.58	0.45	0.47	0.69	0.66	0.60	0.48	0.42	0.28	0.32	0.36	0.30	0.17	0.13	0.13	0.11	0.05
fam. proc.					0.05	0.29	0.55	0.58	0.70	0.62	0.48	0.52	0.52	0.60	0.67	0.69	0.58	0.41	0.24	0.49	0.57
ascending	0.86	0.84	0.83	0.81	0.78	0.79	0.84	0.91	0.94	0.91	0.79	0.62	0.40	0.19	0.10	0.03	0.00	0.00			
lateral	0.95	0.99	0.98	0.93	0.86	0.73	0.55	0.41	0.34	0.36	0.49	0.63	0.82	0.92	0.96	0.97	0.94	0.83	0.71	0.53	0.38
descending	0.00	0.02	0.07	0.18	0.35	0.53	0.70	0.82	0.85	0.83	0.78	0.73	0.74	0.72	0.72	0.71	0.72	0.73	0.80	0.88	0.92

Table 3f Proportion co-residing with kin, data ca. 1960

Kin	Exact age of ego (years)																				
	0	5	10	15	20	25	30	35	40	45	50	55	60	65	70	75	80	85	90	95	100
husband	1.00	0.98	0.97	0.97	0.12	0.45	0.68	0.76	0.80	0.79	0.78	0.74	0.66	0.56	0.45	0.33	0.19	0.09	0.04	0.02	
parent	0.98	0.97	0.95	0.92	0.85	0.52	0.29	0.19	0.12	0.09	0.05	0.03	0.00								
father	1.00	0.98	0.96	0.93	0.76	0.44	0.23	0.13	0.06	0.04	0.02	0.01									
mother	1.00	0.98	0.96	0.93	0.80	0.47	0.25	0.17	0.10	0.08	0.04	0.02									
sibling	0.70	0.84	0.92	0.92	0.77	0.46	0.23	0.13	0.09	0.07	0.06	0.06	0.05								
brother	0.51	0.65	0.74	0.75	0.62	0.34	0.15	0.08	0.05	0.03	0.03	0.03	0.02								
sister	0.51	0.63	0.74	0.75	0.59	0.32	0.16	0.09	0.06	0.05	0.04	0.04	0.03								
child					0.05	0.29	0.55	0.69	0.74	0.76	0.74	0.68	0.59	0.50	0.41	0.35	0.31	0.28	0.27	0.26	
son					0.03	0.20	0.39	0.53	0.60	0.62	0.59	0.53	0.43	0.35	0.26	0.20	0.18	0.16	0.15	0.14	
daughter					0.03	0.15	0.36	0.50	0.56	0.59	0.55	0.50	0.40	0.28	0.22	0.18	0.16	0.15	0.15	0.14	
grandparent	0.01	0.01	0.01	0.01	0.01																
grandfather	0.01	0.01	0.01	0.01	0.00																
grandmother	0.01	0.01	0.01	0.00	0.00																
grandchild									0.00	0.00	0.00	0.01	0.01	0.01	0.01	0.01	0.00	0.00	0.00	0.00	
grandson									0.00	0.00	0.00	0.00	0.00	0.00	0.00	0.00	0.00				
granddaughter																					
gr-grandparent																					
gr-grandfather																					
gr-grandmother																					
gr-grandchild																					
gr-grandson																					
gr-granddaughter																					
aunt/uncle	0.01	0.01	0.01	0.00	0.00																
aunt	0.01	0.01	0.00	0.00	0.00																
uncle	0.01	0.00	0.00	0.00	0.00																
first cousin				0.00	0.00	0.00	0.00	0.00	0.00	0.00	0.00										
nephew/niece						0.00	0.00	0.00	0.00	0.00	0.00										
nephew				0.00	0.00	0.00	0.00	0.00	0.00												
niece				0.00	0.00	0.00	0.00	0.00	0.00												
fam. or.	1.00	0.99	0.99	0.99	0.87	0.54	0.31	0.21	0.15	0.12	0.10	0.08	0.05	0.04	0.03	0.02	0.01	0.01	0.00	0.00	
fam. proc.					0.12	0.45	0.68	0.77	0.83	0.85	0.85	0.83	0.79	0.74	0.64	0.56	0.44	0.35	0.30	0.28	
ascending	1.00	1.00	0.99	0.98	0.86	0.52	0.29	0.19	0.12	0.09	0.05	0.03	0.00								
lateral	0.70	0.84	0.92	0.92	0.77	0.46	0.23	0.13	0.09	0.07	0.06	0.06	0.05								
descending				0.00	0.01	0.00	0.00	0.00	0.00	0.00	0.00	0.01	0.01	0.01	0.01	0.01	0.00	0.00	0.00	0.00	

Table 4a   Mean number of living kin, data ca. 1985–1990

Kin	Exact age of ego (years)																				
	0	5	10	15	20	25	30	35	40	45	50	55	60	65	70	75	80	85	90	95	100
husband					0.1	0.5	0.7	0.8	0.8	0.9	0.8	0.8	0.7	0.7	0.5	0.4	0.3	0.1	0.1	0.0	0.0
parent	2.0	2.0	2.0	1.9	1.9	1.8	1.7	1.6	1.3	1.1	0.8	0.5	0.1								
father	1.0	1.0	1.0	1.0	0.9	0.9	0.8	0.7	0.6	0.4	0.3	0.1	0.0								
mother	1.0	1.0	1.0	1.0	1.0	0.9	0.9	0.9	0.8	0.6	0.5	0.4	0.1								
sibling	0.8	1.1	1.4	1.5	1.5	1.5	1.5	1.4	1.4	1.4	1.4	1.3	1.3	1.2	1.0	0.8	0.6	0.3	0.1	0.1	0.0
brother	0.4	0.6	0.7	0.8	0.8	0.8	0.8	0.8	0.7	0.7	0.7	0.7	0.6	0.6	0.5						
sister	0.4	0.5	0.7	0.7	0.7	0.7	0.7	0.7	0.7	0.7	0.7	0.6	0.6	0.6	0.5						
child					0.0	0.4	0.9	1.2	1.5	1.5	1.5										
son					0.0	0.2	0.4	0.6	0.7	0.8	0.8										
daughter					0.0	0.2	0.4	0.6	0.7	0.8	0.8										
grandparent	3.2	2.9	2.4	1.9	1.4	0.9	0.4	0.2	0.1	0.0	0.0										
grandfather	1.5	1.3	1.0	0.8	0.5	0.3	0.1	0.0	0.0	0.0	0.0										
grandmother	1.8	1.6	1.4	1.2	0.9	0.6	0.3	0.1	0.0	0.0	0.0										
grandchild												0.7	1.2	1.7	2.0	2.2	2.4	2.4	2.4	2.4	2.3
grandson												0.3	0.6	0.9	1.1	1.2	1.2	1.3	1.3	1.2	1.2
granddaughter												0.3	0.6	0.8	1.0	1.1	1.1	1.1	1.1	1.1	1.1
gr-grandparent	0.9	0.4	0.2	0.0	0.0	0.0															
gr-grandfather	0.3	0.2	0.0	0.0	0.0	0.0															
gr-grandmother	0.6	0.3	0.1	0.0	0.0																
gr-grandchild														0.0	0.1	0.2	0.5	1.1	1.8	2.4	2.9
gr-grandson														0.0	0.0	0.1	0.3	0.6	0.9	1.2	1.4
gr-granddaughter														0.0	0.1	0.1	0.3	0.5	0.9	1.2	1.5
aunt/uncle	3.0	3.0	2.9	2.9	2.8	2.7	2.5	2.3	2.0	1.6	1.1	0.7	0.4	0.1	0.0	0.0	0.0				
aunt	1.4	1.4	1.4	1.4	1.4	1.3	1.3	1.2	1.0	0.8	0.6	0.4	0.2	0.1	0.0	0.0	0.0				
uncle	1.6	1.5	1.5	1.5	1.5	1.4	1.2	1.1	0.9	0.7	0.5	0.3	0.1	0.1	0.0	0.0	0.0				
first cousin	2.4	3.2	3.8	4.2	4.4	4.4	4.4	4.3	4.3	4.2	4.1	3.9	3.6	3.2	2.8	2.2	1.6	1.1	0.7	0.3	0.1
nephew/niece			0.0	0.1	0.3	0.6	1.1	1.5	1.9	2.0	2.1	2.1	2.1	2.1	2.1	2.1	2.0	1.9	1.8	1.7	1.5
nephew			0.0	0.0	0.1	0.3	0.6	0.8	1.0	1.1	1.1	1.1	1.1	1.1	1.1	1.1	1.1	1.0	0.9	0.8	0.7
niece			0.0	0.0	0.1	0.3	0.5	0.7	0.9	0.9	1.0	1.0	1.1	1.0	1.0	1.1	1.1	0.9	0.9	0.8	0.7
fam. or.	2.8	3.1	3.4	3.4	3.3	3.3	3.2	3.0	2.8	2.5	2.2	1.8	1.4	1.2	1.0	0.8	0.5	0.3	0.2		0.0
fam. proc.						0.8	1.6	2.1	2.3	2.4	2.4	2.3	2.3	2.2	2.0	1.9	1.7	1.5	1.4	1.2	1.1
ascending	9.1	8.3	7.5	6.8	6.1	5.4	4.7	4.1	3.4	2.7	1.9	1.2	0.5	0.1	0.0						0.1
lateral	3.2	4.3	5.2	5.7	5.8	5.9	5.8	5.8	5.7	5.6	5.5	5.2	4.9	4.4	3.8	3.0	2.2	1.4	0.8	0.4	0.1
descending			0.0	0.1	0.3	0.6	1.1	1.5	1.9	2.1	2.4	2.8	3.3	3.8	4.2	4.5	4.9	5.4	5.9	6.4	6.7

Table 4b Proportion having living kin, data ca. 1985–1990

Kin	Exact age of ego (years)																				
	0	5	10	15	20	25	30	35	40	45	50	55	60	65	70	75	80	85	90	95	100
husband					0.08	0.48	0.71	0.83	0.85	0.86	0.85	0.80	0.75	0.67	0.54	0.41	0.26	0.13	0.06	0.01	0.00
parent	1.00	1.00	1.00	1.00	0.99	0.99	0.98	0.96	0.90	0.79	0.62	0.37	0.15	0.02							
father	1.00	0.99	0.97	0.95	0.92	0.86	0.81	0.69	0.57	0.43	0.29	0.13	0.04	0.00							
mother	1.00	1.00	1.00	0.98	0.96	0.95	0.92	0.87	0.77	0.65	0.51	0.32	0.12	0.02							
sibling	0.53	0.70	0.82	0.81	0.81	0.81	0.81	0.80	0.80	0.80	0.79	0.78	0.76	0.74	0.68	0.58	0.41	0.27	0.15	0.03	0.00
brother	0.35	0.46	0.56	0.56	0.56	0.56	0.55	0.55	0.55	0.54	0.53	0.50	0.49	0.46	0.44	0.33	0.21	0.12	0.07	0.01	0.00
sister	0.30	0.43	0.52	0.53	0.53	0.53	0.53	0.52	0.52	0.52	0.52	0.52	0.50	0.51	0.51	0.51	0.50	0.29	0.15	0.03	0.00
child					0.03	0.29	0.55	0.68	0.74	0.75	0.75	0.74	0.74	0.74	0.74	0.74	0.73	0.72	0.70	0.67	0.60
son					0.02	0.17	0.35	0.46	0.52	0.54	0.54	0.53	0.54	0.54	0.54	0.53	0.52	0.50	0.48	0.44	0.37
daughter					0.02	0.16	0.33	0.45	0.50	0.51	0.52	0.52	0.52	0.51	0.51	0.51	0.50	0.50	0.49	0.48	0.42
grandparent	1.00	0.99	0.94	0.88	0.74	0.55	0.33	0.15	0.07	0.02	0.00										
grandfather	0.93	0.86	0.77	0.62	0.43	0.29	0.12	0.05	0.01	0.01											
grandmother	0.99	0.96	0.90	0.81	0.65	0.47	0.28	0.13	0.06	0.01	0.00										
grandchild									0.00	0.00	0.16	0.35	0.50	0.59	0.65	0.67	0.68	0.68	0.68	0.67	0.67
grandson										0.01	0.08	0.24	0.39	0.47	0.54	0.57	0.58	0.58	0.58	0.57	0.57
granddaughter										0.01	0.10	0.24	0.35	0.45	0.51	0.55	0.56	0.56	0.56	0.56	0.56
gr-grandparent	0.48	0.27	0.10	0.04	0.01	0.00															
gr-grandfather	0.26	0.14	0.04	0.01	0.00																
gr-grandmother	0.39	0.21	0.08	0.03	0.01	0.00															
gr-grandchild														0.01	0.03	0.13	0.23	0.36	0.48	0.56	0.60
gr-grandson														0.01	0.01	0.08	0.16	0.29	0.39	0.46	0.51
gr-granddaughter															0.02	0.08	0.17	0.27	0.39	0.47	0.52
aunt/uncle	0.96	0.96	0.96	0.96	0.96	0.95	0.94	0.92	0.87	0.78	0.63	0.44	0.26	0.12	0.03	0.01	0.00				
aunt	0.79	0.79	0.78	0.78	0.77	0.76	0.75	0.70	0.66	0.58	0.44	0.30	0.17	0.07	0.02	0.01	0.00				
uncle	0.82	0.82	0.81	0.81	0.80	0.79	0.75	0.70	0.63	0.52	0.39	0.23	0.13	0.06	0.02	0.00	0.00				
first cousin	0.74	0.84	0.89	0.90	0.91	0.91	0.91	0.91	0.91	0.90	0.90	0.89	0.89	0.86	0.85	0.79	0.67	0.52	0.38	0.21	0.12
nephew/niece			0.01	0.05	0.18	0.34	0.51	0.62	0.68	0.71	0.71	0.71	0.70	0.70	0.70	0.70	0.69	0.69	0.67	0.64	0.60
nephew			0.01	0.03	0.11	0.23	0.38	0.48	0.55	0.57	0.58	0.58	0.57	0.57	0.57	0.57	0.56	0.55	0.52	0.49	0.45
niece			0.00	0.03	0.11	0.20	0.32	0.43	0.49	0.53	0.54	0.54	0.54	0.54	0.54	0.53	0.52	0.52	0.51	0.48	0.44
fam. or.	1.00	1.00	1.00	1.00	1.00	1.00	1.00	1.00	0.99	0.98	0.94	0.88	0.81	0.74	0.68	0.58	0.41	0.27	0.15	0.03	0.00
fam. proc.					0.08	0.48	0.71	0.83	0.87	0.89	0.90	0.89	0.89	0.87	0.86	0.83	0.80	0.77	0.73	0.67	0.61
ascending	1.00	1.00	1.00	1.00	1.00	1.00	1.00	1.00	0.99	0.95	0.86	0.65	0.37	0.14	0.03	0.01	0.00				
lateral	0.87	0.95	0.98	0.99	0.99	0.99	0.99	0.99	0.99	0.99	0.98	0.98	0.98	0.97	0.96	0.91	0.78	0.62	0.46	0.24	0.12
descending			0.01	0.05	0.18	0.34	0.51	0.62	0.68	0.71	0.76	0.82	0.86	0.88	0.89	0.89	0.89	0.89	0.89	0.87	0.86

Table 4c   Mean age of living kin, data ca. 1985–1990

Kin	Exact age of ego (years)																				
	0	5	10	15	20	25	30	35	40	45	50	55	60	65	70	75	80	85	90	95	100
husband	31.6	36.5	41.5	46.4	25.7	28.5	32.9	37.3	42.0	46.5	50.9	55.7	60.5	65.0	69.3	73.7	77.2	79.2	80.3	79.1	82.1
parent	33.0	37.9	42.8	47.7	51.3	56.1	60.9	65.4	69.8	73.8	77.7	81.3	84.1	86.3							
father	30.2	35.2	40.2	45.1	52.5	57.3	61.9	66.2	70.7	74.5	78.1	81.6	84.9	86.1							
mother	30.2	35.2	40.2	45.1	50.1	55.1	59.9	64.7	69.2	73.3	77.4	81.1	83.9	86.4							
sibling	5.5	7.9	10.9	15.4	20.4	25.3	30.3	35.3	40.3	45.3	50.3	55.2	60.0	64.7	69.3	73.3	76.5	79.7	83.1	85.5	87.0
brother	5.4	8.0	11.0	15.5	20.5	25.5	30.5	35.5	40.5	45.5	50.5	55.4	60.1	64.8	69.1	73.2	76.5	79.4	83.1	86.6	87.0
sister	5.6	7.7	10.9	15.2	20.1	25.1	30.1	35.1	40.1	45.1	50.1	55.1	59.9	64.7	69.4	73.4	76.5	79.9	83.0	85.0	87.0
child					1.5	2.3	4.5	7.5	10.8	15.2	20.1	25.1	30.1	35.1	40.1	45.1	50.0	54.9	59.8	64.5	69.0
son					0.9	2.2	4.4	7.4	10.7	14.9	19.8	24.8	29.8	34.9	39.8	44.8	49.7	54.6	59.3	64.0	68.5
daughter					1.9	2.4	4.6	7.5	11.0	15.4	20.4	25.4	30.4	35.4	40.4	45.4	50.3	55.3	60.2	65.0	69.4
grandparent	60.9	64.9	68.7	72.2	75.6	78.7	81.0	82.9	85.4	82.8	85.6										
grandfather	61.6	65.5	69.0	72.5	75.9	79.5	81.2	83.6	86.6												
grandmother	60.3	64.5	68.4	72.0	75.4	78.3	81.0	82.7	85.1	82.8	85.6										
grandchild									2.1	2.5	2.9	4.3	6.3	8.7	11.6	15.3	19.4	24.2	29.1	34.1	39.0
grandson										2.7	2.7	4.1	5.9	8.5	11.4	15.0	19.0	23.8	28.8	33.7	38.6
granddaughter									2.1	2.2	3.1	4.5	6.7	8.9	11.8	15.6	19.8	24.6	29.6	34.6	39.5
gr-grandparent	78.8	81.1	82.9	84.7	86.2	89.0															
gr-grandfather	79.0	81.4	83.4	83.7	84.0																
gr-grandmother	78.8	81.0	82.6	84.9	86.9	89.0															
gr-grandchild														1.6	2.6	3.3	4.6	5.9	7.7	10.1	12.8
gr-grandson														1.6	3.6	3.6	4.7	5.8	7.8	10.2	13.0
gr-granddaughter															1.8	3.0	4.6	6.0	7.7	10.0	12.5
aunt/uncle	31.7	36.6	41.5	46.4	51.2	55.9	60.3	64.6	68.6	72.1	75.0	77.5	80.0	82.3	84.1	85.4	85.7				
aunt	32.2	37.2	42.1	46.9	51.8	56.5	61.1	65.5	69.4	72.8	75.5	78.0	80.5	82.6	85.2	87.0					
uncle	31.2	36.1	41.0	45.8	50.6	55.3	59.4	63.8	67.7	71.4	74.5	76.9	79.2	81.8	82.8	83.1	85.7				
first cousin	9.2	11.3	14.1	17.5	21.6	26.2	31.1	36.0	40.8	45.6	50.2	54.7	59.0	63.1	67.0	70.2	73.0	75.9	78.2	79.6	81.8
nephew/niece			1.5	2.8	3.5	5.1	6.6	9.0	11.9	15.6	20.0	24.8	29.6	34.6	39.5	44.4	49.3	54.0	58.6	63.0	67.1
nephew			1.4	2.6	3.5	5.0	6.4	8.9	11.9	15.6	20.1	24.9	29.8	34.8	39.6	44.6	49.5	54.1	58.6	63.0	67.3
niece			2.1	3.0	3.5	5.3	6.8	9.2	11.8	15.6	19.9	24.7	29.3	34.3	39.3	44.2	49.0	53.9	58.5	62.9	67.0
fam. or.	24.3	26.2	28.8	33.1	37.8	42.4	46.9	51.0	54.6	57.6	60.2	61.8	62.7	65.1	69.3	73.3	76.5	79.7	83.1	85.5	87.0
fam. proc.					18.2	17.1	17.3	19.5	22.3	26.5	31.1	35.6	40.1	44.2	47.8	51.2	54.2	57.0	60.6	64.7	69.1
ascending	46.6	48.7	51.2	53.9	56.8	59.7	62.4	65.8	69.4	72.8	76.1	79.1	81.3	82.8	84.1	85.4	85.7				
lateral	8.3	10.4	13.2	17.0	21.3	26.0	30.9	35.8	40.6	45.5	50.3	54.8	59.3	63.5	67.6	71.0	73.8	76.7	79.2	80.2	81.9
descending					3.5	5.1	6.6	9.0	11.9	15.4	18.3	20.0	21.3	23.2	25.4	27.9	30.0	31.1	31.8	32.8	33.9

Table 4d Mean number of dependent kin, data ca. 1985–1990

Kin	Exact age of ego (years)																				
	0	5	10	15	20	25	30	35	40	45	50	55	60	65	70	75	80	85	90	95	100
husband					0.1	0.1	0.4	0.8					0.2	0.4	0.4	0.4	0.2	0.1	0.1	0.0	0.0
parent			0.0	0.0	0.0	0.1	0.2	0.4	1.1	1.1	0.8	0.4	0.2	0.0							
father			0.0	0.0	0.0	0.1	0.2	0.4	0.5	0.4	0.3	0.1	0.0	0.0							
mother							0.0		0.6	0.6	0.5	0.3	0.1	0.0							
sibling	0.8	1.0	1.0	0.7	0.3	0.1															
brother	0.4	0.5	0.5	0.3	0.2	0.0															
sister	0.3	0.5	0.5	0.3	0.2	0.0															
child					0.0	0.4	0.9	1.2	1.1	0.7	0.3	0.0									
son					0.0	0.2	0.4	0.6	0.6	0.3	0.2	0.0	0.1								0.8
daughter					0.0	0.2	0.4	0.6	0.6	0.3	0.1	0.1	0.0								0.3
grandparent	1.0	1.4	1.7	1.6	1.3	0.9	0.4	0.2	0.1	0.0											
grandfather	0.5	0.7	0.8	0.7	0.5	0.3	0.1	0.0	0.0												
grandmother	0.5	0.8	1.0	1.0	0.8	0.6	0.3	0.1	0.0												
grandchild										0.0	0.2	0.6	1.1	1.4	1.4	1.1	0.7	0.4	0.1	0.0	0.0
grandson										0.0	0.1	0.3	0.6	0.7	0.7	0.6	0.4	0.2	0.1	0.0	0.0
granddaughter										0.0	0.1	0.3	0.5	0.7	0.6	0.5	0.3	0.2	0.1	0.0	0.0
gr-grandparent	0.9	0.4	0.2	0.0	0.0																
gr-grandfather	0.3	0.2	0.0	0.0	0.0																
gr-grandmother	0.6	0.3	0.1	0.0	0.0																
gr-grandchild																0.2	0.5	1.1	1.5	1.8	1.8
gr-grandson																0.1	0.3	0.5	0.8	0.9	0.8
gr-granddaughter																0.1	0.3	0.5	0.8	0.9	0.9
aunt/uncle	0.1	0.0	0.0	0.1	0.2	0.4	0.8	1.1	1.3	1.3	1.0	0.6	0.4	0.1	0.1	0.2	0.5				
aunt	0.0	0.0	0.0	0.0	0.1	0.2	0.4	0.6	0.7	0.7	0.5	0.4	0.2	0.1	0.0	0.1	0.3				
uncle	0.0	0.0	0.0	0.0	0.1	0.2	0.3	0.5	0.6	0.6	0.5	0.3	0.1	0.1	0.0	0.0	0.3				
first cousin	2.0	2.3	2.2	1.8	1.2	0.7	0.3	0.1	0.1	0.1	0.1	0.6	1.0	1.4	1.7	1.6	1.4	1.1	0.6	0.3	0.1
nephew/niece			0.0	0.1	0.3	0.6	1.0	1.2	1.3	0.9	0.6	0.3	0.1	0.0	0.0	0.0	0.0	0.1	0.4	0.7	0.9
nephew			0.0	0.0	0.1	0.3	0.6	0.7	0.7	0.5	0.3	0.1	0.1	0.0	0.0	0.0	0.0	0.1	0.2	0.4	0.5
niece			0.0	0.0	0.1	0.3	0.5	0.8	0.6	0.4	0.3	0.1	0.1	0.0	0.0	0.0	0.0	0.3	0.2	0.0	0.5
fam. or.	0.8	1.0	1.0	0.7	0.4	0.2	0.4	0.8	1.1	1.1	0.8	0.5	0.5	0.6	0.7	0.8	0.5	0.3	0.2	0.0	0.0
fam. proc.							0.9	1.2	1.1												
ascending	2.0	1.9	1.9	1.8	1.5	1.4	1.6	2.1	2.5	2.4	1.8	1.1	1.3	2.0	2.4	2.4	1.9	1.4	0.8	0.3	0.1
lateral	2.7	3.3	3.2	2.5	1.5	0.7	0.3	0.1	0.1	0.1	0.3	0.7	1.3	2.0	2.4	2.4	1.9	1.4	0.8	0.3	0.1
descending			0.0	0.1	0.3	0.6	1.0	1.2	1.3	1.0	0.8	0.9	1.2	1.5	1.5	1.3	1.3	1.6	2.1	2.6	2.7

Table 4e   Proportion having dependent kin, data ca. 1985–1990

Kin	Exact age of ego (years)																				
	0	5	10	15	20	25	30	35	40	45	50	55	60	65	70	75	80	85	90	95	100
husband									0.00	0.00	0.02	0.05	0.16	0.39	0.43	0.37	0.25	0.12	0.06	0.01	0.00
parent			0.01	0.02	0.05	0.12	0.31	0.57	0.79	0.78	0.62	0.37	0.15	0.02							
father			0.01	0.02	0.04	0.09	0.23	0.39	0.49	0.43	0.29	0.13	0.04	0.00							
mother				0.01	0.01	0.06	0.19	0.36	0.62	0.63	0.51	0.32	0.12	0.02							
sibling	0.53	0.70	0.69	0.48	0.27																
brother	0.35	0.44	0.44	0.29	0.16																
sister	0.30	0.40	0.39	0.28	0.15																
child					0.03	0.29	0.55	0.67	0.62	0.41	0.23	0.08	0.01								
son					0.02	0.17	0.35	0.45	0.44	0.26	0.15	0.05	0.01								
daughter					0.02	0.16	0.34	0.44	0.37	0.26	0.12	0.03	0.00								
grandparent	0.61	0.76	0.85	0.84	0.73	0.55	0.33	0.15	0.07	0.00											
grandfather	0.44	0.54	0.61	0.56	0.43	0.29	0.12	0.05	0.01												
grandmother	0.43	0.60	0.73	0.74	0.63	0.47	0.28	0.13	0.06												
grandchild										0.00	0.16	0.35	0.50	0.55	0.56	0.48	0.34	0.20	0.11	0.02	
grandson											0.08	0.24	0.38	0.42	0.44	0.36	0.24	0.16	0.07	0.01	
granddaughter											0.10	0.24	0.35	0.40	0.41	0.34	0.23	0.12	0.05	0.01	
gr-grandparent	0.48	0.27	0.10	0.04	0.01	0.00															
gr-grandfather	0.25	0.14	0.04	0.01	0.00																
gr-grandmother	0.39	0.21	0.08	0.03	0.01	0.00															
gr-grandchild														0.01	0.03	0.13	0.23	0.36	0.48	0.52	0.52
gr-grandson														0.01	0.01	0.08	0.16	0.28	0.37	0.42	0.41
gr-granddaughter															0.02	0.08	0.17	0.27	0.37	0.41	0.43
aunt/uncle	0.06	0.02	0.02	0.05	0.12	0.28	0.50	0.68	0.76	0.74	0.62	0.44	0.26	0.12	0.03	0.01	0.00				
aunt	0.03	0.01	0.01	0.02	0.09	0.17	0.34	0.46	0.53	0.52	0.43	0.30	0.17	0.07	0.02	0.01	0.00				
uncle	0.04	0.01	0.01	0.03	0.05	0.16	0.27	0.41	0.47	0.46	0.37	0.23	0.13	0.06	0.02	0.00					
first cousin	0.71	0.78	0.76	0.68	0.50	0.33	0.17	0.07	0.05	0.10	0.19	0.34	0.53	0.67	0.76	0.74	0.65	0.52	0.37	0.21	0.11
nephew/niece			0.01	0.05	0.18	0.33	0.50	0.57	0.54	0.45	0.32	0.17	0.07	0.02	0.01	0.00					
nephew			0.01	0.03	0.11	0.23	0.37	0.43	0.44	0.33	0.20	0.11	0.04	0.01	0.00						
niece			0.00	0.03	0.11	0.20	0.31	0.37	0.37	0.30	0.22	0.11	0.05	0.02	0.01						
fam. or.	0.53	0.70	0.69	0.49	0.32	0.18	0.31	0.57	0.79	0.78	0.62	0.44	0.41	0.46	0.55	0.57	0.41	0.27	0.16	0.03	0.00
fam. proc.					0.03	0.29	0.55	0.67	0.62	0.46	0.42	0.46	0.54	0.57	0.58	0.55	0.54	0.62	0.67	0.73	0.76
ascending	0.90	0.89	0.88	0.87	0.83	0.78	0.81	0.89	0.95	0.92	0.81	0.58	0.33	0.13	0.03	0.01	0.00				
lateral	0.86	0.94	0.92	0.81	0.62	0.37	0.17	0.07	0.05	0.10	0.20	0.37	0.63	0.81	0.89	0.88	0.77	0.61	0.46	0.24	0.12
descending			0.01	0.05	0.18	0.33	0.50	0.57	0.54	0.46	0.42	0.46	0.54	0.57	0.58	0.55	0.54	0.62	0.67	0.73	0.76

Table 4f Proportion co-residing with kin, data ca. 1985–1990

Kin	Exact age of ego (years)																				
	0	5	10	15	20	25	30	35	40	45	50	55	60	65	70	75	80	85	90	95	100
husband	1.00				0.08	0.48	0.71	0.82	0.85	0.86	0.85	0.80	0.75	0.66	0.53	0.41	0.26	0.13	0.06	0.01	
parent	0.96	0.96	0.96	0.95	0.87	0.49	0.27	0.16	0.11	0.08	0.06	0.03	0.01	0.01							
father	1.00	0.95	0.93	0.91	0.81	0.40	0.21	0.11	0.07	0.05	0.02	0.00									
mother	1.00	0.96	0.95	0.93	0.84	0.46	0.25	0.14	0.09	0.06	0.06	0.03	0.00								
sibling	0.53	0.68	0.79	0.78	0.63	0.28	0.12	0.03	0.01	0.01	0.01										
brother	0.35	0.44	0.54	0.53	0.44	0.19	0.09	0.01	0.00	0.00	0.00										
sister	0.30	0.42	0.50	0.47	0.36	0.16	0.06	0.02	0.00	0.00	0.00										
child					0.03	0.29	0.55	0.67	0.73	0.71	0.65	0.53	0.39	0.27	0.18	0.12	0.11	0.10	0.09	0.08	
son					0.02	0.17	0.35	0.46	0.53	0.52	0.46	0.35	0.25	0.16	0.09	0.06	0.05	0.05	0.04	0.03	
daughter					0.02	0.16	0.33	0.45	0.49	0.47	0.42	0.32	0.22	0.14	0.10	0.07	0.06	0.05	0.05	0.05	
grandparent	0.04	0.03	0.03	0.03	0.02	0.01	0.00	0.00	0.00												
grandfather	0.03	0.03	0.03	0.02	0.02	0.01	0.00	0.00	0.00												
grandmother	0.04	0.03	0.03	0.03	0.02	0.01	0.00	0.00	0.00												
grandchild												0.00	0.00	0.00	0.00	0.00	0.00	0.00	0.00	0.00	
grandson												0.00	0.00	0.00	0.00	0.00	0.00	0.00	0.00	0.00	
granddaughter																					
gr-grandparent																					
gr-grandfather																					
gr-grandmother																					
gr-grandchild																					
gr-grandson																					
gr-granddaughter																					
aunt/uncle	0.02	0.02	0.01	0.00	0.00	0.00															
aunt	0.02	0.01	0.00	0.00																	
uncle	0.01	0.01	0.01	0.00	0.00	0.00															
first cousin																					
nephew/niece							0.00	0.00													
nephew							0.00	0.00													
niece								0.00													
fam. or.	1.00	0.97	0.97	0.96	0.89	0.50	0.28	0.16	0.11	0.08	0.06	0.03	0.01	0.01	0.00	0.00	0.00	0.00	0.00	0.00	
fam. proc.					0.08	0.48	0.71	0.83	0.87	0.89	0.89	0.87	0.82	0.73	0.61	0.46	0.33	0.23	0.15	0.10	
ascending	1.00	1.00	0.99	0.98	0.90	0.50	0.27	0.16	0.11	0.08	0.06	0.03	0.01	0.01							
lateral	0.53	0.68	0.79	0.78	0.63	0.28	0.12	0.03	0.01												
descending							0.00	0.00	0.00	0.00	0.00	0.00	0.00	0.00	0.00	0.00	0.00	0.00	0.00	0.00	

Bibliography

Abellán, Antonio (1994), 'Hogar y familia', *Revista de Gerontología*, 4(2), 112–13.

Aceves, Joseph (1971), *Social Change in a Spanish Village*, Cambridge, Mass., Schenkman Publishing Co.

Åkerman, Sune (1981), 'The importance of remarriage in the seventeenth and eighteenth centuries', in J. Dupâquier, E. Hélin, P. Laslett, M. Livi Bacci, and S. Sogner (eds.), *Marriage and Remarriage in Populations of the Past*, London, Academic Press, 163–76.

Alberdi, Christina, and Alberdi, Inés (1982), 'La institución matrimonial: Su lugar en la constelación familiar. Aspectos jurídicos y sociales del divorcio', in R. Conde (ed.), *Familia y cambio social en España*, Madrid, Centro de Investigaciones Sociológicas, 177–97.

Alberdi, Inés (1977), *¿El fin de la familia?*, Barcelona, Bruguera.

——(1982), 'Un nuevo modelo de familia', *Papers. Revista de Sociología*, 18, 87–112.

——(1994), *Informe sobre la situación de la familia en España*, Madrid, Ministerio de Asuntos Sociales.

Almeida, Elisabet, and Flaquer, Lluis (1993), 'La monoparentalidad en España: Claves para un análisis sociológico', *Document de Treball*, Institut d'Estudis Socials Avançats, Universitat Pompeu Fabra.

Alonso Martínez, M. (1947), *El Código Civil en sus relaciones con las legislaciones forales*, Madrid, Editorial Plus-Ultra.

Anderson, Michael (1974), *Family Structure in Nineteenth Century Lancashire*, Cambridge, Cambridge University Press.

——(1976), 'Marriage patterns in Victorian Britain: An analysis based on registration district data for England and Wales, 1861', *Journal of Family History*, 1, 55–78.

Andorka, Rudolf, and Faragó, Tamás, 'Pre-industrial household structure in Hungary', in R. Wall (ed.), *Family Forms in Historic Europe*, Cambridge, Cambridge University Press, 65–104.

Angeli, Aurora, and Belletini, Athos (1979), 'Strutture familiari nella campagna Bolognese a meta' dell'Ottocento', *Genus*, 35, 155–72.

Arana-Goiri, Sabino (1980), *Obras Completas*, 2nd edn., Donostia (San Sebastian), Sendoa Argitaldaria.

Arango, Joaquín (1980), 'La teoría de la transición demográfica y la experiencia histórica', *Revista Española de Investigaciones Sociológicas*, 10, 169–98.

——(1987), 'La modernización demográfica de la sociedad española', in J. Arango *et al.* (eds.), *La economía española en el siglo XX: Una perspectiva histórica*, Barcelona, Editorial Ariel, 203–36.

Aranzadi, Engracio de (1932), *La casa solar vascao Casa y tierras del Apellido Zarauz*, Zarauz, Editorial Vasca.

Arbaiza, Mercedes (1994), *Estrategias familiares y transición demográfica en Vizcaya (1825–1930)*, doctoral diss., Universidad del País Vasco, Leioa, Vizcaya.

Arbelo Cuberlo, A. (1962), *La mortalidad en la infancia en España, 1901–1905*, Madrid, Consejo Superior de Investigaciones Científicas.

Ardit, Manuel (1991), 'Un ensayo de proyección inversa de la población valenciana (1610–1899)', *Boletín de la Asociación de Demografía Histórica*, 9(3), 27–48.

Arejula, Juan Manuel de (1806), *Breve descripción de la fiebre amarilla padecida en Cádiz y los pueblos comarcanos en 1800, en Medina-Sidonia en 1801, en Málaga en 1803, y esta última plaza y varias otras del reyno en 1804*, Madrid: Imprenta Real.

Ariès, Philippe (1960), *L'Enfant et la vie familiale sous l'ancien régime*, Paris, Librairie Plon; trans. into English as *Centuries of Childhood: A Social History of Family Life* (1962), New York, Vintage Books.

Baines, Dudley (1985), *Migration in a Mature Economy: Emigration and Internal Migration in England and Wales 1861–1900*, Cambridge, Cambridge University Press.

Barbagli, Marzio (1984), *Sotto lo stesso tetto: Mutamenti della famiglia in Italia dal XV al XX secolo*, Bologna, Il Mulino.

——and Kertzer, David (1990), 'An introduction to the history of Italian family life', *Journal of Family History*, 15, 369–83.

Barreiro Mallón, Baudilio (1973), *La jurisdicción de Xallas en el siglo XVIII: Población, sociedad y economía*, Santiago, Universidad de Santiago de Compostela.

Barrera González, Andrés (1990), *Casa, herencia y familia en la Cataluña rural*, Madrid, Alianza Editorial.

——(1993), 'Sucesión unipersonal y familia troncal en la Cataluña y el norte de la Península Ibérica', in D. Comas d'Argemir and J. F. Soulet (eds.), *La família als Pirineus*, Andorva, Conselleria d'Educació, Cultura i Joventud of Andorra, 140–57.

Becker, Gary S. (1981), *A Treatise on the Family*, Cambridge, Mass., Harvard University Press.

Behar, Ruth (1986), *Santa Maria del Monte: The Presence of the Past in a Spanish Village*, Princeton, Princeton University Press.

——and Frye, David (1988), 'Property, progeny, and emotion: Family history in a Leonese village', *Journal of Family History*, 13, 13–32.

Bengtsson, Tommy (1984), 'Harvest fluctuations and demographic response: Southern Sweden, 1751–1859', in T. Bengtsson, G. Fridlizius, and R. Ohlsson (eds.), *Preindustrial Population Change*, Stockholm, Almquist and Wiksell, 329–55.

Benitez Sánchez-Blanco, Rafael (1992), 'Familia y transmisión de la propiedad en el País Valenciano (siglos XVI–XVII). Ponderación global y marco jurídico', in F. Chacón Jiménez and J. Hernández Franco (eds.), *Poder, familia y consanguinidad en la España del Antiguo Régimen*, Barcelona, Anthropos, 35–70.

Berkner, Lutz K., and Mendels, Franklin F. (1978), 'Inheritance systems, family structure and demographic patterns in Western Europe, 1700–1900', in C. Tilly (ed.), *Historical Studies in Changing Fertility*, Princeton, Princeton University Press, 209–33.

Bernabeu Mestre, Josep (1991), 'Enfermedad y población: Una aproximación crítica a la epidemiología histórica española', *Revisiones en Salud Pública*, 2, 67–88.

——(1994), 'Problèmes de santé et causes de décès infantiles en Espagne, 1900–1935', *Annales de Démographie Historique*, 61–78.

——Pérez Moreda, Vicente, and Reher, David (1994), *Mortalidad infantil y juvenil en Madrid, Castilla-La Mancha y Valencia: Resultados provisionales de un proyecto de investigación*, working paper, Instituto de Demografía, Madrid.

Berthe, Maurice (1984), *Famines et épidemies dans le campagnes navarraises à la fin du moyen age*, Paris: S.F.I.E.D.

Bestard-Camps, Joan (1991), 'La familia: Entre la antropología y la historia', *Papers. Revista de Sociología*, 36, 79–91.

Bongaarts, John (1987), 'The projection of family composition over the life course with family status life tables', in J. Bongaarts, T. Burch, and K. Wachter (eds.), *Family Demography: Methods and their Application*, Oxford, Clarendon Press, 189–212.

Bourdieu, P. (1962), 'Célibat et condition paysanne', *Etudes Rurales*, 5–6, 32–135.

——(1972), 'Les stratégies matrimoniales dans le système de reproduction', *Annales, E.S.C.*, 4–5, 1105–25.

Bourgeois Pichat, Jean (1951), 'La mesure de la mortalité infantile', *Population*, 6, 233–48, 459–80.

Brandes, Stanley H. (1971), *Migration, Kinship and Community: Tradition and Transition in a Spanish Village*, New York, Academic Press.

Braudel, Fernand (1966), *La Méditerranée et le monde méditerranéen à l'èpoque de Philippe II*, 2 vols., Paris, Librairie Armand Colin.

Breschi, Marco, and Livi-Bacci, Massimo (1986*a*), 'Saison et climat comme constraint de la survie des enfants', *Population*, 1, 9–36.

——(1986*b*), 'Stagione di nascità e clima come determinanti della mortalità infantile negli Stati Sardi di Terraferma', *Genus*, 42, 87–101.

——(1994), 'Le Mois de naissance comme facteur de survie des enfants', *Annales de Démographie Historique*, 169–86.

Brettell, Caroline B. (1986), *Men Who Migrate, Women Who Wait: Population and History in a Portuguese Parish*, Princeton, Princeton University Press.

——(1988), 'Emigration and household structure in a Portuguese parish, 1850–1920', *Journal of Family History*, 13, 33–58.

——(1991), 'Property, kinship, and gender: A Mediterranean perspective', in D. I. Kertzer and R. P. Saller (eds.), *The Family in Italy from Antiquity to the Present*, New Haven, Yale University Press, 340–54.

Burguière, A. (1986), 'Pour une typologie des formes d'organsation domestique de l'Europe moderne (XVI–XIX siècles)', *Annales, E.S.C.*, 3, 639–55.

Cabourdin, Guy (1981), 'Le remariage en France sous l'Ancien Régime (seizième–dix-huitième siècles)', in J. Dupâquier, E. Hélin, P. Laslett, M. Livi-Bacci, and S. Sogner (eds.), *Marriage and Remarriage in Populations of the Past*, London, Academic Press, 273–86.

Cabré, Anna (1989), *La reproducciò de les generacions catalanes 1856–1960*, doctoral diss., Barcelona, Universitat Autónoma de Barcelona.

——(1993), 'Volverán tórtolos y cigüeñas', in L. Garrido Medina and E. Gil Calvo (eds.), *Estrategias familiares*, Madrid, Alianza Editorial, 113–31.

——(1994), 'Tensiones imminentes en los mercados matrimoniales', in J. Nadal (ed.), *El mundo que viene*, Madrid, Alianza Editorial, 32–60.

——and Pujadas, Isabel (1987), 'La fecundidad en Cataluña desde 1922: Análisis y perspectivas', paper given at the I Congrés Hispano-Luso-Italià de Demografia Històrica, organized by the Asociación de Demografía Histórica (ADEH) and the Società Italiana di Demografia Storica (S.I.DE.S.), Barcelona.

——and Torrents, Angel (1991), 'La elevada nupcialidad como posible desencadenante de la transición demografica en Cataluña', in M. Livi Bacci (ed.), *Modelos regionales de la transición demográfica en España y Portugal* (Actas del II

Congreso de la Asociación de Demografia Histórica, Vol. 2), Alicante, Instituto de Cultura Juan Gil Albert, 99–120.

Cachinero Sánchez, Benito (1982), 'La evolución de la nupcialidad en España, 1887–1975', *Revista Española de Investigaciones Sociológicas*, 20, 81–99.

——(1985), 'Estimating levels of adult mortality in eighteenth century Spain', *Historical Methods*, 20, 63–70.

Cain, Mead (1981), 'Risk and insurance: Perspectives on fertility and inequality in rural India and Bangladesh', *Population and Development Review*, 7, 435–74.

——(1983), 'Fertility as an adjustment to risk', *Population and Development Review*, 9, 688–702.

Caldwell, John C. (1976), 'Toward a restatement of demographic transition theory', *Population and Development Review*, 2, 321–66.

——(1981), 'The mechanisms of demographic change in historical perspective', *Population Studies*, 35, 5–27.

——(1982), *Theory of Fertility Decline*, London, Academic Press.

Campo Urbano, Salustiano del (1974), *La política demográfica en España*, Madrid, Editorial Cuadernos para el Diálogo.

——(1991), *La 'nueva' familia española*, Madrid, Eudema.

——and Navarro, Manuel (1985), *Análisis sociológico de la familia española*, Barcelona, Ariel.

Camps-Cura, Enriqueta (1985), *La formació d'una ciutat catalana sota l'impuls de la industrialització*, Master's thesis, School of Economics, Universidat Autònoma de Barcelona.

——(1990a), *Migraciones internas y formación del mercado de trabajo en la Cataluña industrial en el siglo XIX*, doctoral diss., European University Institute of Florence.

——(1990b), 'La teoría del capital humano: Una contrastación empírica. La España Industrial en el siglo XIX', *Revista de Historia Economica*, 2, 305–34.

——(1990c), 'Urbanización y migraciones durante la transición al sistema fabril: El caso catalán', *Boletín de la Asociación de Demografía Histórica*, 7(2), 73–96.

——(1990d), 'La evolución del salario real en el sector textil algodonero. La "España Industrial S.A.", 1850–1913', paper given at the XV Simposio de Análisis Económico, Barcelona.

——(1995), *La formación del mercado de trabajo industrial en la Cataluña del siglo XIX*, Madrid, Ministerio de Trabajo y Seguridad Social.

Caro Baroja, Julio (1958), *Los vascos*, Madrid, Ediciones Minotauro.

——(1972), *Etnografía histórica de Navarra,* vol. 2, Pamplona, Editorial Aranzadi.

——(1976), *Baile, familia, trabajo*, San Sebastián, Editorial Txertoa.

Carr, Raymond, and Fusi, Juan Pablo (1981), *Spain: Dictatorship to Democracy*, Allen & Unwin, London.

Caselli, Graziella (1991), 'Health transition and cause-specific mortality', in R. S. Schofield, D. S. Reher, and A. Bideau (eds.), *The Decline of Mortality in Europe*, Oxford, Clarendon Press, 68–98.

——(1994), *National Differences in the Health Transition in Europe*, working paper, Population Research Institute, Indiana University.

Casey, James, and Vincent, Bernard (1987), 'Casa y familia en la Granada del Antiguo Régimen', in J. Casey *et al.* (eds.), *La familia en la España mediterránea (siglos XV–XIX)*, Barcelona, Editorial Crítica, 172–211.

Celaya Ibarra, A. (1993), 'El régimen jurídico de la familia en las regiones pirinaicas (vertiente sur)', in D. Comas d'Argemir and J. F. Soulet (eds.), *La família als Pirineus*, Andorra, Conselleria d'Educació, Cultura i Joventud of Andorra, 20–33.

Centro de Investigaciones sobre la Realidad Social (Cires) (1994), *La realidad social en España, 1992–1993*, Madrid, Ediciones B.

Cerdà, Ildefonso (1867), *Teoría general de la urbanización: Reforma y ensanche de Barcelona*, facsimile edn., 3 vols. (1968–71), Madrid, Instituto de Estudios Fiscales.

Chacón Jiménez, F. (1983), 'Introducción a la historia de la familia española: El ejemplo de Murcia y Orihuela (siglos XVII–XIX)', *Cuadernos de Historia*, 10, 235–66.

——(1987a) (ed.), *Familia y sociedad en el Mediterráneo occidental: Siglos XV–XIX*, Murcia.

——(1987b) (ed.), 'Notas para el estudio de la familia en la región de Murcia durante el Antiguo Régimen', in J. Casey *et al.* (eds.), *La familia en la España mediterránea (siglos XV–XIX)*, Barcelona, Editorial Crítica, 129–71.

——and Hernández Franco, Juan (1992) (eds.), *Poder, Familia y consanguimidad en la España del Antiquo Régimen*, Barcelona, Anthropos.

Chayanov, A. V. (1925 [1966]), *The Theory of Peasant Economy*, ed. D. Thorner, B. Kerblay, and R. E. F. Smith, Homewood, Ill, R. D. Irwin.

Christian, William A. (1972), *Person and God in a Spanish Valley*, New York, Seminar Press.

Clayton, Richard R. (1979), *The Family, Marriage, and Social Change*, Lexington, Mass., D. C. Heath.

Coale, Ansley J. (1971), 'Age patterns of marriage', *Population Studies*, 25, 193–214.

——(1977), 'Demographic effects of below-replacement fertility and their social implications', in *Below-Replacement Fertility in Industrial Societies*, suppl. to vol. 12 of *Population and Development Review*, 203–16.

——(1986), 'Demographic effects of below-replacement Fertility and their social implications', in K. Davis, M. S. Bernstam, and R. Ricardo-Campbell (eds.), *Below-Replacement Fertility in Industrial Societies: Causes, Consequences, Policies*, suppl. to vol. 12 of *Population and Development Review*, 203–16.

——and Demeny, Paul (1966 [1986]), *Regional Model Life Tables and Stable Populations*, New York, Academic Press.

——and McNeill, R. M. (1972), 'The distribution by age of the Frequency of First marriage in a female cohort', *Journal of the American Statistical Association*, 67, 743–9.

——and Treadway, Roy (1986), 'A summary of the changing distribution of overall fertility, marital fertility, and the proportion married in the provinces of Europe', in A. J. Coale and S. C. Watkins (eds.), *The Decline of Fertility in Europe*, Princeton, Princeton University Press, 31–181.

——and Watkins, Susan Cotts (1986) (eds.), *The Decline of Fertility in Europe*, Princeton, Princeton Unversity Press.

Comas d'Argemir, Dolors (1984), 'La família troncal en el marc de les transformacions socio-econòmiques del Pirineu d'Aragó', *Quaderns de l'Institut Català d'Antropologia*, 5, 44–68.

——(1988), 'Household, family, and social stratification: Inheritance and labor strategies in a Catalan village (nineteenth and twentieth centuries)', *Journal of Family History*, 13, 143–63.

——(1991), 'Casa y comunidad en el Alto Aragón: Ideales culturales y reproducción social', *Revista de Antropología Social*, 0, 131–50.

Comas d'Argemir, Dolors (1992), 'Matrimonio, patrimonio y descendencia: Algunas hipótesis referidas a la península Ibérica', in F. Chacón Jiménez and J. Hernández Franco (eds.), *Poder, familia y consanguinidad en la España del Antiguo Régimen*, Barcelona, Anthropos, 157–76.

——(1993), 'Els canvis recents del sistema familiar al Pirineus: Les pautes del matrimoni i solteria', in D. Comas d'Argemir and J. F. Soulet (eds.), *La família als Pirineus*, Andorra, Conselleria d'Educació, Cultura i Joventud of Andorra, 232–47.

——and Pujadas, Joan J. (1980), 'Sistema d'herencia i estratificació social: Les estratègies herditàries al Pirineu Aragonès', *Quaderns de l'Institut Català d'Antropologia*, 2, 25–55.

Comunidad de Madrid (1992), *Encuesta demográfica de la Comunidad de Madrid de 1991*, Madrid, Comunidad de Madrid.

——(1994), *Censos de población y vivienda de 1991 de la Comunidad de Madrid. Tomo 5: Hogares, familias y núcleos: Características demográficas básicas*, Madrid, Comunidad de Madrid.

Contreras, J. (1991), "Los grupos domésticos: Estrategias de producción y reproducción', in J. Prat *et al.* (eds.), *Antropología de los Pueblos de España*, Madrid, Taurus, 343–80.

Cornell, Laurel L. (1994), 'The gender/labor balance hypothesis', Working Paper No. 34, Indiana University, Population Institute for Research and Training.

Corsini, Carlo (1981), 'Why is remarriage a male affair? Some evidence from Tuscan villages during the eighteenth century', in J. Dupâquier, E. Hélin, P. Laslett, M. Livi-Bacci, and S. Sogner, *Marriage and Remarriage in Populations of the Past*, London, Academic Press, 385–96.

Costa, Joaquín (1902*a*), 'La comunidad doméstica del Alto Aragón', in J. Costa (ed.), *Derecho consuetudinario y economía popular de España*, vol. 1, Barcelona, Manuel Soler, 30–47.

——(1902*b*), 'Los desposorios en la Mancha', in J. Costa (ed.), *Derecho consuetudinario y economía popular de España*, vol. 2, Barcelona, Manuel Soler, 167–81.

Cruz Mundet, José Ramón (1991), *Rentería en la crisis del Antiguo Régimen (1750–1845): Familia, caserío y sociedad rural*, Rentería, Ayuntamiento de Rentería.

Czap, P. (1983), ' "A large family: The peasant's greatest wealth": Serf households in Mishino, Russia, 1814–1958', in R. Wall (ed.), *Family Forms in Historic Europe*, Cambridge, Cambridge University Press, 65–104.

Da Molin, Giovanna (1990*a*), 'Family forms and domestic service in southern Italy from the seventeenth to the nineteenth centuries', *Journal of Family History*, 15, 503–27.

——(1990*b*), *La famiglia nel passato: Strutture familiari nel Regno di Napoli in età moderna*, Bari, Cacucci Editore.

Delgado Pérez, Margarita (1987), 'El reciente descenso de la fecundidad en España: Un análisis por provincias', paper given at the I Congrés Hispano-Luso-Italià de Demografia Històrica, organized by the Asociación de Demografía Histórica (ADEH) and the Società Italiana di Demografia Storica (S.I.DE.S.), Barcelona.

——(1993), 'Cambios recientes en el proceso de formación de la familia', *Revista Española de Investigaciones Sociológicas*, 64, 123–54.

——(1994), *La fecundidad de las adolescentes*, Madrid, Centro de Investigaciones Sociológicas-Instituto de Demografía.

——and Livi-Bacci, Massimo (1992), 'Fertility in Italy and Spain: The lowest in the world', *Family Planning Perspectives*, 24, 162–71.

Delille, Gérard (1985), *Famille et propriété dans le Royaume de Naples (XV–XIX siècles)*, Rome, Édition de l'École des Hautes Études en Sciences Sociales.

——(1990), 'La famiglia contadina nell'Italia moderna', in P. Bevilacqua (ed.), *Storia dell'Agricoltura Italiana in Età Contemporanea: Uomini e Classi*, Venice, Marsilio Editori, 507–34.

Del Panta, Lorenzo (1991), 'Modelos de desarrollo demográfico en Italia entre los siglos XVIII y XIX: Problemas e hipótesis de investigación', *Boletín de la Asociación de Demografía Histórica*, 9(3), 9–26.

Dewerpe, A. (1985), *L'industrie aux champs: Essai sur la proto-industrialisation en Italie du Nord (1800–1880)*, Rome, Édition de l'École des Hautes Études en Sciences Sociales.

Díez Nicolás, Juan (1971), 'La transición demográfica en España, 1900–1960', *Revista de Estudios Sociales*, 1, 89–158.

——(1985), 'La mortalidad en la Guerra Civil española', *Boletín de la Asociación de Demografía Histórica*, 3(1), 41–55.

Dopico, Fausto (1987a), 'Nupcialidad y familia en España (siglos XVI–XX)', paper given at the I Congrés Hispano-Luso-Italià de Demografia Històrica, organized by the Asociación de Demografia Histórica (ADEH) and the Società Italiana de Demografia Storica (S.I.DE.S.), Barcelona.

——(1987b), 'Regional Mortality Tables for Spain in the 1860s', *Historical Methods*, 20, 173–9.

——and Rowland, Robert (1990), 'Demografia del censo de Floridablanca: Una aproximación', *Revista de Historia Económica*, 8, 591–618.

Douglass, William A. (1971), 'Rural exodus in two Spanish Basque villages: A cultural explanation', *American Anthropologist*, 73, 1100–14.

——(1973), *Muerte en Murélaga: El contexto de la muerte en el País Vasco*, Barcelona, Barral.

——(1975), *Echalar and Murelaga: Opportunity and Rural Exodus in Two Spanish Basque Villages*, London, C. Hurst.

——(1988a), 'Iberian family history', *Journal of Family History*, 13, 1–12.

——(1988b), 'The Basque stem family household: Myth or reality', *Journal of Family History*, 13, 75–90.

Drake, Michael (1981), 'The remarriage market in mid-nineteenth century Britain', in J. Dupâquier et al. (eds.), *Marriage and Remarriage in Populations of the Past*, New York, Academic Press, 287–96.

Dubert García, Isidro (1987), *Los comportamientos de la familia urbana en la Galicia del Antiguo Régimen: El ejemplo de Santiago de Compostela en el siglo XVIII*, Santiago, Universidad de Santiago de Compostela.

——(1992a), *Historia de la familia en Galicia durante la época moderna, 1550–1830 (Estructura, modelos hereditarios y conflictividad)*, A Coruña, Ediciós do Castro.

——(1992b), 'El fenómeno urbano en la Galicia interior: Características económicas y demográficas del ámbito semiurbano (1571–1850),' *Obradoiro de Historia Moderna*, 1, 13–44.

Dyson, Tim, and Murphy, Michael (1991), 'Macro-level study of socio-economic development and mortality: Adequacy of indicators and methods of statistical analysis', in

J. C. Cleland and A. G. Hill (eds.), *The Health Transition: Methods and Measures*, Canberra, Health Transition Centre, The Australian National University, 147–64.

Echeverri Dávila, Beatriz (1993), *La gripe española: La panedemia de 1918–1919*, Madrid, CIS-Siglo XXI.

Elder, Glen H., Jr. (1987), 'Families and lives: Some developments in life-course studies', *Journal of Family History*, 12, 179–99.

Elliott, John H. (1986), *The Count-Duke of Olivares: The Statesman in an Age of Decline*, New Haven, Yale University Press.

Elorza, Antonio (1978), *Ideología del nacionalismo vasco*, San Sebastian, L. Haranburu. *Enciclopedia universal ilustrada europeo-americana (1907–30)*, Barcelona, J. Espasa.

Etzioni, Amitai (1977), 'The family: is it obsolete?', *Journal of Current Social Issues*, 14 (Winter), 4–9.

Fernandez, James W., and Fernandez, Renate Lellep (1988), 'Under One Roof: Household Formation and Cultural Ideals in an Asturiau Mountain Village', *Journal of Family History*, 13, 123–42.

Fernández Cordón, Juan Antonio (1987), 'Análisis longitudinal de la fecundidad en España', in A. Olano Rey (ed.), *Tendencias de la Fecundidad y Planificación Económica*, Madrid, Ministerio de Economía y Hacienda, 49–75.

——(1994*a*), *La fecundidad de las generaciones en España*, Working Paper No. 12, Instituto de Demografia, Madrid.

——(1994*b*) (ed.), *Proyección de la población española: España 1991–2026, Comunidades autónomas 1991–2006, Provincias 1991–2006*, vol. 1, Madrid, Instituto de Demografia-Consejo Superior de Investigaciones Científicas.

——(1994*c*), 'Spain: Adjusting to the new family structures', in W. Dumon (ed.), *Changing Family Policies in the Member States of the European Union*, Bonn, Commission of the European Community, 105–22.

Fernández Cortizo, Camilo (1982), 'A una misma mesa y manteles: La familia de Tierra de Montes en el siglo XVIII', *Cuadernos de Estudios Gallegos*, 23, 237–76.

——(1988), 'En casa y compañía: Grupo doméstico y estrategias familiares en la Galicia Occidental a mediados del siglo XVIII', in J. C. Bermejo (ed.), *Parentesco, familia y matrimonio en la historia de Galicia*, Santiago, Tórculo, 145–65.

Fernández Martínez, Rafael (1953), *Realidad de la casa asturiana*, Oviedo, Diputación de Asturias.

Ferrer i Alòs, Llorenç (1987), *Pagesos, rabassaires i industrials a la Catalunya central*, Barcelona, Publications of the Abby of Montserrat.

——(1991), 'Familia y grupos sociales en Cataluña en los siglos XVIII y XIX', in F. Chacón Jiménez, J. Hernández Franco, and A. Peñafiel Ramón (eds.), *Familia, grupos sociales y mujer en España (s. XV–XIX)*, Murcia, Universidad de Murcia, 119–37.

——(1992), 'Estrategias familiares y formas jurídicas de transmisión de la propiedad y el estatus social', *Boletín de la Asociación de Demografía Histórica*, 10(3), 9–14.

——(1993), 'Fratelli al celibato, sorelle al matrimonio: La parte dei cadetti nella riproduzione sociales dei gruppi agiati in Catalogna (secoli XVIII–XIX)', *Quaderni Storici*, 83, 527–54.

——(1994), 'L'ús de la família per la burgesia de la Catalunya central', in S. Ponce and L. Ferrer (eds.), *Família i canvi social a la Catalunya contemporània*, Vic, Eumo, 15–44.

—— (1995), 'Notas sobre el uso de la familia y la reproducción social', *Boletín de la Asociación de Demografía Histórica*, 13(1), 11–27.

—— (forthcoming), 'The use of the family: Inheritance systems and social groups in Catalonia during the seventeenth and eighteenth centuries', *Journal of the History of the Family*.

Fildes, Valerie A. (1987), *Breasts, Bottles and Babies: A History of Infant Feeding*, Edinburgh, Edinburgh University Press.

Flaquer, Lluis (1990), 'La familia española: Cambio y perspectivas', in S. Giner (ed.), *España: Sociedad y Política*, Madrid, Espasa Calpe, 509–49.

—— and Soler, Juan (1990), *Permanencia y cambio en la familia española*, Estudios y Encuestas 18, Centro de Investigaciones Sociológicas, Madrid.

Fleury, Michel, and Henry, Louis (1956), *Des registres paroissiaux à l'histoire de la population. Manuel de dépouillement et d'exploitation de l'état civil ancien*, Paris, Institut National d'Études Démographiques.

Flinn, M. W. (1974), 'The stabilisation of mortality in preindustrial western Europe', *The Journal of European Economic History*, 3, 258–318.

Fraga Iribarne, Manuel, Velarde Fuertes, Juan, and Campo Urbano, Salustiano del (1973), *La España de los años 70. Vol. II: La economía*, Madrid, Editorial Moneda y Crédito.

Freeman, Susan Tax (1970), *Neighbors: The Social Contract in a Castilian Hamlet*, Chicago, Chicago University Press.

—— (1979), *The Pasiegos: Spaniards in No Man's Land*, Chicago, Chicago University Press.

Gacto, Enrique (1987), 'El grupo familiar de la Edad Moderna en los territorios del Mediterráneo hispánico: Una visión jurídica', in J. Casey *et al.*, *La familia en la España mediterránea (siglos XV–XIX)*, Barcelona, Editorial Crítica, 36–64.

Galloway, Patrick R. (1986), 'Differentials in demographic responses to annual price variations in pre-revolutionary France: A comparison of rich and poor areas in Rouen, 1681 to 1787', *European Journal of Population*, 2, 269–305.

—— (1988), 'Basic patterns of annual variations in fertility, nuptiality, mortality, and prices in pre-industrial Europe', *Population Studies*, 42, 275–303.

—— (1992), 'Changements séculaires des freins de court terme à la croissance démographique en Europe de 1460 à 1909: Frein preventif, frein positif et frein de température', in A. Blum, N. Bonneuil, and D. Blanchet (eds.), *Modèles de la démographie historique*, Paris, Institute National d'Études Demographiques, 193–240.

—— (1993), 'Short-run population dynamics among the rich and poor in European countries, rural Jutland, and urban Rouen', in D. S. Reher and R. S. Schofield (eds.), *Old and New Methods in Historical Demography*, Oxford, Oxford University Press, 84–108.

—— (1994), 'Secular changes in the short-term preventive, positive, and temperature checks to population growth in Europe, 1460 to 1909', *Climatic Change*, 26, 3–63.

Garrabou, Ramón, Pujol, J., and Colomé, J. (1991), 'Salaris, us i explotació de la força de treball agrícola (Catalunya 1818–1936)', *Recerques*, 24, 23–52.

Garrido Arce, Estrella (1992a), ' "Casa y compañía": La familia en la Huerta de Valencia, siglo XVIII. Algunas reflexiones teóricas y metodológicas', *Boletín de la Asociación de Demografía Histórica*, 10(3), 63–82.

—— (1992b), 'La imposible igualdad: Familia y estrategias hereditarias en la Huerta de

Valencia a mediados del siglo XVIII', *Boletín de la Asociación de Demografía Histórica*, 10(3), 83–104.

Garrido Arce, Estrella (1995), 'El *ciclo Familiar* y el *tiempo de vida* en la Huerta de Valencia, 1747–1800', *Boletín de la Asociación de Demografía Histórica*, 13(1), 29–52.

Gaunt, David (1983), 'The property and kin relationships of retired farmers in northern and central Europe', in R. Wall, J. Robin, and P. Laslett (eds.), *Family Forms in Historic Europe*, Cambridge, Cambridge University Press, 249–80.

Gelles, Richard J. (1995), *Contemporary Families: A Sociological View*, Thousand Oaks, Calif., Sage Publications.

Gilmore, David D. (1980), *The People of the Plain: Class and Community in Lower Andalusia*, New York, Columbia University Press.

Giri Brown, Beatriz A., Ortiz Bascuñana, Rita, and Peinado Bascuñana, Inmaculada (1985), 'Análisis agregativo de la población de Pedro Muñoz, 1875–1972', working paper presented in the Facultad de Ciencias Políticas y Sociolgía, Universidad Complutense de Madrid.

Goldschmidt, W., and Kunkel, E. J. (1971), 'The structure of the peasant family', *American Anthropologist*, 73, 1058–76.

Goldstone, Jack A. (1986), 'The demographic revolution in England: A re-examination', *Population Studies*, 40, 5–34.

Gómez-Cabrero Ortiz, Angel, and Fernández de la Iglesia, María Soledad (1991), 'Sociedad, familia y fecundidad en Mocejón (1600–1719): Una reconstrucción de familias, *Boletín de la Asociación de Demografía Histórica*, 9(1), 65–88.

Gómez Redondo, Rosa (1992), *La mortalidad infantil española en el siglo XX*, Madrid, Siglo XXI-CIS.

Gurría García, Pedro (1984), 'Observaciones sobre la estructura familiar camereana en época moderna', in *Cuadernos de Investiqación del Coleqio Universitario de la Rioja*, 10(1), 57–70.

Hajnal, John (1953), 'Age at marriage and proportions marrying', *Population Studies*, 7, 111–36.

——(1965), 'European marriage patterns in perspective', in D. V. Glass and D. E. C. Eversley (eds.), *Population in History*, London, Edward Arnold, 101–46.

——(1982), 'Two kinds of preindustrial household formation system', *Population and Development Review*, 8, 449–94.

Halpern, Joel M. (1972), 'Town and countryside in Serbia in the nineteenth century: Social and household structure as reflected in the census of 1863', in P. Laslett and R. Wall (eds.), *Household and Family in Past Time*, Cambridge, Cambridge University Press, 401–28.

Hamilton, Earl J. (1934), *American Treasure and the Price Revolution in Spain, 1501–1650*, Cambridge, Mass., Harvard University Press.

——(1947), *War and Prices in Spain, 1651–1800*, Cambridge, Mass., Harvard University Press.

Hammel, Eugene A., and Laslett, Peter (1974), 'Comparing household structure over time and between cultures', *Comparative Studies in Society and History*, 16, 73–103.

——and Mason, Carl (1993), 'My brother's keeper: Modelling kinship links in early urbanization', in D. Reher and R. Schofield (eds.), *Old and New Methods in Historical Demography*, Oxford, Clarendon Press, 318–42.

——McDaniel, C. K., and Wachter, Kenneth W. (1979), 'Demographic consequences of incest prohibitions', *Science*, 205, 972–7.

——Mason, Carl, and Wachter, Kenneth (1990), *SOCSIM II: A Sociodemographic Microsimulation Program, Revision 1.0: Operating Manual*, Berkeley, Calif.

——Wachter, Kenneth, Mason, Carl, Wang, Feng, and Yang, Haiou (1991), 'Rapid population change and kinship: The effect of unstable demographic changes on Chinese kinship networks, 1750–2250', in United Netions (ed.), *Consequences of Rapid Population Growth in Developing Countries*, New York, Taylor and Francis, 243–71.

Hansen, Edward C. (1977), *Rural Catalonia under the Franco Regime*, Cambridge, Cambridge University Press.

Hareven, Tamara K. (1971), 'The history of the family as an interdisciplinary field', *Journal of Interdisciplinary History*, 2, 399–414.

——(1987), 'Family history at the crossroads', *Journal of Family History*, 12, ix–xxiii.

——(1991), 'The history of the family and the complexity of social change', *American Historical Review*, 96, 95–124.

——and Plakans, Andrejs (1987) (eds.), *Family History at the Crossroads*, Princeton Princeton University Press.

Harrison, Mark (1977), 'The peasant mode of production in the work of A. V. Chayanov', *Journal of Peasant Studies*, 4(2).

——(1981), 'Chayanov y la economía del campesinado ruso', in A. V. Chayanov *et al.* (eds.), *Chayanov y la teoría de la economía campesina*, Mexico City, Editoria Pasado y Presente, 153–89.

Henry, Louis (1981), 'Le fonctionnnement du marché matrimonial', in J. Dupâquier, E. Hélin, P. Laslett, M. Livi-Bacci, and S. Sogner (eds.), *Marriage and Remarriage in Populations of the Past*, London, Academic Press, 191–8.

Hicks, W. Whitney, and Martínez-Aguado, Timoteo (1987), 'Los determinantes de la fecundidad dentro del matrimonio en España', *Revista Española de Investigaciones Sociológicas*, 39, 195–212.

Hurtado Martínez, J. (1987), 'Análisis del hogar en una comunidad murciana durante la segunda mitad del siglo XVIII: Lorca, 1761–1771', in *Actas del I Congrés Hispano-Luso-Italià de Demografia Històrica*, Barcelona, 520–7.

Ibañez Gómez, Maite, Ortega Berruguete, Arturo R., Santana Ezquerra, Alberto, and Zabala Llanos, Marta (1994), *Casa, familia y trabajo en la historia de Bergara*, Bergara, Ayuntamiento de Bergara.

Iglesias de Ussel, Julio, (1988) (ed.), *Las familias monoparentales*, Madrid, Ministerio de Asuntos Sociales-Instituto de la Mujer.

——and Flaquer, Lluis (1993), 'Familia y análisis sociológico: El caso de España', *Revista Española de Investigaciones Sociológicas*, 61, 57–75.

Imhof, Arthur E. (1981), 'Remarriage in rural populations and in urban middle and upper strata in Germany from the sixteenth to the twentieth century', in J. Dupâquier, E. Hélin, P. Laslett, M. Livi-Bacci, and S. Sogner (eds.), *Marriage and Remarriage in Populations of the Past*, London, Academic Press, 335–46.

INE (Instituto Nacional de Estadística) (1952), *Tablas de mortalidad de la población española. Años 1900–1940*, Madrid, INE.

——(1978), *Tablas de mortalidad provinciales (1969–1972)*, Madrid, INE.

——(various years), *Movimiento natural de la población española*, Madrid, INE.

——(1993), *Encuesta sociodemográfica 1991. Tomo II. Resultados Nacionales, Volumen 1. Hogar y Familia*, Madrid, INE.

International Labour Office (various years), *Yearbook of Labour Statistics*, Geneva, ILO.

Iriso Napal, Pedro Luis, and Reher, David S. (1987), 'La fecundidad y sus determinantes en España, 1887–1920: Un ensayo de interpretación', *Revista Española de Investigaciones Sociológicas*, 39, 45–118.

Iszaevich, A. (1984), 'Població, vinicultura i urbanització social a la villa de Barberá', in B. Escandell and I. Terrades (eds.), *Història i Antropologia a la memoria d'Angel Palerm*, Montserrat, Abadía de Montserrat, 237–50.

Kertzer, David I. (1984), *Family Life in Central Italy, 1880–1910*, New Brunswick, NY, Rutgers University Press.

——and Brettell, Caroline (1987), 'Advances in Italian and Iberian family history', *Journal of Family History*, 12, 87–121.

Keyfitz, Nathan (1987), 'Form and substance in family demography', in J. Bongaarts, T. Burch, and K. Wachter (eds.), *Family Demography: Methods and Their Application*, Oxford, Clarendon Press, 3–16.

Kintner, H. J. (1985), 'Trends and regional differences in breastfeeding in Germany from 1871 to 1937', *Journal of Family History*, 10, 163–82.

Knodel, John (1988), *Demographic Behaviour in the Past: A Study of Fourteen German Village Populations in the Eighteenth and Nineteenth Centuries*, Cambridge, Cambridge University Press.

——and Kintner, H. (1977), 'The impact of breast feeding patterns on the biometric analysis of infant mortality', *Demography*, 14, 399–419.

Kunstadter, P., Westoff, C., and Stephen, F. F. (1963), 'Demographic variability and preferential marriage patterns', *American Journal of Physical Anthropology*, 21, 511–9.

Lanza García, Ramón (1988), *Población y familia campesina en el Antiguo Régimen: Liébana, siglos XVI–XX*, Santander, Universidad de Cantabria.

——(1991), *La población* y el crecimiento económico de Cantabria en el Antiguo Régimen, Madrid, Universidad Autónoma de Madrid/Universidad de Cantabria.

Lasch, Christopher (1977), *Haven in a Heartless World: The Family Besieged*, New York, Basic Books.

Laslett, Peter (1972), 'Introduction', in P. Laslett and R. Wall (eds.), *Household and Family in Past Time*, Cambridge, Cambridge University Press, 1–90.

——(1983), 'Family and household as work group and kin group: Areas of traditional Europe compared', in R. Wall, J. Robin, and P. Laslett (eds.), *Family Forms in Historic Europe*, Cambridge, Cambridge University Press, 513–63.

——(1987), 'The character of familial history, its limitations and the conditions for its proper pursuit', *Journal of Family History*, 12, 263–85.

——(1988), 'Family, kinship and collectivity as systems of support in pre-industrial Europe: A consideration of the "nuclear hardship" hypothesis', *Continuity and Change*, 3(2), 153–76.

——(1989), *A Fresh Map of Life: The Emergence of the Third Age*, London, Weidenfeld and Nicolson.

——and Clarke, Marilyn (1972), 'Houseful and household in an eighteenth-century Balkan city: A tabular analysis of the listing of the Serbian sector of Belgrade in

1733–4', in P. Laslett and R. Wall (eds.), *Household and Family in Past Time*, Cambridge, Cambridge University Press, 375–400.

——and Wall, Richard (1972) (eds.), *Household and Family in Past Time*, Cambridge, Cambridge University Press.

Lázaro Ruiz, Mercedes, and Gurría García, Pedro A. (1992), 'La familia y el hogar en logroño durante el siglo XVIII', *Boletín de la Asociación de Demografía Histórica*, 10(3), 105–14.

Leasure, W. (1963), 'Factors Involved in the Decline of Fertility in Spain 1900–1950', *Population Studies*, 16, 271–85.

Le Bras, Hervé (1973), 'Parents, grandparents, bisaïeux', *Population*, 28, 9–37.

——(1981), 'Le remariage rival du mariage', in J. Dupâquier, E. Hélin, P. Laslett, M. Livi-Bacci, and S. Sogner (eds.), *Marriage and Remarriage in Populations of the Past*, London, Academic Press, 199–210.

——(1993), 'Simulation of change to validate demographic analysis', in D. Reher and R. Schofield, Roger (eds.), *Old and New Methods in Historical Demography*, Oxford, Clarendon Press, 259–79.

Lee, Robert (1988), 'Infant, child, and maternal mortality in Western Europe: A critique', in A. Brändström and L. G. Tedebrand (eds.), *Society, Health, and Population during the Demographic Transition*, Stockholm, Almqvist and Wiksell International, 9–23.

Lee, Ronald D. (1974), 'Estimating series of vital rates and age structures from baptisms and burials: A new technique with applications to pre-industrial England', *Population Studies*, 28, 495–512.

——(1981), 'Short-term variation: Vital rates, prices, and weather', in E. A. Wrigley and R. S. Schofield, *The Population History of England 1541–1871: A Reconstruction*, Cambridge, Mass., Harvard University Press, 356–401.

——(1985), 'Inverse projection and back projection: Comparative results and sensitivity tests for England', *Population Studies*, 39, 233–48.

——(1993), 'Inverse projection and demographic fluctuations. A critical assessment of new methods', in D. S. Reher and R. S. Schofield (eds.), *Old and New Methods in Historical Demography*, Oxford, Oxford University Press, 7–28.

Lefaucher, N. (1988), '¿Existen las familias monoparentales?', in J. Iglesias de Ussel (ed.), *Las familias monoparentales*, Madrid, Ministerio de Asuntos Sociales-Instituto de la Mujer, 153–162.

Le Play, Frédéric (1858), *Les ouvriers des deux monders*, Tours, Mame.

——(1864), *La réforme sociale. Vol. 3: La Famille*, Tours, Mame.

——(1867), *Réforme sociale en France déduite de l'observation comparée des peuples européens*, Paris, Dentu.

——(1877–9), *Les ouvriers européens: L'Organisation des familles*, 6 vols., Tours: Mame.

——(1990), *Campesinos y pescadores del norte de España*, Clásicos Agrarios, Madrid, Ministerio de Agricultura, Pesca y Alimentación. Edición, introducción y notas a cargo de José Sierra Alvarez.

Lesthaeghe, Ron (1980), 'On the social control of human production', *Population and Development Review*, 6, 527–48.

Lisón Tolosana, Carmelo (1966), *Belmonte de los Caballeros: A Sociological Study of a Spanish Town*, Oxford, Clarendon Press.

——(1971), *Antropología cultural de Galicia*, Madrid, Siglo XXI.

Lisón Tolosana, Carmelo (1976a), 'Estructura antropológica de la familia en España', in R. Carballo *et al.* (eds.), *La familia, diálogo recuperable*, Madrid, Karpos.
——(1976), 'The ethnics of inheritance', in J. G. Peristiany (ed.), *Mediterranean Family Structures*, Cambridge: Cambridge University Press, 305–15.
——(1977), *Invitación a la antropología cultural de España*, La Coruña, Editorial Adara.
——(1987), 'Estrategias matrimoniales, individuación y *Ethos* lucense', in J. C. Perístiany (ed.), *Date y matrimonio en los países mediterráneos*, Madrid, Centro de Investiqationes Sociológicas/Siglio XXI, 79–106.
——(1991), 'Antropología de los pueblos del Norte de España: Galicia', *Revista de Antropología Social*, 13–29.
Livi Bacci, Massimo (1968), 'Fertility and nuptiality changes in Spain from the late 18th to the early 20th century', *Population Studies*, 22, 83–102 and 211–34.
——(1971), *A Century of Portuguese Fertility*, Princeton, Princeton University Press.
——(1977a), *A History of Italian Fertility during the Last Two Centuries*, Princeton, Princeton University Press.
——(1977b), 'Can anything be said about demographic trends when only aggregate vital statistics are available?', in R. D. Lee (ed.), *Population Patterns in the Past*, New York, Academic Press, 311–36.
——(1978), *La société italienne devant les crises de mortalité*, Florence, Dipartimento Statistico, Universita degli studi di Firenze.
——(1981), 'On the frequency of remarriage in nineteenth century Italy: Methods and results', in J. Dupâquier, E. Hélin, P. Laslett, M. Livi-Bacci, and S. Sogner (eds.), *Marriage and Remarriage in Populations of the Past*, London, Academic Press, 347–62.
——(1988), 'La Península Ibérica e Italia en vísperas de la transición demográfica', in V. Pérez Moreda and D. S. Reher (eds.), *Demografía histórica en España*, Madrid, Ediciones E1 Arquero, 138–78.
——and Reher, David S. (1993), 'Other paths to the past: From vital series to population patterns', in D. S. Reher and R. S. Schofield (eds.), *Old and New Methods in Historical Demography*, Oxford, Oxford University Press, 66–83.
López Moran, Elías (1902), 'León', in J. Costa (ed.), *Derecho consuetudinario y economía popular de España*, vol. 2, Barcelona, Manuel Soler, 231–331.
McCaa, Robert (1993), 'Benchmarks for a new inverse population projection program: England, Sweden, and a standard demographic transition', in D. S. Reher and R. S. Schofield (eds.), *Old and New Methods in Historical Demography*, Oxford, Oxford University Press, 40–56.
——and Pérez Brignoli, Héctor (1985), *'Populate': From Births and Deaths to the Demography of Past, Present and Future*, Minneapolis.
Macías Hernández, Antonio M. (1991), 'La demografia de una población insular atlántica: Gran Canaria, 1680–1850', *Boletín de la Asociación de Demografía Histórica*, 9(3), 49–66.
McKeown, Thomas (1976), *The Modern Rise of Population*, London, Edward Arnold.
Madoz, Pascual (1845–50), *Diccionario geográfico-estadístico-histórico de España y sus posesiones de ultramar*, Madrid, Est. tip. de P. Madoz y L. Sagasti.
Martín-Ballestero y Costea Luis (1949), *La casa en el derecho aragonés*, Zaragoza, Consejo Superior de Investigaciones Científicas.
Martínez Carrión, José Miguel (1983), *La población de Yeste en los inicios de la*

transción demográfica, 1850–1935, Albacete, Instituto de Estudios Albacetense, 645–70.

——(1988), 'Peasant household formation and the organization of rural labor in the Valley of Segura during the nineteenth century', *Journal of Family History*, 13, 91–110.

Martínez Rodríguez, Enrique (1992), 'La mortalidad infantil y juvenil en la Galicia urbana del Antiguo Régimen: Santiago de Compostela, 1731–1810', *Obradoiro de Historia Moderna*, no. 1, 45–78.

Martín Rodríguez, Manuel (1984), *Pensamiento económico español sobre la población*, Madrid, Ediciones Pirámide.

Mendels, Franklin (1978), 'La composition du ménage paysan en France au XIXe siècle: Une analyse économique du mode de production domestique', *Annales, E.S.C.*, 4, 780–802.

Miguel, Amando de (1992) (ed.), *La sociedad española, 1992–93: Informe sociológico de la Universidad Complutense*, Madrid, Alianza Editorial.

Mikelarena Peña, Fernando (1992*a*), 'Estructuras familiares y sistemas sucesorios en Navarra: Una aproximación crítica desde las ciencias sociales a las perspectives tradicionales', *Revista Jurídica de Navarra*, 14, 119–45.

——(1992*b*), 'Las estructuras familiares en la España tradicional: Geografía y análisis a partir del Censo de 1860', *Boletín de la Asociación de Demografía Histórica*, 10(3), 15–62.

——(1992*c*), 'Modelos de matrimonio y regímenes de herencia en Navarra a finales del siglo XVIII', *Príncipe de Viana*, 53, 19–33.

——(1993), 'Regímenes demográficos, sistemas sucesiorios y estructuras familiares en Navarra a finales del siglo XVIII', in D. Comas d'Argemir and J. F. Soulet (eds.), *La família als Pirineus*, Andorra, Conselleria d'Educació, Cultura i Joventut of Andorra, 206–21.

——(1995), *Demografía y familia en la Navarra tradicional*, Pamplona, Institución Príncipe de Viana.

Moll Blanes, Isabel (1988), 'La estructura familiar del campesinado de Mallorca, 1824–1827', in *La familia en la España Mediterránea, siglos XV–XIX*, Barcelona, Crítica, 212–57.

Moore, Barrington, Jr. (1958), *Political Power and Social Theory*, Cambridge, Mass., Harvard University Press.

Moral, Carmen del (1974), *La sociedad madrileña fin de siglo y Baroja*, Madrid, Ediciones Turner.

Morassi, L. (1979), 'Strutture familiari in un comune dell'Italia settentrionale alla fine del secolo XIX', *Genus*, 35, 197–217.

Moreno Almárcegui, Antonio (1992), 'Pequeña nobleza rural, sistema de herencia y estructura de la propiedad de la tierra en Plasencia del Monte (Huesca). 1600–1855', in F. Chacón Jiménez, and J. Hernández Franco, Juan (eds.), *Poder, familia y consanguinidad en la España del Antiguo Régimen*, Barcelona, Anthropos, 71–106.

——and Torres Sánchez, Rafael (1993), 'La composición de la casa y las estrategias de herencia en Plasencia (Huesca), siglos XVI–XIX', in D. Comas d'Argemir and J. F. Soulet (eds.), *La família als Pirineus*, Andorra, Conselleria d'Educació, Cultura i Joventut of Andorra, 182–207.

Moreno Navarro, Isidoro (1972), *Propiedad, clases sociales y hermandades en la Baja*

Andalucía, Madrid, Siglo Veintiuno.

Mueller, Eva (1976), 'The economic value of children in peasant agriculture', in R. G. Ridker (ed.), *Population and Development: The Search for Selective Interventions*, Baltimore, The Johns Hopkins University Press, 98–152.

Muñoz Pérez, Francisco (1987), 'Le déclin de la fécondité dans le Sud de l'Europe', *Population*, 42, 911–42.

——(1991), 'Les naissances hors mariage et les conceptions prénuptiales en Espagne depuis 1975: 1. Une période de profonds changements; 2. Diversité et évolution régionales', *Population*, 46, 881–912 and 1207–48.

Muñoz Pradas, Francisco (1990), *Creixement demogràfic, mortalitat i nupcialitat al Penedès (segles XVII–XIX)*, doctoral diss., Universitat Autònoma de Barcelona.

——(1991), 'Proyección inversa y estimación indirecta de la mortalidad: Resuldos para un grupo de localidades catalanas', *Boletín de la Asociación de Demografía Histórica*, 9(3), 67–86.

Nadali Oller, Jordi (1956), 'Demografia y economía en el orígen de la Cataluña Moderna. Un ejemplo local: Palamós (1705–1839)', *Estudios de Historia Moderna*, vi, 281–309. Also published recently in Nadal (1992) 149–74.

——(1984), *La población española (Siglos XVI a XX)*, corrected and expanded edn., Barcelona, Ariel.

——(1992), *Bautismos, desposorios y entierros: Estudios de historia demográfica*, Barcelonia, Ariel.

——and Sáez, Armaud (1972), 'La fecondité à Sant Joan de Palomós (Catalogne) de 1700 à 1859', *Annales de Démographie Historique*, 105–13.

Netting, Robert (1981), *Balancing on an Alp: Ecological Change and Continuity in a Swiss Mountain Village*, Cambridge, Cambridge University Press.

Nicolau Nos, Roser (1991), 'Trayectorias regionales en la transición demográfica española', in M. Livi Bacci (ed.), *Modelos regionales de la transición demográfica en Españay Portugal* (Actas del II Congreso de la Asociación de Demografia Histórica, Vol. 2), Alicante, Instituto de Cultura Juan Gil Albert, 49–65.

Olivares, Castillo, and Vinal, Teresa (1988), 'El comportamiento de la mortalidad en los inicios de la transición demográfica (Aproximación al caso del Bajo Segura, 1850–1935)', in C. Pérez Aparicio (ed.), *Estudis sobre la població del País Valencià*, vol. 2, Valencia, Edicions Alfons El Magnànim/Instidut d'estudis Juan Gil Albert, 645–68.

Omran, A. R. (1971), 'The epidemiologic transition: A theory of the epidemiology of population change', *Milbank Memorial Fund Quarterly*, 49, 509–38.

O'Neill, Brian Juan (1984), *Propietários, lavradores e jornaleiros: Desigualdade social numa aldeia transmontana 1870–1978*, Lisbon, Publicaçoes Dom Quixote.

Ortega Berruguete, Arturo R. (1989), 'Matrimonio, fecundidad y familia en el País Vasco a fines de la Edad Moderna', *Boletín de la Asociación de Demografía Histórica*, 7(1), 47–74.

——Erauzkin, L., Eiguren, M., and Begoña, M. (1988), 'Troncalidad, matrimonio y estructura familiar en Bizkaia a fines del siglo XIX', in *II Congreso Mundial Vasco: Historia de Euskal Herria*, vol. 2, Vitoria, Vitoria, 127–43.

Palli, H. (1983), 'Estonian households in the seventeenth and eighteenth centuries', in R. Wall (ed.), *Family Forms in Historic Europe*, Cambridge, Cambridge University Press, 207–16.

Parish, W. L., and Schwartz, M. (1972), 'Household complexity in nineteenth century France', *American Sociological Review*, 37, 154–73.

Pascua, Marcelino (1934), *La mortalidad infantil en España*, Madrid, Dirección General de Sanidad.

Pedregal y Cañedo, Manuel (1902), 'Asturias, derecho de familia', in J. Costa (ed.), *Derecho consuetudinario y economía popular de España*, vol. 2, Barcelona, Manuel Soler, 99–106.

Pérez Díaz, Victor (1966), *Estructura social del campo y éxodo rural: Estudio de un pueblo de Castilla*, Madrid, Editorial Tecnos.

Pérez-Fuentes Hernández, Pilar (1993), *Vivir y morir en las minas. Estrategias familiares y relaciones de género en la primera industrialización vizcaína: 1877–1913*, Bilbao, Universidad del País Vasco.

Pérez García, José Manuel (1979), *Un modelo de sociedad rural del Antiguo Régimen en la Galicia costera: La península del Salnés*, Santiago, Universidad de Santiago de Compostela.

——(1988*a*), 'La familia campesina en la Huerta de Valencia durante el siglo XVIII', *Boletín de la Asociación de Demografía Histórica*, 6(2), 5–28.

——(1988*b*), 'Demografía coyuntural y factores autorreguladores en la Huerta de Valencia: El ejemplo de Benimaclet (1720–1855)', in C. Pérez Aparicio (ed.), *Estudis sobre la població del País Valencià*, vol. 1, Valencia, Edicions Alfons El Magnàním/ Institut d'estudis Juan Gíl Albert, 397–417.

——(1989), 'Elementos configuradores de la estructura familiar campesina en la Huerta de Valencia, siglo XVIII', *Estudios Humanísticos*, 11, 121–49.

Pérez Moreda, Vicente (1980), *Las crisis de mortalidad en la España interior, siglos XVI–XIX*, Madrid, Siglo XXI.

——(1985*a*), 'La evolución demográfica española en el siglo XIX (1797–1930): Tendencias generales y contrastes regionales', in Società Italiana di Demografia Storica, *La popolazione italiana nell'ottocento: Continuità e mutamenti*, Bologna, Editrice Clueb, 45–113.

——(1985*b*), 'La modernización demográfica, 1800–1930: Sus limitaciones y cronología', in N. Sánchez Albornoz (ed.), *La modernización económica de España 1800–1930*, Madrid, Alianza, 25–62.

——(1986), 'Matrimonio y familia: Algunas consideraciones sobre el modelo matrimonial español en la Edad Moderna', *Boletín de la Asociación de Demografía Histórica*, 4(1), 3–51.

——(1988), 'Respuestas demográficas ante la coyuntura económica en la España rural del Antiguo Régimen', *Boletín de la Asociación de Demografía Histórica*, 6(3), 81–118.

——and Reher, David S. (1985), 'Demographic mechanisms and long-term swings in population in Europe, 1200–1850', *IUSSP International Population Conference*, iv, 313–29.

Pinnelli, Antonella, Nobile, Annunziata and Lapinch, Andis (1994), 'La mortalité infantile dans les pays développés et les Républiques de l'ancienne Union soviétique: Tendances et facteurs', *Population*, 49, 369–94.

Piquero, Santiago (1991), *Demografía guipuzcoana en el Antiguo Régimen*, Bilbao, Universidad del País Vasco.

Pitt-Rivers, J. A. (1961), *The People of the Sierra*, Chicago, Chicago University Press.

Plakans, Andrejs (1984), *Kinship in the Past: An Anthropology of European Family Life 1500–1900*, Oxford, Blackwell.

Pollard, Sidney (1978), 'Labour in Great Britain', *The Cambridge Economic History of*

Europe. Vol. 7, pt. 1: Britain, France, Germany, and Scaudinavia, M. M. Postan and P. Mathizs (eds.), Cambridge: Cambridge University Press.

Popenoe, David (1988), *Disturbing the Nest: Family Change and Decline in Modern Societies*, New York, Aldine de Gruyter.

Poppel, Frans van (1992), *Trouwen in Nederland: Een historisch-demografische studie van de 19e en vroeg-20e eeuw*, A.A.G. Bijdragen 33, Stichting Nederlands Interdisciplinair Demografisch Institu, Landbouwuniversiteit, Wageningen.

Poza Martín, María del Carmen (19825), 'Nupcialidad y fecundidad en Valle de Tabladillo entre 1787 y 1860: Una nota de investigación', *Boletín de la Asociación de Demografía Histórica*, 3(2), 32–50.

Prados de la Escosura, Leandro (1993), 'Spain's real gross domestic product, 1850–1990: A new series', *Documentos de Trabajo*, Madrid, Dirección General de Planificación, Secretaría de Estado de Hacienda, Ministerio de Economía y Hacienda.

Preston, Samuel H. (1976), *Mortality Patterns in National Populations with Special Reference to Recorded Causes of Death*, New York, Academic Press.

——and Haines, Michael R. (1991), *Fatal Years: Child Mortality in Late Nineteenth Century America*, Princeton, Princeton University Press.

——Keyfitz, Nathan, and Schoen, R. (1972), *Causes of Death: Life Tables for National Populations*, New York, Seminar Press.

Prieto Bances, Ramón (1976) (ed.), *Obra escrita*, vol. 2, Oviedo, University of Oviedo.

Pujadas, Isabel, and Solsona, Montserrat (1987), 'Evolución reciente y modelos de nupcialidad en España (1970–1981)', *Papers de Demografia*, Barcelona, Centre d'Estudis Demogràfics, Universitat Autónoma de Barcelona.

Pullan, Brian, and Woolf, Stuart J. (1978), 'Plebe urbane e plebe ruvalis Da poveri a proletari, in Autori Vari, *Storia d'Italia. Annali, I: Dal feudalesímo al capitalismo*, Turin, Einaudi.

Pullum, Thomas W. (1987), 'Some mathematical models of kinship and the family', in J. Bongaarts, T. Burch, and K. Wachter (eds.), *Family Demography: Methods and their Application*, Oxford, Clarendon Press, 267–84.

Rabell Romero, Cecilia (1994), 'Trayectoria de vida familiar, razo y género en Oaxaca Colonial', in P. Gonzalbo and C. Rabell Romero (eds.), *La familia en Iberoamérica*, Mexicocity, El Colegio de Mexico.

Reeves, Jack H. (1987), 'Projection of number of kin', in J. Bongaarts, T. Burch, and K. Wachter (eds.), *Family Demography: Methods and their Application*, Oxford, Clarendon Press, 228–48.

Reher, David S. (1988), *Familia, población y sociedad en la provincia de Cuenca, 1700–1970*, Madrid, Siglo XXI-Centro de Investigaciones Sociologicas.

——(1989), 'Urban growth and population development in Spain, 1787–1930', in R. Lawton, Richard and R. Lee (eds.), *Urban Population Development in Western Europe from the Late Eighteenth to the Early Twentieth Century*, Liverpool, Liverpool University Press, 190–219.

——(1990a), *Town and Country in Pre-industrial Spain: Cuenca, 1550–1870*, Cambridge, Cambridge University Press.

——(1990b), 'Urbanization and demographic behaviour in Spain, 1860–1930', in A. van der Woude, J. de Vries, and A. Hayami (eds.), *Urbanization in History: A Process of Dynamic Interactions*, Oxford, Clarendon Press, 282–99.

——(1991*a*), 'Marriage patterns in spain, 1887–1930', *Journal of Family History*, 16, 7–30.

——(1991*b*), 'Dinámicas demográficas en Castilla la Nueva 1550–1900: Un ensayo de reconstrucción', in J. Nadal i Oller (ed.), *La evolución demográfica bajo los Austrias* (Actas del II Congreso de la ADEH, vol. 3), Alicante, Instituto de Cultura Juan Gil Albert, 17–75.

——(1992), '¿Malthus de nuevo? Poblacióny economía en México durante el siglo XVIII', *Historia Mexicana*, 41, 615–64.

——(1993), 'Una perspectiva comarcal y regional de España en 1887', in D. S. Reher, B. Nogueras, and N. Pombo San Miguel *España a la luz del Censo de 1887*, Madrid, Instituto Nacional de Estadística, 33–114.

——(1995), 'Wasted investments: Some economic implications of childhood mortality patterns', *Population Studies*, 49, 519–36.

——and Ballesteros-Doncel, Esmeralda (1993), 'Precios y salarios en Castilla la Nueva: La construcción de un indice de salarios reales, 1501–1991', *Revista de Historia Económica*, 10(1), 101–51.

——and Camps-Cura, Enriqueta (forthcoming), 'Considerations on family economies in Spain', in R. Wall and O. Saito (eds.), *The Economic and Social Aspects of the Family Life-Cycle: Europe and Japan, Traditional and Modern*, Cambridge, Cambridge University Press.

——and Iriso Napal, Pedro L. (1989), 'Marital fertility and its determinants in rural and in urban Spain, 1887–1930', *Population Studies*, 43, 405–27.

——Nogueras, Beatriz, and Pombo San Miguel, Nieves (1993), *España a la luz del Censo de 1887*, Madrid, Instituto Nacional de Estadística.

——Bernabeu Mestre, Josep, and Pérez Moreda, Vicente (1994), 'Mortalidad infantil y juvenil en Madrid, Castilla-La Mancha y Valencia. Resultados provisionales de un proyecto de investigación', Working Paper (Serie Documentos de Trabajo), Instituto de Demografía, Madrid.

Requena y Díez de Revenga, Miguel (1990), 'Hogares y familias en la España de los ochenta: El caso de la Comunidad de Madrid', *Revista Española de Investigaciones Sociológicas*, 51, 53–78.

Rodríguez Cancho, Miguel (1981), *La villa de Cáceres en el siglo XVIII (demografía y sociedad)*, Cáceres, Caja de Ahorros.

Roigé i Ventura, X. (1989), *Família, grup doméstic i estratégies residencials al Priorat*, Lérida, Estudi General de Lleida.

——(1993), '"En çò des aranesi" evolució de les formes de residéncia i de la família troncal a la Val d'Aran', in D. Comas d'Argemir and J. F. Soulet (eds.), *La família als Pirineus*, Andorra, Conselleria d'Educació, Cultura i Joventud of Andorra, 158–78.

Roussel, Louis (1986), 'L'Évolution récente de la structure des ménages dans quelques pays industriels', *Population*, 41, 913–34.

——(1992), 'La Famille en Europe occidentale: Divergences et convergences', *Population*, 47, 133–52.

Rowland, Robert (1984), 'Sistemas familiares e padrões demográficos em Portugal: Questões para uma investigaçao comparada', *Ler História*, 3, 13–32.

——(1987*a*), 'Nupcialidade, familia, mediterraneo', *Boletín de la Asociación de Demografía Histórica*, 5(2), 128–43.

Rowland, Robert (1987b), 'Mortalidad, movimientos migratorios y edad de acceso al matrimonio en la Península Ibérica', *Boletín de la Asociación de Demografía Histórica*, 5(2), 128–43.

——(1987c), 'Matrimonio y familia en el Mediterráneo Occidental: Algunas interrogaciones', in F. Chacón (ed.), *Familia y sociedad en el Mediterráneo Occidental: Siglos XV–XIX*, Murcia, University of Murcia, 243–62.

——(1988), 'Sistemas matrimoniales en la Península Ibérica (siglos XVI–XIX): Una perspectiva regional', in V. Pérez Moreda and D. S. Reher, *Demografía Histórica en España*, Madrid, Ediciones El Arquero, 72–137.

Rowntree, Benjamin Seebohn (1901), *Poverty: A Study of Town Life*, London, Macmillan.

——(1910), *Land and Labour: Lessons from Belgium*, London, Macmillan.

Rudolph, Richard L. (1992), 'The European family and economy: Central themes and issues', *Journal of Family History*, 17, 119–38.

Ruggles, Steven (1987), *Prolonged Connections: The Rise of the Extended Family in Nineteenth-Century England and America*, Madison, University of Wisconsin Press.

——(1990), 'Family demography and family history: Problems and prospects', *Historical Methods*, 23, 23–30.

——(1994a), 'The transformation of American family structure', *American Historical Review*, 99, 103–28.

——(1994b), 'The origins of African-American family structure', *American Sociological Review*, 59, 136–51.

Saavedra Fernández, Pegerto (1985), *Economía, política y sociedad en Galicia: La provincia de Mondoñedo, 1480–1830*, Santiago, Xunta de Galicia.

——(1988), 'Casa y comunidad en la Galicia interior', in José Carlos Bermejo Barrera (ed.), *Parentesco, familia y matrimonio en la historia de Galicia*, Santiago, Tórulo, 95–143.

——(1992), 'Datos para un estudio da mortaldade de "párvulos" en Galicia (fins do XVII–mediados do XIX)', *Obradoiro de Historia Moderna*, no. 1, 79–96.

Sabean, David Warren (1990), *Property, Production, and Family in Neckarhausen, 1700–1870*, Cambridge, Cambridge University Press.

Sahlins, Marshall D. (1972), *Stone Age Economics*, Chicago, Aldine-Atherton.

Sallares i Pla, Juan (1892), *El trabajo de las mujeres y los niños: Estudio sobre sus condiciones actuales*, Sabadell (Barcelond), A. Vives.

Sánchis Avalos, Santiago, and Madril Muñoz, Alfons (1990), 'Nupcialitat i fecunditat a la vila de Xulilla al segle XVII', *Afers. Fulls de recerca i pensment*, 9, 62–88.

Sardon, Jean-Paul (1992), 'La primo-nuptialité féminine en Europe: Éléments pour une typologie', *Population*, 47, 855–92.

Schofield, Roger, and Reher, David (1991), 'The decline of mortality in Europe', in R. Schofield, D. Reher, and A. Bideau (eds.), *The Decline of Mortality in Europe*, Oxford, Clarendon Press, 1–17.

Schurer, Kevin, and Moll-Blanes, Isabel (1990), 'Working lives: Rhythms of household income in early twentieth-century Mallorca', paper given at the Tenth International Economic History Conference, Leuven.

Segalen, Martine (1981), *Sociologie de la famille*, Paris, Armand Colin Éditeur. Also published in English as *Historical Anthropology of the Family* (1986), Cambridge and Paris, Cambridge University Press and Maison des Sciences de l'Homme.

——(1985), *Quinze générations de Bas-Bretons: Parenté et société dans le Pays Bigourden Sud 1720–1980*, Paris, Presses Universitaires de France.

Sharlin, Allan (1986), 'Urban-rural differences in fertility in Europe during the demographic transition', in A. J. Coale and S. C. Watkins (eds.), *The Decline of Fertility in Europe*, Princeton, Princeton University Press, 234–60.

Shorter, Edward (1976), *The Making of the Modern Family*, New York, Basic Books.

Simón Tarrés, Antoni (1987), 'La familia catalana en el Antiguo Régimen', in J. Casey *et al.*, *La familia en la España mediterránea (siglos XV–XIX)*, Barcelona, Editorial Crítica, 65–93.

Smith, Daniel Scott (1993), 'The curious history of theorizing about the history of the western nuclear family', *Social Science History*, 17, 325–53.

Smith, James E. (1981), 'How first marriage and remarriage markets mediate in the effects of declining mortality on fertility', in J. Dupâquier, E. Hélin, P. Laslett, M. Livi-Bacci, and S. Sogner (eds.), *Marriage and Remarriage in Populations of the Past*, London, Academic Press, 229–43.

——(1984), 'Widowhood and ageing in traditional English society', *Ageing and Society*, 4(4).

——(1987), 'The computer simulation of kin sets and kin counts', in J. Bongaarts, T. Burch, and K. Wachter (eds.), *Family Demography: Methods and their Application*, Oxford, Clarendon Press, 249–66.

——and Oeppen, Jim (1993), 'Estimating numbers of kin in historical England using demographic microsimulation', in D. Reher and R. Schofield (eds.), *Old and New Methods in Historical Demography*, Oxford, Clarendon Press, 280–317.

Smith, Richard M. (1981), 'Fertility, economy and household formation in England over three centuries', *Population and Development Review*, 7, 595–622.

——(1983), 'Hypothéses sur la nuptialité en Angleterre aux XVIIIe et XIXe siécles', *Annales, E.S.C.*, 38, 107–36.

——(1984), 'Some issues concerning families and their property in rural England 1250–1800', in R. M. Smith (ed.), *Land, Kinship and Life Cycle*, Cambridge: Cambridge University Press, 1–73.

——(1988), 'Welfare and management of demographic uncertainty', in M. Keynes, D. Coleman, and N. Dimsdale (eds.), *The Political Economy of Health and Welfare*, New York, Macmillan Press, 108–35.

Soler Serratosa, Juan (1985), 'Demografia y sociedad en Castilla la Nueva durante el Antiguo Régimen: La Villa de los Molinos, 1620–1730', *Revista Española de Investigaciones Sociológicas*, 32, 141–90.

Sorokin, Pitrim (1937), *Social and Cultural Dynamics*, vol. 5, New York, E. P. Dutton.

Stone, Lawrence (1977), *Family, Sex, and Marriage in England, 1500–1800*, New York, Harper and Row.

——(1981), 'Family history in the 1980s', *Journal of Interdisciplinary History*, 12, 51–7.

Strumingher, L. S. (1977), 'The artisan family: Tradition and transition in XIXth century Lyon', *Journal of Family History*, 2, 211–22.

Tenorio, Nicolás (1982), *La aldea gallega*, Vigo, Ediciones Xerais de Galicia.

Terradas Saborit, Ignasi (1980), 'Els origens de la institució d'hereu a Catalunya: Vers una interpretació contextual', *Quaderns de l'Institut Català d'Antropologia*, 2, 64–97.

——(1984), *El món històric de les masies*, Barcelona, Curial.

Tilly, Louise A. (1979), 'Individual lives and family strategies in the French proletariat', *Journal of Family History*, 4, 137–52.

Tilly, Louise A. and Scott, J. W. (1978), *Women, Work and Family*, New York, Holt, Rinehart and Winston.

Torrents i Rosès, Angels (1992), 'La preponderancia del hogar troncal en una población industrial catalana: Sant Pere de Riudebitlles, 1849', in V. Montojo Montojo, (ed.), *Linaje, familia y marginación en España (ss. XIII–XIX)*, Murcia, Universidad de Murcia, 93–115.

——(1993), *Transformacions demogràfiques en un municipi industrial català: Sant Pere de Ruidebitlles, 1608–1935*, doctoral diss., Universitat de Barcelona, Facultat de Goegrafia i Història.

UNESCO (various years), *Statistical Yearbook*, Paris, UNESCO.

Urrutikoetxea Lizarraga, José (1992), *'En una mesa y compañía': Caserío y familia campesina en la crisis de la 'sociedad tradicional'. Irún, 1766–1845*, San Sebastián, Universidad de Deusto.

——(1993), 'La familia troncal campesina vasco-húmeda: De mecanismo de regulación social a soporte ideológico tradicionalista', in D. Comas d'Argemir and J. F. Soulet (eds.), *La família als Pirineus*, Andorra, Conselleria d'Educació, Cultura i Joventud of Andorra, 246–61.

Valero Lobo, Angeles (1984), 'Edad media de acceso al matrimonio en España: Siglos XVI–XIX', *Boletín de la Asociación de Demografía Histórica*, 2(2), 39–48.

——(1991), 'Evolución del hogar y de la estructura familiar en Madrid, 1970–90', *Boletín de la Asociación de Demografía Histórica*, 9(1), 89–122.

Vallés, José Miguel S. (1992), 'Los jóvenes y la constitución de los nuevos hogares y familias', in A. de Miguel (eds.), *La sociedad española 1992–93*, Madrid, Alianza Editorial, 151–73.

Vallin, Jacques (1991), 'Mortality in Europe from 1720 to 1914: Long-term trends and changes in patterns by age and sex', in R. Schofield, D. Reher, and A. Bideau (eds.), *The Decline of Mortality in Europe*, Oxford, Clarendon Press, 38–67.

Viazzo, Pier Paolo (1989), *Upland Communities: Environment, Population and Social Structure in the Alps since the Sixteenth Century*, Cambridge, Cambridge University Press.

——and Albera, Dionigi (1990), 'The peasant family in northern Italy, 1750–1930: A reassessment', *Journal of Family History*, 15, 461–82.

Vicens Vives, Jaume (1954), *Noticia de Catalunya*, Barcelona, Destino.

Vilquin, Eric (1978), 'La mortalité infantile selon le mois de naissance au XIX siécle', *Population*, 6, 1137–53.

Wachter, Kenneth W. (1987), 'Microsimulation of household cycles', in J. Bongaarts, T. Burch, and K. Wachter (eds.), *Family Demography: Methods and their Application*, Oxford, Clarendon Press, 215–27.

——Hammel, Eugene A., and Laslett, Peter (1978), *Statistical Studies of Historical Social Structure*, New York, Academic Press.

Wall, Richard (1978), 'On the age of leaving home', *Journal of Family History*, 3, 181–202.

——(1983), 'Introduction', in R. Wall (ed.), *Family Forms in Historic Europe*, Cambridge, Cambridge University Press, 1–63.

Watkins, Susan Cotts (1986), 'Regional patterns of nuptiality in Western Europe, 1870–1960', in A. J. Coale and S. C. Watkins (eds.), *The Decline of Fertility in Europe*, Princeton, Princeton University Press.

——(1991), *From Provinces into Nations: Demographic Integration in Western Europe, 1870–1960*, Princeton, Princeton University Press.

Watson, John (1928), *Psychological Care of Infaut and Child*, New York, Norton.

Weir, David (1984), 'Life under pressure: France and England, 1670–1870', *Journal of Economic History*, 54(1), 27–47.

Wheaton, Robert (1987), 'Observations on the development of kinship history, 1942–1985', *Journal of Family History*, 12, 285–302.

Woods, Robert I., and Hinde, P. R. A. (1985), 'Nuptiality and age at marriage in nineteenth-Century England', *Journal of Family History*, 10, 119–44.

——Watterson, P. A., and Woodward, J. H. (1988–9), 'The causes of rapid infant mortality decline in England and Wales', *Population Studies*, 42, 343–66 and 43, 113–32.

——(1986), *The Poor in Western Europe in the Eighteenth and Nineteenth Centuries*, London, Methuen & Co.

Wrigley, E. Anthony (1977), 'Births and baptisms: The use of Anglican baptism registers as a source of information about the numbers of births in England before the beginning of civil registration', *Population Studies*, 31, 281–312.

——(1981), 'Population history in the 1980s', *Journal of Interdisciplinary History*, 12(2), 207–26.

——and Schofield, Roger (1981), *The Population History of England, 1541–1871: A Reconstruction*, Cambridge, Mass., Harvard University Press.

Yaben y Yaben, Hilario (1916), *Los contratos matrimoniales en Navarra y su influencia en la estabilidad de la familia*, Madrid, Jaime Ratéz.

Zulaika, Joseba (1984), *Basque Violence: Metaphor and Sacrament*, Reno, Nev., University of Nevada Press.

Index